A HISTORY OF MODERN BRITAIN IN 12 CRISES

Christopher Kirkland

First published in Great Britain in 2026 by

Bristol University Press
University of Bristol
1-9 Old Park Hill
Bristol
BS2 8BB
UK
t: +44 (0)117 374 6645
e: bup-info@bristol.ac.uk

Details of international sales and distribution partners are available at bristoluniversitypress.co.uk

DOI: 10.51952/9781529232028

British Library Cataloguing in Publication Data
A catalogue record for this book is available from the British Library

ISBN 978-1-5292-3199-1 hardcover
ISBN 978-1-5292-3200-4 paperback
ISBN 978-1-5292-3201-1 ePub
ISBN 978-1-5292-3202-8 ePdf

Cover design: Nicky Boroweic
Front cover image: AdobeStock/ad_hominum

Contents

Preface

The motivation for this book stems from my experiences as both a student and teacher of British political history. Political history is frequently concerned with how things should or do work. Crises are often seen through this lens as a deviation. They are easily dismissed as representing short-term challenges which, due to their temporal nature, offer only limited conceptual use. They are problems to be solved, and once solved can be dismissed as being of no further importance – possibly aside from political point-scoring.

Upon becoming a lecturer I was keen to develop a module covering crises as objects of study in their own right. I have been fortunate enough to be permitted to develop and teach on the module 'Britain in Crisis'. Teaching on this module has given me the opportunity to think about the similarities and differences that exist within crises. Through this I have encouraged students to think not just about what went wrong in times of crises, but also how crises manifest themselves, and how power is utilised in times of crisis. Asking these questions helps link what happened to explanations of how it happened and predictions of what might happen in the future. These questions, and the discussions in class, prompted the writing of this book.

Writing this book has further given me a chance to reflect on how such transitions occur, what shapes them and how they impact upon broader, contemporary, politics. In offering a comparative approach I have been keen to explore the commonalities and differences that exist within crises. Doing so has encouraged me to think more holistically about how contemporary British politics has been shaped, about where the drivers of policy originate and how our understanding(s) of both crises and non-crises are shaped by previous narrations.

Crises can offer much to the study of contemporary politics. They are moments which have the potential to shape and reshape politics as much as elections or changes in government. Crises offer answers to questions of what worked and what did not work and challenge existing conceptualisations of policy. Even where remedies are seen as short term, they can also leave lasting legacies.

Crises are not immune from broader tensions within the policy-making process. They do not, in and of themselves, offer or promote a natural or single policy but are contested. Deciding what policies to implement rests upon notions of blame and exclusion of ideas that are seen to have failed. Different narratives offer different understandings of blame, which in turn can be influenced by the ability of those incorporated into the crisis to levy or deny such accusations.

Crises can also be personal, even for those not directly connected to the crisis. Many years after events people still recall where they were when the news of a crisis broke or their initial responses to it. Such understandings have definitely shaped my interest in exploring crises. I recall the impromptu school assembly held following the 9/11 bombings, and, having grown up in North London, watching the unfolding news coverage of the 7/7 London bombings. My undergraduate degree was heavily shaped by the Global Financial Crisis, which in turn became the subject of my PhD. The ideas and early planning of this book were undertaken as the COVID-19 crisis spread, changing my daily routine.

In addition to the four crises listed above, Brexit, climate change, migration populism and the two elections of President Trump, to name a few, give increasing credence to the idea of a world in flux and notions of continual or permanent crises. I was born in 1989. Throughout my time studying history and politics the world has become more prone to (the language of) crises.

These are the reasons why I wanted to write this book. Crises have shaped both British politics and our lived experience of it. Yet they have not been explored in the same depth as 'normal policy making' (however defined). As I demonstrate here, thinking holistically about these events offers much to our understanding. These are not homogenous though, and different actions may yield different results. Understanding the drivers of change within crises is important and helps us reflect on how contemporary politics has been shaped. Doing so might also shed some light on the peculiarities of future crises and what we might be able to expect from these. As the following chapters demonstrate, this is not meant to be an exhaustive list of crises in modern Britain but rather a means of exploring how crises can and do shape British political history.

The book owes much to many. I would like to thank the production team at Bristol University Press and in particular Zoe Forbes and Stephen Wenham. This book has been subject to several delays – all my fault – and I have been immensely grateful for their patience. I would like to thank colleagues who have supported me in its writing and been willing to discuss the issues with me. I thank the two anonymous reviewers for their comments on an earlier draft of the manuscript. I would also like to thank my students, particularly those who have taken my final year undergraduate module on 'Britain in Crisis', which initially inspired the book. This book is the product of many debates and discussions with both students and fellow academics. It has been a project that I have wanted to do for a long time and writing it has undoubtedly aided my own teaching.

The final thanks I owe is to my family. Like crises, academic research often requires immediate action and takes priority over competing pressures. I am very grateful for the patience and support they have shown, especially my wife Jacqueline and daughters Allegra, Charlotte and Jasmine, born in the very final stages of production. I hope that me writing this book is as close to a crisis as any of you will ever come.

As ever, although many people have made the book possible, any mistakes remain mine and mine alone.

1

This All Sounds Very Familiar

In 1979, the then Prime Minister Jim Callaghan was misquoted by a national newspaper as saying, 'Crisis? What Crisis?' – an attempt by the paper to present the government as out of touch and unable to govern. This was by no means the first crisis (see, for example, King, 1975; Brittan, 1977), or the first attempt to portray the government as inept in the wake of such a crisis, but the quote became symbolic of wider government failure.

In the last decade events have increasingly been described as crises, from Brexit to COVID-19 to the economic turmoil under Liz Truss's short tenure as Prime Minister. Each of these relates to specific, time-bound events, but other underlying 'crises' have also been mooted, for example in relation to the National Health Service (NHS), housing (supply or policies), education (funding) and so on, particularly in the wake of austerity – itself a legacy of the 2008 Global Financial Crisis (GFC, see Chapter 13). Undoubtedly such narratives sometimes employ vastly different understandings of the term crisis, but nonetheless multiple crises are now spoken of and largely accepted as coexisting. Observers may be excused for posing a similar, but distinct, question to that attributed to Callaghan in 1979: 'Crisis? *Which* Crisis?'

In part, this is due to the nature of the media. The (UK) media consists primarily of private companies (the BBC being an exception to the rule). Newspapers, television and online news services rely upon their ability to sell either physical copies of the newspaper or, much more commonly, advertising space, which in turn depends on audience share. Here, then, a product (news) is needed to attract people's attention. People are unlikely to consume news from a particular outlet if all they are told is what they already know or is unlikely to make a difference to their lives. While we may all have preferences for a world where nothing bad happens or where everything remains constant, such a world would make for bad newspaper sales.

Eye-catching stories that form the front pages of newspapers or appear first on television or in radio bulletins can be 'hyped up' – sensationalised – to exaggerate their effects. These are designed to keep the reader or viewer interested, as it is widely accepted that the news stories which follow will be of lesser importance.

Media outlets are, after all, private companies that seek to monetarise and profit from the reporting of news items, either by selling access to the news or through subjecting their readers/viewers to paid advertisements. Notions of crisis fit within this context, encouraging greater engagement with the media outlet. Although a more detailed understanding of the term 'crisis' will be offered in the next chapter, it is fair to say that the term is an emotive one. Describing an event as a crisis places significant emphasis upon the event. It also implies a number of related questions – for example, 'What's gone wrong?' or 'What can be done?' Here, crises or the reporting of crises will catch the attention of the would-be viewer more than other, non-crisis-related stories.

These understandings are oversimplified, but, as Chapter 2 highlights, there is a tendency to overuse the term 'crisis'. While acknowledging that crises are unequal entities and what one person might consider to be a crisis of the utmost importance others may view as less important, any growth in the number of (potential) crises poses questions for policy makers and citizens alike, relating to notions of '(un)governability' (King, 1975).

This book is not, however, a reflection of modern Britain or an attempt to bemoan (non-)decisions made by policy makers in recent years. Nor is it the first attempt to situate Britain's problem in a comparative context. Commentaries such as those which called Britain 'the sick man of Europe' in the 1970s compared the economic fortunes of Britain with its (Western) European neighbours; in the 1990s, scholars spoke of a more terminal decline (see Chapter 15). This resonated with one of the underlying messages of Labour's 1997 general election campaign – 'things can only get better'.

Rather, this book acknowledges that such discourse is not new. By guiding the reader through a number of historic crises in British politics, it highlights similarities between them. In doing so, it asks: 'Why are (similar) crises repeated?'

This book explores 12 crises in British politics. In doing so, it seeks to unpack not just a story about British political history, but also something about the nature of crises – how they occur and how they are understood and contested – by drawing upon literature concerning the pathology of crises. One key argument of the book is that the two are interconnected; you cannot fully understand any singular crisis, British or otherwise, without also understanding how crises are formed, shaped and evolve.

The similarities that exist between these crises are important. Edward Heath's famous question, 'Who governs?', was explicitly asked in the wake of mounting industrial unrest and questions over government capacity; but it could also be applied to the relationship between the House of Commons and House of Lords in 1909–10, or the tension between financial markets and the Labour governments of both 1931 and 2008–10. A not dissimilar question, 'Who *should* govern?', could also be aptly applied to the questions of Irish Home Rule (1912–14, and even beyond) and to both world wars – which were fought in defence of democratic government. Governments further highlighted/drew upon this question during the General Strike of 1926 and the Miners' Strike of 1984–85.

Studying crises also offers a means through which we can understand post-crisis changes. Chapter 2 demonstrates that crises offer a mechanism through which new policies are instigated, including those that subsequently form new paradigms (Hall, 1993). As the chapter also shows, within crises, timings are paramount, and responses are needed to alleviate the impact of the crisis. Formed by politicians and media outlets, the need for a quick response can lead to divergence between schools of thought – for example, Pirie (2012) highlights the differences between the academic literature and government and media responses to the 2008 GFC.

Crises challenge understandings. They seek primarily to determine what worked and what didn't, encouraging policy makers to focus on the former and rectify the latter. Solutions must be found as quickly as possible and have the propensity to become the new norm for policy. Such understandings, at least in democratic societies, are often guided not by lengthy academic debates or inquiries but through resonating with our 'everyday experiences', confirmed by voters in times of elections. Elections can and do have large impacts upon crises; the elections of 1931 and 2010 ushered in periods of austerity, and 1979 confirmed the anti-union narratives of Thatcher and the Conservative Party. During both world wars, deliberation, discussion and critical debate were seen as incompatible with an effective crisis resolution, and elections were postponed. Other anti-democratic measures, such as the suppression of protests, were also imposed. Similar restrictions were implemented during the COVID-19 pandemic, when again individual health/security was prioritised ahead of (elements of) democratic governance.

Given such timings, stabilisation and success can often be conflated post-crisis. To continue the arguments made by Pirie (2012), and as Chapter 13 highlights, austerity came to be viewed as the solution to the 2008 crisis, despite much protestation from within academic circles (for example, Blyth, 2013b; Hay, 2013).

Scope then exists to ask how such disparities occur, or why policy making becomes entrenched within a specific narrative even when the narrative is challenged outside formal politics. Why, for instance, did the Labour Party accept notions of excessive government spending following its electoral defeat in 2010?

Other crises produced similar examples of key figures and groups significantly reversing their policies on issues following crises, for instance the Labour Party's acceptance of Thatcher's anti-union legislation in the 1980s; the Conservatives' acceptance of the primacy of the House of Commons post the Constitutional Crisis of 1910; and both political parties' acceptance of Britain's (relative) decline in global power after Suez.

Another aspect of crises, which is often missed through conceptualisations that view these as deviations rather than events in their own right, is the comparative element. Crises offer not just a means of understanding what has happened; they also act as a means of understanding similar events moving forward. Any resolution(s) to crises, if they are to be successful, do not just alleviate the immediate problems faced but offer a framework for preventing any recurrence. In doing so, they offer a new framing of events, which becomes the 'default' for understanding similar events in the future. Such comparisons often appear implicitly (for example, the language used to report on industrial actions such as the 2022 Summer of Discontent and the 1979 Winter of Discontent), while others represent a logical continuation (for example, the Second World War following the First World War, given the similar participants in the conflict).

Not all crises can be included in a single book. This leads to questions about which crises to include and, conversely, which to exclude. As the following chapters demonstrate, crises are inherently subjective, and this also applies to the selection and omission of crises. Inevitably, different actors will assign different levels of salience to each series of events (including rejecting terminology that defines events as 'crises'). Some crises, such as the Second World War, are almost universally accepted as having had a significant impact upon British politics, yet others are disputed depending on the positions and ideologies of those comparing the crises. The severity of a crisis may depend upon a person's location (for example, Irish Home Rule Crisis or the immediate impact of the 7/7 London bombings), their profession (for example, the Miners' Strike 1984–85) or health status (for example, COVID-19).

Here, then, the focus on just 12 crises is a product of time and space constraints within the book. It goes without saying that other events and crises, and indeed non-crisis periods, also contribute to the history of Britain.

This book seeks to situate these crises within their historical context. This presents two methodological points. The first is a desire to view the crises from the perspective of contemporaries. Doing so enables a consistent application of the term 'crisis'; as Chapter 2 notes, the term cannot only be applied retrospectively. It would be insufficient to simply dismiss a particular crisis as being 'unimportant' based solely upon its ending or resolution. Such a dismissal would ignore or overlook the fact that this crisis could still offer some understanding of the nature of crises or their resolution. For example, those which are resolved quickly might aid our understanding of how to overcome, or even prevent, similar crises in the future. Rather, crises need to be understood as contemporary events. While it is easy to dismiss the importance of (some) crises from the vantage point of history, policies must be deliberated, contested and enacted before any outcomes are known.

Following on from this, the second methodological point is that crises are not simply past events, but ones that are experienced first-hand. People live through crises and must be able to acknowledge their position within a crisis to declare it as such. If such capacities did not exist, then there would be no means for understanding contemporary times as crises.

These methodological points are developed further in Chapter 2 but are raised here as they pertain to the choice of crises to be included. The crises contained in the book, when viewed from the vantage point of history, shaped Britain to differing degrees, but each, I contend, had the potential to radically alter British history. For example, few beyond those with a keen interest in the UK Constitution might consider the 1909–10 crisis (see Chapter 3) to be of significance today, but it is not difficult to see how alternative decisions within such a crisis might have significantly affected the monarchy or the development of Parliament.

In an increasingly globalised world, a further critique may point to the relatively restrictive geographical approach taken. Each of the crises contained in this book either occurred solely within the UK or affected UK policy. The globalised nature of events is limited in scope. Chapters covering the First and Second World Wars (Chapters 5 and 8) and Suez (Chapter 9) explicitly include the actions of other countries, other chapters do not – here the Irish Home Rule crisis (Chapter 4) is very much couched within the 'domestic' or devolved political agreements that existed within Ireland at the time, rather than an exploration of any relationship between two equal countries. Given the constraints of time and space, the international aspects of crises may be overlooked (for example, the global nature of COVID-19 or 'terrorism' beyond the 7/7 bombings) – other publications do this, but in doing so lose the comparative elements of exploring multiple crises.

One could point to other crises which have had implications for British politics. For example, the 9/11 terrorist attacks in the US or the migration crisis which dominated the priorities of the EU in 2015–16. The Cold War dominated foreign policy more than the events explored in this book – the Suez Crisis can be seen as a manifestation of that war, but one would be hard-pressed to argue the reverse. We could also point to global warming, which by its nature affects every nation on the planet (albeit in an unequal manner). Such crises have been omitted from this book, and again, this is a subjective decision. Links between these events – and others – and British politics/policy have been documented elsewhere.

Creating an objective ordering of crises, along the lines of which is most important, would involve making judgements, not only about the effects of crises but also about comparing across sub-fields of politics; for example, deciphering between the Constitutional Crisis of 1909–10 and the Suez Crisis of 1956 involves not just exploring the events themselves but also comparing domestic and foreign policy.

I do not claim to have achieved this, but I highlight it to demonstrate how time-consuming/cumbersome establishing such a hierarchy would be. Rather, within this book, I have sought to include national crises which I, as the author, see as important in understanding British political history, drawing upon my experiences as both a student and a teacher of the subject matter and working within the confines of a single book. I acknowledge that these choices leave open the prospect for criticisms such as 'Why include a chapter on X, but omit one on Y?' which are to be expected and welcomed. However, this is only part of the story of this book; another, arguably more important, aspect is the links that exist between these crises (and indeed any others that readers wish to also explore). Again, due to the omission of certain crises these may not be as complete as they otherwise could be, but this should not detract from the links made within the following chapters.

Similarities exist in terms of: actions taken within crises; the importance of prevailing norms, which offer a means of understanding, framing and responding to crises; or the means of resolving crises, through instigating new norms or paradigm shifts (Hall, 1993); notions of blame, and framing within crises and how such narratives shape our understanding of 'What is to be done?' within the crisis itself. Similarities also exist in how crises are remembered and how they define subsequent events (including future crises). For example, through the use of particular lexicons, conceptual frameworks and 'new' paradigms.

Another key argument contained within the book is that crises are inherently unequal. This is true not just in their effects but also in terms of the policies and outcomes that they produce. As Chapter 2 notes, labelling an event as a crisis is not an objective process, but one laden with political connotations. In this regard, crises are not simply 'reset buttons'; policies such as the lockdowns imposed during COVID-19 or the rationing of the Second World War could not simply replace the pre-crisis inequalities. Specific policies were enacted, such as the government's homelessness policy during COVID-19, which offered temporary accommodation to the vast majority of those living rough (on this, see Grube, 2022, pp 198–9), as prerequisites for the 'shared experiences' associated with lockdowns and restrictions on movement.

The book is not a historical account for its own sake. Drawing upon an interdisciplinary approach offers a more holistic understanding of crises as it is informed by both disciplines; here, (political) history is not explored in an attempt to gain a complete set of knowledge. Rather, the purpose of doing so, as Riley (2021, p 280) notes, is that 'history should always be rewritten'. A constant rewriting of history allows us to incorporate new voices and/or perspectives – including those which have previously been marginalised within academia or similar debates – and new sources to allow for earlier interpretations to be challenged and, where necessary, corrected. Doing so also helps to inform us about our current situation, as it sheds a light on the assumptions and prejudices of those who are writing the history and also of those consuming such versions of events. Riley (2021, p 293) argues that although public figures often have a preoccupation with how history will judge them, learning *about* the past is very different from learning *from* the past.

Riley (2021, p 280) further notes that such rewriting is not the monopoly of the historian. This book, itself a wider reflection of my teaching, is intended as a very small part of this. By comparatively exploring crises in this manner, I hope to shed light on an otherwise overlooked aspect of history. Although each crisis in and of itself has been studied previously through comparing these events, I hope to encourage further debate surrounding both our understanding of historic events and our expectations and behaviours within contemporary crises. Reflecting on the lessons and outcomes of crises – even if policies have been implemented – is important in understanding how future crises may manifest themselves and how we both can and should respond to such events.

Outline of the following chapters

The remainder of the book applies the notions of crises, blame and framing to specific events and explores how each was defined and presented by politicians and the media. It offers 12 case studies, which have all been defined elsewhere as crises. Importantly, this is not intended to be an exhaustive list of all crises within Britain over the last 120 years. Rather, the crises explored here demonstrate how such narratives came to define each crisis, how politicians responded to these understandings and how crises can be resolved.

In unpacking each crisis, Chapters 3–14 follow a similar pattern, allowing for comparisons to be drawn. Each chapter first establishes the causes of the crisis, outlining what happened. Second, it asks how such events were portrayed within the contemporary media and by key stakeholders such as politicians or blamed agents. The chapter then moves on to discuss the resolution to the crisis, exploring what policies were adopted to overcome the crisis. The final section in each chapter is devoted to the legacy of the crisis, asking to what extent the crisis and any shared/collective memories have also impacted British politics. The ending of each chapter contains some selected further reading. Suggestions of this type cannot be exhaustive, but I hope to facilitate the reader to engage with further materials, combining a mix of academic sources and also contemporary accounts of the crisis, emphasising the lived experiences of the events in question.

Chapter 2 sets out a theoretical introduction to the term 'crisis'. It highlights how the term is used in different discourses, from academic study to media and political narratives. Doing so offers a theoretical framework for understanding the subsequent chapters in this book and a means of comparing and contrasting events which have come to be accepted, by various actors, as crises.

Chapter 3 explores the House of Lords' decision to block the Liberal government's budget of 1909. It highlights how this use of the veto became defined as a constitutional crisis, involving not only Parliament but the monarchy as well.

Chapter 4 looks at the passage of the Third Irish Home Rule Bill, and opposition to the bill in Ulster. It highlights how this became a crisis underpinned by notions of nationalism and identity before exploring how such opposition almost brought civil war to Ireland in 1914. This crisis is unique within the book, as its 'ending' came about due to more pressing concerns relating to the onset of the First World War, rather than a definitive resolution to the crisis itself.

Chapter 5 analyses the First World War. It looks at how the state was mobilised for wartime purposes. It also considers how the war led to the formation of a coalition government and explores questions of financing as the government increased its role in the domestic economy.

Chapter 6 focuses on the 1926 General Strike, which involved more than 1.5 million workers over nine days and was the largest strike in British history, in sympathy with coal miners. It highlights the difficulties that both the government and the trade unions had in promoting their messages following the printing press strike. The government promoted narratives of revolution and presented it as a threat to British democracy.

Chapter 7 explores the Great Slump of 1931. It highlights how financial problems became defined as a spending crisis and how both the Labour and

National governments sought to address this. It notes how the formation of a National government, despite maintaining the same Prime Minister and Chancellor, liberated politicians from some of the structural constraints faced by the Labour administration that had been elected in 1929, offering a means of crisis resolution.

Chapter 8 assesses the onset of the Second World War and the expansion of the British state. Just as in the First World War, the conflict saw a vast expansion of the state, necessary to support the war effort. It then asks to what extent such an expansion of the state was accepted in the post-war settlement.

Chapter 9 looks at the Suez Crisis of 1956. It highlights the Eden government's response to President Nasser's nationalisation of the Suez Canal and the decision of the UK, along with its French and Israeli counterparts, to retake the canal by force. In doing so, the chapter explores tensions between foreign and economic policy, which ultimately led to the withdrawal of British forces in December 1956.

Chapter 10 focuses on the 'Winter of Discontent', so called due to the number of days lost to industrial action in the winter of 1978–79. The longest period of industrial action since the 1926 General Strike was, in many respects, reminiscent of the wider political and economic problems of the 1970s. The crisis expedited the shift towards monetarist economic policy and the end of the Callaghan government.

Chapter 11 analyses the Miners' Strike of 1984–85. This is the final case study that is explicitly about industrial relations. The strike had numerous parallels with British industrial relations in the 1970s. It was seen as a key test of the Thatcher government and divided not only communities but also the mining industry. The government's victory in the strike was seen as removing a key obstacle to economic reforms, which gathered pace in Thatcher's second term in office.

Chapter 12 explores the terrorist attacks in London on 7 July 2005 and the attempted attacks two weeks later. This was the worst terrorist attack on UK soil since the 1988 Lockerbie bombing and the first by perpetrators claiming to follow the Islamic religion. This chapter draws parallels between the UK government's involvement in, and rhetorical uses of, 'the war on terror' and government communication in both the First and Second World Wars, as well as assessing the tensions between policies aimed at defending freedoms and national security.

Chapter 13 centres upon the GFC of 2007–8. It identifies two clear narratives presented by the Labour and Conservative parties respectively – that of a global crisis and a crisis of debt – before highlighting how the former was redefined as the latter. Important distinctions between notions of structure and agency are drawn to help demonstrate how narratives prevented a paradigm shift.

The final crisis to be explored in Chapter 14 is that of COVID-19. Although global in nature, the timing of the pandemic differed between countries and led to different policies being pursued. Here, just as in the case of the Irish Home Rule Crisis, setting a precise date for the 'end' of the crisis is difficult – not least as the disease continues to lead to hospitalisations and fatalities and long-term effects are still being discovered. This chapter highlights tensions within different areas of government policy through contrasting health and economic perspectives. It further asks what impact such measures have had on the prevailing economic orthodoxy of austerity, developed in response to the GFC explored in the previous chapter.

Although each chapter serves as a stand-alone case study of a single crisis in British history, the final, concluding chapter will offer some remarks on how these case studies contribute to the notions of blame, framing and crisis resolution. These remarks will expand upon the theoretical considerations outlined in this chapter before making some comments about the nature of crises in British politics.

2

Understanding Crises

Overview

This chapter explores the understanding of crisis to be utilised within the book. It traces the etymology of crises from the medical term to its use in social sciences. In doing so it argues that the term poses both objective and subjective properties and highlights some of the similarities which exist in times of crisis.

It traces the pathology of crises, suggesting that a similar pattern emerges in times of crisis. Such pathologies rest upon the relationship between framing, agenda-setting, blame and resolution. While not every crisis follows exactly the same pattern, some commonalities can be identified; crises are seen as taking priority in the political agenda and require immediate action or resolution. They are also a reflection of something going wrong and in need of correcting. Such understandings offer notions of blame and require action to be taken to limit the ability of those blamed (either agents or structures) to cause similar problems in the future. The final link is that of crisis resolution, which can only occur after a crisis has been identified. This links to the notions of paradigm shifts which can symbolise widespread change following crises.

Introduction

The term 'crisis' has been used so widely by various philosophers and politicians that the concept has become 'one of the most allusive, imprecise and generally unspecified concepts within the theoreticians' armoury' (Hay, 1999a, pp 317–18). Gamble (2010a, p 6), speaking about the 2008 'GFC' (Global Financial Crisis), notes that 'when events as large and complex as this occur it is not easy to establish their causes or to assess their significance, in part because that is determined over time by the political responses to them'.

The term 'crisis' stems from ancient Greek, and has its origins in medicine (Gamble, 2009, pp 38–9). Embodied within a longer process – a disease – the crisis represents a turning point, 'when a change takes place which is decisive for recovery or death'. Habermas (1998) argues that those caught up in the crisis require liberation; crises also 'always involve an element of suspense. In a crisis, people are waiting to see what will happen … [the] outcome is not fore-ordained, and there is more than one way in which [the crisis may] be resolved'.

Scholars in other fields have varying methods and means of analysing crises (Dutton, 1986; Kindleberger and Aliber, 2005, p 24). Crises are portrayed as being exceptional and therefore often synonymous with immediate action; they can thus be viewed as turning points (Gamble, 2009, pp 38–9). Gamble draws on differences between the crisis and the cause of the crisis, noting that the 'crisis is the turning point in that disease, the moment in which the body either starts to shake off the disease or succumbs to it'. The separation of crises from their causes is key here. It is the effect of an event (or events) which generates a crisis, rather than the event per se. This can be exemplified by thinking about natural events, which are only declared crises in so far as they affect humans. It is not the natural event itself, which is not a product of any human decisions, that merits the term 'crisis'; the shifting of tectonic plates under the sea is in and of itself insufficient to be labelled as a crisis; however, should the shifting plates generate an earthquake or tsunami which impacts upon settlements, then a crisis may be declared. Debates concerning the crisis might relate to previous decisions about the location of settlements and the quality of building materials, where choices (however limited) existed.

What unites each crisis is the idea that crises must have a point of reference. When we talk of a crisis, on an aggregate level, we speak of an *x* crisis, such as a banking crisis or a financial crisis. Such referencing is often implicit rather than explicit – and, for example, others have spoken about a financial crisis (Davies, 2011), a missile crisis (Allison, 1969) or a crisis within a relationship (Minkin, 1974, p 20). A further distinction exists between natural and man-made crises. 'Industrial crises are disasters caused by human agencies and the social order; natural disasters are acts of nature' (Shrivasta et al, 1988, p 287). References, however, are not static and can change within crises – for example, the competing portrayals of COVID as a health and a financial crisis (see Chapter 14) or the tensions between narratives describing the 2008 crisis as one of a lack of growth and those depicting it as one of excessive government spending (see Chapter 13).

Crises are negative events (O'Connor, 1987), but negative events per se are not sufficient to warrant the label 'crisis'. Crises (at least in a political sense) pose a challenge to existing norms and understandings. In this context, we can think of events that are not included in this book, one recent example being Brexit. While opinion polls suggest that many now view this as a suboptimal event, defining it as a crisis, rather than the cause of one, is more problematic. Though some wish to portray Brexit as a constitutional crisis (see, for example, Grieve, 2018), this is conceptually problematic. It is less clear what aspects of the UK's (albeit uncodified) Constitution prohibit or are 'threatened' by Brexit and are thus in need of 'liberation' (Kirkland and Deva, 2023).

Crises involve both objective and subjective understandings. Jessop (2018, p 49) notes that crises contain both dangers and opportunities for those able to frame the debates. Jessop outlines five distinct features for analysing crises. First, crises have 'both objective and subjective aspects ... objectively crises occur when a set of social relations cannot be reproduced in the old way. Subjectively, crises tend to disrupt accepted views of the world and create uncertainty on how to 'go on' within it'. Second, crises 'do not have predetermined outcomes: how they are resolved, if at all, depends on the actions taken in response to them'. Third, crises may be 'deliberately exaggerated or even manufactured ... based on mis-perception or mis-recognition of real world events and processes. Sometimes crises may be manufactured, or at least exaggerated, for strategical or tactical purposes'. Fourth, it is this subjective moment that facilitates 'decisive action'; without it, disinterested observers 'will have insufficient resonance ... to spur them into efforts to take decisive action'. Fifth, crises are 'complex, objectively overdetermined moments of subjective indeterminacy, where decisive action can make a major difference to the future'.

Jessop's notion of crises as constituting both a subjective and objective understanding links to Gilbert's (2002, p 195) assertion of a '"crisis without an enemy" ... [which] characterise[d] the situation in which is a crisis is to a large extent produced by the reactions of people in charge dealing with the problem as well as by the interplay of the many other actors and organisations intervening directly or indirectly'.

This definition has distinct constructivist aspects: events can be real or perceived, constraints may be anticipated (as opposed to being visible), and crises can be defined in relation to future events, which can only be predicted *if* x or y happens/does not happen. This conditionality may be expressed implicitly or explicitly.

If it is the means by which liberation is sought (though not necessarily achieved) that determines a state of crisis, rather than the outcomes (of such events), then crises can be seen as processes (Hay, 1995). As the term implies, any 'resolution' of a crisis may only occur after a crisis has first been acknowledged.

Understanding crises as constructed is important. As Colin Hay (2010, p 465) has argued, crises 'are above all public constructions, which need bear no direct correspondence with the symptoms they narrate'. This is not to say that they are false or that the events they describe are not real and serious, but they require an active process of narration, in which the 'raw materials' of crisis are bound together and given meaning (Saunders, 2012, p 25).

Here then, in order to understand crises and their impact, we need to explore more than just the events themselves. Rather, we also need to assess and analyse the importance of the narrations surrounding such events. This book attempts to do that by engaging with the narratives of both politicians and the media.

Narratives of crises

Such understandings of crises, whereby competing interests do battle through notions of blame, agenda-setting and framing, are important. Seeing crises as processes, rather than simply assessing their outcomes, acknowledges that crises may not always be 'resolved'; indeed, many narratives of crises emerge while they are ongoing. Nor can we assume that any 'resolution' will be positive. To return to the medical definition and Habermas's notion of liberation, the 'crisis' may be resolved through death – and, indeed, many crises do result in death. Although death could conceivably be viewed as liberation, this is clearly an alternative 'liberation' than if the organism were to heal.

Understanding crises as constructed further compels us to explore narratives of events rather than the events per se. Hay (2014, p 60) notes that 'it is a necessary but not in itself a sufficient condition of getting the responses to the crisis right that we get our diagnosis of the crisis right'. Failure to do so may lead to misallocation of blame and 'new' policies that will not lead to the resolution of the crisis (or will risk worsening it).

Distinguishing between suboptimal events is more complicated. Jessop's (2018) five criteria demonstrate that defining events as crises is not simply an objective exercise; the crisis must hold both subjective and objective claims. There is no objective measure by which an event or series of events can be termed a crisis; rather, by accommodating Jessop's subjective factors, the narratives that become accepted do so by resonating with 'everyday experience'. Narratives and myths become a part of our collective understanding, not by appealing to an objective measure of validity but by 'providing a simple and flexible story that succinctly links together a series of "symptoms" with a cause while attributing blame' (Stanley, 2014, p 900). The notion of resonating is important; individuals have little direct engagement with a number of events that collectively form crises.

Nor do crises exist in isolation. The causes of crises, contested as they are, are often interlocked and interwoven. Responses to one crisis can lead to or exacerbate others (Richards, Smith and Hay, 2014). Crises – which themselves require the prioritisation of resources – can be seen as being in competition with one another. For example, the responses to environmental crises, which require, in part, lower consumption, stand in direct opposition to responses to economic crises, which are often presented as requiring greater (increased) economic activity. Which crisis (or crises) takes precedence adds a further layer of agenda-setting.

Two themes are important here, both of which have the propensity to cloud attempts to obtain a correct diagnosis. First, there may be an assumption that only a single crisis exists at any given time. Hay (2014, pp 60–61) alludes to this when he asks if the 2007–8 crisis was 'the UK's crisis or a global crisis or perhaps a crisis of the West, or perhaps a crisis of the Eurozone and its immediate hinterland from the UK is largely exempt'. By selecting just one of these – as contemporary narratives often did – other conceptualisations were excluded.

Focusing on one crisis leads to a single narrative, which in turn leads to a single set of policies aimed at resolving the crisis. Here, policies and paradigms must compete with one another. For example, when the Conservatives came to power in 2010, they abandoned Labour's Keynesian understandings in favour of austerity, and they did not seek to amalgamate the two policy responses.

Likewise, Labour in government between 2008 and 2010 rejected Conservative understandings of a debt crisis and the need to rapidly curtail existing spending.

Second, as Hay (2014, p 61) argues, plausible narratives could be offered for each of these understandings, yet each represents only half the story. Dissecting the crisis in terms of geographical area encourages us to emphasise a single focal point, which in turn leads us to overlook underlying causes – what Hay identifies as weaknesses in the Anglo-American growth model (on this, also see Hay, 2013, and Chapter 13). Ultimately, this means that even plausible narratives may not lead to effective resolutions. As the narratives themselves are contested, so too can the outcomes or any successes stem the policies to resolve them. If, for example, the medical definition of a crisis was not one of science but subjective, in the same way that political crises are, then treatments may be mis-administered. Undertaking surgery on a person's leg may not cure problems elsewhere in the body, and thus a positive response to the crisis may become unobtainable.

Successful narratives do not simply tell a story. Often, they involve simplifying complex accounts. Hay (2001, p 204) notes that indeed their 'success' as narratives generally resides in their ability to provide a simplified account that is sufficiently flexible to 'narrate' 'a great variety of morbid symptoms while unambiguously appropriating blame … crisis narratives must make sense to individuals of their experiences of the crisis'.

Narratives of crises may not lead to widespread changes for two reasons. First, blame may be misallocated. This can occur due to a lack of information (either suppressed by those who otherwise would be blamed or willingly/inadvertently missed) and/or if a 'jury' (for example, politicians, regulators, electorates) fails to assign blame to the correct groups. Here, the electorate may re-elect politicians who generated a crisis if they place blame elsewhere or view the crisis as less salient than other policy areas. Such a scenario is unlikely to promote a paradigm shift (Kirkland, 2017, p 30). However, it is worth noting that just because events do not pertain to a crisis in one sector does not entail that they cannot be considered a crisis in an alternative (policy) area. Such understandings relate to notions of causation. It is consistent to reject notions of Brexit as a constitutional crisis (Kirkland and Deva, 2023) while maintaining that it is a part of wider/broader crises involving different actors/institutions. Jessop (2017, p 133) argues that Brexit is not by itself a crisis, but a manifestation of a 'continuing organic crisis of the British state and society'. Likewise, Caporaso (2018) argues that (from the EU's perspective) Brexit, the Eurozone crisis and the refugee crisis are all intertwined, and Virdee and McGeever (2018) situate Brexit within a wider 'financial and political crisis'.

The second reason why narratives of any specific crisis may not lead to large-scale changes is that such responsibility may be confined to a small group or individual – the 'bad apples' argument. Here, narratives of blame may focus on individuals at the expense of overarching structures or processes. Such understandings emphasise notions of immorality stemming from the actions or agency of the 'apple' (or individual) itself. Once this blame has been cast and measures have been taken to deal with the issue, notions (understandings) of crisis resolutions often suggest that searching for further problems is unnecessary. The problem was simply the singular apple – it is not a product of the tree or the wider conditions in which the apple grew or was cultivated. After all, if we accept the implicit causation that 'one bad apple can spoil the barrel', we cannot simultaneously also argue that bad barrels (structures) spoil the otherwise good apples.

Just as in the case of crisis (narrative) formation, deciding which crises gain traction, and when, is a subjective process. Despite accepting and promoting narratives of crises relating to the environment or climate change, during economic downturns politicians often prioritise the latter over the former. Burns and Tobin (2016) highlight this in respect to the EU's environmental policy, but the same is also true of national governments. The issue of climate change has been on the domestic political agenda for the last three decades, with varying levels of salience, during which time it has frequently been labelled a 'crisis'. Yet policies aimed at overcoming the 2007–8 economic crisis and COVID-19 were formed and framed in a political space that at best ignored, and at worst exacerbated, such understandings of a climate crisis by pursuing economic growth at the expense of environmental concerns.

Such processes are influenced by groups such as the media and politicians. The choice of what to publicise emphasises the privileged position of the media within society. The ability to act as gatekeepers (Berkowitz, 1997; Shoemaker, 1997; White, 1997) can come through either publicising or suppressing the reporting of events. Journalists and/or editors can select what information is presented to readers/viewers/listeners. These decisions, to disseminate information or not, can be highly subjective. Bennett and Kottasz (2012, p 131) support this idea of the gatekeeper, noting that 'media coverage is a major source of knowledge about business crises and an important determinant of public attitudes towards them. Indeed, in the absence of first-hand experience, the news media are likely to have been a person's primary source of information'. If media coverage is a person's primary source of information, it follows that if the media does not report such information, the public may be unaware of it.

Cohen and Young (1973, p 97) note that news 'is manufactured by journalists through interpreting and selecting events to fit pre-existing categories, themselves a product of the bureaucratic exigencies of news agencies'. The same news stories appear in different outlets in very different manners, with the focus of the stories depending very much upon the journalists, editors, or intended audience. The subjective nature of the media is not confined to the wording of news items; the amount of space or time devoted to an issue and the salience of the issues or news within a newspaper or TV bulletin also are subjective – for example, it may be assumed by consumers of news that issues which are front-page news or the first item on the bulletin are more important than those which are tucked away in the middle of a newspaper or appear later on the television programme.

Cohen, quoted by Dearing and Rodger (1996, p 1, original emphasis), also notes: 'The press may not be successful much of the time in telling people what to think, but it is stunningly successful in telling its readers what to think *about*'. The notions of gatekeeping and issue prevalence are important, as 'attention to an issue, whether by media personnel, members of the public, or policy makers represents power by some individuals or organizations to influence the decision making process' (Dearing and Rodger, 1996, p 3).

Key events can lead to shifting discourses within crises. For example, the election of the Conservative-led coalition government in 2010 helped usher in a new understanding of the economic problems Britain faced. The dominant narrative of these events, advocated by the incumbent Labour government, was as a 'Global Financial Crisis'. Once in government, the coalition was able to redefine the crisis as one of excessive spending, offering a justification for austerity policies (Kirkland, 2017).

Such understandings are linked to the subjective nature of crises; 'depending on the vantage point of the observer(s) and their interest, crises may generate different outcomes. Allocating resources in times of crises can be politicised and even being blamed may not necessarily prevent agents or institutions receiving resources' (Kirkland, 2022, p 21).

Change and paradigm shifts

Crises, in this sense, can be posited against 'normal policy making' (Hall, 1993). Given the 'failures' associated with crises and the additional resources required to alleviate them, there are advantages in declaring particular scenarios to be crises. Declaring a crisis in the NHS, for example, presents an argument for exceptional increases in resources to the sector. Some agents have motivations for declaring a crisis – to attract attention to particular issues or causes, or to divert resources to a particular policy area.

Hall (1993) outlines how crises can change policies through the notion of paradigm shifts. Paradigm shifts can be seen as 'advancing' understandings (for example, through Hall's understanding of social learning). They can develop and draw upon, but importantly transform, existing policies. Hall (1993, p 277), in outlining the transition from policy at time-0 to policy at time-1, cites Sack, who argues: 'the most important influence in this learning is previous policy itself'. If no social learning occurs, then the policies at these two times will be the same. However, during paradigm shifts, one replaces the other because existing means of understanding are unable to conceptualise/capture current understandings. Implicit here is an important notion that policy at time-1 is at least as good as, if not better than, policy at time-0.

Hall (1993, p 278) warns that social learning may take 'different forms'; it normally involves three 'central variables; the overarching goals that guide policy … the techniques or policy instruments used to attain those goals, and the precise setting of these instruments'.

In outlining the transition from Keynesianism to monetarism in the 1970s and 1980s, Hall (1993, p 284) notes that when such a paradigm shift occurred:

> there was a radical shift in the hierarchy of goals guiding policy, the instruments relied on to effect policy, and the setting of those instruments.

> Moreover, these changes were accompanied by substantial changes in discourse employed by policy makers in the analysis of the economy on which policy was based.

Hall argues that the economic challenges of the 1970s left the Keynesian paradigm unable to explain rising inflation and unemployment, which hitherto were seen to hold a negative relationship. The breakdown in this understanding, conceptualised as 'stagflation', encouraged new means of thinking and understanding to gain prominence and allowed monetarist theory to become the dominant way of understanding the economy. For its proponents, monetarist theory was 'presented as a doctrine that could restore the authority of the government as well as resolve Britain's economic problems' (Hall, 1993, pp 284–5, 287). The resolution to the crisis of the 1970s saw inflation, rather than unemployment, become the key macroeconomic indicator of the economy. According to the newly dominant monetarist ideology, controlling inflation was central to achieving economic stability and growth. Successive governments emphasised inflation targets rather than alternative measures such as unemployment figures.

Third-order change occurs when existing paradigms fail to effectively conceptualise the world. Crises can require new paradigms, with distinct narratives, to emerge to explain what is happening and how such crises can be resolved. Monetarism offered an understanding of stagflation (and how to overcome such problems), which enabled it to replace Keynesianism as the dominant paradigm in the late 1970s/early 1980s.

Hall (1993, p 275) argues that social learning only occurs in third-order change, which is distinct from 'normal policy making'. However, he also points out that such social learning is contested and presents the question of who is able to determine what is in the 'national interest'. In assessing the paradigm shift of the 1980s, Hall (1993, p 288) argues that 'macroeconomic issues became the subject of an intense political debate' and the 1979 general election offered voters the option to replace Keynesian economics with monetarism.

If crises offer the ability to pursue different policies, then they must also 'be able to generate means of differentiating (and deciding) that which worked (particular policy, agents, etc.) and that which didn't [or failed]' (Kirkland, 2017, p 14). Here, new paradigms are not only expected to offer 'better' policies, but also theoretical understanding/conceptualisations where previous paradigms failed. Crises can, and do, lead to changes not only in policies but in overarching understandings or paradigms. This, in turn, suggests that more than one viable policy option must be present before a crisis.

Akin to crises, paradigm shifts are also contested. Although we often see history as a linear collection of ideologies with eventual winners and losers, paradigms do not simply disappear once replaced, but rather can still contest the narratives/assumptions of any new paradigm. The example offered by Hall of the shift from Keynesianism to monetarism bears this out – although monetarism became dominant in the 1980s and guided British economic policy for almost three decades, neither it nor Keynesianism was 'conclusively proved nor disproved' (Blyth, 2013a, p 204). A testimony to this is the resurgence of Keynesianism following the 2008 economic crisis, as both a solution to the problems faced in 2008 and a critique of austerity policies (Gamble, 2009; Boyer, 2012).

Crises as unequal

We can also add to this the importance of choice in the decisions that led to the onset of the crisis. Crises can be seen to legitimise particular policy actions, as indicated by Rapport's (1962) definition of a crisis as a call to action.

In addition to the replacement of one crisis by another, seemingly more important, crisis on the political agenda, we can also point to deliberate attempts to suppress or dispel notions of crises. Four reasons may exist why individuals or organisations might wish to suppress notions of a crisis: to avoid blame, to shift discourse(s), to prevent resource allocation, or to defend the status quo. These factors are not mutually exclusive – those seeking to avoid narrations of a crisis emerging may hold multiple reasons for advocating such positions.

Not all crises follow a set pathology or are indeed equal. The failure of the existing paradigm to sufficiently explain events often leads to a plurality of 'alternatives', not all of which can be implemented. Different actors possess different powers during what Hall (1993) identifies as 'normal policy making' – such as wealth, influence, and ability to publicise their narratives – and these can be magnified during crises. During crises, greater attention is afforded to political leaders (for example, during both world wars) or those with particular specialisms (for example, medical professionals during COVID-19).

The time horizons of events/responses within crises can also differ significantly. The London Bombings of 7/7 (see Chapter 12) occurred within minutes of each other, while other crises, such as both world wars (Chapters 5 and 8) lasted years, and questions remain as to whether or not the threats posed by crises such as COVID-19 have dissipated four years after first being realised (see Chapter 14). Indeed, Gamble (2009, p 40) notes that the term 'crisis' can refer to 'an impasse, or deadlock, in society or institution, which can persist for a very long time before it is decisively resolved'.

Additionally, similar events, natural or man-made, may lead to different policy outcomes. One recession may not be the same as another, and the difference in responses or effectiveness of responses may lead to one being declared a crisis and the other not.

Linked to this, we can differentiate between different groups caught up within the crisis. We can distinguish, for example, between those blamed and those not, those able to contribute to policy-making decisions and those not, and between groups that may be affected to differing degrees. While there may exist some overlap between such groups – and such distinctions are not exhaustive – they are not mutually exclusive. It is not a precondition of being blamed that an institution or agent will be excluded from the decision-making process; in the wake of the 2007–8 GFC, much was made of the expertise and technical knowledge that those employed within the banking sector could offer to policy makers (McDonnell and Valbruzzi, 2014).

Political or aggregated (as opposed to individual) crises have different impacts upon different actors or agents. Although it is a 'cliché, [it is true that] in times of emergency people turn to both state and nation'. The scale of the crisis means that the state becomes the primary response vehicle. The state can 'provide the resources required for security [and] use its sovereign powers to intervene in a way that no other institution can' (Stanley, 2022, p 160). For example, during both the GFC and the COVID-19 pandemic, the government organised the printing of 'extra' money through a process known as quantitative easing – something that would be illegal if any other group or individual sought to do it. State control expanded in both world wars as the pressures of total war required that the state become responsible for the organisation of industries essential to the war effort. The state also acted to nationalise elements of the banking sector, which was deemed 'too big to fail' in the wake of the GFC. On a lesser scale, the state mobilised the army to ensure vital supplies during the General Strike of 1926.

Particular groups may also benefit from crises; for example, crises offer the state additional powers. Historically, crises allow 'reformist policy makers powers to bypass legislative gridlock and entrenched interests' (Mulder, 2020) They can allow (or be used to legitimise) the suspension of governance norms (including democratic elections) in order to fight a larger, common enemy. For example, in the Second World War, the House of Commons voted to extend its life beyond the normal 4–5 years – and for longer than the 7 years permitted by the 1911 Parliament Act. In other countries, such as Greece and Italy, the Eurozone crisis led to the imposition of technocratic governments and the suspension of democratic elections (McDonnell and Valbruzzi, 2014).

3

The Constitutional Crisis of 1909–10

Overview

This chapter analyses the Constitutional Crisis of 1909–10. This crisis emanated from the House of Lords' opposition to the Liberal budget of 1909. Opposition stemmed from the notion that the Liberal government – which had won a landslide in 1906 – had extended the normal parameters of the budget to include policies that had previously been vetoed by the upper chamber. This led the Lords to veto the budget, challenging the convention that money bills, passed by the lower house, should pass unopposed. The Lords' veto led to a constitutional crisis and generated a political deadlock. The crisis extended beyond the legislature and executive to incorporate the monarchy, following George V's guarantee that should the Liberals win a second election in late 1910, he would create hundreds of new Liberal peers to ensure the passage of the budget. This prompted two elections in 1910 – the first explicitly on the issue of the budget and a second on House of Lords reform. The Liberals won both due to the support of the Irish Parliamentary Party; they passed the budget and, in 1911, passed the Parliament Act, explicitly limiting the powers of the House of Lords and confirming the primacy of the House of Commons.

Introduction

The UK Constitution is often noted for its flexibility, not being codified like other constitutions, such as that of the US. The UK's Constitution has evolved through a number of Acts of Parliament and conventions. However, this process has not been linear or uncontroversial. As the events of 1909–10 demonstrate, drawing upon historical conventions can lead to different interpretations of the Constitution and its operation. Such differences were clear in the Edwardian period, and it was unclear whether or not the Constitution could be updated to reflect the wider changes within British politics or if the Constitution itself had become obsolete.

The key change of the nineteenth century was the extension of the franchise to more males. This weakened the monopoly of the upper classes over British politics and led to new items being placed onto the political agenda, though such changes were not equal across institutions. As the franchise was extended to a greater proportion of the population throughout the late nineteenth century, the divisions between the elected House of Commons and the unelected House of Lords became starker. The primacy of the elected House of Commons was by no means accepted or even guaranteed; at the turn of the twentieth century, the Conservative Prime Minister, the 3rd Marquess of Salisbury, sat in, and governed from, the House of Lords. Salisbury, although acknowledging that the power of the House of Commons had risen over the nineteenth century, 'knew little' about it. His first-hand experience of the lower chamber was limited – he had sat 'for a pocket borough during the few years he spent' in the Commons; he interacted with elected MPs during Cabinet meetings, but he sought to minimise such interactions and he 'loathed in the deepest way having to kowtow to an electorate whose intellectual and moral qualities he despised' (Bentley, 2001, pp 170–71).

Along with broader themes of powers, some specific instruments were also questioned and tested. The tradition of the House of Lords not altering (or indeed rejecting) money bills dates back to Commons resolutions of 1671 and 1678, the latter of which stated: 'it is the undoubted and sole right of the Commons to direct, limit, and appoint in such bills the ends, purposes, considerations, conditions, limitations, and qualifications of such grants, which ought not to be changed or altered by the House of Lords'. Yet the Lords had 'never explicitly admitted the claims of the Commons [though] they had in fact submitted to them. The right of the Lords to reject a money bill remained, on the tacit assumption that it would not be exercised' (Le May, 1979, p 132; Parliament, 2023).

Such a process was tested in 1860, when the Lords rejected Gladstone's proposals to abolish the duty on paper, making printing more accessible to working-class authors and ideas, though this rejection 'did not provoke a major Constitutional crisis because the Cabinet was divided' (Le May, 1979, p 132). This meant that the proposals could easily be dropped without significant political repercussions. The Prime Minister, Lord Palmerston, quoted in Le May, told the Queen that 'the opinion of the great majority of the public is that the Lords have done a right and useful thing'.

Tensions over the powers of both chambers and, importantly, their relationship with one another, led to partisan understandings not just of the legislature, but of wider constitutional arrangements. Liberal writings and interpretations of the Constitution were at odds with Conservative understandings of the authority commanded by institutions such as the House of Lords or the monarchy (Bentley, 2001, p 159). Here, the Lords 'joined hands with the people to save them from manipulation by a short-sighted, self-centred and faction riddled system of "democracy"'. The House of Lords, according to Conservatives, could, if necessary, 'act as a barrier against harm until the electors had their chance to comment more fully at a general election' (Bentley, 2001, p 169).

Rising unemployment and the prospect of a recession were seen as quickly draining government support in favour of alternatives to the Liberals' fiscal policies, namely tariff reforms. The Unionists offered little acceptance or support for the election result of 1906. Speaking a few months later in June, former Prime Minister and leading Conservative MP, Arthur Balfour (quoted in Le May 1979, p 190) stated that it was the duty of the Unionist Party 'in or out of office to continue to control the destinies of this great empire'. Such duty was exercised when the party was out of office, through their large majority in the House of Lords. For Balfour and the Conservatives, the House of Lords offered stability. Unlike the Commons, which due to its democratic nature was prone to fluctuations, the Lords represented a bulwark against large, but ultimately short-lasting, shifts in public opinion.

Balfour's position was born out of a constitutional understanding of the role of the House of Lords. Speaking in Manchester in October 1907 Balfour (quoted by Le May, 1979, p 190) argued that the Lords' powers, 'which [they] undoubtedly ought to exercise, is not to prevent the people of this country having the laws they wish to have, but to see that the laws are not … the hasty and ill-considered offspring of one passionate election'.

With such dominance also came a particular view of the UK Constitution. The House of Lords, collectively, saw themselves as guardians of the public's (as opposed to the electorate's) will – against a Commons that was still elected by only a minority of the adult population.

The Liberal Party won the 1906 election with a landslide majority on an unprecedented 10.6 per cent swing from the Conservatives. The Liberals won 401 out of the 670 seats and, in addition, would be supported by the 83 Irish Nationalists and the 29 Labour MPs (Murray, 1980, p 55). Such a victory enabled the party to plan radical legislation, which further exacerbated tensions between the now Liberal-dominated House of Commons and the Conservative-dominated House of Lords. Asquith, quoted in Cross (1963, p 24), wrote to the King's Private Secretary: 'Unless I am greatly mistaken the election of 1906 inaugurates a new era.'

The composition of the Commons was now radically different from that of the House of Lords, where the Conservatives held a large majority, with 355 seats compared to the Liberals' 88 (and could further be expected to be supported on key issues by 124 Liberal Unionists). The composition of the House of Lords reduced the prospect for a radical programme to emerge, certainly on the most salient issue of the day – Irish Home Rule. Divisions over the issue of Irish Home Rule left the Liberal Party with less than 15 per cent of MPs in the upper house (Norton, 2012, pp 446–7).

The Liberal government that assumed office in 1906 was markedly different from that which had left office in 1885. New liberal thinkers such as J.A. Hobson and L.T. Hobhouse were successful in inspiring a new generation of liberal thinking and justified the taxation of a particular class for the 'immediate benefit of another'. Such ideas led the Liberals to propose new forms of direct taxation, such as differentiating between earned and unearned incomes, increasing death duties and taxation on land values (Murray, 1980, pp 32–34).

Yet there was little to suggest that the government that assumed office was likely to be revolutionary. As Paul Thompson (1992, pp 210–11, 222) notes, prior to the extension of the franchise in 1918, Parliament was not seen exclusively as a vehicle for radical reform or change. Formal politics was not universal; less than one third of adults were registered voters, with women and the working classes largely excluded. The Parliament that was elected in 1906 reflected this bias against the working class: 'a sixth of [its] members were Old Etonians, a third had been to Oxford or Cambridge. A fifth were landowners; nearly two-fifths active businessmen; and nearly half involved in finance or insurance. A mere tenth were working class, most trade unionists'. Nor were such biases simply a product of the Conservative Party; although there were fewer 'officers and country gentlemen' among the ranks of Liberal MPs than there were in the Conservative opposition, Asquith's parliamentary party retained more barristers, solicitors and businessmen, to the extent that 'a quarter [of Liberal MPs] were men of great wealth' (Cook, 1976, p 43).

Throughout the 1906–10 Parliament, the House of Lords rejected an education bill and a plural voting bill that had been passed in the Commons, as well as land bills and a licensing bill, which was rejected in support of the commercial interests of brewers (Powell, 1996, p 44).

Conservatives and Unionists highlighted the lack of mandate for such policies, which were designed to appeal to only a selection of the population. The Liberal Party, for example, did not incorporate debates about pensions into their official campaign in 1906, and indeed, the bill faced opposition from the government's own backbenchers (Cross, 1963, p 68). The Liberal MP for Preston, Harold Cox, claimed that 'no member of the House [of Commons] had a mandate for' the legislation that he claimed would cost £26 million per annum (Hansard, 1907). Cox argued that, rather than standing on a platform of pensions, the Liberals had promised a reduction in taxation – something that would be unaffordable should pensions be introduced.

The Lords, for their part, exercised restraint in determining which bills to block. Although this was not an easy strategy, they were able to block certain bills that were deemed partisan, while avoiding 'open collision with working-class interests', to the extent that the editor of the *Spectator* argued that 'my quarrel with the House of Lords is not that they pass too few Liberal measures but that they pass too many' (Blewett, 1972, pp 60–61). The Lords successfully managed to block measures that were seen as sectional or had little public support, while 'measures that favoured the working class, and that could have engendered a real peers-versus-people struggle, were let through, not least the Trades Disputes Bill, the Old Age Pensions Bill, and the Eight Hours Bill' (Norton, 2012, p 449).

In response, the Liberal government in 1907 introduced a motion (quoted by Norton, 2012, p 449), which stated:

> That, in order to give effect to the will of the people as expressed by their elected representatives, it is necessary that the power of the other House to alter or reject bills passed by this House should be so restricted by law as to secure that within the limits of a single Parliament the final decision of the Commons shall prevail.

Although this motion passed by 432 votes to 147, the government did not pursue any further action or bring forward legislation to that effect. The issue of the Lords had not been salient in the 1906 election campaign and therefore any moves would likely be rejected by the Lords. Nor was there appetite for another election; the Liberals had suffered a number of by-election losses throughout the Parliament, which led the Conservative Central Office by 1909 to predict a Unionist majority of 20 in any future election. Liberal predictions, too, acknowledged that the government was 'doomed' to defeat (Blewett, 1972, p 62; Norton, 2012, p 449).

In 1909, the twin pressures of German militarisation and social welfare spending left the government with a deficit of £16.5 million. Pensions, introduced in 1908, cost £8.75 million and purchasing four new Dreadnought battleships amounted to a further £8.75 million (Morgan, 2009, p 28).

To overcome these costs, the Liberals proposed a budget which would raise £16 million in revenue through a combination of increasing income tax from 1s to 1s 2d in the pound, imposing a supertax of 6d in the pound on incomes over £5,000, increasing duty on tobacco by half a penny and duties on whisky by 6d a bottle. New taxes on cars and petrol were introduced, along with controversial land taxes (Cook, 1976, p 48).

The Chancellor, Lloyd George, one of the great political orators of British history, presented this budget as a 'war budget', designed to 'wage implacable war against poverty and squalidness' as well as funding naval rearmament through the purchase of new Dreadnoughts (Cook, 1976 pp. 46–8).

The Finance Bill, introduced in April, only passed its last stages in the House of Commons on 4 November 1909. It passed by 379 votes to 149, following an unprecedented 70 days of parliamentary debate and 554 divisions. It then went to the House of Lords, where it was rejected on 30 November by 350 votes to 75.

Two days later, in the Commons, Asquith (quoted in Powell, 1996, p 48) carried a motion declaring that the Lords' actions in blocking the budget represented '"a breach of the Constitution and a usurpation of the rights of the Commons". He sought and obtained a dissolution from the King and the focus of the budget battle shifted from Parliament to the country, with a general election to be held in January 1910'.

Questions of representation became paramount. The budget was not designed to instigate a battle with the Lords, but as a workaround to the Lords' veto, constructed on the assumption that the peers 'would not dare to tamper with a finance bill'. Though he acknowledged that this was a possibility, Lloyd George devised the budget as 'something of a "catch-all" that would serve to promote the Liberal cause irrespective of what happened to his proposals in the Lords' (Murray, 1973, p 555).

The Lords defended their position, maintaining that the bill that was presented extended beyond the remit of a budget and was being used to circumvent their expressed opposition in policy areas such as temperance measures and paving the way for new taxes based upon land values. It was argued that the Liberals did not possess a mandate for these reforms, and by rejecting the plans, the Lords sought to force a general election, which would act as a de facto referendum on the issues (Sayle, 2021). Such views, held by the radical right within the Unionist parties, linked to notions of the legitimacy of the aristocracy but also the upper chamber as acting as a constitutional safeguard against the House of Commons – ensuring that legislation passed reflected the will of the people. On this issue, opponents to the bill gambled that they, better than the elected House of Commons, understood the public mood/will.

Ridley (1992) argues that contemporary and initial understandings of the decision to reject the budget for short-term political motivations are too simplistic. Rather than agreeing with narratives, epitomised in Lloyd George's assertion that the House of Lords was 'Balfour's poodle', which suggest that the Conservatives and Balfour simply allowed proposals that would support the Labour movement while rejecting sectional Liberal proposals, Ridley argues that the differences stemmed from an understanding of the Constitution that had emerged from the 'constitutional revolution' between 1882 and 1902. Here, as the executive took a greater control over the timetable of the House of Commons – encouraged by Liberal and Conservative Prime Ministers alike – the House of Lords remained a genuinely free debating chamber which could provide the necessary scrutiny to bills that passed in the Commons. Compounded with these changes, the Liberals' landslide victory in 1906 reinforced the Conservative argument for checks upon the Commons.

The Lords' decisions to block the budget represented a break from convention, which, in lieu of either side backing down, drew other actors such as the monarch, who was normally passive in parliamentary decision making, into the debate. The former Conservative Chancellor of the Exchequer, Michael Hicks Beach, warned Balfour against allowing the Lords to reject the budget. Quoted by Daunton (2007, p 265), he stated:

> The 'interference of the Lords with taxation' will give the government the very cry they want and deprive us of the chance of success we should have had without it … the wisest policy would be, to let it [the budget] be tried. Let people suffer a bit by radical legislation: they will soon put an end to it. But I am convinced we shall be beaten on the issue that would now be presented, and to incur such a risk for the sake of what we might gain by the rejection of this budget for a time, seems to me the worst gamble I have ever known in politics.

Asquith asked Edward VII to create up to 500 new peers to try and resolve the issue. To overcome such tensions, the government sought to appeal not to the electorate but to the monarch to break the impasse. Such a proposal suggested that the traditional method of appointing peers could be circumvented. As the rationale for creating new peers would be explicitly to ensure the legislative passage of the budget, an overtly political act, it directly challenged existing constitutional arrangements establishing the distribution of power, such as the relationship between the two chambers or the power of the monarch to make political appointments in the House of Lords (Kirkland and Deva, 2023, p 616).

This action prompted Unionists to argue that such moves were themselves unconstitutional and violated the neutrality of the monarch. Lord Curzon (quoted by The Earl of Ronaldshay, 1928, p 55), who led the opposition from the Lords, told a crowd in Reading: 'the idea that the House of Lords can be intimidated, or coerced, or cajoled by the threat of the creation of five hundred peers to act in a manner inconsistent with its own conviction or conscience appears to me a fantastic dream'.

The crisis of 1909–10 differed from previous crises relating to the roles of the House of Commons and House of Lords as there was no agreed mechanism for resolving this dispute as there had been in 1830 or 1832. The crisis tested the monarch's relationship with the executive and legislature, as the government appealed to the King to create new Liberal peers to ensure the smooth passage of their political agenda, threatening the constitutional neutrality of the monarch. In previous crises, the 'unquestioned Prerogative of the Crown was an accepted means of resolving a political deadlock; now the prerogative itself was a matter of dispute' (Le May, 1979, p 189).

The crisis then escalated beyond the measures announced in the budget. The crisis was not born out of economics but was constitutional in nature. Norton (2012) exemplifies this, arguing that the issue at stake was whether the Unionist-dominated House of Lords was willing to exert in full the powers afforded to the House. The crisis went to the very heart of the UK Constitution, to the extent that it was 'doubtful' whether the Constitution was accepted by 'those who govern' and conversely 'whether Britain possessed the minimum conditions necessary for Parliamentary government'. Both sides in the debate believed the other had 'broken the Constitution' – the Liberals argued that the Lords' blockage of the budget did so, while the Unionists challenged the promises Asquith had sought and received from the King.

Creating new peers would affect decisions beyond the budget of 1909. With no scope to retire or resign (such provisions only came into effect following the passage of the Peerage Act 1963 and the House of Lords Reform Act 2014), those appointed would remain members. Equally, as life peers were not created until 1958 (under the Life Peerages Act), it is more than conceivable that any new appointments would be hereditary and would permanently increase the size of the upper chamber. Such changes would be permanent (at least until the Conservatives could create a sufficient number of peers to counter the expansion), meaning that the Liberals would be able to push through other controversial measures such as Irish Home Rule (see Chapter 4).

Framing the crisis

For the Liberals in government, the decision to block the budget represented an overextension of the role of the Lords as a revising chamber. Lloyd George (1909) publicly campaigned in the summer of 1909 on the issue of the budget. Addressing an audience of 4,000 in his Limehouse Speech, he defended the economics of the New Liberalism: 'it is rather a shame for a rich country like ours – probably the richest in the world, if not the richest that the world has even seen – that it should allow those who have toiled all their days to end in penury and possibly starvation'. On land tax, Lloyd George justified the government's position by linking economic inputs to outputs. He drew upon a hypothetical example in the coal industry, whereby two prospectors spend large sums of money in an attempt to mine coal. Neither finds coal, having spent £250,000 and £100,000 in the process. Along comes a third prospector, who succeeds in obtaining coal. The outcomes, Lloyd George continued, were that:

> The first man failed; but the landlord got his royalty; the landlord got his dead rent – a very good name for it. The second man failed, but the landlord got his royalty. These capitalists put their money in, and I said 'When the cash failed what did the landlord put in?' He simply put in the bailiffs.

Such a system – whereby certain groups were excluded or insulated from economic risk – was unsustainable in the long term and went against the traditional understanding of stewardship, which was defined as 'the security and defence of the country. Looking after the broken in their villages and its neighbourhoods'. Lloyd George summarised his position: 'No country, however rich, can permanently afford to have quartered upon its revenue a class which declines to do the duty which it was called upon to perform since the beginning.'

In a later speech in Newcastle-upon-Tyne in October, Lloyd George (quoted by Cook, 1976, p 49) went further, asking: 'Who ordained that a few should have all the land of Britain as a prerequisite, who made 10,000 people owners of the soil, and the rest of us trespassers in the land of our birth?'

Press coverage of the issues during the elections was 'both massive and highly partisan in treatment' to the extent that many newspapers over the period 'may have deliberately reported the speeches of opponents inaccurately' (Blewett, 1972, p 301; Blaxill, 2013, p 320). For example, the *London Evening Standard* (1910) in making its position on House of Lords reform asserted that 'Mr Lloyd George is talking utter nonsense' and that Lloyd George was 'at his old game of humbugging the people', while the Conservative Press 'assiduously propagated' ideas of a Liberal and Labour pact, despite both parties denying it and Labour standing more candidates in January 1910 than it had done in 1906 (Porritt,

1910). Similar themes of open hostility emerged in the liberal press; the *Liverpool Daily Post* (1910) ran a headline 'Lordly Lawbreakers' with a subheading 'The Vagueness of Mr Balfour'.

In such reporting the press moved beyond discussions of 'normal policy' making (see Chapter 2 and Hall, 1993) through highlighting the wider importance of constitutional issues. In August 1909, discussion of the budget was repudiated in favour of tariff reform in the Unionist-supporting press, which included the *Daily Telegraph*, the *Morning Post*, the *Standard* and the *Observer* (Blewett, 1972, p 82). By the time of the election in January, the Unionist press was split over the salience and issue of tariff reform. The *Spectator* demonstrated 'antipathy' to the issue, advising its readers to 'choose the lesser evil and therefore vote for the Tariff Reformer rather than the Liberal'. Others, such as the *Sunday Times*, 'virtually ignored tariff reform, devoting its election leaders mainly to a bravura defence of the House of Lords'. By December, as public support waned, 'many Unionist editors, faced with the second election, believed that only drastic remedies could bring success. The Unionist Press became riddled with men convinced that one such remedy was … the excision of Tariff Reform … from the party programme' (Blewett, 1972, pp 306–7).

The unfolding constitutional crisis displaced the issue of tariff reform as the most salient issue of the day. This was exemplified by calls to support the House of Lords even if this meant abandoning/weakening positions on tariff reform. This links to the arguments that crises come to dominate political agendas and divert political resources (see Chapter 2).

Such coverage is akin to the notion of crises as highly salient events, requiring (or enabling) a 'call to action' (Rapport, 1962). As Chapter 2 demonstrated, crises shift agendas, replacing normal policy-making processes. Each of the elections of 1910 extended beyond the budget provisions of 1910 but pertained to constitutional questions about what powers the House of Lords *should* hold.

As Chapter 2 also noted, the ability to disseminate ideas was unequal; Unionist papers had a circulation advantage of just under a million, with the independent *Daily Mirror* alone possessing a circulation of around 630,000. However, any 'advantages which may have accrued from the Unionist preponderance in the national daily press were considerably dissipated by poor relations between the party organisation and the press, and a lack of solidarity amongst the Unionist Press itself' (Blewett, 1972, p 303).

In contrast, the relations between the Liberal Party and the press were carefully managed by Sir Henry Norman, MP for Wolverhampton and a former journalist, who by the time of the January election 'had established a relationship with the press which was the envy of the Unionists' (Blewett, 1972, pp 301–3). In addition to this, the press was, in both elections, 'characterised by an extraordinary preoccupation with things electoral. For eight weeks from 3 December 1909, and for a month following 19 November 1910 the press was literally dominated by the elections'.

Resolving the crisis

The Liberals lost 123 seats in January 1910, leaving them with two seats more than the Conservatives, who had recovered from their electoral nadir of 1906 to win 272. Importantly, and due to the UK's first past the post electoral system, the Conservatives gained 46.8 per cent of the vote in contrast to the Liberals' 43.5 per cent. The Liberals could only form a government with the support of the Irish Parliamentary Party, which held 71 seats (11 fewer than it had won in 1906).

Throughout the election, Liberal leaders argued that House of Lords reforms were needed. The issue of the House of Lords united the anti-Unionists (Blewett, 1972, p 105). The Liberal manifesto of January 1910 argued that the Lords, through blocking the budget, had 'violated the Constitution', while the Labour Party manifesto explicitly stated, 'The Lords must go' (a line that was also repeated in its December manifesto).

Yet, given the parliamentary arithmetic, this could only be achieved through working with other parties. The slim majority afforded to the Liberals was a far cry from the majority seen in 1906; while the Liberals could rely on the support of the Labour Party, which had won 40 seats, a wider coalition was needed, incorporating the Irish Parliamentary Party. In appealing to the Irish Parliamentary Party, Asquith promised reform of the House of Lords (that is, removing its veto powers) in return for their support to pass the budget. Akin to the Lords' self-defined 'constitutional role' demonstrated in the 1909 budget, the Conservative-dominated upper house had previously blocked proposals for Irish Home Rule under Gladstone, arguing that the government did not possess an explicit mandate for such a provision. The prospect of removing such a power therefore appealed to the Irish Parliamentary Party, which reached an agreement with Asquith in April (Pugh, 2012, p 19). The budget was passed in the Commons on 27 April and in the Lords the following day without a division (Cook, 1976, p 53).

The passage of the budget, however, left the issue of the House of Lords unresolved. Asquith planned to bring a bill forward limiting the powers of the Lords, removing their veto. Those opposed to reforming the upper chamber argued that the Liberals and their allies, the Irish Nationalists, still lacked a majority for such reforms, as the January election gave only a mandate for the passage of the budget. The King, Edward VII, informed the government that he would not create new Liberal peers to ensure the passage of the Parliament Act without an election being held first (Dutton, 2004, p 26).

Preparations for a summer election, however, were postponed following the sudden death of the King on 6 May 1910. In the 'hiatus of mourning … politicians stepped back from the brink' and Asquith proposed to find a solution through dialogical means. Balfour, for the Conservatives, accepted the opportunity and a 'constitutional conference' of 12 meetings followed in June and July, with further meetings after the summer recess in October and November (Powell, 1996, pp 52–3). Keen to try and resolve the situation without embarrassing the new monarch, George V, Asquith and Balfour sought to work together to find an agreeable solution. Negotiations were covered in much secrecy, to the annoyance of the Irish Parliament Party, which saw this as an attempt to sideline the issue of Home Rule. Although both sides genuinely attempted to find amicable solutions, these talks broke down, primarily over questions of Irish Home Rule, and because of Lloyd George's unsuccessful proposal to form a National government (Morgan, 1971, pp 150–55; Dutton, 2004, pp 26–7; Pugh, 2012, p 20).

This issue was further complicated by the agreement that Asquith reached with the Irish Parliamentary Party, securing their support for the budget (which the party was otherwise inclined to vote against) in return for promises to abolish the Lords' veto, which in turn would pave the way for Home Rule (see next chapter). This widening of the issue affected the discussions held over the summer. As Powell (1996, p 54) notes: 'the only way in which the conference could have succeeded was if the two front benches had been prepared to come together to produce not simply a joint plan for dealing with reform to the House of Lords, but an agreed solution to the Irish Question as well'.

After the collapse of the talks, Asquith, along with Lord Crewe, the Lord Privy Seal, met with King George V, and issued a Cabinet memorandum calling for guarantees to create Liberal peers or face a dissolution. The danger for the King was that this risked political neutrality. The former was to take a position on a bill before Parliament, in the case of the latter, Lord Crewe (quoted by Marriott, 1931, p 585) warned 'it would be practically impossible, however anxious we naturally should be to do it, to keep the Crown out of the controversy'.

Such arguments link to supporting Jessop's (2018) objective criteria that existing social relations could not continue in the existing manner and Hall's (1993) notion of a paradigm shift – namely that a new understanding of the relationship between the chambers and even their relationship with the monarch, which since the reign of William III had operated under notions of parliamentary supremacy (Kirkland and Deva, 2023), was required to break the impasse.

Despite two elections pertaining to the crisis, the solution was to be found within Parliament itself. When compared to previous constitutional crises, such as the riots of the Reform crisis of 1830–32, 'the events of 1911 certainly lacked … direct public engagement … the temper of the times was different … and excitement did not reach quite that fever pitch' (Powell, 1996, p 62). Here, those advocating blame – the government – knew that they were unable to simply marginalise and bypass those blamed – the Lords, who were required to vote on any legislation. The threat to manufacture 500 or so Liberal peers is testimony to this acceptance of the constitutional role afforded to the House of Lords, which also appealed directly to the public through actively campaigning in the general elections of 1910. This supports the assertions made in Chapter 2 that blame does not necessarily exclude parties from engaging in, or even shaping, the resolution(s) to the crisis.

Despite fears of extra-parliamentary means being needed to resolve the crisis, it was Parliament, through agreeing on a further election in December, which was able to find a resolution to the crisis. Both Kings (Edward VII and George V) were spared the political decision of creating more peers and acting in a manner that would inevitably change the relationship between the executive, legislature and monarchy.

The Liberals lost a further two seats in December, taking their tally at the end of the year to 272. The Conservatives, having gained 116 seats in January, despite losing one in December, ended the year with just one fewer seat (having gained more popular votes) than the Liberals. The Irish Parliamentary Party was the third largest at Westminster, winning 71 and 74 seats in the respective elections, while the Labour Party won 40 and 42 seats.

In 1911, with the help of the Irish Nationals, the Liberal government passed the Parliament Act, which sought to limit the powers of the House of Lords. It put on the statute book the primacy of the House of Commons over financial legislation. The House of Lords' absolute veto over legislation in most areas was replaced by a suspensory veto of approximately two years and the Act reduced the maximum duration of a Parliament from seven years to five (Ballinger, 2011).

Moving the bill on 24 July, to jeers and cries of 'traitor' from opposition benches, Prime Minister Herbert Asquith reiterated the threat of 'packing' the House of Lords:

> A situation has been created from which there is only one constitutional way of escape, and that is unless the House of Lords will consent to restore this Bill, if you like with reasonable amendments consistent with its principle and purpose, we shall be compelled to invoke and exercise the Prerogative of the Crown. I am anxious not to do so, but if we are forced – it is the determination of the Government, and, as I believe, the vast majority of the people of this country, that without further delay this Bill should take its place on the Statute Book. (Hansard, 1911)

The blame directed at the House of Lords and, to an extent, confirmed by the two elections of 1910, meant that it was no longer in a position to dominate political narratives. Speaking for the government in the House of Lords, Lord Morley (quoted in Powell, 1996, p 62) reinforced this argument, claiming that should the Lords attempt to defeat the bill the King would assent 'to a creation of peers sufficient in number to guard against any possible combination of the different parties in opposition'. The acceptance of this threat as genuine was sufficient to persuade enough peers to support the bill in the House of Lords. The Lords, however, attempted to amend the bill in committee stages, but their proposals were rejected in the Commons on 8 August. The House of Lords eventually accepted the Parliament Bill by 131 votes to 114 on 10 August 1911.

Although the Liberals were able to pass the Parliament Act, this can be seen as bringing about only limited change, as Powell (1996, p 67) notes that this crisis, although resolved in terms of the bicameralism of the UK Parliament, did not represent an outright victory. Despite narratives of 'peers versus the people', the Liberals were 'reluctant to push the attack on the Lords to its limit for fear of destabilising the delicate mechanisms of the governing system'. While tipping the balance of power away from the Unionists, this lack of an overarching victory meant that the events of 1909–11 were simply a 'prelude' or 'sideshow' to the 'gathering clouds of the [Irish independence] storm' (see next chapter).

Such a view was shared in the immediate post-war period. Chase (1929, p 570) labelled the bill as a 'compromise' between 'believers in completely popular government and those who distrusted the people'. As part of the Act, limitations were placed upon the government to balance the weaker House of Lords. The key limitation was to require new elections every five years, reducing the maximum life span of a government from seven to five years. This was designed to ensure that a democratic mandate was offered to a legislative programme and to allow for unpopular governments to be removed from office effectively.

Both Left and Right could find solace in the legislation; for progressives, the bill increased the power of the House of Commons, and for Conservatives, it upheld privilege. Although the Liberals were able to 'pass some of their most important legislation' free from the last remaining veto of the Lords, 'they discovered that the Parliament Act was working so as to give them a free hand only during the first two years of each Parliament' (Chase, 1929, p 570).

The provision in the Act that the opposition of the Lords might be overridden after a two-year delay has, however, subsequently been used on seven occasions. It was used twice by the Liberal government of 1910–14, first with respect to the Welsh Churches Act and later to the question of Irish Home Rule (for a fuller discussion of this, see the next chapter). The third related to the nationalisation of iron and steel introduced in the 1948–49 parliamentary session, and the Parliament Act of 1949 (Jenkins, 1954, pp 188–9). The final four bills, the War Crimes Act (1991), European Parliament Elections Act (1999), Sexual Offences (Amendment) Act (2000) and the Hunting Act (2004), also drew upon the provisions contained within the Parliament Act of 1949 (Parliament UK, 2024).

For Jenkins (1954, p 188), however, the compliance of the House of Lords with its new position as subordinate to the Commons stemmed not from the legislative changes arising from the Parliament Act of 1911, or even 1949 which reduced the Lord's veto to just one year, but to the 'wider political climate'. Further reforms of the House of Lords under New Labour have seen an inverse relationship between the powers of the Lords and the willingness to oppose the government (Russell and Sciara, 2007).

In addition to this, it is important to note that the House of Lords still retains its position as the second chamber, and is required to pass any legislation including reforms to the House of Lords itself – unless the government is willing to wait two sessions to see its legislation passed. Without wider changes to politics, emphasising greater democracy and broader notions of representation (for example, the extension of the franchise) combined with shared or lived experiences such as the two world wars and the economic problems of the 1930s, the debates surrounding the powers of the Lords might not have progressed in the same manner. The two chambers could not agree on a reformed House of Lords in 2003, with the Lords voting only in favour of maintaining a wholly unelected upper house (McLean, Spirling, and Russell, 2003, p 299).

Conclusion

The Constitutional Crisis of 1909–10 was fundamentally a crisis between the component parts of government. It was constitutional in the sense that it challenged the contemporary relationship between the House of Commons, the House of Lords and the monarch. As in other crises, key actors took on additional roles, such as the Lords who actively campaigned in the elections to the House of Commons. Here, unlike in crises such as the 1984–85 Miners' Strike or the London Bombings (see Chapters 11 and 12 respectively), blamed agents were able to use their positions to contribute to deliberation and discussions surrounding a resolution to the crisis.

However, unlike some later crises (see the next chapter on Irish Home Rule or chapters on the First and Second World Wars), all of those involved in the crises committed themselves to finding a parliamentary response, which, after two elections in 1910, enabled the passing of both the Liberal budget and the 1911 Parliament Act, which put into law the supremacy of the House of Commons.

Further reading

Godfrey Le May (1979) in *The Victorian Constitution* explores the position of both the Liberal and Conservative parties vis-à-vis the constitution and House of Lords. This offers a useful background to the crisis. The Conservative dominance, and expectations, of the House of Lords is also the theme of Roy Jenkins's (1954) book *Mr Balfour's Poodle.*

Some good overviews of the crisis can be found in the works of Bruce Murray (1980) *The People's Budget 1909/10* and David Powell (1996) *The Edwardian Crisis Britain 1901–1914.* Both help chart the pathology of the crisis and how it spread from the House of Commons to engulf the monarchy and UK Constitution.

Other books emphasise different aspects of the crisis; Neal Blewett's (1972) *The Peers the Parties and the General Elections of 1910* offers a detailed account of the two election campaigns that took place in 1910. On the issue of House of Lords reform, Peter Dorey and Alexandra Kelso's (2011) *House of Lords Reform since 1911: Must the Lords Go?* offers a historical overview of the changes to the upper chamber. The difficulties in achieving further reform are further outlined in Chris Ballinger's (2012) *The House of Lords 1911–2011: A Century of Non-Reform.*

One useful contemporary account of the events of 1909–10 is provided by Sir Austen Chamberlain (1936) in his *Politics from the Inside.* This work publishes a series of letters which outline the Conservative opposition to the budget and 1911 Parliament Act. Although very few contemporary politicians wrote memoirs, there have been a number of biographies written covering leading figures, such as Lloyd George and Herbert Asquith. The most useful of these is Thompson's *Official Biography of Lloyd George* (1948) written in collaboration with Frances, Countess Lloyd-George, which offers an in-depth account of the budget and its key provisions.

4

The (Third) Irish Home Rule Crisis, 1912–14

Overview

This chapter explores the Irish Home Rule Crisis, which stemmed from the Third Irish Home Rule Bill that was laid before the British Parliament in 1912. It was the response to this legislation which eventually saw the creation of two armed forces on the island of Ireland, one to support the legislation passed at Westminster and one opposing it, bringing the country to the brink of civil war. This challenged assumptions of 'normal policy making', such as the rule of law or the state's monopoly over the legitimate use of force. Unlike other crises, such challenges to the rule of law were not confined to those defined as 'political extremists' (as in the case of fascism in the Second World War or the 7/7 terrorist attacks). Rather, they were supported by some within the Conservative Party, which formed His Majesty's Most Loyal Official Opposition within Parliament.

This crisis is closely linked to others in the book, emphasising the points made in Chapter 2 about crises not being mutually exclusive and being potentially linked to one another; its origins stem from the Liberal–Irish Parliamentary Party alliance created following the January 1910 general election to pass the 'people's budget' and the subsequent 1911 Parliament Act (see Chapter 3). Many of the debates covered in the crisis replicated those surrounding the nature of the Constitution, the relationship between the branches of the legislature, and the relationship between the legislature and monarchy a few years earlier. The end point of the crisis (taken here to be 1914) links to a further crisis, that of the First World War, which in September 1914 displaced the Irish Question as the most salient issue of the day and encouraged many of the would-be combatants to switch their focus from Ireland to the Western Front.

Introduction

Unlike other crises in this book, the dates of any (singular) Irish Home Rule Crisis are contested. As this chapter demonstrates, questions about Irish Home Rule were being asked long before 1912 and were by no means settled by 1914, when war in Europe diverted attention from Ireland. Hart (2002, p 17), for example, makes these points, asking: 'What do we call the events of 1916–23? Or should it be 1912–22 or 1917–21? Do these events form a unity or are they better understood discretely as a succession of crises, rebellions and wars?' It should be noted that in asking the question, Hart is concerned with the notion of revolution, and he himself acknowledges that there are distinct periods contained within the aforementioned dates. Although he goes on to explicitly argue that the 'Home Rule Crisis of 1912–1914 was [not] even potentially revolutionary' (Hart, 2002, p 19), this still denotes the existence of a distinct crisis, on which this chapter will focus. This is in keeping with the wider academic literature, which sees the onset of the First World War in 1914 as a break or end point from the legislative crisis (see, for example, Murphy, 1986; Doherty, 2014a).

However, splitting this period, or wider themes of Irish Home Rule, into multiple crises is not without its dangers. Although discrete events can be identified – for example, the Easter Rising of 1916 or the Irish Civil War of 1922–23 – this is not to deny linkages between them. As Jackson (2004, pp 320–22) demonstrates, there are important continuities between the ideas of the first Home Rule Bill in 1886 and the return to direct control from Westminster in 1973 or the Belfast Agreement of 1998. If the policies in the early twentieth century can be described as 'the Irish Question', then subsequent evolution of the relationship between the island of Ireland and the rest of the UK can be termed 'the unresolved question' (Mansergy, 1965, 1991).

Although such linkages are frequently identified by Irish historians, they have often been overlooked by scholars with a British focus. Such arguments have also been made relative to UK governments; Fanning (1985, p 2) argues that 'the Irish policy of the British government in the nineteenth and twentieth centuries may best be interpreted as a series of responses to a succession of intermittent and often long-separated crises'. Furthermore, Fanning argues, such crises are often situated within a broader crisis of British–Irish relations; he points to the international crisis of the late eighteenth century, following the French Revolutionary Wars, which set in motion forces which led to the formation of the United Kingdom of Great Britain and Ireland, and the First World War, which led to the breakup of the union, the independence of Ireland and the reconstruction of the United Kingdom of Great Britain and Northern Ireland). Alongside this emphasis upon the British state, the asymmetry of power between participants within debates relating to Irish Home Rule has meant that, despite differing views on policy (and tactics to achieve this), 'all alike identify the persuasion of the British government to their point of view as the first object of policy'.

Fanning's arguments are important and link to questions of prioritisation. As Chapter 2 suggested, multiple crises may exist simultaneously and overall. It also noted that we cannot only speak of a crisis after it has been resolved; that there must exist the possibility that crises are not resolved (at least in the short term): individual crises may lose salience within public discourse/consciousness without remedies being (fully) found or implemented. The Irish Home Rule Crisis bears these points out, certainly from the vantage point of the modern day. The Great War of 1914 led not only to the UK government, but also both the Ulster Volunteer Force (UVF) and the Irish Republican Army (IRA), turning their attention to continental affairs, demonstrating the fragility of the status quo. Peace, which had hitherto been maintained throughout the crisis, was punctuated by events such as the Easter Rising of 1916, and the end of hostilities in Europe saw a civil war, which had been avoided up to 1914, in the face of the Anglo-Irish war.

Ireland had been governed from Westminster since the Act of Union (1800), which created a new state, 'the United Kingdom of Great Britain and Ireland'. However, the inclusion of Ireland into the new, English-dominated state was not a 'systematic conquest'. Rather, unlike other colonies of the British Empire, in the face of rebellion and civil war the British government persuaded the Irish Parliament to disband itself in exchange for representation at Westminster (Boyce, 1996, p 3). The Act directly linked the state of Ireland to that of the rest of the United Kingdom. Ireland sent 100 MPs to Westminster to sit alongside their English, Scottish and Welsh counterparts and replace the Irish Parliament. Although Irish MPs were more numerous than their Scottish or Welsh counterparts, the dominance of Englishness was unquestionable (Innes, 2003).

Such arrangements made Ireland distinct from other states that formed the British Empire. Although under the Act of Union Ireland remained distinct from Britain, Ireland was not governed by 'empowered local elites' as in the rest of Britain, but rather by 'an executive appointed by the [Westminster] government', based in Dublin Castle. Such government was 'highly centralized ... emphatically a form of imperial government, maintained by a mixture of state patronage and force' (Kelly, 2013, p 583).

The constitutional arrangements with respect to Ireland were significantly different from other British overseas territories. Over the course of the nineteenth century, territories such as Australia, Canada and New Zealand were afforded some form of local government control (Taylor, 2003). The constitutional and governance structure of Ireland, however, remained based on the 1800 Act. Ireland sent MPs to sit in the Westminster Parliament, a body that by virtue of its sovereignty could, and did, make laws. Irish MPs were a part of this, but their representation was insufficient to make changes without the support of a UK (English) political party. Conversely, it was also 'clear that Britain could legislate for Ireland in ways that she could not legislate for remote colonies'. Boyce (1996, pp 2–3) continues, noting that it is neither a compliment nor a complaint to suggest that 'no other country would have handled the kind of political problems that Ireland seemed to present to British politicians in the nineteenth and twentieth centuries'.

The issue of Irish Home Rule, or the 'Irish Question', was not new at the turn of the twentieth century. The start of the 'struggle for Irish independence from Britain' was not in 1912 or even 1800, but can be traced back to 1641, even if the term 'Home Rule' can only be dated as far back as 1873 (Tonge, 2005, pp 9–10; Bartlett, 2014, p 28). Large differences continued to exist between Ireland and the rest of the United Kingdom, not only in terms of identity and religion but also wealth and industrialisation. Ireland was predominantly Catholic, and the economy was based upon agriculture, while Britain had a largely Protestant population and an industrial economy. The exception was the 'rapidly expanding City of Belfast' which, due to its prominence in the shipbuilding trade, was central to Irish economic growth but was more akin to English cities such as Liverpool than Irish cities such as Dublin (Anderson and O'Dowd, 2007, p 941).

Two previous attempts to legislate for Home Rule, both introduced by Liberal governments, were defeated in 1886 and 1893. Each of these proposed a different governance arrangement; the first proposed a bicameral system whereby MPs would be elected under the franchise established by the 1884 Reform Act and an upper chamber that would be elected upon a more restrictive £25 franchise. However, Westminster would retain control over a range of policies such as 'policing, military, defence, foreign affairs, and commerce ... Under the first bill there would [also] be no representation of MPs at Westminster, raising the spectre of taxation without representation'. The second bill, although broadly 'adher[ing] to the provisions of the first bill ... retained Irish representation at Westminster' and proposed a bicameral Irish Parliament. The lower house would retain the current 103 MPs, elected on the existing franchise, while the upper house would comprise 48 members, again elected by a much more restrictive franchise: voters 'who owned or occupied land with an annual valuation of £200 or more' (Kelly, 2013, pp 588–9).

Following the death of Campbell-Bannerman in 1908, the Liberal Party's leadership appeared to have a more imperialist outlook and were more preoccupied with social and welfare issues, such as those contained in the 'people's budget' (see previous chapter) than notions of Irish independence or devolution (Jackson, 2004, p 123). The issue of Irish Home Rule was omitted from both Liberal manifestos of 1910 and did not feature prominently within the election campaign itself.

The low salience afforded to Irish politics was not new. Irish issues had only been discussed previously when part of a broader British issue/crisis (Boyce, 1996). The same occurred following the Constitutional Crisis of 1909–10, which reignited the issue of Home Rule. This crisis had linked the question of Irish Home Rule to that of reforms to the House of Lords in two ways, first through the coalition forged to pass the budget and Parliament Act; the Liberal government promised the Irish Nationalists that they would bring forward an Irish Home Rule bill in exchange for support to pass the 'people's budget' of

1909, and second through removing a key obstacle to Irish Home Rule – the veto of the House of Lords.

Following the passage of the Parliament Act of 1911, the dominance of the House of Commons over the House of Lords was confirmed. The House of Lords, unlike the Commons, had a large Unionist majority. When the Lords' veto powers were replaced with the powers to delay only (see previous chapter), the prospect of Home Rule became closer. It was this constitutional crisis that 'revive[d]' the Liberal's 'half-dormant ... commitment to Home Rule' (Kelly, 2013, p 596).

While limiting the powers of the House of Lords was deemed necessary for the Liberals' wider political agenda, supporting the Irish Parliamentary Party and its leader, John Redmond, was less so. Liberal doubts could be seen in the general elections of 1910; just nine of the 16 ministers who 'issued addresses made no reference to Home Rule, and only 84 out of 272 successful Liberal candidates mentioned it in the December campaign' (Boyce, 1996, p 54).

The 1911 King's Speech opening Parliament promised: 'a measure for the better government of Ireland' (O'Day, 1998, p 246). However, the government was acutely aware of the potential problems of implementing Home Rule. Asquith would later write to George V, informing him:

> [I]f in light of such evidence or indication of public opinion, it becomes clear as the Bill proceeds that some special treatment must be provided for the Ulster counties, the Government will be ready to recognise the necessity, either by amendment of the Bill, or by not pressing it on under the provisions of the Parliament Act. In the meantime, careful and confidential inquiry is to be made as to the real extent and character of Ulster resistance. (O'Day, 1998, p 247)

The government brought forward the third Home Rule Bill in April 1912. This proposed a bicameral parliament, similar to the proposals in the 1893 Bill. It would create a lower house of 164 MPs and a 40-member senate, with members to be nominated by the government, a quarter of whom would retire every two years. Just as in earlier bills, the scope of legislation was to be restricted; the Home Rule Bill offered a 'derisory amount' of control to Ireland:

> Matters relating to the monarchy, marriage, the military, peace or war, foreign affairs, coinage, the law of treason, and trade and navigation ... were to be outside its remit, while others such as policing, tax collection, old age pensions, land purchase, national insurance and even the Post Office could possibly be delegated to Dublin, but only after a period of years. (Bartlett, 2014, p 23)

Although there was a history of radicals on the left of British politics supporting Irish nationalism (O'Connor, 2016), many of the ideas behind Irish Home Rule were not as radical as they might first appear. According to Kelly (2013, pp 582–3), those advocating Home Rule did not have independence as their primary goal. Home Rulers wished for 'an Irish Parliament under the Crown, parallel rather than subservient to the Westminster Parliament'. Such a government would represent a system of devolution which would grant powers to Dublin akin to the post-1997 settlements with Scotland and Wales, whereby an 'Irish executive [would be] formed from, and answerable to, an elected Irish parliament'.

This posed problems for both the Liberals, as it risked their alliance with the Irish Parliamentary Party. The coalition of those favouring Home Rule was thus an uneasy one. Divisions within the Liberal benches were apparent from the outset: upon the tabling of the bill, one Liberal MP, Agar-Robartes, put forward an amendment that would exclude the counties of Armagh, Antrim, Down and Londonderry (Boyce, 1996, p 50).

If the government's position was unclear, then so too was that of the opposition. The Conservative Party was divided and 'lacked an integrated and consistent political ideology'. Previous discussions had considered plans for further devolution to the rest of the United Kingdom. Loughlin cites Leo Amery's comments in the House of Commons: 'Not a soul throughout these debates ever says anything to suggest that he feels the United Kingdom is really a nation and that Irish nationalism in any shape or form means the end of United Kingdom nationalism' and his conclusion that fundamentally the crisis arose from 'the failure to "invent a single name for the United Kingdom in 1800"'. The crisis in many ways forced both sides to adopt more precise positions and 'jettison' more contentious issues such as Tariff Reform or compulsory military service (Loughlin, 1995, pp 50, 52; see also Murphy, 1986).

The Conservatives, now under Bonar Law, supported Thomas Agar-Robartes's amendment, largely for political reasons, drawn more from the need for party unity and safe in the knowledge that the amendment would fail. The Conservatives were also split over the issue, and the amendment was initially opposed by a large group of backbenchers. The opposition was led by Walter Long, who represented the Strand constituency in London but had previously been MP for Dublin County South. Those opposing the amendment argued that they were committed to protecting Unionists in both the North and South who opposed it.

However, Conservative Party support did not represent a turning point; it did not represent the point at which the Conservatives focused their attention exclusively on Ulster (Murphy, 1986, p 224). The composition of the House of Commons, combined with the weakened powers of the House of Lords, pushed Unionists to seek alternative methods for opposing the bill. Long, supported by up to 80 backbenchers, remained willing to work outside the party to foster new parties and alliances to oppose Irish Home Rule.

The legislative passage of the bill seemed guaranteed; the government, with the support of the Irish Parliamentary Party, had sufficient votes to secure the legislation. Cross-party agreements for amendments were not forthcoming; in addition to the failure of the Agar-Robartes amendment in December 1912, Edward Carson tabled his own amendment to permanently exclude the counties of Ulster from the provisions of the bill, but this was supported by just one Liberal MP (McConnel, 2013, p 272).

The crisis, just as the constitutional crisis discussed in the previous chapter, also involved the monarch, George V. The preamble to the 1911 Parliament Act (see previous chapter) stated the intention 'to substitute for the House of Lords … a second chamber constituted on a popular instead of a hereditary basis'. Yet such a change had not (and still has not) been completed, leaving opponents of the bill to claim that the Constitution was 'in a state of suspense'. Given that the balance of power between the two chambers had been altered, opponents of Home Rule argued that the veto powers previously held by the Lords 'must necessarily devolve upon the King' (Nicolson, 1953, p 117).

The monarch was 'more open' to the views of the opposition than the government (McLean, 2001, p 171), in terms of partition and an exemption for Ulster, though he had no 'personal desire at all' for a change in government. In a letter to Asquith, dated August 1913, he lambasted the 'very embarrassing position' in which he had been placed. In the same letter, he expressed frustration and feelings that the 'government is drifting' (quoted by Nicolson, 1953, p 223).

> The Parliament Act, the King feared, placed him 'in a false position and in one never contemplated by the framers of our Constitution'. As I regard it, the King alone can now compel a government to refer to the Country any measure which hitherto would have been so referred by the action of the Lords. (Bogdanor, 1997, p 124)

Framing the crisis

For proponents of Home Rule, the establishment of an Irish Parliament was the 'thin edge of the wedge', and its powers would increase over time. John Redmond, leader of the Irish Parliamentary Party, saw future concessions as being able to compensate for the limited provisions contained within the Home Rule Bill (Mansergy, 1991, p 53; Bartlett, 2014, p 26).

The demands for Home Rule, however, highlight a tension in Nationalist thinking. Redmond, like other Nationalists, rejected notions of partition, though this was in part due to misunderstanding the opposition in Ulster. Yet if such partition was to be denied, a paradox arose whereby anti-partitionist arguments favoured 'the application of the principle of self-determination to one part of the population … accompanied by its denial, backed by force, to the remainder' (Wilson, 1989, p 36).

The Home Rule Bill left unanswered questions of minority rights for the Protestant population, largely confined to Ulster. One Liberal Unionist MP, Harry Lawson (quoted in Bew, 1998, p 1), asked in Parliament, 'How are you in these days, these democratic days, in this democratic age, in this democratic country, to force a million of men into a system which they refuse to join … How are you going to expel the Irish minority from citizenship of the UK?'

In Ulster, Home Rule was seen as the first step – a Trojan horse – on a pathway to separation. It was feared that the Vatican would replace Westminster and promote a cardinal state under the control of the Catholic Church. In 1912, around 500,000 men signed the 'Ulster Covenant' which committed to using 'all means which may be found necessary' to defeat Home Rule. Signatures were also collected within Britain, and the Covenant was signed in cities such as Bristol, Edinburgh, Glasgow, London, Manchester and York.

Initially, the government overlooked or ignored the protests of Ulster's population and its supporters (Jalland, 1980, p 78). On the first reading of the Bill, a third of Liberal speakers (two out of six) ignored the Ulster question 'entirely' and a further two made 'exceptionally brief references to the problem', with only Asquith and Birrell (Chief Secretary for Ireland) attempting to consider the issue 'at all seriously' (Jalland, 1980, p 83). Asquith (quoted by Jalland, 1980, p 83) declared: 'We cannot admit, and we will not admit, the right of a minority of the people, and a relatively small minority … to veto the verdict of the vast body of their countrymen.'

Overlooking minorities was not the exclusive domain of those promoting Home Rule; in turn, those opposing the bill focused solely on Ulster. Although the position was 'consistent, forceful and clear', the problems of the 'Protestant Unionist minority in the south and west of Ireland [were] carefully ignored by almost all Unionist speakers during the early stages of the debate' (Jalland, 1980, p 81).

Opposition to Home Rule situated events within a broader framework. For the Conservatives, still licking their wounds after the Parliament Act, the bill was unconstitutional: the two elections of 1910, after all, had been about resolving the previous constitutional crisis (see Chapter 3). The lack of salience afforded to the issue in either January or December 1910 meant that the Liberals, according to their political opponents, 'had not received a proper mandate … for Home Rule' (Walker, 2004, p 29).

Fears also centred upon notions of decline. Drawing upon experiences of the British Army in South Africa during the Boer wars and the granting of independence to Australia (1901), New Zealand (1907), South Africa (1910) and Newfoundland (1907 – Canadian independence having been started in 1867), those opposed to Irish Home Rule linked it to a wider concern over the breakup of the Empire and notions of declining global status. Such fears were further stoked by Germany's expansive naval programme.

MPs sympathetic to the policy of Home Rule united with journalists to present the case. Stephen Gwynn, MP for Galway, headed the Irish Press Agency from 1908. Gwynn and other nationalist MPs wrote for both Irish and English audiences. This generated a circular exchange, which meant that the 'rhetoric in the British Liberal press was indistinguishable from the Irish nationalist position and, as often as not, written by a nationalist' (Doherty, 2014b, pp 82–4).

Despite such arguments dominating Westminster, public interest in notions of Home Rule did not match the importance politicians placed upon the issue. The English public was apathetic on such issues in 1912 (Loughlin, 1995, p 54). Similar reports of apathy can be found elsewhere; speaking about the early years of the 'crisis', Wheatley (2005, p 156) describes the situation in Ireland in similar terms:

> for much of the supposed 'crisis', contemporary writers instead wrote of apathy, while nationalists routinely had to rebut Unionist charges that their quiet meant they did not care. As late as September 1913, Redmond had to deny publicly that nationalists were apathetic, conceding that they had been nearly silent, but seeing this as proof that they had instead been 'law abiding and orderly'.

The *Irish Times* (quoted by McConnel, 2013, p 223), for its part, noted in April 1912 the 'remarkable lack of general interest in the … Bill is manifesting itself … So far as Dublin is concerned the Bill … has fallen like a stick from a spent rocket'. One contemporary even suggested that nationalists had been 'so long demanding Home Rule that it is not to be wondered that the expression … has become … almost devoid of meaning to the man in the street' (Horgan, 1911, p 1). The Royal Irish Constabulary (quoted by McConnel, 2013, p 223) reported that 'the Irish government is not much discussed by the people who seem to care little where parliament is'.

Despite the apparent lack of interest, the rise of new journalism and cheaper printing saw an expansion of publications in Ireland. Such titles were utilised by both sides:

> Unionist newspapers, such as the *Belfast News Letter*, *Northern Wing* and *Belfast Evening Telegraph*, as well as local publications like *Derry People* and *Tyrone Courier*, printed sympathetic coverage of Unionist activities, including the signing of the Ulster Covenant and the Larne gun-running. Advertisements were also placed in newspapers to recruit citizens to the Ulster Volunteers. (O'Hagan, 2020, p 333)

The crisis itself contained two important elements: first, just as in the case of the previous chapter, the crisis could be seen as a constitutional one. 'The Conservatives stoked up Unionist defiance, arguing that the Liberals were abusing their power by threatening to use the Parliament Act to push through the Lords a bill for which they had no mandate' (Kelly, 2013, p 587).

However, unlike in the case of the 'people's budget', the Conservative-led opposition was prepared to use extra-parliamentary means to prevent Home Rule for Ireland and the breakup of the island of Ireland. As in 1909–10, such appeals noted the limitations of Parliament to reflect public opinion. Bonar Law (1912, quoted by Powell, 1996, p 147) argued that there

> were 'things stronger than Parliamentary majorities' and that, in this particular conflict, the Unionist Party would 'not be guided by the considerations ... which would influence us in any ordinary political struggle'. 'I can imagine no length of resistance to which Ulster can go' he asserted 'in which, in my belief, they would not be supported by the overwhelming majority of the British people.'

The Ulster Volunteer Force (UVF) was created in January 1913 to 'safeguard the union'. This was led by Carson to resist attempts at Home Rule and was supported by the Conservative Party. Its initial membership was reported as 85,000, though at its height it boasted a membership of 110,000 (Bowman, 2007; Kelly, 2013, p 596). However, such aggregated figures have subsequently been shown to conceal 'a much more patchy local reality', with questions over the commitments and prioritisations of many members (Jackson, 1992, pp 173–4).

Such a force was 'illegal' according to Edward Carson, though this was not a concern of Carson or other members. Having previously told a Unionist crowd: 'you cannot carry out opposition to a policy of this kind without illegal acts', Carson (quoted by Bew, 1998, p 95) informed a UVF demonstration:

> Drilling is illegal. Only recently, I was reading the Act of Parliament forbidding it. The volunteers are illegal, and the Government knows they are illegal, and the Government does not interfere with them. And the reason is this, the Government knows that the moment they interfere with you, you will not brook their interference; the knowledge will be brought home to them that every man is not only in earnest but that you are prepared to make any sacrifice to maintain your liberties. The moment that is understood, the Government will know their game is up. Therefore, don't be afraid of illegalities. Illegalities are not crimes when they are taken to assert what is the elementary right of every citizen – the protection of his freedom.

The Irish Volunteers were established later that year in November to safeguard the provisions in the Home Rule Bill. Martin (1963) notes that the Irish Volunteer movement 'could not have been launched' had it not been for the UVF. Though wary of the support being offered to Carson, the leadership of the Irish Volunteers denied that such a group was a response to the UVF. Rather, leaders such as MacNeill and Pearse argued that they would form the army of Ireland.

This was deemed necessary as it was suspected that the British Army would be reluctant to defend the notion of Irish Home Rule, fears which seemed justified in March 1914 following the Curragh 'mutiny'. The Liberal government sought to invoke the army to defend peace in Ireland amid rising tensions. However, the army, largely comprised of Protestants, refused to carry out the actions, with many soldiers making it clear that they would rather be dismissed than suppress the Ulster Volunteers (O'Domhnaill, 2004, p 82).

In the summer of 1914, the Irish Parliamentary Party endorsed the Irish Volunteers as 'the "army of the nation"' and MPs actively sought to strengthen 'links with local units, as far as was consistent with constant Parliamentary attendance' (McConnel, 2013, p 291). At the same time, tensions escalated. In July 1914, the UVF landed guns at Howth, and a larger shipment of rifles in Dublin a few weeks later (McConnel, 2013, p 269).

In 1914, Carson argued that exemptions should be made for the nine counties of Ulster. This proposal was rejected by the government in March 1914. Asquith instead proposed that the counties of Ulster that did not want to be subjected to Home Rule could veto the measure for six years. Carson (quoted in Walker, 2004, p 37) replied angrily, saying that they did not want 'a sentence of death with a stay of execution'. A conference was called at Buckingham Palace in June 1914, though this provided no breakthrough in the talks.

Law (quoted by Smith, 1993, p 162) argued that 'the government are trying to carry through the measure in an entirely unconstitutional way and they cannot be prevented from succeeding unless action is taken by us which goes much beyond ordinary Parliamentary opposition'. Earlier, in 1912, he argued (quoted in O'Domhnaill, 2004, p 80) that the Home Rule agenda was part of a 'corrupt Parliamentary bargain'; Unionists, in defence of what Law termed their 'birthright', would 'be justified in resisting [Home Rule] by all means in their power, including force'.

Although such remarks have traditionally been seen as stoking tensions, Smith (1993) argues that they were reflective of Law's leadership position within the Conservative Party, which was weak, and his response to the events in Ireland reflected this weakness. He was not as reckless or militant as others have presented him, but rather sought to exploit the crisis by both stoking tensions within Ulster and blocking any Liberal compromise. Doing so would prolong the crisis until a point when the Liberals would have to face the electorate, which would reject notions of Home Rule.

Irrespective of whether or not the comments were born out of weakness or a desire to utilise such extra-parliamentary means, they offered an alternative understanding of the Constitution. Unlike in 1910, at the height of the 'people's budget' impasse, where the Conservative Party could be seen as upholding the rule of law and thus the UK Constitution, such speeches were not part of an appeal to the Lords, a part of the legislature, but rather to those willing to take up arms. This rhetoric was not confined to the fringes of political discourse, expressed by a fringe or radical party, but was being espoused by the leader of the second largest parliamentary party (in terms of seats in the House of Commons).

Events in Ireland threatened to escalate further than a governance, legislative or constitutional crisis might imply. The former Chief Secretary for Ireland and leader of the Ulster Unionist Party, Walter Long (quoted by Smith, 1993, p 161), would write in July 1914: 'After all this is no ordinary crisis – it is not merely the question of the fate of parties or the result of a general election – it is something more terrible than this, namely, is there to be a civil war or not.'

By the summer of 1914, amid political deadlock, two armed groups threatened to face each other over the impending legislation. Conferences over the summer had failed to find an amicable solution, especially to the Ulster question. Given the different interpretations each side held of the Constitution, there did not exist a strong possibility that dialogue would be able to resolve the issue. With the Ulster Volunteers promising to reject the Home Rule Bill and the Irish Volunteers willing to use force to ensure that the legislation was adhered to, Ireland seemed braced for a civil war.

Resolving(?) the crisis

Before the crisis could escalate further, events in Europe warranted more pressing action. Upon the declaration of war with Germany, the leaderships of both the Ulster Volunteers and the Irish Volunteers urged their members to join the war effort. The implementation of the Irish Home Rule Bill, which received royal assent on 18 September 1914, was postponed 'for twelve months or such later date – not being later than the end of the present war – as may be fixed by his Majesty by order in council' (Harkness, 1996, p 21), temporarily preserving the status quo. Such a sudden shift away from one crisis to focus on another is captured by Margot Asquith's (2014, pp 13–14, original emphasis) diary entry for 4 August 1914:

> all happened in such a short time. On 30th July, everyone was talking of Ireland. The cry of 'Civil War! Civil War!' to which the Times and the Tories treated us every day has been stilled in five days, and we now read in tears a silenced press, with the sound of *real* war wavering like wireless telegraphy round our heads.

Both the Ulster Volunteers and the Irish Volunteers were encouraged to support British troops fighting Germany. Redmond (quoted by Jackson, 2004, p 168) told them to go 'wherever the firing line extends, in defence of right, of freedom and of religion in this war'. Jackson (2004, p 168) argues that promoting such behaviours was not a betrayal of nationalism but rather an acknowledgement that the war offered the chance for reconciliation between Britain and Ireland, and was reflective of the popular belief that the war in Europe was to be short. It was also a reflection of the fact that if Britain were to lose the First World War (certainly if it were invaded), then neither side would be able to secure the future it wished for Ireland.

In November 1914, the Irish Volunteers split into two groups: the National Volunteers, under Redmond, and the Irish Volunteers, under Eoin MacNeill. The latter, although under 10,000 strong, initiated a campaign 'to stir up ill feeling against England and sympathy with Germany, and to prevent Nationalists [from] enlisting in the Army' (Campbell, 2005, p 198). Robert Blake (quoted by Fanning, 2013, p 130) noted that 'paradoxically, it was the outbreak of the First World War which, although it imperilled Britain's very existence, probably alone saved Britain's institutions from disaster'.

Such events delayed, rather than prevented, a paradigm shift. Although for the most part the First World War de-escalated tensions relating to the issue of Home Rule, it did not remove these completely (the Easter Rising of 1916 being an obvious exception); tensions resumed much more explicitly after the Armistice of 1918 (Caulfield, 1995). The years immediately after the end of the First World War saw two conflicts relating to issues of governance in Ireland: the Anglo-Irish War (also referred to as the Irish War of Independence) and a civil war. Any reconciliation of the type advocated by Redmond was only partial and largely short-lived.

The legacy of the crisis

Legacies are often synonymous with resolutions to crises. Outcomes often shape our understanding of the events or tactics used in such events. For example, the defeat of the General Strike in 1926 shaped understanding of the effectiveness of the tactic (see Chapter 6) while victories in both world wars (see Chapters 5 and 8) subsequently framed understandings of remembrance, togetherness and nationalism while confirming accounts of blame.

The crisis explored in this chapter lacks the same definitive 'end' or resolution of other crises, making it more difficult to assess its legacy. In 1914 there was no decisive victory for one side or the other, despite the passage of the Home Rule Bill. At the outbreak of war, negotiations were still ongoing as to how this could be implemented. The abrupt 'pausing' of the Third Irish Home Rule Bill in 1914 is in part symbolic of its legacy, certainly within British (as opposed to Irish) politics and history. Other events overshadowed the prospect of civil war in Britain and tensions were overlooked in the face of a common enemy.

> The reasons for such an imagination gap – our inability to figure out why people were so upset by the 1912 Bill – depend to an extent on the tragic events that characterised the immediate aftermath of the Ulster crisis. The latter was still going on when it was dwarfed by the unparalleled carnage of the First World War, in comparison with which even the Irish wars of 1919–23 were little more than 'troubles'. Drowned in a sea of blood, in Britain the memory of the Third Home Rule Bill was then buried under the rubble of the Great Slump of 1929–39, and wiped out by the Second World War, the Cold War and the demise of the British Empire. (Biagini, 2014, p 415)

Biagini (2014, p 423) further notes that the First World War fundamentally changed British politics. It changed not only the fortunes of the Liberal Party (see next chapter) but also public perceptions of religion, land and Ireland. If the two elections of 1910 were about the House of Lords, the election of 1918 was called by Lloyd George to maximise public support for victory in the war, meaning that the question of Ireland was never tested at the ballot box (Burton, 2019). Burton (2019, p 102) notes that this was not just true of English or English-dominated parties but also that neither 'Sinn Féin nor the Irish Parliamentary Party fully faced up to the Ulster problem'.

This is, of course not to say that the issues of Home Rule, independence, partition or Ulster did not present themselves elsewhere in British and Irish politics. The inter-war period saw the Irish War of Independence (1919–21) and the Irish Civil War (1922–23). It saw the separation of Ireland, with 26 counties from outside Ulster forming the Irish Free State, which formed a dominion within the British Empire until independence was granted in 1937, while the six counties of Ulster remained directly governed from London.

One notable legacy of the crisis was the introduction of military forces to exert political pressure. Opposition to bills from England was not new, especially opposition to Home Rule from within Ulster, yet what was new was 'the organisation of that [opposition] into a military force, armed, trained and officered, claiming to dictate to both Ireland and the English Government, and declaring its readiness to enforce its dictation by military measures' (Hobson, 2013, p 19).

Such links between military groups and political objectives continued to dominate Irish politics after the First World War, up to the signing of the Good Friday Agreement in 1998. The methods used to oppose Home Rule in the pre-First World War period were popularised as the groups became important political and cultural forces during later decades of violence (Campbell, 2017, pp 96–7).

Conclusion

The Irish Home Rule Crisis exemplified many of the issues explored in Chapter 3. This was a further constitutional crisis born out of the alliance forged to pass the 'people's budget' of 1909 and the 1911 Parliament Act (see Chapter 3). The successful passage of legislation relating to Home Rule was only made possible by the latter of these acts, which limited the role of the House of Lords. Given the lack of parliamentary power to obstruct or oppose the legislation, the Conservative Party offered its support to extra-parliamentary means and, in doing so, undermined the rule of law and the capacity of the state to find a peaceful solution to the crisis.

This distinguishes the crisis from others where the state is seen to be at risk of invasion (as in the Second World War, see Chapter 8), revolution (as was argued during the 1926 General Strike, see Chapter 6), or a decline in economic and political power (as was understood during the Suez Crisis, see Chapter 9). In each of those crises the threats to the state came from external forces (respectively, fascist regimes, notably in Germany, the trade unions, the US's plans to sell sterling), yet in the case of Irish Home Rule those who sat in the Westminster Parliament openly supported and encouraged, if not created in the first instance, such threats.

The crisis further demonstrates the argument made in Chapter 2 that crises must exist prior to any resolution. The crisis, when looked at from the vantage point of 1914, had not been resolved. While there had not been any serious outbreaks of violence, it was widely known and understood that both the UVF and the Irish Volunteers were preparing for such a scenario.

Further reading

For the key themes and debates surrounding Home Rule, David Boyce's (1996) *The Irish Question and British Politics 1868–1986* offers a good and accessible historical overview, tracing the debates about the status and role of Ireland within the British Isles from the nineteenth century. For a discussion about the role of the British state or British politics, see David Powell's (1996) *The Edwardian Crisis: Britain 1901–1914*, which links the Irish Home Rule Crisis to the passage of the 1911 Parliament Act, or Patricia Jalland's (1980) *The Liberals and Ireland: The Ulster Question in British Politics to 1914*, which explores the issue of devolution and Home Rule within the Liberal Cabinet under Asquith.

On the role of the Irish Parliamentary Party see James McConnell's (2013) *The Irish Parliamentary Party and the Third Home Rule Crisis*. The collection of works in Gabriel Doherty's (2014a) *The Home Rule Crisis 1912-14* and James Doherty's (2019) *Irish Liberty, British Democracy: the third Irish Home Rule crisis, 1909-14* both offer an Irish perspective on the crisis. The role of Ulster/Northern Ireland following the crisis has also been explored in works such as Thomas Wilson's (1989) *Ulster: Conflict and Consent*.

As in the case of the previous chapter, few contemporary accounts exist of the Irish Home Rule Crisis. In addition to the works mentioned previously (see Chapter 3), A.T.Q. Stewart's (1981) autobiography of Edward Carson and Keith Layborn's (2002) *Fifty Key Figures in Twentieth-Century British Politics* contains entries for key actors, such as Herbert Asquith, Bonar Law and Edward Carson offering insights into the key actors involved within the crisis.

5

The First World War

Overview

This chapter explores the First World War. It notes how the British state expanded during the war in a manner not seen before. The state expanded into private industry and introduced new policies such as conscription. It also took on an enhanced role in promoting propaganda and increased regulation of the national press to build morale and ensure continued public support for the war effort.

The war posed different challenges to different groups, demonstrating the inequalities that crises pose. The fortunes of the Liberal and Labour parties differed significantly, with the latter able to overcome pre-war divisions and the former beset by divisions over issues such as conscription. The war impacted other groups differently as well, such as those on the 'Home Front' as opposed to those who fought on the Western Front.

The chapter also discusses the legacy of the First World War and how this has been reshaped by both subsequent generations and subsequent events, most prominently the Second World War, which commenced two decades later. Unlike other events, the popularisation of war themes in popular culture has impacted how these are understood and shaped different generations' understanding of the events covered here.

Background

On 4 August 1914, Britain declared war on Germany in defence of Belgian neutrality. The escalation of what became known as the 'Great War' was sparked by a range of interwoven alliances and acts across European states, which were triggered by the shooting of Archduke Franz Ferdinand of Austria in Sarajevo on 28 June 1914.

The war provided an initial test to the governing Liberal Party, the majority of whom were opposed to war until Germany declared war on Belgium on 3 August 1914 (David, 1970, p 510), and the broader ideology of liberalism. Asquith, as leader of the Liberal Party and Prime Minister, initially used the threat of coalition to persuade colleagues from resigning. This threat, along with the safe parliamentary majority stemming from the government's commitment to Home Rule legislation (see previous chapter), allowed Asquith to lead a single-party government from the onset of the war into 1915, despite internal opposition, further aided by a disproportionate number of Unionist MPs being absent in the forces (Pugh, 1974, p 815; Turner, 1992, p 56).

Opposition to the war was limited. Following the declaration of war, Ramsay MacDonald, who opposed the government's foreign policy, stepped down as Leader of the Labour Party to be replaced by Arthur Henderson. This meant that all parties officially supported the government's position of declaring war and reduced the need for a change from single-party government in the short term. Outside of Westminster, solidarity towards the German working classes also evaporated to the extent that international solidarity 'proved to be little more than a slogan'. Others who opposed the government, such as the suffragettes, also felt it was prudent to minimise dissent and 'maintain a public silence' (Searle, 2004, p 665). As the previous chapter demonstrated, the unity brought about by the onset of the First World War was sufficient to avert civil war in Ireland, albeit temporarily.

Initially, the government pursued a 'business as usual' approach to the war, assuming that Britain's role in the conflict could be limited to supplying French and Russian soldiers and states with ammunition and other wartime supplies while avoiding combat. Conscription was ruled out as politically impossible in August 1914, and as late as December 1914, men were enlisted entirely voluntarily, 'taken as and when they were prepared to enlist'. This lack of state planning led not only to labour shortages in the domestic economy but also feelings among Britain's allies that it was not 'bearing a fair share of the fighting' (Burk, 1982, pp 20–21).

While questions have been asked about the accuracy of describing the conflict as a 'total war', purely in economic terms the scale of the war effort ensured that the 'term is not too misleading' (Broadberry and Howlett, 2009, p 206). The main economic impact of the First World War was the expansion of the state. Spending on defence had been a key point of contention in the 'people's budget' (see Chapter 3), but once the war commenced, further increases in spending were required. Britain's defence budget increased from £72.5 million in 1912–13 to £1.4 billion by 1915–16, where it remained until 1918–19 (Ellison, Sargent, and Scott, 2019, pp 59–60).

Framing

Initial expectations were that the war would not last long. Margot Asquith (2014, p 4) recalled a dinner on 24 July where everyone was 'discussing how long the war would last. The average opinion was 3 weeks to 3 months'. Lord Kitchener's assertion that the war would last over a year was the exception rather than the rule, and common narratives of the war being 'over by Christmas' were popularised. Recruitment of military personnel was the key priority of the state; success in this regard relied upon a political and social consensus and required 'an active, communicative relationship among both civilians and soldiers … [a] communicative relationship between the Home Front and the battlefront' (Finn, 2010, p 522).

Those who reportedly predicted a short conflict included not only soldiers and politicians, but also those, such as George Bernard Shaw and John Maynard Keynes, who were influenced by arguments relating to the economic irrationality of the war. Against this backdrop, however, Lord Kitchener initially argued that the war could last three years. Others who dissented from this view included journalists; the *Daily Mirror*, for example, reminded its readers of 'a supposedly common belief' in the Second Boer War of 1899, a conflict that would last until 1902, 'that the war would end by Christmas, and warned against the same feeling this time around' (Halifax, 2010, p 109).

Government attitudes towards the working class conditioned their understanding of the conflict. Aside from Kitchener, the government promoted the notion of a short or quick war because they thought, incorrectly, 'that the proletariat would not support any other type of war'. Such ideas were ignorant of the working classes and ignored the fact that the nation had been exposed to the prospect of a European war for the last decade. The press publicised 'jingoistic and Germanophobic articles, while creative writers frightened many into contemplating the consequences of a German invasion of Britain'. In addition, organisations such as the National Service League, founded in 1902, 'inoculated a whole generation of young men … with a certain set of values that were to be important to the strength of British support for the coming war' (Clark, 1996, pp 39–40).

The *Daily Mail* was synonymous with Germanophobia. In the pre-war period, it had run the infamous 'Made in Germany' campaign against German industrial 'dumping' and had, in 1906, serialised William Le Queux's infamous *Invasion of 1910* (Gregory, 2008, p 47). The latter was to be of some importance. The descriptions of German retaliatory shootings and indiscriminate bombardments of civilians helped set a script for 'expected' German behaviour in 1914. It also proved fairly accurate in grasping the style in which the German Army actually waged war in Belgium in 1914 (Gregory, 2008, p 47).

Such understandings were further enhanced by reporting of German atrocities in Belgium in the autumn of 1914, citing the 'barbarity' of German soldiers, including 'allegations that neither women and children had been spared and … multiple cases of rape, torture and mutilation'. Such examples were considered to be allied propaganda in the immediate aftermath of the war and based upon 'unverified evidence from unreliable witnesses'. However, later historians have suggested that the allegations were 'essentially true' (Horne and Kramer, 1994, pp 1–3).

National newspapers supported the war effort. The historian of the *Times* (quoted in Morris, 2015, p 175) noted that war correspondents 'could seldom be other than *laudatores temporis acti* – praisers of what had happened, cheerleaders who eagerly sought to find any element of advantage in any stalemate and minimised or excused defeat'.

Local newspapers played an important role in fostering a sense of community; they had relatively high readerships compared to national titles and operated largely outside the influence of the Press Bureau, established at the start of the war to censor news (Finn, 2010, p 522). Finn (2010, p 524), drawing upon the example of the *Formby Times*, notes how local newspapers advertised for readers to submit to the paper any letters 'receive[d] from the front'.

The war epitomised the link between the media and individuals. Newspapers could offer a substitute for the lack of first-hand information much of the British public had about the conflict. In this sense, they provided the lexicon of possibilities from which the general public tried to understand the death, destruction and deprivation. Local newspapers carried lists of the fallen: pages of portrait-style images of men who had died or were missing, dressed in their uniforms, were presented for local communities to remember, revere and feel gratitude towards. As the local press remained uncensored during the conflict its letters pages consequently became a cultural space in which otherwise voiceless individuals could speak. They articulated a range of views about the war and who should be commemorated. For example, in March 1915, Mrs Pitts, a mother of three in Evesham, Worcestershire, whose husband was shot at dawn, used the pages of the local newspaper to contest ideas about who should be remembered. She positioned her husband, like the lists of the fallen, as a victim of war and wrote to the *Evesham Journal* to quell rumours about his death. She explained that he had written to her in November and December 1914, complaining that he was deaf, lost and struggling to find his regiment (Andrews, 2019, pp 297–8).

This localisation of news allowed local communities to shape narratives of the war and associated myths of combat and heroism long before national framing emerged. The absence of national reporting – such as the BBC – ensured that localism fused with notions of the everyday (Finn, 2010, pp 537–8), but also that multiple stories emerged.

The lack of frontline news at the national level increased the need for and salience of propaganda. Fictitious stories, some of which received public backing, were created to fantasise about what was going on. Public appetite for such stories was 'very strong: people had a craving to know about the fighting and to see their faith in the moral and physical strength of the allies reflected in an accessible form'. Stories such as the passage of Russian troops through Britain in sealed trains towards the Westen Front, or stories of the heroism of a British soldier involving a London vegetarian restaurant and invoking the spirit of the bowmen of Agincourt were published in newspapers and eagerly accepted by a 'gullible and uncritical' public (Buitenhuis, 1987, pp 102–3).

Writers were incorporated into the war effort as early as September 1914. Twenty-five of 'England's most influential writers' were invited by the Liberal MP C.F.G. Masterman to support the war effort. Twenty-four of these (and others who joined later) 'position[ed] themselves as concerned citizens … [to] publish books under their own names through well-known commercial and university presses that were secretly subsidized by the government' (Wollaeger, 2006, p 14).

Masterman had extensive contacts in the fields of both literature and journalism. In a second meeting, he exploited the latter of these and agreed on four resolutions:

> That censorship should be minimal, there should be a government coordinator for giving out government news; that the government should help journalists to report on the dominions and neutral countries; and that British diplomats should enlist the help of journalists to correct the errors in foreign news reporting. (Steed, 1996, p 25)

In addition to keeping the origins of such propaganda secret, Masterman operated on the basis of factual accuracy; such requirements of verification resulted in Masterman limiting the number of German atrocities reported and being labelled as unpatriotic. He also used selective distribution based upon region/area, prioritising certain geographical areas, the most important being the United States, with other specialist offices supporting targeted propaganda campaigns in Scandinavia, the Netherlands and Italy, and Switzerland (Steed, 1996, pp 25–6).

Such propaganda and support for the war effort did not ensure a harmonious relationship between the government and the media. As casualty lists appeared, press influence and circulation grew. In the absence of adversarial politics within Parliament, the media offered the only forum for dissenting opinions. Taylor (1965, p 26) quotes Lloyd George, who noted in 1916 that 'the press has performed the function which should have been performed by Parliament, and which the French Parliament has performed'. Tensions existed between ministers and the press. Kitchener's relationship with Charles Repington, the war correspondent for the *Times*, soured after the paper reported Kitchener's assertion of a prolonged war. According to one newspaper study during the war, Kitchener 'never liked or trusted the press and complained incessantly of inconsistencies. He called it "newspaper embroidery"' (Morris, 2015, pp 174, 179).

Repington was the leading war correspondent in the country, largely by virtue of his own experience. Here, he could offer expertise (and thus legitimacy) that only a few members of the Cabinet could do; aside from Churchill and Kitchener, no minister had personal experience of war. Even without the links to Kitchener, Repington did not lack 'reliable War Office information' (Morris, 2015, pp 177–8).

Repington visited France and the front line and, in contrast to other newspaper correspondents, reported on events from there. In May 1915 he wrote about a shortage of shells and its effects on a British attack on Aubers Ridge. This report, which bemoaned a lack of ammunition, was published on Friday 14 May and headlined 'A Lesson from France'. It named no individual soldier or politician, but the message could not have been clearer. 'The attacks', which were the responsibility of the French, had been 'well planned'. They had failed for 'want of an unlimited supply of explosives'. That was the responsibility of Kitchener and the War Office (Morris, 2015, p 183).

On 21 May, the *Daily Mail* ran a leading article under the headline 'The Tragedy of the Shells. Lord Kitchener's Grave Error', which again linked the crisis to Kitchener. Such was the blame that when the King met Asquith, he 'urged him, when forming his new Cabinet, to create a separate Ministry of Munitions under Mr Lloyd George and thus relieve Lord Kitchener of all work and responsibility in regard to ammunition' (Nicolson, 1953, pp 262–4).

Blame for the 'shell scandal' quickly extended beyond one individual. It resonated with, and amplified, narratives that the government was not fully supporting the war effort. Burk (1982, p 24) argues that the significance of the story was that it enabled Liberals within the new coalition to resist Conservative plans to move Lloyd George from the Treasury and instead presented the opportunity for Lloyd George to 'implement his vision of a total war economy'.

Resolution

Throughout the early stages of the war, the majority of Liberals wished to promote a 'business as usual strategy' to a 'liberal war', applying ideological principles to the conduct of the war. Opposed to this was Lloyd George, who sought to put the economy onto a wartime footing. By May 1915, it was clear that Lloyd George had won the argument. The government had intervened to control the production of munitions and direct the engineering industry to maintain frontline supplies. In March 1915, limitations were placed upon wartime profits, and trade union activities were suspended (Packer, 2006, p 171). However, even here it could still be argued that Lloyd George's plan was not a renunciation of liberalism, but compatible with previous policies. After all, while Liberals had generally wished to maintain the operations of a free market before 1914, they had made significant exemptions to this policy in the field of social reform and direct taxation. Arguably, it was only an extension of these developments to suggest increased government controls of production and trade in wartime, especially as a temporary expedient (Packer, 2006, p 171).

In the Parliament Act of 1911 Asquith had limited a parliamentary sitting to just five years; given the last election was December 1910, Asquith faced the prospect of a wartime general election before the end of the year (possibly held on the same basis as the 'khaki election' of 1900). Pugh (1974, p 816) argues that such considerations explain the swift formation of a coalition in May 1915.

By May 1915 tensions had emerged within the Cabinet, particularly between key figures such as Lord Kitchener, Secretary of State for War, Lloyd George, Chancellor of the Exchequer, and Winston Churchill, First Lord of the Admiralty, aided by concerns about the conduct of, and seriousness attributed to, the war effort in government (Lloyd George, 1938). Such fears were supported by the story in the *Times*, reporting shell shortages on the Western Front (Pelling, 1960, p 72). Asquith, having received assurances from Kitchener, who in turn consulted Sir John French, categorically denied such shortages in Newcastle on 20 April. On 1 May, the *Express* (quoted by Koss, 1976, p 181) informed its readers that this was 'a speech calculated to lull the nation into a fool's paradise … are mischievous to a degree. The country does not yet realise the significance of the war, and the fault is the government's'.

Lloyd George (1938, pp 136–42) notes that the deliberations over forming a coalition took just 15 minutes, though negotiations over ministerial posts went on for longer, with the details of the Cabinet being published on 26 May. The coalition preserved Asquith as leader, but highlighted divisions within the party, particularly over the National Registration Bill of 1915, which was (correctly) seen as moving towards a system of conscription, and the budget of the same year, which was opposed by those who favoured free trade (David, 1970, p 511).

The decision to introduce conscription in 1916 was seen as a triumph of Conservative values over Liberal ones. This was the first time the country had mandated that individuals served in the armed forces (it would later be used in the Second World War as well), and such legislation prioritised the role and defence of the state over that of the individual. Initial understandings thus saw this as 'a triumph of the Tory right-wing over orthodox liberalism' (Adams, 1986, p 244).

The Military Service Act was passed in 1916. This required all single men between the ages of 18 and 41 to enlist, with exceptions for certain professions or those deemed medically unfit. Yet introducing this form of conscription was insufficient; 'Asquith faced calls for additional measures of conscription beginning almost immediately after the passage of the January National Service Act, and they were to persist until May' (Adams, 1986, p 261).

While Conservative supporters defended the bill on grounds of the nation and national defence, it became ideologically a bigger test for liberalism. As one Liberal MP (quoted by Johnson, 2008, p 400) noted, Liberals had supported the war as 'a fight for Liberty against bureaucracy, for British ideals and Liberalism in its widest sense against Prussian Militarism and Tyranny'. As Searle (2004, p 832) summarised, 'the Liberals underwent a crisis of morale as they came to realize the incompatibility between their ideology and what actions they needed to take to secure victory'.

However, far from representing a total defeat for liberalism, the issue of conscription split the party. Some within the party, Lloyd George and Winston Churchill for example, were supportive of the measure. There was also support from some backbench Liberals, such as the Liberal War Committee, founded in January 1916, though most in the party voted for conscription 'without enthusiasm' (Johnson, 2008, p 400). On 5 December, several key allies, including Lloyd George, but also leading Unionists Lord Curzon, Lord Robert Cecil and Austen Chamberlain, signalled declining cross-party support for Asquith, who resigned the following evening (Toye, 2007, pp 168–9).

The change in government in December 1916 is described by Lloyd George (1938, p 616), who led the coalition government, as 'the end of an epoch in the progress of the War'. In terms of the fighting, this was the point at which the allied forces were 'at their lowest ebb', with three allied powers, Belgium, Romania and Serbia, 'completely knocked out [and a] fourth [Russia] – and one of the greatest – had also been practically put out of action' while the 'Central Power Federation was intact'.

Lloyd George (1938, pp 620–21) noted the opposition to his ministry, spanned political parties. He estimated that he held only the support of 136 out of 260 Liberals, with the remainder still loyal to Asquith. The Irish Parliamentary Party was united in its support for Asquith, and 'the Labour Party were divided between supporters of the war and out and out pacifists'. Conservatives who were ministers in the previous administration initially opposed Lloyd George, but reluctantly accepted the new administration as it became a reality.

Lloyd Geroge was a key advocate of moving away from a 'business as usual' approach to a full wartime state. Under his premiership, the government assumed an increased role in the economy. Government revenue doubled between 1915/16 and 1917/18, while expenditure grew almost as quickly. This was funded by an increase in borrowing, from 12.5 per cent of gross national product (GNP) to over 50 per cent (Tomlinson, 1990, pp 46, 50). By the end of the war, Britain's debts stood at £7,481 million, more than ten times the 1913/14 figure and 127.5 per cent of gross domestic product (GDP) (Broadberry and Howlett, 2009, p 219).

Despite population growth of just 2 per cent, the total employment in 1918 was 5.2 per cent higher than in 1913. Though the civilian labour force declined by almost 15 per cent by 1918, there was a 50 per cent increase in the number of women employed, rising from 3.3 million to 4.9 million in July 1918 as the state mobilized the means of production (Broadberry and Howlett, 2009, p 207).

Wars promote technological change and development. Between 1914 and 1918 the nature of conflict changed dramatically, in terms of both the geographies of war and the tactics and equipment used. The conflict of 1914–18 was the first to be branded as a global (world) war. Although its origins were very much in Europe, the number of participants too was greater than in previous conflicts; apart from just Spain, Switzerland, the Netherlands and 'the three Scandinavian countries', all of Europe was involved, as were 'virtually all independent states of the world'. This was a marked change from the previous 100 years, which often saw one-sided conflicts between two nations (Hobsbawm, 1994, pp 23–4).

Technological innovations are common in wartime, not least as states increase funding for innovation and research in a bid to defeat 'the enemy' (the same was also true of the pursuit of vaccinations in response to the COVID-19 pandemic; see Chapter 14). A war that started with rows of cavalry charging at each other soon developed into one where machine guns and tanks were used in a new type of warfare, 'trench warfare'. The war also saw the first use of chemical weapons (which would later be banned as part of the Geneva Protocol in 1925).

While such changes may have influenced military tactics and foreign policy, there is less evidence of large-scale shifts in domestic politics, despite the war being seen as a disruption to prevailing socio-economic norms. The effects of war transcended the political, economic and social spheres. However, such shifts were temporary; just as there were narratives of the war being short-lived, so too there were expectations that upon the end of the war, Britain, along with other combatant nations, would return to a pre-war setting/economy (Hobsbawm, 1994, p 89). Such understanding reduced the need, or political appetite, for a paradigm shift. For example, at the end of the war, many assumed that the debt needed to be repaid, and debates centred upon the ratio of tax increases and spending cuts needed to achieve this. Key institutions such as the Bank of England and the Treasury advocated prioritising repaying such debts.

The economist Pigou argued that any method of repayment would establish a precedent for not only repayments but encourage further increases in government borrowing and spending. After rejecting options for defaulting on the loans, Pigou (1918, pp 136–9) argued that there existed three means of repaying: raising a short-term levy, increasing taxation to pay the interest plus a small amount of capital each year, or a combination of the two. He noted that there were no problem-free solutions, but advocated the third option, a mix of the two, in part due to fears of how a new government – particularly a Labour government – could exercise such levies in the future.

However, in breaking with previous economic assumptions, the size of the state did not fall back to pre-1914 levels (it was 25 per cent of GNP throughout the 1920s), as increases in housing and unemployment spending were difficult to reverse in the inter-war period (Tomlinson, 1990, pp 50–52). Britain's First World War debts were only repaid under the Conservative-led coalition government of 2010–15.

One area responsible for increasing government expenditure after the war was unemployment. Between 1914 and 1920, unemployment averaged 2.2 per cent, half of the pre-war figure between 1904 and 1913, when it was 4.7, but rose a staggering 10 percentage points between 1920 and 1928 (Broadberry, 1986, p 4). Though short-term factors such as deaths due to the war and the subsequent Spanish influenza of 1918 contributed to these figures, rising unemployment would come to symbolise the weakness of the UK economy in the 1920s and 1930s (see Chapters 6 and 7).

Any 'social learning' identified by Hall (1993) did not relate to domestic or economic policy. Rather, according to contemporaries, the mechanism needed to prevent a future war lay in ensuring that the belligerent countries (that is, those that lost, and principally Germany) could never again wage war in Europe. This was the premise of the Treaty of Versailles and the reparations clause, which placed limits on the size of the German armed forces and, through blaming Germany for the onset of the war, made provisions for payments to the allied countries to help with costs of reconstruction.

The coalition manifesto, written by Lloyd George and Bonar Law, argued that before any substantive changes in fiscal policy, the country first needed 'to return to normal industrial changes'. Others, too, pressed for a return to the pre-war economy; in August 1918, the 'Committee on the Currency and Foreign Exchanges after the War' advocated for the 'early return to the gold standard' (Boyce, 1988, p 174).

The starkest political paradigm shifts came in foreign policy. The war cemented the rise of the US as the world's leading economic powerhouse, as demonstrated by the asymmetry of war loans. While Britain was lending money to its European allies, the US refused to lend to riskier nations and would only loan money to Britain, which then acted as an intermediary, borrowing money from the US to lend to Belgium, France, Russia, Italy and Serbia. The risk was that Britain would have to repay these loans even if it failed to receive its own repayments – these fears were played out following the Russian Revolution of 1917, and in *The Economic Consequences of the Peace* Keynes (1920, p 272) argued that Russian loans 'cannot, by any stretch of imagination, be considered good'. Keynes, who worked at the Treasury, expressed concerns relating to this shift in economic power. Fuller and Whitten (2017, p 4) quote two such expressions: 'on October 10 [1916], "The American executive and the American public will be in a position to dictate to this country" ... In December 1917, he observed that Britain had "forfeited the claim we had staked out in the New World and in exchange this country will be mortgaged to America".'

The inter-war period, in which the US adopted a more isolationist stance, helped to disguise such shifts, allowing Britain to continue to act as a global superpower. However, later crises, particularly the Suez Crisis of 1956 (see Chapter 9), which represented the first major disagreement between American and British interests, would bear out such shifts.

Legacy

Unlike some other crises in this book, the memory of the First World War has been incorporated into public discourse. The memory of the war has been sponsored by the state – for example, through the creation of monuments and funding of museums. This has generated opportunities for shared or public remembrance, such as through Remembrance Sunday in November.

However, the state does not have a monopoly on such memory, allowing multiple narratives to emerge: 'there does not exist a singular, popular memory of the First World War in Britain, but a means of remembering through an intangible heritage which can be used to discuss issues far removed from the context of 1914–1918' (Wilson, 2015, p 466). It has also been incorporated into a wide plurality of news and entertainment mediums (Korte, 2001; Hanna, 2009). Nor has the framing of the memory been uncontroversial; historians have questioned the reliability of the 'myths and memories' used to frame the basis for remembrance (Sheffield, 2002).

Such memories are further distinguished along the lines of age, gender, nationality and race (Andrews, 2019, pp 296–7; Olusoga, 2019). Subsequent generations have been keen to present the notion of a naïve population, willing to engage in 'war enthusiasm' and keen to enlist for a conflict that was predicted to be 'over by Christmas in order to avoid missing the "fun"'. Such narratives became popularised in 'fiction memoirs and histories', despite what Halifax (2010, p 103) identifies as 'a more complex picture than simple naïve faith in the imminent success of British and Allied arms'.

Contemporary accounts, those of newspapers and military leaders were traditionally associated with propagating such understandings of a short conflict; however, as Halifax (2010, p 107) later notes:

> Where references to the war's projected duration appeared in the national press, however, they were reports of the official government line that the war could last up to three years or occasional reports of existing rumours about the war's duration. National and local newspapers reproduced soldiers' letters containing predictions for the war's end, but reporting of early predictions that the war would end before Christmas largely related to the failure of German plans to win the war quickly rather than any British preconceptions of an early victory.

As with other historical events, understandings of the First World War have been subject to revision. Over time, the war has gone from being 'immensely popular' at its outbreak, to one which 'few people today would regard as anything remotely like a "just war"' (Taylor, 1999, p 1).

The subsequent revisions and portrayals of the First World War in an increasingly negative light emphasise the changing levels of salience afforded to events but also the importance of another legacy of the First World War, the rise of state propaganda. Taylor (1999, p 2) argues that this is the answer to the rhetorical, but important, question: 'How could what subsequent generations came to know about the war and the way it was fought not be so blatantly apparent to people living through it at the time?' Subsequent generations, well versed in their own contemporary conflicts, may see propaganda as an inevitable part of war (or indeed wider political conflicts – for example, the Cold War), yet such understandings were not commonplace prior to 1914. By the end of the First World War, propaganda represented a form that would be commonplace in contemporary understandings of the topic, with the state being seen as the key distributor (Messinger, 1992, p 1). This propaganda helped to present to contemporaries a narrative of the war as being essential to preserve British independence or notions of liberty and democracy. Such narratives may have been accepted by contemporaries, but others, including the next generation who lived and fought in the Second World War, viewed such understandings with a greater degree of scepticism, drawing upon their own experiences of conflict.

Todman (2013, p 224) notes that five different generations have now sought to understand, unpack and define the events of 1914–18. These five generations, from the grief-stricken parents of those involved to the great-grandchildren, have each been responsible for 'creating, passing on, developing and forgetting myths about the war'. Importantly, despite dominating such discourses, veterans' memories of the war were also 'extremely varied', not only at the time but also afterwards.

One difference between the crisis here and other crises considered in this book – with the possible exception of the 2008 Global Financial Crisis (GFC) – is the almost immediate unravelling and contesting of some narratives, beyond the patriotism evoked by the war. As early as August 1914, the First World War was labelled the 'war to end all wars' by H.G. Wells in his book *The War That Will End War* (Gregory, 2008, p 5). Yet by the end of the war, and as a result of the terms of the peace treaties, Keynes (1920) was predicting another conflict within the next generation. The Second World War subsequently proved Keynes correct and this conflict further shapes our understanding of the 1914 conflict.

> The public rhetoric of Remembrance Day brackets the First and Second World Wars together, the poppy is worn in remembrance of the dead of *both* wars, and we are told incessantly that the dead of both wars sacrificed their lives to preserve our freedom. But the British public does not believe this. It believes that the dead of the Second World War did this, but that the dead of the First World War died in vain. In schools, the First World War is taught more as tragic poetry than as history. Not one in a hundred people in Britain could likely name a single British battlefield victory of the First World War, while many people could name at least three victories from the Second World War: the Battle of Britain, El Alamein and D-Day. (Gregory, 2008, p 4, original emphasis)

Contemporary narrations were also subsequently incorporated into the Second World War and its legacy, with the conflict of 1914–18 overlooked or ignored completely; for example H.G. Wells's description of the war as 'the people's' war, has subsequently become associated with the Second World War (Gregory, 2008, pp 5–6).

In other areas, too, the war failed to produce radical changes. Tanner (1990, p 351) argues that the First World War failed to 'create a homogenous working class, or uniform class experience'. Certainly, 1918 is not seen as a turning point or critical juncture in the same way as 1945 came to be understood (see Chapter 8). The end of the wartime coalition and expansion of suffrage in 1918 to all men over the age of 21 and women over the age of 30 was mitigated by the decision of Lloyd George's coalition Liberals to fight what became known as the 'coupon election' alongside the Conservatives, and the 1918 Redistribution Act, which gave the Conservative Party 'at least seventy safe seats in the home counties and other middle class areas' (Schwarz, 1985, p 52). The decision to prolong Lloyd George's coalition in peacetime ensured there was no change of Prime Minister, and many of the issues prevalent prior to the conflict in 1914 returned to dominate the political agenda. The questions of Irish Home Rule (see Chapter 4) re-emerged, leaving little room for new ideas.

However, this is not to deny that politics after the war looked different to the pre-war period. The Liberal Party split of 1916, along with Lloyd George's continuation of the coalition in the December 1918 election, ensured that in the post-war period the Labour Party, rather than the Liberals, became the main left-wing challenger to the Conservatives (Kirkland, 2022, pp 33–4).

As Chapter 2 explained, crises are not equal; they present different groups and institutions with both challenges and opportunities. Such inequalities may transcend notions of blame, as the different experiences of the Liberal and Labour parties demonstrate. The outbreak of the war 'immediately gave Labour's leaders … a very different and much enhanced stance. For they now came to be needed as brokers and intermediaries between the government and a labour force whose acceptance of a new industrial discipline was an essential condition for military success' (Miliband, 2009, p 47).

Conclusion

The First World War epitomises many aspects of crisis discussed in Chapter 2. The rise of propaganda emphasised the importance of controlling media narratives; the crisis, eventually, saw the expansion of the state through a much more active role in economic management. It also highlights how inequalities exist within crises, as seen in the splits generated in the Liberal Party which led to a change of government and rifts that engulfed the party for the next two decades.

The war also marked a turning point. The notion of a 'short' twentieth century takes as its starting point the year 1914 (see for example Hobsbawm, 1994), replicating the different approaches to modernity outlined in Chapter 1. Such themes are not specific to Britain. The Labour MP Emanuel (Manny) Shinwell (1973, p 11) argued that

> it is generally accepted that 1914 marked the end of an age for the whole world. Nearly a century had passed with only minor wars to disturb the confidence of the ruling and middle classes in Britain and Europe. The interminable series of crises – international, economic, and social – which has bedevilled civilization since 1914 offered a challenge to governments. Yet invariably they have hesitated, floundered, and in seeking to extricate themselves, created the crisis of the next confrontation between theory and practice.

Unlike other crises explored in this book, this one, generated by an existential force, was able to unite, rather than divide, political parties from the outset. This is most notable in the case of debates over Ireland, which had almost reached boiling point in 1914 (see Chapter 4), but also through the forming of coalition governments, which would last until 1922.

Further reading

A number of sources exist relating to the battles and military history of the First World War. In keeping with the themes explored in the book these have been omitted in favour of books covering the domestic politics of 1914–18.

John Turner's (1992) *British Politics and the Great War: Coalition and Conflict 1915–18* explores the coalition government during the war and the tensions that arose within the Liberal Party. Other books are important for focusing on different aspects of the war – for example, the issues relating to the role of the state and of financing the war are covered in Stephen Broadberry and Peter Howlett's (2009) chapter in *The Economics of World War I* and Jim Tomlinson's (1990) *Public Policy and the Economy since 1900*.

On the importance of the media and propaganda and the First World War, see Phillip Taylor's (1999) *British Propaganda in the 20th Century: Selling Democracy* or Andrew Morris's (2015) book *Reporting the First World War: Charles Repington, The Times and the Great War*, which traces Charles Repington's career as a military journalist from the Boer War to the First World War.

Alongside Morris's biography of Repington, key political figures have published their own work. David Lloyd George's (1938) *War Memoirs of David Lloyd George: Volume I* traces the roles he played in the Liberal government of 1914–16 and then as Prime Minister of a coalition government from 1916–18. Alongside this, the diaries of Margot Asquith (2014), wife of Herbert, have been published for the period 1914–16 in *Margot Asquith's Great War Diary 1914–1916*.

6

The General Strike of 1926

Overview

This chapter explores the General Strike in 1926, which remains the largest coordinated strike action ever undertaken in Britain. For nine days in May, 1.75 million workers undertook industrial action in support of 1 million coal miners who had been locked out after refusing to accept pay cuts of between 10 and 25 per cent (Laybourn, 1996, p 1). The Trades Union Congress (TUC) attempted to put pressure on the government to find a last-minute solution to the dispute in the mining industry – as it had done temporarily in July 1925 through offering a subsidy – by asking its members to support a General Strike in defence of the miners. However, negotiations to avert such a strike were torpedoed by unofficial action at the *Daily Mail*. The decision by printworkers to refuse to print an editorial, denouncing the strike as a revolutionary act, was seen as an attack on democracy and the freedom of the press and led to the collapse of talks between the government and the TUC. With the collapse of talks, the strike started at 1 minute to midnight on 3 May and lasted for nine days until 12:20 pm on 12 May.

In the absence of print media, following strikes by the printers, both the government and the TUC sought to control narratives through their own newspapers, the *British Gazette* and the *British Worker*. Throughout the strike, the government, drawing on emergency wartime legislation, coordinated and used blackleg labour and the military to help essential supplies move around the country and drafted in the army to secure vital supplies. After nine days, the TUC called off the strike having received no concessions for miners. The miners, for their part, returned to work in the autumn, under significantly worse conditions than in April, again having won no concessions from either government or mine owners.

Introduction

The crisis of 1926 was born out of structural weaknesses in the UK economy. Although a victor in the First World War, Britain owed £1.4 billion to the

US, and its 'gold and foreign currency reserves had been severely depleted'. Throughout the 1920s, the British economy suffered from acute deflation and high levels of unemployment. GDP in 1929 was just 11 per cent higher than it had been in 1913, a third of the growth of France and just over half that of Germany. Annual productivity increases were also poor by international standards; British productivity grew at just 0.3 per cent per annum, compared to 0.8 per cent in Germany and 2.4 per cent in the US (Foster, 2004, pp 16–17).

The First World War increased the importance of the trade unions in the UK. Membership had increased dramatically, from 4 million in 1914 to 6 million in 1918 and increased further to over 8 million by 1920 (Laybourn, 1993, p 13). The slump at the end of the war, however, placed strains on industrial relations. Although methodological issues relating to the counting of unemployment exist, both trade union figures and official government figures demonstrate that unemployment grew dramatically between 1920 and 1921 (Garside, 1990, p 4).

The General Strike stemmed from a dispute in the coal industry. Coal, which had seen demand peak during the First World War, subsequently saw international demand fall following the peace and a stagnant domestic economy in the 1920s, resulting in reduced profits. In addition, further downward pressure was placed upon the price British exports could command on the international market by the supply of cheaper foreign coal, particularly from the coalfields of Europe. The industry had been nationalised during the First World War, and trade unionists wanted to maintain such arrangements after the war. In 1919, the government established the Sankey Commission to explore the problems and (re)organisation of the coal industry.

Despite important wartime changes relating to 'London's position as an international banker' and the growing importance of the US, with decline in the value of sterling vis-à-vis the dollar (the majority of Britain's wartime loans had to be repaid in dollars), post-war official government policy – drawing upon the Cunliffe Committee – was that Britain should return to the gold standard at the earliest possible opportunity (Morgan, 1952, pp 359–60; see also Chapter 7). Britain returned to gold at the pre-war parity of £1 = $4.86. Keynes (1978, p 207), in his essay 'The Economic Consequences of Mr Churchill', argued that this overvalued sterling by 10 per cent, making exports relatively more expensive. In order to mitigate these additional pressures, mine owners sought to reduce wages and simultaneously asked workers to work longer days.

The Commission produced four reports, the majority report (signed by six members and decided by a casting vote of the chairman) suggested that 'the principle of state ownership of the coal mines be adopted'. Such a system would be organised at a local level, with a Minister of Mines, responsible to Parliament, overseeing a three-tier system of organisation split between national, district and local councils. However, power between the three tiers was asymmetric, with the bulk of power being confined at the district level. National and local councils were limited to 'advisory functions', advising the manager of the mines or the Minister of Mines, respectively. The recommendations also outlined that the Treasury would 'not be entitled to interfere with, or have any control over, the appropriations of moneys derived from the industry' (H.D.H., 1919). It was notable that this was a suggestion, not a recommendation. In any event, Lloyd George decided that as the report only passed by one vote – that of the chairman – this was insufficient (despite previously giving an 'undertaking to implement the majority report'). This left a sense of 'betrayal' in the mining communities, a theme that would 'dominate the industry for many years to come' (Laybourn, 1990, p 112). Of the other three reports, one was accepted by five members of the committee and the other two by just two each (Clegg, 1985, p 246).

In June 1925, the government gave one month's notice that it planned to end the subsidy of coal. The General Council of the TUC, on 25 July, ordered members not to move coal from midnight on 31 July. This was different from a strike; it would be harder for the government and mine owners to counter, while the miners themselves did not risk their wages, pensions or jobs (Renshaw, 1982, p 108).

In order to avert such a strike, the government, on 'Red Friday', 31 July 1925, pending the outcome of a Royal Commission, agreed to continue to subsidise the coal industry for a period of nine months. These nine months were crucial to both the government's and miners' preparedness for the General Strike when it was to arrive in May 1926. In September 1925, the TUC, at its conference in Scarborough, passed a resolution allowing the TUC to call a General Strike, yet the unions made few preparations on the ground for a prolonged strike.

The government was ill-prepared for a strike in 1925. When asked why he offered a subsidy in 1925, Baldwin told his biographer bluntly 'We were not ready' (Mason, 1969, p 3). In 1925, 'there were no serious preparations by the government on the use of state measures against strikes [or] the organisation of a blackleg army to counter the effects of a strike' (Taaffe, 2006, ch 3). However, precedents existed for both; in 1919 the government, using legislation from the First World War, had used the army to transport food amid the railway strike and in 1924 the Labour government had contemplated using emergency powers in relation to a dock workers' strike (Millis, 1928, p 312; Mason, 1969, pp 3–4).

By May 1926, this had changed considerably. In September 1925 the government had created the Organisation for the Maintenance of Supplies, which drew upon 100,000 volunteers – more than the government actually needed to employ during the strike. The government further stockpiled resources and strengthened contact with local authorities and other voluntary bodies to the extent that the Home Secretary informed Cabinet in February 1926 that ' "little remained to be done" in respect of the threatened strike' (Laybourn, 1996, p 9).

In contrast, however, the TUC did not use the time to effectively prepare for industrial action in 1926. Although there was an acceptance of the need for 'unity', there existed a 'lack of machinery and commitment to fulfil that need' (Laybourn, 1993, pp 27–8).

In March, the Royal Commission, headed by Sir Walter Samuel, recommended longer working hours and a reduction in miners' pay. It noted that the output per miner fell from 289 tons of coal between 1899 and 1903 to a provisional estimate of 217 tons for 1925. It offered three methods of reducing costs: a state subsidy, an extension of the working day, or a reduction in wage rates (Jones, 1926, pp 285–6).

The report suggested reorganisation of the industry, but not nationalisation, and an end to the government's subsidy. The government, which stated that it would accept the report if others did, had far less to lose than miners, who had seen their pay almost halve between 1920 and 1925 (Mitchell and Deane, 1971, p 351; Dimsdale, 1981, p 319). The terms were deemed unacceptable to the miners. At the end of April 1926, to avert the lock-out, the government's offer to the miners was a reduction in the minimum payment from 33 per cent above the 1914 figure to just 20 per cent, if daily working hours were extended from seven to eight for a minimum of three and a half years (Cook, 1926, p 6).

In April, mine owners posted 'lock-out' notices, which stated that once the government subsidy ended after the last shift on 30 April, miners could either accept the new terms of employment (longer hours, lower pay) or would be locked out of their employment. Given the failure of collective bargaining within the coal industry, the TUC met government representatives on 30 April to 'explore the possibility of a coal settlement', erroneously believing that they had guarantees from the miners' unions that the TUC and government could meet over the weekend to compile a formula for such reductions. However, on Sunday 2 May, the miners rejected the terms of wage reductions. The Cabinet was also unhappy at the formula used to calculate the new wages, believing it gave 'the impression that the Government had yielded to TUC pressure', and the talks between the TUC and government were terminated (McDonald, 1975, pp 66–9).

Even into the evening of 2 May, there was still hope for a resolution that would avert a General Strike. However, hearing that workers at the *Daily Mail* in London had refused to run an editorial denouncing a strike torpedoed talks. Negotiations between the TUC and government were 'promptly suspended and the government demanded the repudiation of the actions that had taken place and an immediate and unconditional withdrawal of the instructions for a General Strike'. The editorial, which read 'a General Strike is not an industrial dispute. It is a revolutionary movement which can only succeed by destroying the government and subverting the right and liberties of the people', ran in the Manchester edition (James, 1969, p 235; Laybourn, 1996, p 53). Further attempts to find a resolution by Ernest Bevin on 3 May failed due to government demands that threats of a General Strike were called off prior to entering negotiations, and the miners' 'intransigence' (McDonald, 1975, p 69).

The lack of agreement placed the TUC in an impossible position.

> The TUC had hoped right up to the last minute for a settlement which the miners would accept. In a sense, the government's action postponed, for nine days, a tortuous dilemma upon which the TUC was impaled. Its whole policy of support for the miners was based upon the belief, with history as the justification, that pressure could be exerted upon the

> government, which would then intervene in the dispute and engineer a settlement that the miners would accept. No actual General Strike would be needed. However, when the government refused to give way to threats and chose instead to oppose the strike as a threat to the Constitution, the TUC was cornered. It could either retreat and be humiliated or stand and fight, for which it was totally unprepared. A short General Strike, called off as soon as it could be, was an ironic compromise. (Mason, 1969, p 14)

The TUC was caught between wanting to offer support for the miners and following through on its orders and mandate for a General Strike once talks between it and the government broke down. For the TUC, wider industrial action was the logical next (or indeed only) step left to take.

McDonald (1975, p 69) argues that the 'General Strike was the accidental byproduct of an unsuccessful attempt at high level co-operation between the government and the TUC to avert a coal stoppage. Neither the government nor the TUC had consciously planned to have a massive confrontation'; though even if the causes were accidental, this did not mean that the parties entered into the General Strike half-heartedly.

Framing

The government rejected the idea that this was an extension of the industrial action within the mining industry and presented the strike as a revolution. J.C.C. Davidson (quoted by James, 1969, p 235) recounts Baldwin commenting, 'the issue is really quite simple. This is an attempt to take over the functions of government by a body that has not been elected. If they succeed, it will be the end of Parliamentary democracy, which we have taken centuries to build'.

The government portrayed the strike as politically motivated and frequently used terminology such as 'revolution' to outline the dangers of its success. In doing so, the government, despite being present for the talks over the weekend of 1–2 May, distanced itself from the decision to strike and presented itself (along with other, non-union citizens) as a victim of the decision.

Both parties were keen to present themselves as moderates. For the government, this meant working to mediate the dispute in the mining industry. On 3 May, a wireless broadcast quoted Baldwin as saying, 'Owners and miners must find some way, or have some way found for them, of settling their differences without Government intervention, as in the case of other big industries' (Laybourn, 1996, p 56). Through linking the strike to notions of revolution, the government presented itself as defending law and order, without taking normative positions on industrial matters (a similar notion of depoliticising involvement in the strikes was used by the Thatcher government in the 1984–85 Miners' Strike, despite the National Coal Board being a nationalised industry, see Chapter 11).

For the unions, arguments about moderation rested upon notions that much more could have been done to antagonise workers or to bring down the government. J.R. Clynes, then deputy Leader of the Labour Party and trade unionist, argues that the trade unions, far from trying to overturn the Constitution, guaranteed peace during the dispute. Indeed, the trade unions were entitled to a great deal of credit for the order which prevailed. Orders were issued to all strikers not to interfere with essential national services or cause civil disturbances.

> We of the trade unions bought national peace in 1926 at a terrible price. The cost to my own union alone was over £200,000. More than twenty million pounds altogether was lost in wages during the stoppage. We had to make it good; and we did so in order to prevent rioting and as a duty to our members. (Clynes, 1937, p 81)

Recalling the experience of J.H. Thomas of the railwaymen, whose 'duties took him to Buckingham Palace' during the first few days of the strike, Clynes (1937, pp 81–2) notes that George V expressed sympathy for the miners. Clynes further makes the argument that instigating such a revolution would have been easier for the unions:

> Had we been the self-seekers, 'challenging the Constitution' or 'threatening the state' as we were constantly accused of doing, our task would have been much simpler. Recall, we had only to say to the millions of workmen who were on strike: 'Now boys, we've got no more strike-pay for you, and you will starve unless you take to the barricades and get justice and good by force!' Then, revolution would certainly have come.

One significant difference between the framing of the General Strike and other crises such as the Constitutional Crisis of 1910 or the Irish Home Rule Crisis of 1912–14 was that it was the government, rather than opposition groups/parties, that heightened tensions. As Chapter 2 notes, politicians or those with responsibility may be keen to avoid or avert crises, especially if they fear they may be blamed for their onset. Those opposing the government, including journalists, may then have incentives to present narratives of crisis to undermine the government's position. Such tactics were used in 1909–10 and 1912–14 when the Conservative opposition sought to invoke narratives of crisis to help demonstrate the weakness of the Liberal government (and its allies) and bring about a general election on the issues of House of Lords reform and Irish Home Rule. In contrast, in 1926, the government itself arguably presented a narrative of a weaker position. Here, the government used such discourses and narratives to promote a 'call for action' (Rapport, 1962), asking upper and middle class volunteers (including university students) to act as blackleg labour and break the strike (Saltzman, 2018).

The decision to call out the printworkers was something that Glynn and Booth (2020, p 106) suggest may have been a mistake, despite the press being 'almost entirely hostile', as it left the narratives of the strike to the *British Gazette*, a newspaper run by Winston Churchill which advocated the government's position, the *British Worker*, a newspaper run by the TUC, and the BBC radio service, which 'was compelled to bow to government influence'.

No national newspapers ran on 4 May, bar a late and very thin edition of the *Times*. A day later, the government produced the *British Gazette*, with an initial publication of 230,000 copies distributed by plane and by car in London. Although Churchill planned to increase production rapidly, there were serious questions about the paper's readership/cut-through. Harmon (2019, p 197) cites a *Times* article which notes:

> It was a familiar complaint that two copies, one folded inside the other, were thrust into houses where none had been ordered … Its output was palpably far larger than the public demand or the means of effective distribution, and London soon was littered with large bundles of Gazettes that, so far from being read, were never even untied. If there was ever the prospect of a real famine of newsprint, which is very doubtful, this was certainly the way to bring it about.

The prospect of no national newspapers running after Monday 3 May was raised the weekend before, at a meeting of the Newspaper Proprietors Association. It was at this meeting that one resolution passed noted 'in the event of the newspapers being suspended owing to a General Strike … it is advisable in the national interest that the government should print daily bulletins giving essential news' (James, 1969, pp 233–4). From this, the idea of the *British Gazette* was formed. On 3 May, Churchill and Davidson (Financial Secretary to the Admiralty) met with representatives from the Newspaper Proprietors Association, who informed them that they could not jointly publish a newspaper and that the government should produce daily bulletins. Davidson (quoted by James, 1969, p 236) recalls that the government 'were faced on the night of Monday 3 May, with the urgent necessity of creating an organisation for the production and distribution of a daily newspaper which the expert newspaper proprietors confessed themselves unable to produce'.

The publication of the *Gazette* was announced at 6pm on 4 May. J.C.C. Davidson informed everyone that the paper would cost a penny, 'contain authoritative news, and would be in fact a government publication' (Symons, 1987, p 154). The paper was to be run by 'experts' under the leadership of Churchill; however, the reasons for this appointment were less than magnanimous. Although he was the only member of the Cabinet with any journalistic experience (albeit 20 years prior), it was suggested that Churchill's appointment at the *Gazette* was to prevent him from 'disrupt[ing] the government's already-prepared organisation!' Baldwin (quoted by Symons, 1987, p 154) reminded his biographer: 'Don't forget the cleverest thing I ever did … I put Winston in a corner, and told him to edit The British Gazette'.

The *Gazette*, however, was criticised in the House of Commons for being 'propaganda' (Hansard, 1926). Lloyd George described it as 'a first-class indiscretion, clothed in the tawdry garb of third-rate journalism' (quoted by

Layborn, 2002, p 81). Much of the newspaper was devoted – in contrast to other newspapers – to explaining how things were running as normal. One article on the front page of the 10 May edition argues that 'Chief Trades Almost Normal' before outlining the effects in major towns and cities of the Midlands; though the article does note that the position 'is complicated' in Sheffield, where steel workers have caused problems further down the supply chain and 'every day, therefore, sees a further number of men thrown out of work owing to the shortage of raw material and to the stoppage of transport'. The same page also ran an 81-word article entitled 'Postal Service: Very Little Delay in Letter Deliveries' (*The British Gazette*, 1926a). The second page of the same paper presents a call from the Home Secretary for more police volunteers in London and reprints a warning against taking actions akin to the General Strike, drawing upon a speech by former Labour leader J.R. Clynes in 1919.

The *Gazette* framed the strike as a threat to British society, stoking tensions. Baldwin wrote that 'the general strike is a challenge to the parliament and is the road to anarchy', a speech reproduced in the *Daily Express* on 7 May 1926 and a theme picked up in the *Daily Mail*, which on 6 May 1926 managed to publish a short run of the paper using printing works in France. This included the article 'For King and Country', which London printworkers had refused to print. In it, the paper argued that 'a general strike is not an industrial dispute. It is a revolutionary move that can only succeed by destroying the government and subverting the rights and liberties of the people'.

The media, including the *Gazette*, described events drawing upon wartime terminology – for example, on 4 May the government used the BBC to call for volunteers. Critical voices, or those unsupportive of the government, including that of the Labour leader Ramsay MacDonald, were suppressed on the BBC (BBC, 2023; The University of Warwick, 2023). The *Gazette* argued that the strike represented an 'organised attempt to starve the nation' and that the TUC were pointing a 'strike weapon aimed at the daily life of the community' (*The British Gazette*, 1926b) and on 13 May the paper talked about the 'surrender' of workers (*The British Gazette*, 1926c).

The nature of law and order also changed, akin to wartime. New punishments, not normally expected within a democratic society (though the COVID-19 restrictions could also be viewed in this vein, see Chapter 14), emerged, and emphasis was placed upon those. Multiple editions of the newspaper had adverts which appealed for 'special constables' (for example, *The British Gazette*, 1926b, 1926d), written by the Home Secretary. On 10 May, the *Gazette* reported a number of criminal convictions for 'crying false news or making speeches containing untrue statements in regard to the strike situation' (*The British Gazette,* 1926a). It highlights two cases where men convicted of such crimes received punishments of six weeks' hard labour.

Baldwin (quoted by Laybourn, 1993, p 133), speaking on 8 May in a radio address, asked: 'What is it for which the Government is fighting? It is fighting because while the negotiations were still in progress the TUC ordered a General Strike, presumably to force Parliament and the community to heed its will.'

The government's position, expressed in the *Gazette*, was reinforced by the Labour opposition. Despite the links between the party and the trade unions, its leader, Ramsay MacDonald, 'refused to support the strike, instead advocating for Parliament to resolve the issues through legislation' (Kirkland, 2022, p 49).

Narratives of revolution took the TUC by surprise. The instructions given were not for an all-out stoppage, but rather an escalating series of stoppages. The TUC had selected certain groups to take part in action, while many unions were 'instructed to remain at work [including] engineering and shipyard workers, textile and wood workers, the Post Office and the distributive trades' (Bullock, 1960, p 316).

In response to the *British Gazette*, the TUC formed its own newspaper, the *British Worker*, to present its narration of events from 5 May, using the printing services of the *Daily Herald*. Such publication was not uncontested, however; a police raid held up printing on the first day by five hours, while 'turf battles' ensued between various unions, demand outstripped supply and distribution was 'unsystematic and probably restricted largely to the London area' (Phillips, 1976, p 168; Harmon, 2019, pp 195–6).

Throughout the strike, the General Council of the TUC was keen to stress that this was an industrial dispute in support of the 1 million locked-out miners. The chairman of the TUC, Walter Citrine (quoted by Perkins, 2006, p 111), emphasised this point: 'in a technical sense it was never a General Strike. We at the TUC always called it a "national strike". We regarded it as a large-scale sympathetic strike'. Such warnings were heeded, and the strike was undertaken with little violence (Saltzman, 2018, p 5).

The TUC (quoted by Laybourn, 1993, p 4), in defence of later narratives arguing that the strike was tantamount to pursuing revolutionary aims, argued that the strike was 'in support of the miners' and that 'The General Council does not challenge the Constitution'. Laybourn further notes that the terminology surrounding the notion of a general strike was heavily linked to revolutionary goals and aims in many European countries. That such terminology was used in contemporary settings – unlike the Winter of Discontent (see Chapter 10) – heightened the stakes within the crisis. The TUC, despite rejecting such notions, could not ignore these completely as they were fed into public discourse through the *Gazette* and media outlets.

On its first day of publication, the *Worker* set out, on its front page, the TUC's understanding of the strike. While calling upon all of its members to be 'exemplary in his conduct and not to give any opportunity for police interference', the paper 'emphasise[d] the fact that this is an industrial dispute'. It explicitly acknowledged that 'any disturbances would be very damaging to the prospects of a successful termination to the dispute' (*The British Worker*, 1926).

The *Gazette* contained almost three times the content of the *Worker* (defined in terms of word count) and, in doing so, presented the strike as a threat to public order. It portrayed the strike as the work of 'anarchists, Bolsheviks, socialists, communists and agitators' (Harmon, 2019, p 198). It supported and amplified the government message that democracy and the parliamentary government were under threat from the strike.

Taylor (1965, pp 244–5) argues that the government's position over-emphasised the aims of those involved in the strike. He notes that those undertaking action were the same men who had volunteered to fight to preserve British democracy and the British system of governance and 'rallied to the defence of Belgium' just a decade earlier in the First World War. Far from being a revolutionary movement, the strike:

> Was not intended to be general. Transport and railway workers were called out; so to less purpose were printers, workers in heavy industry, in building, and in gas and electricity undertakings. Other workers were held back in 'the second line'. … The strikers asked for nothing for themselves. They did not seek to challenge the government, still less to overthrow the Constitution. They merely wanted the miners to have a living wage. Perhaps not even that. They were loyal to their unions and to their leaders, as they had been loyal during the war to their country and to their generals. (Taylor, 1965, pp 244–5)

The *Daily Mirror* offered a similar line of argument in its reporting of the end of the strike on 12 May, 'workers have been led to take part in this attempt to stab the nation in the back by a subtle appeal to the motives of idealism in them' (Perkins, 2006, pp 229–30). Such narratives denied agency to workers and helped frame the strike as a structural problem of industrial relations.

Such arguments were also made about the broader Miners' Strike and reflected upon notions of 'class consciousness'. The Bishop of Durham, Herbert Hensley Henderson (quoted by Barron, 2010, p 3), who was unsympathetic to such strikes, notes in his diary:

> It is clear than in many cases the men disliked the strike, and that in many cases it hurt their conscience. Nevertheless, they obeyed, they neither resented the behaviour of the TUC in ignoring their wishes nor refused to break their contracts in violation of their professed principles. The education in 'class consciousness' has been so successful that neither self-respect nor religion count for anything against class.

Resolving the crisis

The understanding of the strike as a revolution – rather than an industrial dispute – legitimised the government to incorporate the army into its response (in contrast to this, the Thatcher government's attempts in 1984–85 to present itself as 'neutral' in the dispute were heavily undermined by its allocation of police resources to encourage the movement of coal, see Chapter 11). In addition to 'special' constables, warships were sent to Liverpool and Newcastle, the army was used to safeguard 'key points and vehicles' and 'Territorial Army units, dressed in civilian clothes, supplied with steel helmets and truncheons', were recruited. Although never used, as 'serious outbreaks of violence did not occur', the number of volunteers was dramatic. Recruiting started on 9 May, and within two days, '4,600 reservists had been recruited in London alone'. A day later, there were '12 battalions, one squadron of cavalry, two armoured car companies in use with armed troops posted at various points'. Though the lack of training received by these volunteers was apparent, according to the War Office, 'a "military" incident was avoided more because of the population's good sense than because of the correct use of soldiers by supply and transport authorities' (McDonald, 1975, p 73).

The General Strike lasted just nine days, with workers returning to employment on 13 May. Although historians are split over the effects of the General Strike, with some arguing that it represented a significant defeat for the trade unions, emphasising the enhanced powers afforded to the government following the passage of the 1927 Trade Disputes Act, others argued that little had changed; both agree that the crisis did not represent a paradigm shift.

The end of the strike led to important legislative changes, such as the repeal of the Seven-Hour Day Act and the 1927 Trade Disputes Act, which had four components to it: first, it prohibited strikes other than those 'within the grade or industry in which the strikers are engaged', second it 'limited the right of picketing and declared "intimidation" to be illegal' (Bullock, 1960, p 378). Third, it ended the automatic process of 'contracting in' to the political levy, which was estimated to be worth £200,000 in 1925 and was used to fund the Labour Party (Millis, 1928, p 315). Finally, the Act declared that staff of the civil service could not become members of any organisation affiliated to the TUC. The Act further, 'in purporting to clarify the law on sympathetic strikes, laid over it a cloak of obfuscation that could be interpreted to mean that all but the most narrowly drawn strikes were illegal' (Perkins, 2006, p 262).

The Act demonstrates the power of blame and is important in understanding the government's narrative of the strike. Throughout the strike, as discussed earlier, the government had presented the strike as a revolution or events with revolutionary aspirations. Yet such actions were prohibited by existing legislation. As Millis (1928, p 308) notes:

> Ordinary conspiracy against the state, riot, unlawful assembly, breach of the peace, or sedition remained punishable. Moreover, penalties were imposed upon anyone breaking a contract of service if the result would be to cut off a supply of gas or water or to inflict serious injury on life or property. These prohibitions have not been repealed, and in 1919 were extended to the supply of electric current also.

Moving the bill at the third reading, the Solicitor General was keen to highlight that the government refrained from using the term 'sympathetic strike', as it offered too vague a term, but instead argued that a 'general strike' could be prohibited as it 'is bound to fail'. He continued,

> The reason for that is this, that as soon as you direct a general strike you have to set the workers in array against the whole community. The nation has to fight for its breath. People have to spend their days working for those things of which the general strike has deprived them. (Hansard, 1927)

Through defining the strike as a revolution, or one with revolutionary intent, the government advocated a paradigm-reinforcing narrative. Such narratives delegitimised the actions of the trade unions and created a more restrictive environment for them to operate in. By framing the crisis as one which risked the existing composition of the state, the government left little room for significant post-crisis changes.

If the strikes had been illegal in 1926 (as the government's narrations of revolution implied), then new legislation would have been superfluous – arrests could have been made under existing provisions. Second, through enforcing notions of blame, the government sought to exclude the blame party (the trade unions) from positively contributing to the post-crisis landscape. Such a point is made by Ernest Bevin, in the debates surrounding the repealing of the Act in 1946. Bevin (1946) notes that the passage of the 1927 Act differed from previous trade union legislation, as it was 'the only Trade Union Act carried in the history of this country in regard to which the government of the day refused an inquiry and refused to allow trade unions to state their case'. Foote (1997, pp 123–4) further describes the 1927 Act as 'vindictive' and asserts that its success, along with fears of unemployment, 'led to a drastic decline in union membership, which fell from over eight million in 1920 to under five million by the decade's end'. The Trade Disputes Act was repealed by the post-war Labour government in 1946.

Support for the strike was always likely to be difficult to maintain. Unions cannot command complete loyalty and are reliant upon workers undertaking such action voluntarily. For those going on strike, there are large costs involved. Strikers do not receive wages for days lost due to industrial action, and in 1926 there was no guarantee that after a period of industrial unrest those who withdrew their labour would have a job to return to (Bullock, 1960, p 316).

In her diary on 4 May, Beatrice Webb (quoted by Bullock, 1960, p 345) noted that 'the General Strike will be one of the most significant landmarks in the history of the British working-class'. Bullock (1960, p 345) argues that this was a 'bold forecast' just two days into the strike, but one which 'proved to be fully justified'.

Mason (1969, p 1) argues that the trade unions' defeat at the hands of the government 'successfully discredited the idea of widespread industrial action as a method of obtaining the demands of labour'. Bevan (2008, p 25) makes a similar argument, noting that following the strike, 'the workers of Britain seemed to have exhausted the possibilities of mass industrial action. … The trade union leaders were theoretically unprepared for the implications involved. They had forged a revolutionary weapon without having a revolutionary intention'.

For others on the political left, the strike reinforced existing understandings. G.H.D. Cole, prior to the strike, had concluded that the trade unions were unable to defeat a modern state. Rather, Cole had argued that to change capitalism into socialism, a Labour government had to 'control capital rather than industry' (Beech and Hickson, 2007, p 47).

Legacy

The General Strike, irrespective of motives, demonstrated the limits to extra-parliamentary actions. Both the Labour Party and the TUC post-1926 dropped more radical understandings of social change and how these could be brought about. The Labour Party committed itself to parliamentary rather than revolutionary socialism, while the TUC 'quietly dropped' proposals for radical change and rejected 'massive coordinated industrial action and revolution [which had become] virtually synonymous' (Lovell and Roberts, 1968, p 120; Kirkland, 2022).

The effects of the strike were not confined to those who undertook the industrial action. The coal mining union (the Miners' Federation of Great Britain, from 1944 the National Union of Mineworkers) was particularly affected. The strike was billed as supporting the miners and its defeat made it much more difficult for the miners to win their own industrial dispute. The next national coal miners' strike was not until the 1970s. Church and Outram (1998, p 4) conclude that 'the impoverishment and weakening of the coalminers' trade unions by the events of 1926 took mining industrial relations off the political agenda for many years'.

Laybourn (1993, p 6), however, presents the argument that such a lack of future strikes may not represent a disaster for trade unions, whose members – in addition to employers – bear the financial costs of undertaking industrial action. The General Strike in this vein did not represent a

> turning point in British industrial relations, rather it enforced the existing trend towards the creation of better industrial relations. [However, f]ar from being an unmitigated disaster, the General Strike was, in a sense, a victory for it warned employers of the dangers and economic costs which might arise from industrial conflict. (Laybourn, 1993, p 6)

For Laybourn, the declining number of strikes did not represent weaknesses within the trade union movement. Rather, future industrial action was averted through demonstrating the potential consequences of such strikes, incentivising better relationships between workers and employers.

The memory of the strike, like that of other crises discussed in this book, was very much entwined with later events. Renshaw (1975, p 254) summarised the prevailing thoughts of scholars and trade unionists in the 1970s when he argued in his concluding remarks on the 1926 strike that 'the story of the miners … is still central to an understanding of modern British history'.

However, just a decade later the defeat of the miners in their year-long strike (see Chapter 11) 'broke 1926 loose from its sedimentation in labour history' (Ferrall, 2015, p 185). Following the 1984–85 strike, a new focal point had been created, a new 'year zero', as expressed in David Peace's (2004) novel based on the strike, that could be used as a barometer to judge industrial activity and strategy.

Conclusion

The General Strike demonstrates some of the key themes outlined in Chapter 2. The importance of framing the strike became key as, in the event of limited national media, both the government and the TUC sought to publish their own partisan newspapers. It also demonstrates how inequalities exist in terms of framing: the government's narratives were supported by the BBC, while the printing of the *British Worker* was beset by problems, such as a police raid and a lack of publishing ink (Harmon, 2019).

The crisis also demonstrates how crucial narratives are in shaping outcomes. Victory for the government, which billed the strike as a revolution, led to a paradigm-reinforcing resolution – much akin to the government's appeals for 'business as usual' and resolve following the 7/7 terrorist attacks in London (see Chapter 12). Here, the preservation of the state and existing institutions became the primary goal of those involved – the crisis did not represent the need for social learning or radical changes in legislation, as there had not been – for the government at least – any failure to (re)conceptualise.

The lack of a need for a paradigm shift delegitimised the claims of the TUC, which was blamed for the onset of the crisis. Legislation was passed to punish the unions and limit their powers to prevent further such strikes from taking place.

Further reading

Keith Laybourn's books *The General Strike of 1926* (1993) and *The General Strike Day by Day* (1996) offer an excellent overview of the crisis, through presenting an account of the nature of the strike and its impact upon local communities. For a discussion about the role of the media and the creation of the *British Gazette* and the *British Worker* see Harmon's (2019) journal article in *Labor History*, 'A War of Words: The British Gazette and British Worker during the 1926 General Strike'.

Many accounts of British trade unionism have space devoted to the strike and its aftermath. The best known of these are Hugh Clegg's (1985) *A History of British Trade Unionism since 1889* (Volume II covers the period 1911–33) and Ben Pimlott and Chris Cook's (1982) *Trade Unions in British Politics*. On the defeat of the strike see Geoffrey McDonald's (1975) chapter in Gillian Peele and Chris Cook's *The Politics of Reappraisal*.

One of the best contemporary accounts of the crisis can be found in the papers of the former Conservative Party Chairman John Davidson, who, prior to becoming chairman, managed the *British Gazette* during the strike. His papers have been published in Robert James's (1969) book entitled *Memoirs of a Conservative: J.C.C. Davidson's Memoirs and Papers 1910–37*.

For an alternative account see A.J. Cook, the secretary of the Miners Federation of Great Britain. Arthur Cook (1926) published his account of the strike in *Nine Days: The Story of the General Strike Told by the Miners Secretary*, which directly engages with and counters government narratives of the strike as a revolution.

7

The Great Slump of 1931

Overview

This chapter explores the Great Slump of 1931. Just weeks after winning the 1929 general election (albeit as a minority government), the Labour Party faced the aftermath of the Wall Street Crash and subsequent slump, which in turn led to the US recalling a number of the loans offered to European countries during the First World War and used for reconstruction. This posed budgetary problems for the government, which had been elected to overcome problems of unemployment. Such problems were exacerbated by the decision in 1925 to rejoin the gold standard and the Labour Chancellor Phillip Snowden's desire to maintain a balanced budget.

With unemployment rising, the Labour Party was unable to agree on austerity measures. Snowden attempted to persuade his parliamentary colleagues by establishing a review led by the Liberal Sir George May. However, this report suggested that the government faced a black hole of £120 million, leading the UK's creditors to worry about its financial position and further economic problems as foreign-owned sterling began to be withdrawn from the middle of 1931. The crisis led to a split within the governing Labour Party, and senior Labour figures, such as Prime Minister Ramsay MacDonald, along with Snowden, left the party to form a National government with Conservative and Liberal support. The National government was more willing to implement cuts to spending and reductions in unemployment rates, but also able to leave the gold standard – something that the Labour government had been told by the Treasury was not an option. The National government won a landslide majority in an election in October 1931, with Labour gaining just 52 of the 615 seats.

Introduction

In many respects, the Great Slump of 1931 emanated from some of the same issues as the General Strike of 1926. Although not confined to a single industry, it was a product of Britain's structural economic problems (for example, rejoining the gold standard and unemployment), exacerbated due to international events such as the Wall Street Crash of October 1929. Yet, unlike the Conservative government in 1926, the Labour government, which won the 1929 general election, was a minority, making it harder to pass legislation. In addition, internal disagreements soon materialised within the party over how to tackle the economic problems.

Labour formed its second government in 1929, having gained just 27 seats more than the Conservative Party. However, unlike in 1924, the Cabinet was comprised solely of Labour politicians, and there was no reliance upon agreements with the Liberal Party (which held 59 seats in 1929).

Behind these figures, however, lay an electoral weakness that is often overlooked. Labour, although winning more seats than the Conservatives, received fewer votes, as many seats were won by narrow margins. Any further decline in support for the Liberals, which won 40 of their 59 seats on a minority vote, would vastly disproportionately benefit the Conservative Party. As Stevenson and Cook (2010, pp 112–13) summarise: 'Thus, the 1929 general election, thought a marked step forward for Labour, had hardly been the secure victory that on its surface it appeared.' Labour's chances of further advancement appeared remote, and it was dangerously exposed to 'either a Conservative revival or a Liberal collapse'.

Such notions reflect the calls from the newly elected Labour Prime Minister Ramsay MacDonald for Parliament to work in a 'less partisan fashion and more in the capacity of a council of state' (Ball, 1988, p 173). The weaknesses of the Labour Party led to consistent talk of a coalition government forming – Labour having previously relied upon Liberal support in 1924; though this was initially from fringe figures, and routinely dismissed by Baldwin and other party leaders, by July 1930 there was sufficient press speculation about a 'national government' that:

> the Conservative Party felt obliged to discuss and defend their position once more. None of the shadow Cabinet wanted a coalition, and all sought to avoid it, although it was realised that under the pressure of a crisis or a panic in the City it might become difficult to stand aside. (Ball, 1988, p 173)

Within the Labour Party and the wider Labour Movement, however, the 1929 election results were seen as a great success.

> Initial euphoria permeated almost all sections of the Labour movement. The bulk of the Parliamentary Labour Party (PLP) was 'elated'. The trade unions were also delighted: W.A. Robinson, political general secretary of the National Union of Distributive and Allied Workers (NUDAW), emphasized the overwhelming need for loyalty, and added that he had 'never at any time moved about in such an atmosphere of enthusiasm'. The party activists reflected this mood; the York Divisional Labour Party (DLP) 'congratulate[d] the Working Class on at last becoming the Ruling Class'. (Thorpe, 1991, p 9)

However, such euphoria was short-lived. The Wall Street Crash of October 1929 meant that the US started to recall dollars, crucial for recovery from the First World War, from Western Europe, while unemployment, which in June 1929 stood at 1.16 million (9.6 per cent), by December 1930 had more than doubled to 2.5 million (19.9 per cent) (Cole, 1948, p 235; Office for National Statistics, 1996).

Following the Wall Street Crash, the US government recalled loans made during the First World War. Britain's net borrowing during the war, including acting as a proxy for US loans to European allies (see Chapter 5), had weakened the UK economy and, importantly, the position of the City of London within the gold standard. The post-war domestic economy offered little headroom to use interest rates as a mechanism for maintaining stability within the gold standard – something that 'was the pivot upon which the pre-1914 gold standard had turned' (Williams, 1963, p 520).

Alongside this, the volume of global trade collapsed, and the spending power of individuals plummeted. Even in Britain, where unemployment benefits were most universal, just 60 per cent of the labour force were covered, prompting a further downward spiral as unemployment increased. The crash, then, 'amounted to something very close to the collapse of the capitalist world economy ... where every downward movement of the economic indices [bar unemployment] reinforced the decline in others' (Hobsbawm, 1994, p 91).

The issue of unemployment was crucial for the incoming Labour government. In its 1929 election manifesto, it offered an 'unqualified pledge to deal immediately and practically with this question [of unemployment]' (The Labour Party, 1929). Labour was 'designed to be the representation of the working class and the trade union movement [and as such] saw unemployment as one of the – if not *the* – key indicators of how well society was functioning' (Kirkland, 2022, p 41).

Unemployment and unemployment insurance had been contentious throughout the inter-war period. High unemployment at the start of the decade contributed to a tightening of unemployment insurance. In 1921, the coalition led by Lloyd George uncoupled the links between previous contributions and the unemployment fund; instead, a new requisite based upon seeking work was introduced, which meant that any claimant had to make a real and continuing effort to find work before receiving assistance. Deacon (1976), although identifying regional disparities, notes that some 3 million people were denied funds as a result of this test. Both major parties – Conservatives and Labour – initially supported the test, though backbench opposition forced the Labour government to abolish it in 1930, increasing the number of people claiming, and thus the overall cost of, unemployment insurance.

Labour entered office with only 'one recognised financial expert', Phillip Snowden, who became Chancellor. Snowden's position was unchallenged by senior figures within the Labour Party: 'neither MacDonald nor most of the other members of the Cabinet had any understanding of finance, or even thought they had' (Cole, 1948, p 236).

In 1929, however, Labour did commission a Committee on Finance and Industry (better known as the Macmillan Committee) to investigate the issue

Figure 7.1: Inter-war UK unemployment data

UK unemployment 1918–1939

Unemployment (Yearly Average) %

Year

Source: Office for National Statistics, 1996

of unemployment. The Committee's terms of reference were 'To inquire into banking, finance and credit, paying regard to factors both internal and international which govern their operation, and to make recommendations calculated to enable these agencies to promote the development of trade and commerce and the employment of labour'. Although the depression had led to a recent increase in unemployment, the report noted that 'before the world depression [the UK had] a domestic problem of over a million unemployed ... the committee hence found it necessary to consider proposals relating to both international and domestic monetary policy' (Thomas, 1931; see also Figure 7.1).

The report, not delivered until 1931, was authored by economists such as John Maynard Keynes and highlighted the 'special problems of Great Britain' (Macmillan, 1931; Stamp, 1931, pp 424–5). As in the debt narratives post-2008 (see Chapter 13), attention focused on government policy rather than international conditions.

The Macmillan Committee report concluded that sterling was overvalued – an argument Keynes had made in 1925 (see previous chapter) – and offered solutions of raising international prices or reducing wages. Bevin and Keynes rejected reducing wages, arguing instead for placing tariffs on imports, which could then be used to subsidise exports, 'in effect a form of devaluation through the backdoor, while retaining the existing exchange rate'. The majority report ruled out devaluation itself (Dimsdale and Horsewood, 2014, p 118).

In February 1931, the government established the May Committee, led by the Liberal Sir George May, to explore ways of cutting government expenditure. Although pressured by opposition parties to establish such a committee (Webb, 1932), Snowden saw this as an opportunity to persuade his own party of the need for cuts (Cole, 1948, p 252). The Committee reported on 31 July 1931; it argued that £120 million was needed to balance the budget and recommended £24 million to be raised through taxation and £96 million sourced from spending cuts, including £66.5 million worth of cuts to unemployment relief and £13 million and £3.5 million to the pay of teachers and police respectively.

Far from strengthening Snowden's position, however, the May Committee Report offered to overseas creditors an impression that the British economy was worse than anticipated. Rather than weakening opposition to cuts, as Snowden had hoped, the report generated 'a belief in the insolvency of Great Britain and in the insecurity of the British currency', which in turn made borrowing more difficult/expensive and further emphasised the need for cuts (Ball, 1988, p 174; Kirkland, 2022, pp 40–41).

Foreign firms began to withdraw gold and capital from the UK, believing that the government's 'budgetary position was unsound' (Snowden, 1934, p 936). Publication of the May Committee Report, announcing a 'massive budget deficit', came on the same weekend that it became publicly known that the Bank of England had borrowed £25 million from both the Federal Reserve Bank of New York and the Bank of France (Thorpe, 1991, p 63).

The May Report and its interpretation among Britain's creditors was further amplified by a banking crisis emanating from continental Europe. Between them, these events 'combined to produce a serious run on the gold reserves'. The position of sterling, still linked to gold, could only be saved by obtaining loans in Paris and New York. However, the Bank of England advised the government that such loans would only be forthcoming if creditors' confidence were restored by greater commitments to balancing the budget. This put pressure on the need for cuts, and in particular cuts to unemployment benefit, meaning that 'the crisis had become as much political as financial' (Ball, 1988, p 174).

A run on the pound in August 1931 meant that the meeting of the Cabinet Economy Committee scheduled for the 25th was brought forward by two weeks (to the 12th). During this meeting and the discussions which followed on the 13th, it was decided that the following year's budget should be balanced (Snowden, 1934, pp 936–7). A report to Cabinet the following week estimated that the budget deficit would total £170 million. In order to overcome the deficit, it proposed economies of £78.5 million, of which £28.5 million came from unemployment benefits, and 'new revenue' of £88.5 million (Thorpe, 1988, p 120).

Framing the crisis

Economic problems manifest themselves through different lenses. As occurred following the Global Financial Crisis (GFC) of 2008 (see Chapter 13), there existed a tension between narrations of a financial or budgetary crisis and an unemployment crisis, which Labour identified in its 1929 election manifesto and

Figure 7.2: Inter-war UK inflation data

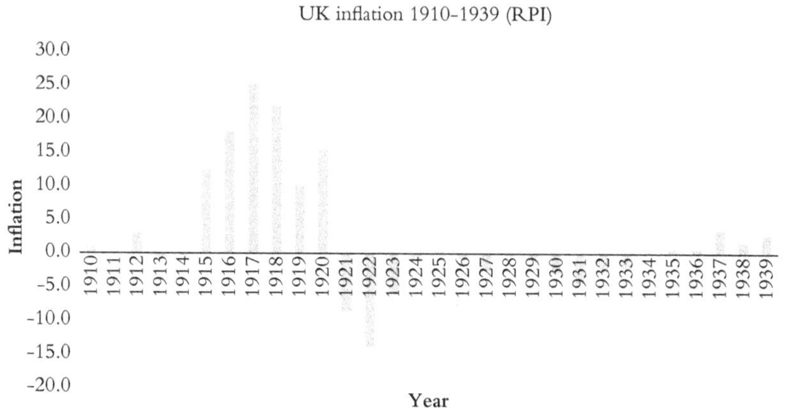

UK inflation 1910-1939 (RPI)

Inflation

30.0 25.0 20.0 15.0 10.0 5.0 0.0 -5.0 -10.0 -15.0 -20.0

1910 1911 1912 1913 1914 1915 1916 1917 1918 1919 1920 1921 1922 1923 1924 1925 1926 1927 1928 1929 1930 1931 1932 1933 1934 1935 1936 1937 1938 1939

Year

Source: Office for National Statistics, 2022a

sought to use the instruments of the state to alleviate. This, in turn, generated a crisis of confidence, which, in order to be resolved, necessitated opposite policies, namely those of state retrenchment.

Juxtaposed against this rise in unemployment was deflation. Alongside high levels of unemployment, the 1920s were characterised by negative inflation rates or deflation (see Figure 7.2), meaning that prices were falling on an annual basis. This placed greater emphasis upon unemployment spending in particular. As wages fell alongside deflation, the protected nature of unemployment insurance meant that those who were out of work were improving their position vis-à-vis those in employment. Additionally, as unemployment climbed, there was a 'lack of work at skilled rates in the most depressed areas; the only jobs which the unemployed might take in the thirties were so often so intermittent and so badly paid that they really were better off on the dole' (Seaman, 1993, p 243). Seaman further notes that the relative safeguarding of unemployment benefits meant that, by 1933, someone unemployed was 'no worse off than an unskilled labourer in work in 1913'.

Themes of 'generous' unemployment benefits were picked up by right-wing newspapers, which placed the blame for government spending upon those in receipt of that spending. Such notions draw upon a distinction between the deserving and undeserving poor. The *Daily Express*, for example, ran a story on 11 July about subsidised fares for 'Dole Excursions', which were reported with no 'mention of whether [such fares] would be taken up by the unemployed'. The article failed to offer a comparison of train fares, which ranged '"from 15s. to 21s." with the rate of weekly unemployment insurance benefit, which was 17s. for an adult male and less for other types of claimant'. Rather, the story was constructed to tally with the '"common sense" of ... the "man in the street"' who might not be unsympathetic to the problems caused by unemployment but nonetheless 'knows that while a good proportion of "his" hard-earned wages will be taken from "him" by the state, others are having "holidays on the dole" subsidised by "his" taxes'. Such understandings were further enhanced by the cartoons of Sidney Strube, which presented a 'respectable, bespectacled figure with his bowler hat and umbrella' who was consistently at the 'mercy of "vested interests" intent on wasting part of his earnings which he paid in taxes' (Brookes, 1985, p 49).

The Labour government was keen to reject the simplistic links between the crisis and government spending. As government spending is 'naturally progressive', any cuts to this would have a disproportionate effect upon the poorest within society, those who were statistically more likely to support Labour than any other political party (Kirkland, 2022, p 41). The Labour government suffered from its 'dual role as a socialist party, with a rhetoric of fundamentally transforming the social order and its short-term role as defender of working-class interests' (Tomlinson, 1990, p 96).

The 'cornerstone' of the Treasury view was that any money spent by the government would 'crowd out' the much more efficient private sector investment. As the economist R.G. Hawtrey (quoted in Cliff, 2015, p 156) wrote to the Macmillan Committee: 'whether the spending comes out of taxes or loans from savings, the increased government expenditure would merely replace private expenditure'. Hawtree further considered a 'radical' idea of 'government spending out of new bank credit' but dismissed this as being inflationary and threatening the gold standard (Klein, 1966, p 46).

The Treasury's insistence upon policies such as the gold standard was an example of a recurring refrain in British political discourse: that there are few, if any, options in the conduct of economic policy. In the 1980s, Prime Minister Thatcher proclaimed that 'there is no alternative'; more recently, George Osborne, Chancellor of the Exchequer under David Cameron, stated that there can be no plan B for economic policy (Kitson, 2013, p 134).

Such themes appear in the final report of the Macmillan Committee – which, although not universally accepted by the authors, read: 'The recent increase in unemployment in every part of the world, accompanied by a decline in production, can in the main be attributed to the fall in the level of prices, unaccompanied by a proportionate reduction of money costs, however brought about' (Stamp, 1931, p 428).

The Labour government thus soon found that promises to tackle the unemployment crisis were contradictory to prevailing economic understandings. This would have presented a challenge during times of non-crisis but became increasingly difficult to pursue given other pressures. Nor was there much support for pursuing radical policies – the government's main priority was to overcome the immediate banking/financial crisis, and longer-term promises or ambitions were displaced by the most salient issues. This was supported by a wider idea within the party that socialism would be achieved from the basis of a strong economy, not out of a crisis of capitalism.

Contemporary literature began to blame the depression on Labour. This traced the problems of unemployment to 'rigidities which prevented the free working of the capitalist system', principally 'obstructions to the downward movement of wages'. Economists such as Edwin Cannan (1932) and A.C. Pigou (1933) advocated wage cuts to increase employment.

Crisis resolution

Unable to pass legislation, against a backdrop of worsening economic problems, Ramsay MacDonald and Philip Snowden sought to forge a coalition to try and implement some of the spending reductions that were unpalatable to the Labour Party. In doing so, they argued that the economic situation required cross-party support and, in August 1931, formed a National government with the support of Conservative and Liberal MPs.

A fortnight after forming the National government, Parliament resumed sitting. The government abridged some political constraints; the new parliamentary majority stood at 497 seats (Stevenson and Cook, 2010, p 11), guaranteeing the passage of legislation – something that the Labour minority government (even when the party was united) could not. Equally, it was not bound by promises made during the 1929 general election campaign. These, as MacDonald and Snowden had advocated, had been superseded by the current economic crisis.

The National government adopted policies that had been perceived as unthinkable in the previous government. On 21 September 1931, Britain left the gold standard, breaking with the prevailing economic orthodoxy to the extent that one Labour MP (quoted in Moggridge, 1969, p 9) bluntly claimed that 'nobody told us we could do that'.

However, as Foote (1997) notes, this underplays the economic orthodoxy that Labour pursued during the crisis. The lack of an alternative narrative/understanding of the crisis – separate from one of government spending – meant that

> the economic policy pursued by Snowden in government in 1929–31 was marked by a respect for orthodoxy worthy of any Tory Chancellor. His acceptance of Hobson's theories of underconsumption was combined with a belief in the Quantity Theory of Money – the theory that any increase in purchasing power without any corresponding increase in productivity would cause inflation ... In other words, the incorruptible socialist, Snowden, was forced to uphold the market and the bankers as the forces determining financial policy. The result was a financial crisis and the desertion of Labour by Snowden and MacDonald. (Foote, 1997, pp 158–9)

Kitson (2013, p 134) argues that the withdrawal from the gold standard had two important benefits: first, devaluing the currency 'replaced persistent deflation'. This made British products more competitive in the international marketplace (until other countries followed suit and also left the gold standard, limiting Britain's relative advantage). Second, the withdrawal from the gold standard allowed an inflationary monetary policy – since money was no longer dependent upon UK gold reserves, the government could pursue policies of 'cheap money' to stimulate the internal market and encourage growth, particularly in the housing sector.

Richardson (1967, pp 184–6) notes that such emphasis on 'cheap money' did not drive Britain to leave the gold standard (indeed, policies of cheap money were attempted in 1930–31 under the Labour government, but failed due to unfavourable underlying conditions). He dates the government's emphasis on 'cheap money' to the middle of 1932, stating that this arose only after 'a further deterioration in the deflationary trend *after* the abandonment of gold and sterling depreciation and because a worldwide demand had arisen for attempts to raise prices' (Richardson, 1967, p 185, emphasis added).

The immediate problems faced by the UK government following the abandonment of the gold standard were inflationary. Bank of England interest rates increased to 6 per cent (up from 2.5 per cent in early 1931) and remained at the higher level for five months (Richardson, 1967, p 187).

The nature and timings of recovery are, unsurprisingly, contested. Richardson (1967, p 22) argues that, compared to other industrial countries, Britain's decline was modest, and its recovery was ensured by 1937. He criticises other characterisations of a 'hesitant and half-hearted' recovery for over-emphasising the issue of unemployment; although it only fell to below 10 per cent in one month (August 1937) in the decade following 1929, 'the similarities between the unemployment levels of 1929 and 1937 show that cyclical unemployment had been eliminated by the middle of 1937'. Here, Richardson distinguishes between the crisis of unemployment, which Labour entered office in 1929 determined to resolve, and the Great Slump, which generated wider economic problems in the 1930s.

Miller (1976, pp 454–6) argues that indicators other than unemployment fell 'only [by] a few percent' during the Slump, while falls in inflation meant an increase in purchasing power for those who remained employed. This questions the impact the Slump had upon individuals. Alongside this, the 20 per cent increase in GDP between 1932 and 1936 enabled the Conservative-dominated national government to emphasise the cyclical nature of the crisis, arguing against a radical or paradigm-shifting policy. In 1934, the Minister of Labour, Oliver Stanley (quoted by Miller, 1976, p 456), proudly noted that British unemployment stood at 'only 2,000,000', a fifth of that in the US, and unemployment in 1940 was predicted to average 21 per cent – the same figure as in 1932.

Although Britain suffered from unemployment, in a relative sense, Britain also held a lot of advantages over its competitors. As Hobsbawm (1994) notes, economic problems were not unique to Britain. That just 60 per cent of those unemployed were entitled to financial assistance from the state seems low compared to the universal welfare system introduced in the 1940s, but it was world-leading in the inter-war period; in addition, Britain's departure from gold standard did not generate the 'downward plunge of the exchange rate' that was predicted. Although the pound fell sharply against the dollar, reaching a trough of $3.14 in December 1932, this did not generate a financial panic or hyperinflation. Indeed, once the dollar left the gold standard in 1933, the pound quickly regained, and exceeded, its parity. 'For most of the 1930s, after the initial shock, capital flowed *into* London. So that the pound, until the imminent threat of war, was a relatively attractive currency to hold in this depressed and politically turbulent decade' (Tomlinson, 1990, pp 98–100).

In addition to favourable international comparisons, others have argued that Britain's experience during the Great Slump was moderated by the weakness of its economy in the preceding decade. Rees (1970, p 40) notes, 'if Britain suffered less than other industrial countries from the shock of the world economic depression it was because depression was already a permanent feature of her economy'.

While this may position Britain in a positive light in terms of the crisis, it also affected its recovery (or at least expectations of what the recovery would encompass/ look like). In Chapter 2, it was noted that crisis resolutions are often benchmarked against a pre-crisis period, which acts as the 'normality' that those embroiled in the crisis seek to return to. The importance of unemployment statistics in the Great Slump is symptomatic of this. High unemployment – which tallied over a million in 1929 – was viewed as a crisis in and of itself upon Labour entering office in 1929. Yet such figures were accepted and amalgamated in the resolution to the Great Slump, to such an extent that returning to the levels of unemployment of the 1920s was seen as a success as the economy resumed growing in the 1930s. By the middle of the decade such concerns were further dropping down the political agenda as they were replaced by security concerns/fears of increasingly militaristic governments in Europe and Japan, which paradoxically reduced the salience afforded to an unemployment crisis but, through rearmament policies, helped to combat the high levels of unemployment which characterised the inter-war period.

Such a distinction is important, as noted by A.J.P. Taylor (1965, p 317), when he writes:

> The nineteen-thirties have been called the black years, the devil's decade. Its popular image can be expressed in two phases: mass unemployment and 'appeasement'. No set of political leaders has been judged so contemptuously since the days of Lord North.

Yet, paradoxically, most English people were enjoying a richer life than any previously known in the history of the world: longer holidays, shorter hours, higher real wages. They had motor cars, cinemas, radio sets and electrical appliance. The two sides of life did not join up.

Although the national economic figures hid wide regional variations (on this point, see Richardson, 1967), they – principally the unemployment figures – contributed to a 'myth' of 'missed opportunities' and 'wasted time'. Such themes were used as late as 1951, during the Labour Party campaign, which drew upon these myths in its election slogan 'Ask your Dad!' Later decades 'hardened and reinforced' this view, not least due to the contrast of full employment achieved in the 1950s and 1960s (Stevenson and Cook, 2010, p 11).

The political, as opposed to economic, crisis is easier to define. Traditional understandings of the crisis of 1931 see 'Labour's defeat in the 1931 election and MacDonald's "betrayal" [as] inseparable' (Stevenson and Cook, 2010, p 110). While it is true that blame has been conferred upon both, and, as Stevenson and Cook go on to note, the Labour Party in government generated public disillusionment prior to the crisis of 1931 and were likely to lose the next election, such an assimilation overlooks the agency that the crisis offered to both groups and how the crisis forged different paths for each.

The positive reception that the National government received also implied that blame for the crisis lay with the Labour government and party. The 'new' government was warmly welcomed by the press, which offered its full support by likening the crisis to a war. Patriotic support for the National government extended across different newspapers. The *Guardian* (1931) noted that 'there is today an emergency of peace which is comparable with that of war. It demands a comparable effort in the form of national unity'. The *Telegraph* (1931) argued that 'what the government have a right to expect from all good citizens is loyal support for the measures taken by them to justify the maintenance of the world's confidence in sterling unimpaired' and the *Daily Mail* (1931) for its part warned that adding 'to the difficulties of the new ministers by displays of political rancour or recrimination would be as bad as treachery in war'.

Labour's large-scale electoral defeats in 1931 and 1935 epitomise this. Just as the crisis of the First World War differentiated between political parties, so too did the Great Slump and the 1930s. Here, the Labour Party, rather than MacDonald or Snowden, felt the immediate repercussions of the crisis. Philip Snowden, who had served as Chancellor throughout the Labour government, remained so until the election of October 1931, in which he did not stand, before being elevated to the House of Lords. From there, he served as Lord Privy Seal in the National government between 1931 and 1932. Ramsay MacDonald remained Prime Minister until 1935, winning a landslide victory in the general election of 1931. Although MacDonald was defeated in the parliamentary seat of Seaham in the general election of 1935, he was returned to the House of Commons in a by-election the following January for the Combined Scottish Universities seat.

In contrast, the Labour Party was heavily fractured by the crisis; those who had joined the National government, such as MacDonald and Snowden, were largely from the right of the party, but those with more authoritarian views also left, including Oswald Mosley, who created the New Party and later the British Union of Fascists. A year later, the Independent Labour Party (ILP) also split from the Labour Party and other left-wing groups such as the Socialist League were founded shortly afterwards (Pimlott, 1977). The remaining party also looked inward at the plurality of groups within it. Some proposed greater alignment with groups such as the Communists, provoking fierce debates and leading to the temporary expulsion of 'several left-wing leaders' (Foote, 1997, p 145).

Such problems continued throughout the decade; in the 1935 election, Labour was unable to inflict even the 'slightest embarrassment' on the National government. Key figures were defeated: Henderson lost his seat in Burnley, as did Clynes (Manchester, Platting), Graham (Central Edinburgh), Morrison (South Hackney) and Alexander (Sheffield, Hillsborough). Just one former Cabinet minister (George Lansbury) and two junior ministers (Clement Attlee and Stafford Cripps) survived (Thorpe, 1991, pp 256–7).

Led by Conservative Prime Ministers from 1935 (Stanley Baldwin and later Neville Chamberlain), the National government was able to govern for much of the 1930s, winning large majorities in both 1931 and 1935, until the creation of the wartime coalition government under Winston Churchill in 1940. In contrast, the Labour Party, which became associated with the failures of the Great Slump, was deeply divided following the split of 1931. Throughout the 1930s, Labour was forced to think more holistically about its programme and how socialism could be introduced to Britain. Elizabeth Durbin (1985, pp 261–2), daughter of the MP Evan Durbin, argued that by the end of the decade the party had 'travelled lightyears in the depth and sophistication of its knowledge of British financial institutions and economic policies … [to the extent that] neither the failure of 1931 nor the failure to deal with depression unemployment was likely to be repeated out of ignorance'. However, as Durbin notes, this was not a smooth transition; rather, the 1930s represented a 'long process of research and debate'. Durbin's claims are not without contestation (see, for instance, Booth, 1996; Foote, 1997; Kirkland, 2022), but do demonstrate the differences between the Labour Party, which was removed from power and forced to reconsider its economic understanding, and the individuals (MacDonald and Snowden) who left the party in the split of 1931, were able to continue in their positions and were not challenged in the same manner.

Legacy

During the crisis Ramsay MacDonald argued that 'it was the system rather than Labour which was on trial. [Yet] he presided over a government which found itself incapable of implementing any economic policy other than the palliatives of Treasury and Bank of England orthodoxy' (Eatwell and Wright, 1978, p 38). This should have led to the possibility of a paradigm shift, as it places emphasis upon structures while exonerating agents. If it is accepted that it was the system, rather than the government, which failed, then social learning would suggest finding an alternative means of conceptualising how the economics can be structured.

The notion of a socialist government faced with a crisis of capitalism may also indicate fertile ground for significant changes, but the actions undertaken by Snowden were far from radical. Key institutions such as the Bank of England, the bureaucracy and the majority of industry were all 'thrown against innovation'. Such institutions, 'in the end, preferred an orthodox Conservative government to any kind of Labour one' (McKibbin, 1975, p 123).

The widespread agreement on economic policy outside of government meant it was difficult to find sympathy for any new or radical ideas. As Tomlinson (1990, p 113) notes, the position of the Bank of England was weakened by the decision to leave the gold standard, yet the Treasury (which became 'the crucial agency in economic policy making') never promoted the issue of unemployment in the 1930s. Here, despite institutional changes, a lack of social learning prevented what Hall (1993) defines as a paradigm shift, at least in the short term, as there existed a lack of alternatives being publicly advocated. Keynes's ideas, although shaped by the slump of 1931, did not penetrate mainstream political thought until their acceptance within the Labour Party in the latter half of the 1930s and were not tested in government until the 1940s.

Blame, then, was linked to the ideology of the Labour Party rather than to individuals such as MacDonald or Snowden. The sterling crisis was prioritised over problems of unemployment, as demonstrated by the decision of the National government to cut unemployment insurance. The National government did not enact a 'New Deal' akin to that in the US or the expansionary policies that were implemented in Europe. Rather, minimal intervention was favoured, ensuring that the government's 'central objective of ensuring that the depression would cause no fundamental changes in existing economic and social relationships' (Miller, 1976, p 453). Such policies and overarching goals prevented any social learning or paradigm shift as identified by Hall (1993).

Regarding the wider Labour Party throughout the 1930s, despite the splits, it remained the second largest party behind the Conservatives – the Labour Party that remained outside of the National government won a far greater percentage of the popular vote and more seats (52), even in 1931, than either Liberal faction (Liberal, 32, or National Liberal, 35) which joined the National government. Though the National government won a landslide victory – gaining 554 seats out of a possible 615 – 470 of these (85 per cent) were Conservative; the National Labour contingent stood at just 13 (Thorpe, 1991, p 255).

Although a smaller party, questions about its ideology did not recede. The experience of 1931 required the party to think more holistically about economic issues. Throughout the 1930s, many thinkers within the Labour Party sought to grapple with economic considerations; broadly, this can be summarised as a debate between those who wished to incorporate Keynesianism into the party (Evan Durbin and Ernest Bevin) and socialist critics (such as G.D.H. Cole and Harold Laski). The party created four new standing committees to shape its policy, two of which dealt directly with economic issues (Brooke, 1992, p 13).

Just as in the case of Irish Home Rule (see Chapter 4), conflict in Europe replaced domestic issues as the most salient issue of the day. From the middle of the decade the international situation took priority, as exemplified by the National government's manifesto of 1935. The manifesto mentions the term 'unemployment' eight times, but six of these are in relation to 'unemployment assistance'. Commitments to lower unemployment were confined to 'special areas' and Scotland (The Conservative Party, 1935).

A similar pattern occurs in the Labour manifesto of the same year. The manifesto mentions the term 'unemployment' fewer times (five as opposed to eight) and, although promising to 'reabsorb idle workers into productive employment by far-reaching schemes of national development', focuses its primary attention upon the levels of unemployment assistance (The Labour Party, 1935).

Conclusion

The crisis of 1931 had both economic and political elements to it. The Labour government that won the 1929 election promising to tackle high levels of unemployment was soon derailed following external events. The lack of economic expertise within Labour left it unable to oppose the orthodoxy of existing institutions such as the Bank of England and the Treasury, combined with political mistakes such as commissioning the May Report.

The crisis further demonstrates how inequalities can materialise within crises and how blame can lead to exclusion. Blaming the Labour government, as opposed to individuals, ensured Labour's exile from power for almost a decade. This differed from MacDonald's and Snowden's continued importance within government through their incorporation into the National government.

As with the Irish Home Rule Crisis (see Chapter 4), the resolution of the crisis relied upon other factors. Nationally, the commitment to rearmament in the late 1930s and the onset of the Second World War in 1939 led to falling unemployment, while the conflict itself offered the Labour Party a route back into government, first in the wartime coalition from 1940 and then as a majority government after winning a landslide in the 1945 general election (see Chapter 9).

Further reading

In their book *The Slump: Britain in the Great Depression*, John Stevenson and Chris Cook (2010) explore the social conditions within Britain in the 1930s and link these to the electoral politics of the decade. Many other accounts of the fortunes of the Labour Party have been written, such as Ben Pimlott's (1977) *Labour and the Left in the 1930s*. In contrast, Chris Wrigley (2012) offers a reappraisal of the Labour government under MacDonald as part of his chapter in John Shepard, Jonathan Davis and Chris Wrigley's edited collection *The Second Labour Government*.

An introduction to the economics of the slump can be found in D.E. Moggridge's (1969) *The Return to Gold, 1925: The Norman Conquest of $4.86*. The impact of the slump and its aftermath paved the way for new economic theories, associated with John Maynard Keynes. Keynes published his *General Theory of Employment Interest and Money* in 1936, which offered a critical account of the failed policies that led up to the slump.

Philip Snowden's (1934) *An Autobiography* offers an account of the crisis and situates this within the wider problems faced by the Labour government of 1929–31. It also offers the insights of the National government and its approach to the crisis. Clement Attlee ([1954] 2019), in *As It Happened*, only briefly touches upon the crisis but offers an insight into Labour's responses to the defection of MacDonald and Snowden. The best critical contemporary accounts of the Labour government's approach to the crisis can be found in Sidney Webb's (1932) *What Happened in 1931* or G.D.H. Cole's (1948) *A History of Labour Party*.

8

The Second World War

Overview

This chapter analyses the Second World War (1939–45). Although the crisis stemmed from foreign policy and external actors, it completely changed Britain not only during the conflict but also afterwards. Following the declaration of war in September 1939, the transition from a consumption-based economy to a wartime economy required a large expansion of the state. The state controlled the means of production and rationed key items such as food and clothing. Further intrusions into normal daily lives were exhibited through conscription, blackouts, media censorship and propaganda. The expansion of the state saw a corresponding reduction in democracy or the rights of citizens, new laws were passed to secure Britain's defences and, along with tighter media regulations, elections were suspended for the duration of the war.

Victory in the war was secured in foreign battlefields but also in the arena that came to be known as 'the Home Front'. Notions of sacrifice were not limited to serving soldiers but included ordinary civilians, and debates within both the armed forces and the civilian population focused attention on what kind of world was to come once peace returned. The 1945 general election – the first in ten years – is often seen as a watershed moment in this regard. Labour's first majority government, something that at the end of the 1930s appeared a far-fetched idea, to its supporters ushered in a 'new Jerusalem'; to its critics – especially those on the left – it largely reverted to the economic understandings of the 1930s.

Introduction

Just as in the case of the First World War (see Chapter 5), the origins of the Second World War encompass both domestic and foreign affairs. The First and Second World Wars, however, were not completely inseparable. Keynes (1920) famously argued that the terms of the peace treaties signed after the First World War helped foster the economic conditions of the 1930s that once again saw war break out on the European continent. He points, in particular, to the reparations clauses and argues that 'Germany's capacity to pay will be exhausted by the direct and legitimate claims which the Allies hold against her' (Keynes, 1920, p 120). This clause amounted to a 'blank cheque', and the final reparations figure, £6.6 billion, was only set two years later (Laffan, 1989, p 82).

In addition to paying this huge sum of money, Germany's ability to repay the debts diminished as through the loss of territories it lost 'much of the country's reserves of iron ore, coal and zinc', a situation that deteriorated further in 1923 when French and Belgian troops invaded the coal-rich Ruhr area. In 1924, a new plan for reparations, the Dawes plan, replaced the terms set out in Versailles. This helped to ease the burden of reparations and, in practice, financed these through US loans to the extent that Germany 'paid less in reparations between 1924 and 1930 than she received in foreign investments' (Laffan, 1989, pp 82, 89).

Throughout the 1930s, Hitler sought to overturn the remaining components of the Versailles Treaty, including extending German military power, remilitarising the Rhineland and achieving *Anschluss* with Austria in March 1938. Further territorial claims followed; in September 1938, the Munich Agreement accepted further German claims, this time in Czechoslovakia. Chamberlain believed this would be the last of Hitler's territorial claims in Europe and famously declared that the deal offered 'peace in our time'.

However, the agreement was short-lived. Chamberlain's appeasement strategy of the 1930s was increasingly placed under strain by more and more demands from a resurgent Hitler. As Churchill argued in the House of Commons on 5 October, '£1 was demanded at the pistol's point. When it was given, £2 was demanded at the pistol's point. Finally, the dictator consented to take £1 17s. 6d. and the rest in promises of good will for the future' (Hansard, 1938).

In 1939, Hitler invaded the remainder of Czechoslovakia. German attention turned to Poland, which sought and received guarantees from Britain and France in August. Britain had used the time following the Munich Agreement to enhance its wartime capabilities, including introducing a limited form of conscription in April 1939 (Dennis, 2021). Two days after Hitler's invasion on 1 September 1939, Chamberlain announced to the nation that Britain was once again at war with Germany, in defence of Poland, starting Britain's involvement in the Second World War.

Criticisms over Chamberlain's appeasement policy or failure to rearm became popularised in historical accounts of the years immediately following 1939. Here, policies of appeasement became synonymous with 'weakness, blindness and even cowardice' (Levy, 2006, p ix). However, such an understanding fails to acknowledge the choices being made and the desire to prevent war. Levy argues that such accounts do not contend that the appeasers were blameless and acknowledges that they made mistakes, but rather that what was attempted was logical policy given Britain's capabilities in the 1930s and the lack of guarantees of US support should a war materialise. Mackay (2003, p 30) offers support for such arguments, noting that public appetite for a second total war within a generation was also very low. In 1933, the Oxford Union had declared that under no circumstances would it 'fight for King and country', and other issues were far more salient within people's minds.

> Mass unemployment meant that millions suffered from poverty, bad housing, ill health and poor nutrition. These were the losers in British society, people who had little cause to feel they had a stake in it. Would they fight for it? The desperation that underlay the hunger marches and demonstrations of the National Unemployed Workers' Movement was an unpromising culture medium for regrowing the national spirit. From the standpoint of our imaginary assessor, the depression's victims must surely be counted as a poor resource in the mobilisation of the nation for total war. (Mackay, 2003, p 30)

Linked to this, the official opposition, the Labour Party, 'gave little or no serious attention to defence problems' prior to 1935. The Labour Party, under Clement Attlee, emphasised the role of the League of Nations in foreign affairs and saw this as the means to achieving peace. Therefore, Labour voted against borrowing large sums of money to fund defence spending and, even in April 1939, against a form of conscription (Attlee, [1954] 2019, pp 97–104; Toye, 2001).

Nor was there any indication that the public mood had shifted towards narratives or support for war. The day after the Munich Conference, the *Times* editorial (cited by Eatwell, 1971, p 122) argued that 'No conqueror returning from victory on the battlefield has come home adorned with nobler laurels than Mr Chamberlain from Munich'; while the *Express* noted that the odds of an early (November) general election were 6–4 (Eatwell, 1971, p 123).

Opposition within the Conservative Party was also muted. Chamberlain had a reputation as a stateman, building upon previous roles before assuming the role of Prime Minister. '[M]ost Conservatives supported Chamberlain's policies of rearmament while advocating peace in Europe.' They 'remained convinced that Chamberlain's was the only viable foreign policy. Not one local association registered any public protest against appeasement, and several constituency parties were still expressing their approval in the summer of 1939' (Jeffreys, 1991, p 365). Resignations over foreign policy, such as Eden's in early 1938, failed to have long-term effects – not least as Lord Halifax, who replaced Eden as Foreign Secretary, was seen as a more senior party figure, and Eden refrained from publicly criticising the government. Even Churchill's opposition to foreign policy was largely limited to air parity, prior to the Munich conference. Attempts by the Labour opposition to form an alliance with disgruntled Conservative MPs 'foundered' (Jeffreys, 1991, pp 365–6).

Despite later coming to represent a more interventionist approach, Churchill was an isolated figure within the Conservative Party, and opposition seemed to be futile. Eatwell (1971, p 123) quotes Harold Macmillan, who abstained in the Munich vote in the House of Commons: 'everyone knew that so great was the strength of the Government in the country nothing could seriously shake them in Parliament'. Macmillan (1966, p 528) argued that the entire country should shoulder some blame, but he acknowledged that the

> House of Commons remained apparently impervious to the steadily deteriorating position. The government neglected their duty. The opposition encouraged them in their neglect; they even spent most of their time in blaming ministers for the very small efforts that they belatedly made to remedy a rapidly worsening situation … There is no precedent in history for a Parliament allowing the country to concede one diplomatic defeat after another.

It is important to assess how the strength of support for Chamberlain, even as late as 1939, could later be transcended and replaced by narratives blaming the Conservative Party, under the leadership of Baldwin and Chamberlain, for a decade of failure, not just in foreign but also in economic and social policy. Here, as events become increasingly suboptimal, narratives aimed at understanding those events and surrounding policies also changed (for the example of the National government abandoning the gold standard in 1931, see previous chapter, or the shift in emphasis upon Britain's debt during the 2008 Global Financial Crisis, see Chapter 13). Events, particularly defeats or retreats in the early stages of the Second World War, would help to shape such shifts in narrative.

Framing

The first 18 months of the war represented a 'phoney war' with little military action in Western Europe. Chamberlain was able to retain his authority despite early mistakes in delaying a declaration of war by reforming his Cabinet, in particular through incorporating Churchill and offering Eden the position of Dominions Secretary, which, although outside Cabinet, saw the return to government of a critic of the appeasement policy. In addition to this, Labour's decision to form a 'patriotic opposition' saddled the party, according to Jeffreys (1991, p 368), with 'the worst of both worlds', whereby they could be accused of being unpatriotic for failing to support the government while at the same time they were criticised by party activists for entering into electoral truces which prevented by-election contests (and gains) for the duration of the war.

However, following events at Dunkirk in 1940, when British servicemen had to be rescued from the northern French coast, blame soon came to be levelled at the appeasement policies pursued by the previous governments. The most famous contemporary account of blame was written over the weekend following the rescue operation by three men later revealed as Michael Foot (Labour), Frank Owen (Liberal) and Peter Howard (Conservative), under the pseudonym CATO. They produced a publication, *Guilty Men*, which blamed 15 individuals for Britain's current predicament. The publication sold over 217,000 copies, despite major stockists such as W.H. Smith refusing to handle it (Aster, 1989, p 234).

The book, a rare contemporary account of blame, notes that Britain's problems did not start in 1939 and begins by blaming the dominance of British politics by Ramsay MacDonald and Stanley Baldwin (later criticism is included for

Chamberlain, who would break this duopoly in 1937). The authors argue that these leaders 'took over a great empire, supreme in arms and secure in liberty. They conducted it to the edge of national annihilation' (CATO, 1940, p 19). Throughout the work, questions of Britain's preparedness remain, especially in relation to air power. Later, the authors note that despite promises in 1934 that Britain's air force should never cease to be superior to Germany's, by 1939, according to then Prime Minister Neville Chamberlain, Germany was 'far superior to [Britain] in arms and equipment' (CATO, 1940, p 110).

Aster (1989, p 239) summarises CATO's arguments: first, that the three Prime Ministers since 1924 had failed to understand the serious nature of the threat posed by Hitler and Mussolini in Europe and thus failed to offer the proper salience to rearmament policies. Second, appeasement had failed to understand the 'aggressive ambitions of Naziism', instead making 'damaging and unnecessary concessions in the vain hope of peace'. Finally, the large parliamentary majorities afforded in both 1931 and 1935 meant that Conservatives were able to pass controversial legislation and suppress opposition or criticism of such policies.

The war saw an increased appetite for news, partly due to a lack of other activities – many leisure activities were curtailed to help with the war effort – but partly due to the centrality of events to people's daily lives. A similar pattern can be seen during COVID-19, when government restrictions further limited individual leisure (and in some cases employment) activities, and the communication between government officials and ordinary citizens increased through daily briefings (see Chapter 14).

It was estimated that by the end of the 1930s, three quarters of the adult population 'read at least one of the eight national daily newspapers, with many people reading more than one' (Marwick, 1982, p 136). During the war, readership expanded across all social groups, including 'the masses – other ranks in the forces and factory workers' (Taylor, 1965, p 548). Alongside cinema viewing figures, radio too exploded; the nine o'clock news on the radio was listened to by approximately 17 million people, and Churchill's speeches attracted 21 million listeners. A record 28 million tuned in for the King's speech on D-Day (Nicholas, 1999, p 62). Radio coverage was near total; over two services the BBC produced 30 hours of content per day, though audience figures varied wildly for different programmes. Throughout the war, 'the function of radio itself changed, from a provider of private or familial enjoyment and self-improvement to a vital instrument of public information and entertainment' (Nicholas, 1999, p 63). As Marwick (1982, p 154) argues, the Second World War has been described as a golden age for each form of media then available. Different media did not seek to replace each other but performed 'slightly different task[s] within a commonality of objectives'.

Just as in the First World War, the means of communication of information was important in maintaining civilian morale, though this goal had to be offset against provisions ensuring that information was not being made readily available to the enemy. Government control of narratives was important (as it had been in 1926, in the face of a very different 'enemy'; see Chapter 6). In September

1939, a full Ministry of Information was created. It was to perform 'five broad functions; … the release of official news; security censorship of the press, films and the BBC; the maintenance of morale; the conduct of publicity campaigns for other departments; and the dissemination of propaganda to the enemy, neutral allied and empire countries'. The Press and Censorship Bureau took over the responsibility for censorship and news between October 1939 and the following April, and the Foreign Office permanently took over control of propaganda to the enemy from October 1939 (McLaine, 1979, p 3).

Another key success of British narratives was their impact on the wider world. Just as in the First World War, British propaganda was not limited to the domestic population but circulated within the empire and the wider English-speaking world, including the United States of America. In the summer of 1940, there were arguments in the US that joining the war on the side of the Allies would be fruitless as German victory was already assured. Such claims were effectively dismissed on the BBC (Buitenhuis, 2000, p 450).

Although US involvement in the Second World War came only after the Japanese attacks on Pearl Harbor in December 1941, the impact of British narratives was clear:

> The United States joined a war that it knew principally through British eyes. During the critical years of 1940 and 1941, practically all of the United States' news about the war passed through London and was shaped either directly by the publicity and censorship structure of the British government or by the partiality of well-cultivated foreign correspondents. (Cull, 1995, p 201)

Beneath these successes, however, McLaine (1979, pp 5–7) paints a picture of a dysfunctional Ministry, constantly undergoing reorganisations, with ministers also initially changing frequently. The Ministry was inward-looking, with little scope for influences from either trade unions or the Labour Party. The third minister to head the department, Duff Cooper, resigned in June 1941 in protest at not being granted additional powers. Such early problems were also identified by Mackay (2003, pp 38–9), who notes that the Ministry of Information was afforded low salience within Cabinet; those whom the Cabinet chose to front the Ministry did so on a part-time basis and had to fit this work alongside other commitments. Such a lack of salience represented a weakness in British communications at the start of the war.

The reality was that by 1939 the cinema and radio were truly media of mass communication, firmly established in the everyday lives of most people. The potential they had for influencing the public mood was evident to all – except, it would seem, the nation's leaders. Chamberlain even spoke of closing the BBC down altogether, as a needless waste of resources. This blind spot in the Prime Minister's knowledge of the world stands in sharp contrast to the great importance attached in Germany to the manipulation of popular feelings through mass communication.

Linked to this was a misunderstanding of key terminology. Debates surrounding the definition and application of 'morale' persisted during the first few years of the Ministry. This meant that for almost 'two years the measures taken by the propagandists were unnecessary and inept, based as they were on a misunderstanding and distrust of the British public, which in turn were products of the class and background of the propagandists themselves' (McLaine, 1979, pp 10–11).

Two new regulations were important to overseeing the media: Defence Regulation 3, which prohibited citizens from 'obtaining, recording, communicating to any other person or publishing information which might be useful to an enemy', and Regulation 39b, which made it an offence 'in any manner likely to prejudice the efficient prosecution of the war to obtain, possess or publish information on military matters' (Marwick, 1982, pp 140–41).

However, this did not entail that newspapers were uncritical, especially in the early years of the war when military defeats outnumbered successes. Following events at Dunkirk, Aneurin Bevan, in *Tribune*, called for an inquiry and the removal of those responsible, while the *Daily Mirror* called for the 'removal of survivors from the "old loitering gang"'. Other papers, including right-wing ones such as the *Daily Mail*, took a similar approach (Addison, 1977, pp 107–8).

One difference between the First and Second World Wars was the use of film as a means of disseminating information. During the 1940s, it was estimated that 80 per cent of Britons went to the cinema at least once a year, and 1,640 million tickets were sold (Harvardi, 2014, p 4). The Second World War is often seen as a 'golden age' of British filmmaking, when the industry produced films that were truly popular while also reflecting traditional British values and culture (Stewart, 1996, p 81). Filmmakers were able to capture in depth daily lives during the war and then project these to mass audiences. Here,

> In their depictions of British society during 'the people's war', many films sought representation of what the British were fighting for; whereas the 'people's peace' remained a far more unfocused proposition, most obviously framed in the notion that 'never again' must conditions return to the poverty and disillusionments of the 1930s. (Burton, 1995, p 73)

Other changes to the means of reporting were also important. Bromley (1999) cites Orwell, who argues that as the market economy was replaced by the wartime economy, prioritising the war effort at the expense of personal or individual consumption, the power held by advertisers disappeared, leaving journalists freer to express their views within the popular press. This was further enhanced by the reduction in the size of newspapers – focusing on the most important issues of the day. Newspapers were reduced by approximately 80 per cent as ink became scarce (Marwick, 1982, p 141).

The war period saw 'the emergence of a democratic, crusading, tabloid newspaper' in the *Daily Mirror* (Thomas, 2004, p 470). Unlike other papers, the

Mirror 'had no proprietor. It was created by the ordinary people on its staff and especially by Harry Guy Bartholomew, a man who worked his way up from office boy to editorial director' (Taylor, 1965, pp 548–9). Taylor (1965, pp 548–9) argues that the paper 'gave an indication as never before what ordinary people in the most ordinary sense were thinking'. However, this radical understanding has been challenged by revisionist historians who note that the change in the *Mirror*'s approach was top-down rather than bottom-up and did not represent a democratisation or pluralism of discourses (Bromley, 1999). The *Mirror*'s links to engaging with working-class ideas and attitudes or bringing these into wider narratives of support for the war have been noted elsewhere. These drew upon the paper's pre-war stances, covering topics such as the Spanish Civil War (Bingham and Conboy, 2009). Other outlets – especially the BBC – also had to diversify their reporting to incorporate more left-wing and working-class voices to enhance morale (Buitenhuis, 2000).

The government, wary of comparison to 1914, were keen to downplay suggestions of a quick or immediate end to the war, even after specific victories in battle. However, the incorporation of such suggestions in public discussions through the media, including on the BBC, was vital. Opposition politicians, especially those on the left of the Labour Party, argued that:

> the promise of a better post-war world would aid morale, and [were] also a determination that the disappointments of the post-1918 period should be avoided. As Attlee put it in November 1939, 'People want to know for what kind of country they are fighting', adding on a personal note, 'many of us remember the hopes that we entertained at the end of the last war and what happened after the peace'. On the left, Nye Bevan went further, believing the war to herald a social revolution: it would be a war for socialism, or socialism realised through war, with fascism abroad and Toryism at home as the two enemies to be fought as part of the same process. In Harold Laski's view, equally, Labour should only support Chamberlain in so far as it was his purpose to defeat Hitler; it should, at the same time, seek to expose his weakness and achieve a victory for socialism as well as for the nation. (Toye, 2001, p 88)

Such freedoms changed following Labour's decision to join a coalition government with the Conservatives under Churchill; however, the theme of post-war society was adopted within the popular press. As early as January 1941, even before the US became involved in the war, the magazine *Picture Post* ran a special edition entitled 'A Plan for Britain'. This contained a number of articles offering 'radical new proposals for a completely fresh approach to employment, social welfare, housing, town planning, the countryside, health and education'. Contained within the articles were pictorial representations of what new towns would look like: high-rise blocks of flats, 'American style highways and flyovers' and different zones for 'housing, leisure and industry' (Stevenson, 1988, p 53).

The same publication argued that at the end of the First World War '[t]he plan was not there. We got no new Britain … This time we can be better prepared. But we can only be better prepared if we think now' (Kynaston, 2008, p 20). This led to a widened debate as the concepts and thoughts began to transcend into popular discourses and daily lives. The year 1942 marked a significant point for such understandings, as the Beveridge Report was published, selling 630,000 copies. The report was compiled in November 1942 (and made public a month later), the same month as Churchill described 'the end of the beginning' of the war, at the Lord Mayor's Day Luncheon (Eada, 1943, p 213). This report identified five evils within British society ('want, ignorance, squalor, idleness and disease') and set out a means for eradicating them in a post-war environment. In doing so, it gave politicians, the media and the public a framework for discussion about what a post-'people's war' future might look like. The report advocated for a social security scheme and welfare system that would protect people from the cradle to the grave.

In 1942, Bromley (1999, pp 95–7) contends that the press demonstrated its popular credentials by calling for the immediate and full publication of the Beveridge Report amid claims that the coalition government was attempting to fudge or dilute some of the contents. This campaign was supported by the *Picture Post* a week later, demonstrating widespread support for a particular vision of post-war reconstruction. Bromley notes that the press, despite different ideological leanings, 'broadly supported' the Beveridge Report. Here, the press transcended traditional political understandings and 'appealed to audiences segmented on a variety of often overlapping levels – age, gender, income, leisure interests, class, as well as politics – which were not simply subsumed by the experiences of war'.

Crisis resolution

The mistakes of the First World War would not be repeated in the Second World War. The war did not represent 'business as usual' (see Chapter 5), and any predictions of a short war were not well publicised. A full wartime economy was launched with immediate effect. The state intervened to ensure price controls through the Price of Goods Act in November 1939 before introducing rationing in January 1940. This attempted to stabilise prices and replaced the market system of determining supply and demand to offer a more equitable distribution (Earley and Lacy, 1942).

In order to effectively manage the economy, estimations for national demand and savings needed to be undertaken. Keynes argued for their inclusion in the budget, which had traditionally been limited to focusing on national incomings and outgoings. The budget of April 1941 incorporated these measures for the first time, transforming the nature of the budget. Although they were 'a little hazardous … they transformed the budget into a key regulator of the market economy'. Such changes, although introduced to help finance the war effort, became entrenched within post-war budgets as the 'chief instrument(s) of economic management' (Addison, 1977, pp 170–71).

Alongside these changes, the budget included sharp increases in income tax, setting a standard rate of 50 per cent and top rate of 97.5 per cent, an excess profits tax of 100 per cent and a compulsory savings scheme. Keynes had persuaded Treasury officials that the war should be financed through taxation rather than accumulating debt (Cooley and Ohanian, 1997, p 445).

Just as in the First World War, a government change led to the creation of a coalition government in 1940, following Germany's invasion of Norway – a country whose strategic importance had hitherto been overlooked by European powers (Kersaudy, 1990, p 9). The events in Norway were debated in the House of Commons on 7 and 8 May, in an event that one historian described as 'the most significant in Parliament's long history' (Ball, 2020). The opposition Labour Party initially did not intend to turn the debate into a vote; it was not tabled as a vote of censure or confidence (Smart, 1998, p 215). However, as key Conservatives withdrew support for the Prime Minister – Leo Amery most famously reciting the words of Oliver Cromwell to the Long Parliament of 1653: 'You have sat too long here for any good you have been doing. Depart, I say, and let us have done with you. In the name of God, go' (Hansard, 1940) – Chamberlain's position seemed increasingly fragile.

Despite many Conservatives criticising the government, Chamberlain won the vote by 281 votes to 200. Although a technical victory, this represented a 'crushing moral defeat' – a far cry from the majority of 222 secured in support of his deal in Munich two years earlier (Addison, 1977, pp 97–8). Such a relative loss of support is often seen as being fatal to Chamberlain and is often uncritically accepted as leading to Churchill becoming Prime Minister (Smart, 1998, p 215).

In fact, Chamberlain's resignation was not immediate; he did not resign until 10 May. The day after the Norway vote, both Attlee and Arthur Greenwood met Chamberlain in Downing Street, where they reinforced the idea of a change of leader. The Labour leader was then asked if his party would form part of a coalition under an alternative leader, to which he replied that he believed they would, but he would go to the party's conference currently being held in Bournemouth and ask delegates. The delegates were asked if they would join a coalition, first under Chamberlain, then under someone else, and replied 'No' to a coalition led by Chamberlain but 'Yes' to one led by someone else. These results were communicated by phone back to Chamberlain. By the time Attlee caught the train back to London, Chamberlain had seen the King and resigned (Attlee, [1954] 2019, pp 113–14). Smart (1998, p 240) concludes that it was 'Labour leaders on their own who brought down Neville Chamberlain'.

Upon Chamberlain's resignation, Churchill was called to the Palace and took on the role of Prime Minister. Attlee, on his way back to London, was diverted to the Admiralty, where he accepted a position in Churchill's War Cabinet, formalising a coalition government. Although Churchill was able to lead the government, the shift to a coalition government and wider war represented a loss of initiative by the Conservatives in home affairs and a repudiation of the record of the National government of 1931–40. Yet this was also to enable a more reformist approach to government. Outside education, where reform had been promised almost two decades earlier, the Conservative appetite for change was non-existent.

For Addison, it was the Labour Party that was the driver of change during the war. He argues that the formation of the coalition government represented 'the crucial change' during the war, replicating and enhancing shifts in public opinion; he also asserts that 1940 'should also go down as the year when the foundations of political power shifted decisively leftwards for a decade' (Addison, 1977, pp 17–18). Not only was the Labour Party incorporated into government, but changes occurred outside of Westminster/formal politics; the TUC and institutions such as the BBC had to respond to the new priority of maintaining the morale and welfare of the working classes. It was during 1940 that a new phrase emerged: 'the people's war'.

Churchill's agency was significant and impacted the success of British propaganda. As well as Prime Minister, he was also Minister for Defence. Widely regarded as a 'great wartime leader', such were his experiences in the First World War and 'bulldog spirit' that Labour insisted he became Prime Minister as a condition of their joining the coalition. His oratory was immortalised in speeches such as 'we will fight them on the beaches'. It was through these speeches that he helped to maintain morale following the fall of France (Laybourn, 2002 p 84).

The popularity of Churchill was distinct from that of the government. In Gallup polls from 1942, over 80 per cent of people routinely 'approved of Churchill as Prime Minister'. However, amid various 'setbacks overseas … for instance by the fall of Singapore or the loss of the North African fortress of Tobruk in 1942, satisfaction with the government fell below 50 per cent' (Pelling, 1980, p 400).

Between 1940 and 1942, attention turned to what a post-war society would look like, aided by publications such as the Beveridge Report. That distinguishes this crisis from others (such as the 7/7 London Bombings or the Suez Crisis), as debates and deliberations about what a post-war society should look like took place during the crisis itself. This meant that alternatives to simply 'returning' to the pre-crisis status quo could be discussed. Here, too, the framing of the war as a total, 'people's' war was important – this was not simply about state survival (which became increasingly secure from mid-1940 onwards).

The resolution to the war was the coming of peace. Germany surrendered on 7 May 1945, ending hostilities in Europe. This allowed a return to the pre-war democratic state and a retreat of state powers. The timing of the election and return of democracy, following victory in Europe (VE), was controversial. In October 1944, there was a debate to renew the truce for another 12 months, though in doing so Churchill acknowledged that the election could come after victory over Germany was secured but before Japan's surrender. There was a desire to avoid a rushed election as had occurred after the First World War. However, after VE Day on 8 May 1945, 'Churchill's Conservative advisers favoured an early election in order, if possible, to capitalize upon his reputation as the architect of victory. This meant June or early July' (Pelling, 1980, p 401).

This was opposed by Labour leaders, who wished 'for precisely the same reason' to wait until the autumn (Pelling, 1980, p 401). Attlee wrote to Churchill on 21 May, arguing that an autumn election would allow an updating of the electoral register following demobilisation, and a conclusion to international conferences, including peace talks (Attlee, [1954] 2019, pp 136–9). This position was confirmed by the Labour Party conference (Pelling, 1980, p 402).

The election, which was set for 5 July, was the first in ten years and signified a return to 'normal' democratic politics. Although the war in the Pacific continued, the external threat to the state was deemed sufficiently neutralised so that deliberation and disagreement could replace the emergency wartime coalition government. Alongside this, 1945 saw the return of greater citizen freedoms and an easing of some regulations, though some policies, such as rationing, were maintained and even extended throughout the latter half of the 1940s (see Kirkland, 2022, p 62).

One notable outcome of the 1945 election was the extent to which the armed forces voted for the Labour Party. This had not been tested in opinion polls, but during the war, 'the mood of the country was changing, most dramatically in the forces. There, the auguries indicated a massive shift of opinion against an incumbent class and the leadership which had stumbled into war' (Mitchell, 1995, p 11). The reasons for this are multifaceted. Conservative MPs and candidates bemoaned the Army Bureau of Current Affairs, while the Labour Party recruited members of the armed forces to stand. Figures such as Roy Jenkins, James Callaghan and Denis Healey all served in the armed forces in the Second World War. In total, Labour stood 'more than 120 candidates' from the 'fighting services', which Attlee ([1954] 2019, p 144) argued in a radio address symbolised Labour's transformation from a class party to a more inclusive one.

The post-war period had changed not only the Labour Party's electoral fortunes from the depths of the 1930s, as demonstrated by the landslide victory in 1945, but also the expectations of government. Such changes were not confined to voters but extended to politicians. As Attlee ([1954] 2019, pp 166–7) notes, the 1945 Labour programme was far 'more extensive than that launched by any peace time government … It would certainly have astonished Members of Parliament of the days before the First World War, when one major measure in a session was thought to be quite enough'.

Nor was this simply an ambition. The war had provided the framework with which this programme could be realised. As Minkin (1991, p 70) notes, unlike its successors, the Labour government of 1945–51 'did steadfastly implement virtually its entire domestic manifesto commitments. It was a feat which future Labour Governments were to find beyond them'.

Addison (1977, p 14) describes this emerging consensus in the 1945 general election. He argues that the three main parties all fought the election committed to principles of 'social and economic reconstruction … A massive new middle ground had arisen in politics … When Labour swept to victory in 1945, the new consensus fell like a branch of ripe plums, into the lap of Mr. Attlee'. The

Conservative Party's acceptance of policies introduced between 1945 and 1951 reinforced notions of consensus in the post-war period. Economic policy, as well as the broad relationship between the state and the economy conceived in the late 1940s, remained largely unchallenged until the International Monetary Fund (IMF) crisis of 1976.

Pimlott argues that the term 'consensus', when related to the immediate post-war period, like 'most historical theories, … is as much about the present as the past. The assumption of harmony in the past is a way of underlining the gulf that is believed to exist in the present' (Pimlott, Kavanagh, and Morris, 1989, p 13). Here, then, the notion of consensus is used to distinguish this period from the more adversarial politics of the 1930s or the 1970s–1980s. Writing from the vantage point of the 'end of consensus', Pimlott (1988, p 130) argues that the term is used to describe more than simply agreement, but a position whereby those involved are 'happy agreeing, are not constrained to agree, and leave few of their number outside the broad parameters of their agreement'.

Pimlott suggests that any consensus necessarily extends beyond policy to encompass values. From here, two arguments can be highlighted to critique the idea of a consensus emerging in the immediate post-war period: differences between notions of equality within Labour and Conservative thought and the failure of the Liberals to gain representation in Westminster. Hickson (2004) criticises each of these, drawing upon a broader definition of consensus, which he dates to 1951 and the Conservative acceptance of the last Labour government's policies. He notes that all governments are constrained by external factors, directly challenging Pimlott's voluntary criteria, and notes that the 'Liberal squeeze' reflects the two larger parties shifting towards the median voter. In this context, he contends that, despite commitments to historic ideologies within each party, both the Labour and Conservative parties 'settled on similar policy positions … [due to how politicians] interpreted both the constraints they were under and the way in which they interpreted their ideological objectives' (Hickson, 2004, p 153).

Labour's rationale for nationalisation supports Hickson's arguments. Though the idea was developed in the 1930s as a response to the Great Slump, the war offered not only the chance to nationalise key industries – to help the war effort – but to defend such policies out of necessity or planning. Here, the central argument for nationalising industries such as coal or railways rested upon notions of productivity, not of workers' control or for ideological purposes. The war vindicated policies of nationalisation but gave little to enhance the rationale for such policies (Brooke, 1992, p 245).

Importantly, the notion of consensus cannot be conflated with one of paradigm change. A consensus could simply emerge within elite politics as one (or more) party accepts a dominant idea. As revisionists note, Labour's programme for government in the post-war period was not simply a product of the war but developed throughout the 1930s, following the splits of 1931 (see previous chapter on the Great Slump). In the 1930s, key Labour figures began to engage seriously with Keynesian ideas (Kirkland, 2022, pp 64–5), to the extent that in 1936 Keynes (quoted by Toye, 2001, p 92) wrote that there was 'little divergence between the political implications of my ideas and the policy of the Labour Party', noting that it was only the internal divisions within the party that prevented him from joining it. Much of the social learning, important in incorporating Keynesian ideas into British macroeconomic policy, occurred in the 1930s prior to the war. Klein (1966) dates the 'Keynesian revolution' to earlier in the decade, and others argue that the breakdown of the pre-Keynesian paradigm occurred in the 1920s (Stirling and Laybourn-Langton, 2017). The war offered not an ideological framework for such a platform – nationalisation had been advanced on the grounds of efficiency prior to the outbreak of the Second World War – but rather a 'political opportunity to assert what was already believed in the party' (Tomlinson, 1996, p 22).

Labour's programme in office was modest. Tomlinson notes that spending on welfare payments rose only marginally, by 2.3 per cent of national income, from its pre-war figure. Although large aspects of the Beveridge Report had been accepted by the wartime coalition government, and Labour when in office remained committed to follow this tradition, the Beveridge Report itself reflected the austere wartime conditions of its publication and, although it came to be seen as a framework for the new post-war society, such planning was 'austere' (Tomlinson, 1998, p 69; see also Harris, 1994). For the Labour government of 1945–51, planning was limited to using inherited controls to 'regulate consumption and the balance of payments' rather than determining levels of outputs and investments as was seen in France or the 'classic Soviet five-year plans'. One example of this was Labour's failure to deliver a National Investment Bank, despite promising to do so in its 1945 manifesto (Tomlinson, 1990, pp 206–7).

Oliver and Pemberton (2004, p 421) have argued that any post-war changes emanated not from political struggles, as Hall (1993) indicates in his exploration of the 1970s and 1980s, but from a gradual acceptance of Keynesian economics. This was due to the 'gradual intellectual conversion of those responsible for economic policy-making, of a battle that occurred not between parties but within the administrative apparatus of government and, crucially, of the exigencies of war'.

Legacy

Remembrance of the Second World War became linked to that of the First World War. On the one hand, the First World War offered a means of remembrance that could subsequently be applied to the Second World War – notions of Remembrance Day, for example. Remembrance Sunday, as it became known after the Second World War, incorporated the war of 1939–45; separate commemorations on VE or Victory over Japan (VJ) Day did not displace the second Sunday in November as Britain's official Remembrance Day. However, this was also partly due to the nature of the war. Military casualties were higher in the First World War than in the Second, but in the latter, civilian populations were just as extensively targeted (Murphy, 2000, p 3).

Just as in the case of the First World War, the memory of the Second World War has been revised through the meaning offered to language (see the earlier debate relating to notions of the post-war consensus). Terminology has become adopted, redefined and epitomised within British society and politics – for example, 'the slogan of "fair shares", sometimes thought to have been invented by Labour propagandists in 1945, originated in fact in the publicity campaign devised by the Board of Trade to popularise clothes rationing in 1941' (Addison, 1977, pp 18–19).

Linked to this is the idea of the 'Dunkirk Spirit': recalling memories of a hasty retreat from France in the summer of 1940 has subsequently been used to symbolise determination in the face of adversity. Contemporary understandings of such phrasing were far from homogeneous.

> [C]onstruction of the memory of Dunkirk in a wide repertoire of media, including Parliamentary speeches, newsreels, radio broadcasts, poetry, memoirs, fiction and, especially, film, was full of contradictions and differences of emphasis. Political leaders and military chiefs had an interest in one kind of representation; left-wing journalists and serving soldiers had a stake in another. The popular memory of Dunkirk in Britain mattered and was subject to contestation: it was never static and fixed, but had to be continually secured. (Summerfield, 2010, p 790)

The political or social legacy of the Second World War is often associated with the Labour government of 1945–51, and in particular the promise to build a 'New Jerusalem'. Notions of the war as a vehicle for change have been accepted by politicians from both the Left and the Right (Morgan, 2001, p 4). Here, 1945 represents a watermark and is frequently seen as the start of modern Britain. Such a view is represented not only in the literature (see, for instance, Richards, 2023; Toye, 2023) but also in popular television shows such as Andrew Marr's (2007) *History of Modern Britain*.

The legacy of the consensus, stemming from the Beveridge Report of 1942 and the Education White Paper of 1944, which laid the foundations for the creation of the NHS and the welfare state, became a framework for both contemporaries and later historians to view and understand the Second World War. As Lowe (1990, pp 154–5) notes, neither of the terms 'consensus' or 'welfare state' was used positively in the immediate post-war period. 'Butskellism', an amalgamation of the names of R.A. Butler, Conservative Chancellor of the Exchequer 1951–55 and his Labour predecessor Hugh Gaitskell, was coined by *The Economist* to indicate the overlap between the Labour and Conservative parties, and was more common than 'consensus'; it was not until 1950 that Attlee used the term 'welfare state' as a term of endearment. Prior to the understanding of a welfare state as a benevolent state, it was used by Conservative backbenchers to denounce the costs associated with welfare programmes.

Conclusion

The Second World War epitomises many of the claims made about crises in Chapter 2. The crisis, like the First World War, saw a large expansion in the role of the state, not just in terms of military preparations but into economic relationships, controlling prices and the supply of non-essential goods.

The state further expanded in terms of propaganda and scrutiny over the media, reinforcing the idea of the importance of narratives. Information was essential to the war effort, in terms of foreign policy (denying opponents access to information while asking friendly or sympathetic nations for support) but also in terms of boosting civilian morale.

The war also serves to demonstrate Hall's (1993) understanding that paradigm shifts can occur over a long period. Although much of the 'social learning' took place prior to the war, certainly within the Labour Party, the post-war environment offered the conditions for the Attlee administration to define British economic policy through a Keynesian lens. Although unescapably austere, this was a distinct approach to economic management which remained central to policy making until the 1970s.

The legacy of the war undoubtedly shaped British politics. Modern British politics is often defined as the post-war period, largely in part because it represents the last war of its kind: one in which British civilians were targeted and killed. Key phrases and terminology, even the darkest elements of the war, have been popularised to demonstrate strength in adversity – for example, 'Blitz spirit' or 'Dunkirk spirit'.

Further reading

Paul Addison's (1977) *The Road to 1945: British Politics and the Second World War* offers a detailed examination of the changes in British politics during the Second World War. Both Nicholas Cull's (1995) *Selling War* and Robert Murphy's (2001) *British Cinema and the Second World War* outline the role of propaganda during the conflict. For a background to British politics in the 1930s see for example Martin Gilbert's (1970) *The Roots of Appeasement* or Nick Crowson's (1997) *Facing Fascism: The Conservative Party and the European Dictators, 1935–1940.*

Stephen Brooke's (1992) *Labour's War: The Labour Party and the Second World War* explores how the war changed the fortunes of the Labour Party. Further accounts of the Labour government of 1945–51 can be found in Richard Toye's (2023) *Age of Hope: Labour, 1945, and the Birth of Modern Britain* and Jim Tomlinson's (1996) *Democratic Socialism and Economic Policy: The Attlee Years, 1945–1951.*

Clement Attlee's ([1954] 2019) *As It Happened* spans both the wartime period and the post-war government which he led. Hugh Gaitskell's diaries have also been published for the period 1945–56 (Williams, 1983). Other Labour Party ministers who have written autobiographies covering the period include Herbert Morrison's (1960) *Herbert Morrison: An Autobiography*. Outside of politicians' accounts, the Beveridge Report of 1942 demonstrated changing social attitudes during the war, while the publication by 'CATO' (1940) of *Guilty Men* defined contemporary understandings of blame in wartime and post-war Britain.

9

The Suez Crisis, 1956

Overview

This chapter explores the Suez Crisis of 1956, which was the first serious test of British foreign policy after the Second World War and a key moment in the Cold War. Compared to other foreign policy crises, Suez did not have an immediate effect on people's everyday lives, but this does not mean it was insignificant.

The crisis was a personal disaster for Anthony Eden, who had served as Foreign Secretary both in the 1930s and following the Conservatives' return to power in 1951, before becoming Prime Minister in 1955. Throughout the crisis Eden's health deteriorated to the extent that he resigned the premiership in January 1957.

The crisis occurred when Britain, along with France and Israel, hatched a secret plan to try and regain control of the Suez Canal, which had been nationalised by the Egyptian government. This involved the UK and France using military personnel to create a dividing line between Israeli and Egyptian forces after the former launched an invasion to strengthen its dominant position in the Middle East.

Plans to garner US support failed, and Eden miscalculated the US opposition to Britain using force to regain the Canal. As the US threatened to sell sterling bonds, the UK's finances, already impacted by the loss of oil imports and access to the Canal, were unable to sustain both military intervention and maintaining the position of sterling. This led to a ceasefire being agreed on 6 November and a full withdrawal of British troops by December.

The crisis and its aftermath reflected Britain's position in the post-war environment. Its reliance on the US in terms of economic support demonstrated that alone it could not compete with the US and the USSR in the bipolar world of the Cold War. Policies of decolonisation, especially in Africa, were extended under Eden's successor, Harold Macmillan.

Introduction

The Suez Canal links the Mediterranean Sea with the Indian Ocean. It was of strategic importance for European countries, such as Britain and France, that wished to trade with the Indian subcontinent and wider Eastern hemisphere. For Britain, it offered an easy route to colonies in the Asian subcontinent rather than navigating around the Horn of Africa. It was important in opening trading routes with South Asia. Going via the Canal rather than around the Western Cape reduced the distance between Liverpool and Bombay by almost half. It further offered more reliable coaling points for the new steamships in the Mediterranean (Fletcher, 1958, p 559).

In 1854, a 99-year lease had been given to Ferdinand de Lesseps to build a sea-level waterway connecting the Mediterranean and Red seas. British involvement dated back to 1875, when Prime Minister Disraeli, ignoring his Chancellor and Foreign Secretary, purchased £4 million of shares in the Suez Canal. Britain had earlier rejected the opportunity to participate in the initial building of the scheme in the 1850s (Gorst and Johnman, 1997, p 1). The status of the Canal was established by the Suez Canal Convention of 1888, which stated, among other things, that the Canal 'was to be free and open whether in war or peace to the vessels of all countries whether mercantile or naval'. In addition to the Convention, changes in geopolitics placed a strain on the governance of the Canal. Although the Universal Company of the Suez Maritime Canal remained 'substantially French, the Entente Cordiale of 1904 removed any future French official interest in the governance of Egypt'. Following the end of the First World War, Egypt became a protectorate of Britain. Despite proclaiming Egyptian independence in 1922, the British government retained responsibility in four areas, at its own discretion: 'protection and security of imperial communications, the defence of Egypt, protection of foreign interests and minorities and the issue of government of the Sudan' (Gorst and Johnman, 1997, pp 6–7). The 1936 Anglo-Egyptian treaty offered the opportunity to extend Britain's powers: it created the Suez Canal Zone, under British control, which was used as a base for Allied forces in the Second World War (Gorst and Johnman, 1997, pp 7–9).

The 1936 treaty provided the basis of British–Egyptian relations until 'in 1951 Egypt unilaterally abrogated 1936 Anglo-Egyptian Treaty of Alliance. Britain's position in Egypt was maintained by force'. The 1936 treaty had allowed a British presence of 10,000 troops, but by the early 1950s this had grown to 80,000 (Morsy, 1993, p 527). The reduced need for external guarantees of Egypt's safety in the wake of the end of the Second World War led to this treaty being presented and labelled as an 'unequal treaty', as it was argued that Egypt was 'not a free agent at the time' (Lloyd, 1980, pp 7–8). In 1954, the British 'agreed, essentially, to evacuate troops from the Canal Zone in return for the right to re-enter in the event of an attack on the Arab states or Turkey', in a move designed to symbolise equality between Britain and Egypt (Louis, 2003, p 43).

The Conservatives returned to power in 1951, having criticised Labour's foreign policy in the Middle East, particularly following Iran's nationalisation of the Anglo-Iranian Oil Company (Kyle, 2011, p 7). Following this nationalisation of a strategic asset, the Attlee administration considered using military force to reclaim the Abadan oil refinery but preferred to seek a legal solution, appealing to the International Court of Justice and later the United Nations, on both occasions without success (Speller, 2003, p 39). Although military options were explored and ready – according to the government – on 20 July, the prospect of undertaking such action had eroded. The US was opposed to military action against the incumbent Iranian government, and any such action would inevitably be met with a 'hostile reaction … in the Arab world' (Speller, 2003, p 62).

The strategic importance of Egypt within the wider context of the Cold War led the UK, along with the US and the World Bank, to take a stake in Egyptian development. In 1955, the three countries entered into discussions over a loan to build a dam at Aswan on the upper Nile. In January 1956, however, fearful about the conditions which limited Egyptian sovereignty, increasing anti-British propaganda emerged in Egypt. Alongside this, President Nasser embarked on several arms deals with the USSR, and rumours emerged that Moscow was also prepared to finance the dam. Such alliances, along with fears over the extent to which Egypt would be able to repay the loans being suggested, led both Britain and the US to, independently, reconsider their support for the dam. On 19 July, it was announced that the US was withdrawing its support for the dam; Eden made a similar announcement two days later (Aster, 1976, pp 141–2).

In response, on 26 July, Nasser announced that the Suez Canal would be nationalised – with compensation payments made at current prices. Nationalising the Canal enabled Nasser to use canal dues – money paid to use the canal – to finance the building of the Aswan Dam instead. This decision effectively reduced British presence in an area of strategic importance; half of Britain's oil imports passed through the Canal, while 75 per cent of Canal shipping belonged to NATO countries. 'In one stroke, Nasser had challenged the entire Western world, and again reaffirmed his leadership of anti-colonialism in the Arab world' (Aster, 1976, p 142).

The Canal's strategic importance was also linked to British economic power. Ironically, the government's determination to adopt a strong position and 'confront Nasser' was partly based on a belief that 'failure to do so would jeopardize both the sterling exchange rate and the very existence of the sterling area' (Kunz, 2003, p 216).

The crisis represented 'the most significant episode in British foreign policy since 1945' (McCourt, 2014, p 58); it 'revealed in stark terms Britain's decline from great power status' rather than predicated such a decline. McCourt (2014, p 58) is skeptical of historical accounts seeing Suez as a decisive event which radically changed British power. He argues that while

> Britain's role as a *great power* was at stake, and that fact led the Eden government to make a series of fateful decisions many would come to

> regret. ... Such judgments also leave important questions unanswered. If Britain was no longer a great power, why did its leaders not recognize that fact and avoid confrontation over Suez? Conversely, if Britain was still a great power in 1956, why did its chosen response not succeed?

Rather than viewing the events in this framework, McCourt (2014) argues that the space for Eden's actions occurred due to understandings of the UK as a '*residual great power*' (original emphasis), with such understandings shaped in part by the US's role as 'Atlantic leader'. Here, the importance attached to British foreign policy is seen as a product of historical factors and now reliant upon its relationship with the US (Blagden, 2021).

Framing

Eden saw the nationalisation as an act of aggression and linked the actions of Nasser to those of Hitler in Europe in the 1930s. For Eden, one of the most important lessons of the immediate pre-Second World War period was that 'a militant dictator's capacity for aggrandizement was limited only by the physical checks imposed upon him' (Aster, 1976, p 141).

The news of the Canal's nationalisation reached Eden during a dinner for the Iraqi King on Friday evening. That evening, he commissioned a wide-ranging meeting with government ministers, representatives of foreign nations and the opposition leader, Hugh Gaitskell (Pearson, 2002, pp 20–21). The following Monday, he told the House of Commons that action in respect to financial sanctions had been imposed on the Egyptian government, but stressed that discussions, including with colleagues from Washington, were continuing (Hansard, 1956).

Upon hearing of the decision, Eden (quoted by McCourt, 2014, p 58) declared Nasser 'must not get away with it'. He further argued (quoted by Kunz, 1991, pp 76–7) that an inability to regain control of the Canal would have 'disastrous consequences for the economic life of the Western powers and their standing in the Middle East'. In correspondence with US President Eisenhower, Eden (quoted by Boyle, 2001, p 167) wrote:

> My colleagues and I are convinced that we must be ready, in the last resort, to use force to bring Nasser to his senses. For our part we are prepared to do so. I have this morning [26 July] instructed our Chiefs of Staff to prepare a military plan accordingly.

A similar reaction spanned the British press, which responded to the nationalisation of the Canal with 'unbridled aggression' and viewed this as a military act. The Labour-supporting *Daily Herald* alongside the Conservative *Daily Mail* and *Daily Telegraph* compared Nasser to Hitler, while the *Daily Mail* advocated immediate reoccupation. The liberal *News Chronicle* argued that 'The British government will be fully justified in taking retaliatory action' (Shaw, 1996, p 23).

Throughout the crisis, the print media was 'consistently more aggressive and more pro-war than was public opinion'. During the crucial first few days of government intervention in Egypt, only a minority of the public supported the government's actions, compared to a majority of the printed media. Even at the peak of the conflict, when 'many people inevitably equated support for the government with loyalty to the troops, the percentage of people in favour of the government's policy was significantly lower than the proportion of national and provincial papers singing Eden's praises' (Shaw, 1996, p 92).

Such belligerence does not entail that the press was homogeneous in its response, however; the prospect and support for military action split the printed press. The *Observer* had adopted an anti-imperialist stance since 1948. It opposed apartheid in South Africa and saw the wider process of decolonisation as inevitable. The initial decision from Nasser to nationalise the Canal was widely condemned by the press, with the *Times* declaring the action a 'coup' (Parmentier, 1980, p 436). Although the *Times* reported that the public supported Eden and the government's handling of the crisis, such reporting was 'inadequate' as it 'implied the British government enjoyed a degree of support which it did not have' (Owen, 1957; Cockett, 1991). Even where the press was sympathetic, it 'never clearly understood the purpose of the government's policy' (Parmentier, 1980, p 435).

The press overlooked important themes such as 'Egypt's legal right to nationalize the Anglo-French Company', which enabled the government 'to concentrate on building up a picture of the enemy as a serious military and ideological threat to Britain and the world'. Doing so resulted in a 'tirade of abuse and threats against a foreign leader the like of which arguably had not been seen since Hitler tore up the Munich Agreement in March 1939' (Shaw, 1996, p 190).

Shaw (1996, pp 92–4) argues that the Suez Crisis represented a watershed in relations between the media and government and that in subsequent crises government would give much more weighting to the role of the media. Shaw rejects the notion that the press was more hostile to the government than the British public and argues that government manipulation of the media influenced this. 'By briefing the appropriate lobbies, for example, the government managed to conduct a war of nerves against a foreign leader on a scale rarely seen and across the whole press spectrum without itself having to come out into the open.'

Yet reports that Eden immediately decided upon taking military action arise from revisionist accounts of the events after Nasser's decision was relayed to the Prime Minister. Eden initially sought to utilise diplomacy rather than force to overturn the decision. However, support, especially from the US, was slow to materialise, and fears of the Soviet Union vetoing an action within the UN limited the attractiveness of that option (Pearson, 2002).

Eden's willingness to pursue military options drew upon the lessons of the 1930s. Eden, previously Foreign Secretary under Baldwin and Chamberlain in the 1930s, had resigned in 1938 over the appeasement policies being pursued. Although not wishing to be a vocal critic of the government, Eden had been critical of offering concessions to Germany over Czechoslovakia and led a young group of about 30 Conservative MPs known as 'the Eden Group' to try and influence government policy (Chapter 8; Aster, 1976, pp 55–6). He argued that although Nasser lacked the domestic political support of Hitler, tolerating the actions of Nasser was akin to the claims that Hitler was 'entitled to do what he liked in his own territory'. Eden argued that Nasser, supported by Russia, was seeking to expand his influence across the Arab world and systematically remove Western influence (Boyle, 2001, pp 169–71).

Crisis resolution

Eden's experiences led him to adopt a tough stance on Nasser. The Cabinet was tasked with 'the primary objective ... to bring the downfall of the Egyptian government', even though Nasser's actions – offering compensation which was 'No more than a decision to buy out the Company's shareholders' – did not represent a breach of the law. This left the UK government with a dilemma: 'How could the British government condemn him as an international criminal whose coup justified the strongest of retaliatory measures, even armed force outside the United Nations?' The response was a combination of 'rapid military preparations allied with a propaganda campaign vilifying Nasser' and drumming up support for military action (Shaw, 1995, pp 321–2). Such a strategy was not without its risks:

If the public were to discover Eden's real purpose, many who trusted him as 'a man of peace' would be alienated. The trick, therefore, was to have the mass media do the government's bidding – wittingly or unwittingly – while ministers stuck to the line that their sole objective was 'restoring' the international status of the Suez Canal (Shaw, 1995).

Eden made special efforts to liaise with the US administration; the American chargé d'affaires attended the hastily arranged meeting on the evening of Eden receiving the news of the nationalisation, and the following day Eden asked for President Eisenhower's help directly to bring 'the maximum pressure to bear on the Egyptian government'. Though this was not akin to letting the US dictate policy, on 27 July, the Cabinet agreed that should the US and France be reluctant to act, then Britain would be 'willing to act alone' (Shaw, 1996, pp 154–6). Macmillan (2003, pp 578–9), in his diaries, noted that Cabinet was 'unanimous' in its view of 'strong and resolute' action, while omitting any indication that this would be predicated on the US.

Boyle (2001, p 168) draws upon Eisenhower's correspondence to suggest that the UK government was prepared to use force 'without delay'. Such plans were thwarted by a lack of US support – Eisenhower noted in his response to Eden that Congress would have to approve any US involvement in a military capacity and warned that this would only be offered if attempts to find a peaceful solution had been tried first.

Although optimistic about the prospects of US support, due in part to its withdrawal of funding for the Aswan Dam and wider pressures in the context of the Cold War, finding common ground in respect to policy in the Middle East had represented a 'tenuous convergence of aims' (Hain, 1991, pp 202–3). However, American support and reaction in the region had previously been harder to gauge. Shaw (1996, p 155) argues that neither side found common ground in regional politics; 'to Washington the British appeared to be out of touch with local issues and political forces, with a dangerous tendency to over-react; to London the Americans all too often wanted the influence but without the necessary commitment', as exemplified by their reluctance to sign the Baghdad pact.

In October, without the knowledge of the US, Eden met in secret with General Challe, Major General of the French armed forces, and Albert Gazier, the French Minister for Labour. At a meeting in Chequers, a plan was hatched that would encourage an Israeli offensive into Egypt. Israeli forces would be given sufficient time to cross the Sinai Peninsula before France and Britain would order both sides to withdraw from the Canal Zone (Thomas, 1986, pp 110–11).

Nor was American opposition expected (Pearson, 2002, p 158). Selwyn Lloyd, the Foreign Secretary, recounted a speech made by US Secretary of State John Foster Dulles in September 1956, in which Dulles (quoted by Lloyd, 1980, p 144) appeared to see force as a legitimate policy tool:

> I do not care how many words are written into the charter of the United Nations about the not using force; if in fact there is not a substitute for force and some way of getting just solutions of some of these problems, inevitably the world will fall back into anarchy and chaos.

Lloyd (1980, p 144) argues that if Nasser rejected a settlement or the UN Security Council failed to find common agreement, anyone listening to Dulles would concur that he would 'accept the use of force, even if the United States themselves did not take part'. A similar understanding was made by Eden, who believed that Eisenhower would not stand in the way of Britain. As late as 30 October, after hostilities had commenced, Cabinet approved a letter to the US President 'asking him to support the action taken to safeguard the Canal and stop the fighting' (Aster, 1976, pp 157–8).

On 29 October, Israeli forces crossed into Egypt and struck across the Sinai Peninsula. British aircraft and French aircraft carriers had departed for the region a few days earlier and were used to monitor the Canal and Egyptian forces. A UN Security Council resolution, requested by the US, calling for the withdrawal of Israeli troops and for all countries to refrain from using force, was vetoed by the British and French, the first time these nations had exercised that power. An ultimatum for both Israeli and Egyptian forces to vacate 10 miles each side of the Canal was issued. Israel – still 100 miles from the Canal – agreed while Egypt 'naturally refused', sparking an air offensive against Egyptian airfields. In retaliation, Nasser ordered the sinking of blockships in the canal (Aster, 1976, pp 157–9).

On 3 November, Britain and France agreed to a ceasefire if a UN peace-keeping force was established until a more permanent settlement could be reached. Despite this proposal, British, French and Israeli forces continued apace, to the extent that 'General Sir Charles Keightley, joint Commander-in-Chief of the Allied forces afterwards estimated that by 12 November Suez could have been occupied'. On the same day, Eden 'issued a public statement supporting the Government and encouraging the Americans to understand the action taken … On the following morning, 4 November, both Eden and Lloyd "were in complete agreement that having got thus far, it would be wrong to call off the operation"' (Aster, 1976, p 161; Pearson, 2002, p 159).

Eisenhower was 'outraged at having been kept in the dark and ultimately duped' (Aster, 1976, p 158). In response, the US was able to exert financial pressure upon the UK, first by imposing economic sanctions, but later by refusing to back Britain and its allies receiving support from the International Monetary Fund (IMF). The lack of US support for military intervention was based upon wider external pressures: the fear that supporting such a move would legitimise the decision by the Soviet government to forcibly crush the Hungarian uprising and considerations of the presidential election which took place on 6 November.

This pressure jeopardised the UK's desire to maintain the exchange rate of transferable sterling within 1 per cent of the rate of parity at \$2.80. This figure was symbolic, as it had 'long been regarded, by both British and American authorities and by financial markets, as the danger point for sterling reserves' (Kunz, 2003, p 226). On 31 October, British reserves stood at \$2,244 million and even optimistic forecasts envisaged this would fall to close to \$2,000 million by the end of the year.

Speculation arose that the Bank of England would have to abandon commitments to maintaining the sterling parity rate of \$2.80, set following devaluation in 1949. A further devaluation risked sterling's position as a reserve currency and, according to the Governor of the Bank of England (quoted by Boughton, 2001, p 435), could potentially lead to 'the breakup of the sterling area (possibly even the dissolution of the Commonwealth), the collapse of [the European Payments Union], a reduction in the volume of trade and currency instability at home leading to severe inflation'.

The UK's financial situation was so serious that:

> Unless all the country's financial resources were mobilised to maintain the fixed rate against the dollar, it was said that it would be necessary to move to a floating exchange. That would, in Macmillan's estimation, end sterling's role as an international currency and destroy the sterling area. The Chancellor warned his colleagues that he expected the loss of gold and dollars to be as high as \$300m during the month of November. (Kyle, 1991, p 335)

The Suez Crisis, then, had escalated into a financial, as well as political or militaristic, crisis. As Boughton (2000, p 280) notes:

> Sterling came under heavy speculative pressure in the form of short-term capital outflows unrelated to the current account. In the absence of that speculation, British reserves would have been stable and adequate; even with the commercial effects of the closing of the canal, the United Kingdom had a current account surplus for both 1956 and 1957. For the other countries, however, the external imbalances arose mainly from the current, not the capital, account.

The economic sanctions, including on oil, shifted the opinions of Chancellor Harold Macmillan. As Sterling began to be sold in increasing quantities Macmillan phoned his US counterpart, who informed him that the US would only support an IMF loan for Britain if a ceasefire was agreed before midnight on 6 November. Lloyd recalled that before the Cabinet meeting, he had spoken to Macmillan, who had told him 'that in view of the financial and economic pressures we must stop'. Macmillan then told Cabinet that he 'could not anymore be responsible for Her Majesty's Exchequer' unless there was a ceasefire (Pearson, 2002, pp 161–2), though Macmillan contests this (see Horne, 1989, p 440). Cabinet called off the operation on 6 November. Eden later recalled that no Cabinet minister was willing to continue (Aster, 1976, p 161).

Such notions are echoed by the US response to events. W. Randolph Burgess, the Under-Secretary to the US Treasury (quoted in Kunz, 2003, p 215), later argued: 'The British had no sooner invaded than they recognized immediately that they couldn't carry on a war of any scale without financial help; and in view of the US position, taken promptly at the United Nations, we were not prepared to finance their war effort.'

Within the economic sphere, too, there had been a westward shift of global power. The 'United States had emerged from the war as the world's largest creditor; Britain had the dubious distinction of being the world's largest debtor' (Kunz, 1991, p 6). In addition to this, although it was denied at the time, the US's blocking of funding from the IMF until a ceasefire was agreed pushed Britain into ending the conflict (Gorst and Johnman, 1997, p 133; Boughton, 2000).

Britain's 'humbling abortion of the Suez intervention in 1956, at the US' behest, encapsulated the impotence of the UK's attempts to pursue independent imperial objectives and spelled the end for UK unilateralism vis-à-vis the US' (Green, 2020, pp 108–10). It pushed the UK towards the Eurobond market; this offered new markets for UK banks as links with the Empire diminished. The position of UK banks was only maintained 'by switching to the dollar', which in turn cemented the hegemony of the dollar as the global currency. The transition to the Eurobond market had regulatory implications. It shifted economic activity 'offshore', which 'effectively split the UK banking system into a much more stringently regulated domestic banking market and a permissive international market'. Here the 'prefix "Euro" is a misnomer, in that it defines what is an offshore currency, held and used outside the country where it acts as legal tender, and traded in a market which exists outside the system of state-prescribed banking jurisdiction' (Burn, 1999, p 226).

Legacy

The crisis was not the first major test of British foreign policy in the Middle East or even the first post-war test in the region (see, for example, Lloyd, 1980, chapter 1). Nor was it a turning point in the history of the Middle East. Yet it proved to be a 'decisive moment' in British (though Thomas uses the term 'English') history (Thomas, 1986, p 9). Post-Suez, the UK embarked on a period of isolationism; US Secretary of State Dean Acheson's famous remark in 1962 (quoted by Martill, 2017) that Britain had 'lost an empire and failed to find a role' came to define foreign policy post-Suez. Following the crisis, Britain embarked on a period of 'muddled' foreign policy – 'half in and half out of Europe, hailing the special relationship with the US and yet with unresolved questions about whether the UK was subservient partner or force in its own right' (Richards, 2023, p 74). Eden was not the only Prime Minister to lose his position due to an inability to resolve the problems identified by Acheson – according to Richards, the same fate befell Thatcher, Major, Cameron and May, all of whom failed to offer a coherent and acceptable relationship with Britain's European partners.

In addition, the Suez crisis strained the relationship between the UK and the US. The humiliating defeat led to a rise in anti-American feeling, particularly on the right of the Conservative Party (Hickson, 2020, pp 32–3). One peer, Lord Lambton, quoted by Hickson, even argued that the 'Anglo-American relationship had always been a myth'. Even on the rare occasions when the UK did adopt a different path to the US – such as Wilson's decision not to support the Vietnam War – this was due to the prioritisation of domestic issues. Leaving unresolved the question of the UK–US relationship, was the UK simply 'a subservient partner or a force in its own right(?)' (Richards, 2023, p 74; see also Vickers, 2008).

The crisis challenged UK–US relations and the 'special relationship'. For almost a decade following the crisis, serious efforts were made to repair the relationship on both sides of the Atlantic. Under Macmillan, the special relationship was quickly restored, until the mid-1960s. Though Suez was not the first test of the relationship that had been forged in the darkest days of the Second World War. The asymmetry of the relationship was exhibited in the exclusion of the UK from the ANZUS defence pact signed in 1951 between the US, Australia and New Zealand, while the US's refusal to join the Baghdad pact in 1955 was seen as a 'refusal to underwrite an alliance which might enable Britain to preserve its political influence with existing states in the third world' (Sanders, 1990, pp 169–70).

McCourt (2014, p 2) argues that 'although it quickly became clear that Britain was not in the same ranks as the United States and the Soviet Union after the end of the Second World War in terms of material power, British policy makers have nonetheless viewed their state as continuing to have a prominent part to play in world politics'. In many respects, the Suez Crisis was symptomatic of a paradigm shift that had already occurred. Eden (quoted in Peden, 2012, p 1084) argued that Suez had 'not so much changed our fortunes as revealed realities'.

Although later historians (Peden, 2012; McCourt, 2014) argue that Britain's decline was visible prior to the crisis, this view was not shared in contemporary policy-making circles or discourses. Northedge (1970, p 37), writing over a decade after Suez, argues that British thought since the end of the Second World War has 'unquestioningly accepted the premise that Britain should continue to rank as a world power of the first order'. Equally, understandings of decline have not been universally accepted; even in the twenty-first century, politicians and military leaders often insist that 'Britain requires the necessary military firepower to exert influence across the world ... Instead, one can expect to hear phrases about the importance of Britain "securing a place at the top table" and "punching above its weight"' (Murphy, 2011, p 33). While such language may owe more to rhetorical strategies than attempts to accurately present an objective understanding of UK power, other understandings of Britain's role in the world also argue, albeit implicitly, that the Suez Crisis was not a moment in which Britain realised its diminished power or role. Rather, for some, joining the European Economic Community (EEC) in 1973, some 17 years after Suez, acted as a 'moment of national surrender, fuelling a "deep sense of loss of prestige", when Britain abandoned a heroic, global identity for a diminished, Continental role' (Saunders, 2020, p 1145).

In the immediate aftermath of the crisis, links between Suez and African decolonisation soon emerged, with the premise being that as Britain's status diminished, it became increasingly difficult to maintain an empire. However, just as McCourt (2014) argues that Suez revealed rather than changed the limitations of British power, moves towards decolonisation had begun prior to the crisis. In 1954 there was cross-party support for policies which would eventually see 'dependent peoples ... managing their own affairs' (Low and Lapping, 1987, p 31).

In terms of military capabilities but also economic reality, Suez had laid the foundation for a new economic paradigm. 'Euromarkets became the crux of a new wave of globalization' and promoted a deepening integration between the UK and the US. This cemented the hegemony of the US dollar as the global reserve currency and tied the UK to wider financial pressures, which themselves would contribute to a further crisis in 2008 (see Chapter 13) (Green, 2020, pp 104–5).

The repercussions of Suez were felt more widely than just by the participants in the crisis, even leaving aside the populations whose independence stemmed from the rapid British and French decolonisation that followed events in 1956. Dietl (2008) argues that the Suez Crisis was not just confined to those who undertook military action but challenged notions of 'Europe' and 'European integration' that developed in the 1940s and the first half of the 1950s. Such notions were linked to the Cold War and (Western) Europe's place as a 'third force' between the US and the USSR. The Suez Crisis, along with the Hungarian Revolution of October–November 1956, saw a 'major upheaval against the institutionalized Western Bloc architecture'. For other European countries such as France, 'the weakness of the European countries relative to the superpowers clearly demonstrated the necessity for greater European solidarity'. This led to a renewed push for European integration and the signing of the Treaties of Rome, laying the foundations of the EEC, later the EU, in 1957 (Vaisse, 1991, p 336).

Despite being a foreign policy crisis, the greatest ramifications (as opposed to realisations), in a UK sense, were domestic; the Suez Crisis 'destroyed' Eden's premiership and became the defining moment of his tenure in Number 10 Downing Street. The crisis was so dominant that Eden is widely understood to have been the worst post-war Prime Minister in British history (Theakston and Gill, 2021). Following the crisis, 'the received impression of Sir Anthony Eden … [became] one of a man wrecked by indecision, living up to his reputation as an habitual Downing Street "ditherer"'. Yet such understandings could not accurately define his initial response to the crisis (Shaw, 1996, p 189). As his biographer Aster (1976, p 165) noted, 'the reputation he had built since 1923 remains identified with one event – the Suez Crisis. It is a cruel fate, even by the harsh standards of politics, to be remembered by one failure and not by numerous achievements'.

Conclusion

The Suez Crisis highlights arguments that crises are both objective and subjective (see Chapter 2). Eden's revelation that the crisis had 'not so much changed our fortunes as revealed realities' (as cited earlier) may have contributed to some areas of policy making, such as pushing Britain, under Eden's successor Harold Macmillan, to a more favourable stance on European integration. It confirmed other aspects of foreign policy, such as decolonisation (Ashton, 2002). Some themes, such as declining global status and power and the asymmetric 'special relationship' with the US have been harder to incorporate into British discourses.

Eden's role in the Suez Crisis holds many parallels with that of Gordon Brown in 2008. Eden had served as Foreign Secretary three times, including in the administration immediately prior to his own, under Churchill between 1951 and 1955. Between 1935 and 1955, Eden was Foreign Secretary for all but eight years – six of which, 1945–51, he spent in opposition as Churchill's 'de facto deputy' (Bale, 2012, p 26), the other period was the 22 months between February 1938 and December 1940. Even as Prime Minister, Eden's relative lack of knowledge of domestic issues and lack of experience in policy coordination meant that he remained 'clearly still in charge of foreign affairs' (Bale, 2012, pp 76–7). A crisis in foreign policy was, therefore, more significant for Eden than a crisis in another policy area, given his responsibilities in shaping British foreign policy for over a decade.

Both Eden and Brown had to wait in the wings for a significant period, despite being promised the leadership of their respective parties by incumbent leaders Churchill (who as early as 1946 wrote to Eden to ensure the handling of the transfer) and Blair – Brown's team believed that he had been promised the leadership as early as 1994 (Kyle, 2011, p 11; Gamble, 2012, p 495). The crisis was one which quickly became personal – just as the economic crisis of 2008 did for the person who had been Chancellor of the Exchequer for over a decade before becoming Prime Minister. Eden's previous position and experience, in many ways, led to him becoming a 'scapegoat' for the crisis (Wilson, 1977, p 303).

Further reading

The Suez Crisis is often discussed in relation to wider UK foreign policy, with the defeat of the UK (along with France and Israel) being viewed as a turning point. However, this should not detract from the good narratives that focus more explicitly upon the events of 1956, such as Thomas's (1986) *The Suez Affair* or Kunz's (1991) *The Economic Diplomacy of the Suez Crisis.*

On this issue of the role of the media see Tony Shaw's (1996) *Eden, Suez and the Mass Meda.* For an analysis of the involvement of key actors (outside of government) in the crisis see Gorst and Kelly's (2000) *Whitehall and the Suez Crisis.*

One key contemporary account is that of Foreign Secretary Selwyn Lloyd. In his 1980 book *Suez 1956*, Lloyd offers an account of the background to the crisis prior to his role as Foreign Secretary in 1955. The diaries of Lloyd's cabinet colleague, Harold Macmillan, also contain an account of the build-up to the crisis from within government, this time the Chancellor of the Exchequer. The events are touched upon in *The Cabinet Years 1950–1957* – but it contains no entries between 5 October 1956 and 3 February 1957. Macmillan claimed he destroyed the entries covering these dates at the behest of Anthony Eden (Macmillan, 2003, p 607).

Outside of politicians, the Washington correspondent for *The Economist*, Keith Kyle, offers an account of the crisis, focusing heavily on Britain, in his books *Suez* (1991) and *Suez: Britain's End of Empire in the Middle East* (2011).

10

The Winter of Discontent, 1978–79

Overview

This chapter explores the Winter of Discontent of 1978–79. Over the course of that winter, 5.4 million days were lost to industrial action as workers in occupations as diverse as the NHS, gravediggers, road haulage and refuse collectors went on strike. Following years of pay restraint, successful negotiations far exceeded the government's official 5 per cent pay cap, leading to a spiral of inflation-busting pay rises.

Set against what soon became termed 'militant, over-powerful' trade unions was a weak government, which lacked a parliamentary majority and appeared to have lost control of its incomes, and wider economic, policy. Callaghan's failure to call an election in the autumn of 1978 to press ahead with a fourth phase of the incomes policy backfired, as inflation soared over the winter.

Although most of the strikes occurred at a local level (for example, the gravediggers in Liverpool), the media homogenised the effects of industrial action. This had the effect of exaggerating the action being taken. Unlike in 1926, the action was not nationally coordinated, yet the media drew upon wartime slogans such as 'the Battle of Britain' and 'Britain under siege' to present such a scenario to the wider public.

Introduction

As Chapter 2 noted, the emergence of crises places new items upon the political agenda. Throughout the 1970s, industrial relations became the most salient issue. As Hartman (1976, p 4) argued, by the mid-1970s, the unions had become so important that 'public attitudes on a range of social and political issues will be conditioned by their perceptions of the industrial relations situation'.

Following a miners' overtime ban and strike, Prime Minister Ted Heath called an election in February 1974 on the issue of 'who governs?' The election saw the Labour Party, led by Harold Wilson, replace the Conservative Party as the largest party in government but short of an overall majority. The Labour

Party came to office promising to work with the trade unions to immediately resolve the dispute in the mining industry but also to mitigate against growing inflationary pressures.

Labour won the February 1974 general election but formed a minority government. A further general election victory in October afforded the party a three-seat majority, though due to by-election defeats, this had evaporated by 1976. Nor was the lack of a workable parliamentary majority the only political problem facing the government; by the mid-1970s, scholars such as Anthony King were arguing that Britain over the last decade had become 'so much harder to govern'. King (1975, pp 164, 168) pointed to an overloaded state in which the number of 'dependency relationships in which government is involved has increased substantially, and … the incidence of acts of non-compliance by other participants in these relationships has also increased substantially'. In short, the 'range of matters for which British governments hold themselves responsible – and for which they believe that the electorate may hold them responsible – has increased greatly over the past ten or twenty years', while their capacity to deliver successful outcomes had diminished.

Linked to this was growing concern among commentators about the growth of the trade union movement. Membership had risen from 10 million to 13 million in 15 years (to 1979), and by January 1979 union density was 55 per cent of the workforce (McIlroy and Campbell, 1999, p 99). Trade unions were also becoming more concentrated; although the number of stoppages was falling, the number of days lost to industrial action was almost four times the figure of the 1950s (Aldcroft and Oliver, 2000, pp 94–5).

Labour's response to the inflationary pressures was to ask for wage restraint from the trade unions in exchange for price controls, in an agreement known as the Social Contract. Although this misrepresented the causes of inflation and, in doing so, blamed wage increases for such pressures rather than the 'fivefold rise of oil prices at a time of very rapid world inflation' (Brittan, 1975, p 131), it offered a framework for slowing price increases. The government would increase some benefits, offer subsidies on food and freeze council house rents in exchange for moderation in pay demands (Thorpe, 2015, p 201).

The rate of inflation increased in 1975 before halving in just three years; however, the extent to which the government had upheld its side of the bargain was disputed. Rogers (2009, p 645) notes that the government adopted a prudent approach to public expenditure. In April 1975 the Chancellor Dennis Healey announced cuts of £1,000 million while the Treasury (quoted in Rogers, 2009, p 645) argued that the government needed to make 'a very substantial reduction in public expenditure for the year 1979 – perhaps more than £3 billion at 1974 prices'.

The crisis and requirements for public spending cuts also led to the collapse of the Social Contract. Healey announced budget cuts of 20 per cent in December 1976 and 'real expenditure on personal social services fell dramatically in 1977–78, and towards the end of the government's life there was increasing talk of the need to "target" benefits, raising the spectre of the means test once again'

(Thorpe, 2015, p 201; see also Kirkland, 2022, p 87). Such was the severity of the cuts that the *Daily Mail* referred to the plans as 'austerity' (Castle, 1993, p 499).

The contract, however, could be viewed as a success for the government. Stage two of the incomes policy produced 'the most severe cut in real wages in twenty years' as inflation rose three times as fast as wages between mid-1976 and mid-1977. But such success proved to be a 'wasted effort' as the pound's devaluation on 28 September forced the government to turn to the International Monetary Fund (IMF) for a loan. This represented 'the worst sterling crisis since the war' (Barnes and Reid, 1982, pp 210–11).

The IMF loan and inflationary pressures allowed the Labour government under Wilson and later Callaghan to instigate a 'fundamental change', shifting from the prevailing Keynesian orthodoxy to a monetarist one (Bogdanor, 2016). Bogdanor quotes Denis Healey's response to rising unemployment figures in 1975, when he argued, 'I do not believe that it would be wise to put unemployment as the central problem'. A year later, Callaghan very publicly broke with the prevailing post-war consensus and stated that inflation, rather than unemployment, was the government's key macroeconomic indicator. At the Labour Party conference in Blackpool that year, he told delegates:

> We used to think that you could spend your way out of a recession and increase employment by cutting taxes and boosting Government spending. I tell you in all candour that that option no longer exists, and that in so far as it ever did exist, it only worked on each occasion since the war by injecting a bigger dose of inflation into the economy, followed by a higher level of unemployment as the next step, higher inflation followed by higher unemployment. We have just escaped from the highest rate of inflation this country has known; we have not yet escaped from the consequences: high unemployment. (Callaghan, 1976)

By the second half of 1978, inflation stood at 8–9 per cent; opinion polls were tightening. Labour having previously trailed the Conservatives by as much as 15 per cent in 1977, the parties were level in July 1978. The economic recovery of 1977–78 made 'Callaghan's administration [look] much more credible' following the IMF crisis of 1976 (Morgan, 1990, p 404). By November, 'Labour had a higher approval rating than [the] Conservatives' (Heath, 1998, p 569; Callaghan, 2006, p 518).

As inflation was beginning to subside, Callaghan was widely expected to call a general election in the autumn of 1978, four years after the last. There was also scepticism that the unions would accept a new pay deal, with one Cabinet minister warning that the proposed 5 per cent figure was 'unrealistically low', while others warned that even if the policy were agreed between unions and the government it could not be sold to the workers (Goodman, 2003, pp 223–5; Dorey, 2016, pp 105–6). Feeding into this assumption, Callaghan announced the next stage of the incomes policy, Phase IV, which would limit wage increases to 5 per cent. However, this target was not shared across Cabinet, and at least two groups of ministers pushed Callaghan to accept a pay round of 7 per cent (Callaghan, 2006, pp 520–22).

Although this decision to postpone an election was 'explicable and rational in terms of the political and calculations at the time', it came to be viewed as 'disastrous … in terms of subsequent developments that unwittingly paved the way for Thatcherism' (Dorey, 2016, p 95). It bounced the trade unions into the 5 per cent pay norm and led to a breakdown in trust between the government and unions. However, this idea was not new in the autumn; Callaghan had floated the idea of a 5 per cent pay norm as early as January 1978. This only became the ceiling for wage settlements following a lack of agreement with the Trades Union Congress (TUC) and the 'need to provide a figure in August for Treasury estimates about public expenditure for the following year'. Such a figure, the Treasury estimated, would result in earning increases of between 9 per cent and 11 per cent (Butler and Kavanagh, 1980, p 119).

At its conference, the TUC rejected the 5 per cent pay cap by a ratio of 4:1 (Benn, 1995, p 449). The conference, held a week before the Labour Party Conference, was set amid an expectation of an autumn election. Callaghan appealed for funding to fight the next election campaign 'whenever that may come'; he rejected the opportunity of confirming an October election, stating that fixing the date too early was not something he wished to do.

At the same conference, the TUC chairman, David Basnet, told Callaghan, 'Prime Minister, you won't tell us your intentions, but I think I ought to tell you what our intentions are. Our intentions are very clear, they are to fight the next election as we've never fought one before'. Such sentiment was echoed by Hugh Scanlon, who said that the TUC was placing itself at the 'disposal of our constituency Labour parties, to work as never before, in the committee rooms by canvassing every day throughout the election campaign and, above all, by mustering our millions to turn out and vote for Labour on whatever date is chosen by the Prime Minister' (LBC/IRN, 1978).

Callaghan's comments a week later that the election would be postponed marked a step change in expectations. Callaghan posed a number of questions in a television broadcast on 7 September – just four days after his speech to the TUC in Brighton:

> Would a general election now make it easier to prevent inflation from going up once more? Would unemployment be any less this winter? Would a general election now solve the problem of how to deal with pay increases during the next few months? Would it bring a sudden, dramatic increase in productivity? No. There are no instant solutions. (Heath, 1998, p 568)

Callaghan noted that the government 'could see the way ahead. I spelled it out this week at Brighton', but omitted references to union opposition to the 5 per cent pay norm. At the Labour Party conference, Callaghan confirmed his decision to postpone the election. Reciting a popular music hall song, he told Thatcher that he 'can't get away to marry you today, my wife won't let me', adding that 'I have promised nobody that I shall be at the altar in October, nobody at all'. Despite these statements, 'trade unions seemed to interpret this as a clear indication that Callaghan was indeed about to call a general election'. Alongside union commitments to the Labour Party offered at Brighton, the decision to push the election back to the spring of 1979 left the unions feeling 'betrayed' and 'infuriated'. Such feelings 'contributed to the bitterness of the Winter of Discontent' (Heath, 1998, p 568; Dorey, 2016, p 114).

The catalyst for the period of industrial action was the industrial dispute at the Ford Motor Company. This strike, which started in September 1978, was in protest at a 5 per cent wage rise, in line with Stage IV of the incomes policy. This was set against a backdrop of the company doubling its profits (to £246.1 million) and its Chairman and Managing Director receiving a salary rise of 80 per cent. The response – walkouts at the Halewood plant – was immediate and was followed two days later by workers at the Belfast and Daventry plants (Lopez, 2014, pp 75–6). On 22 November, Ford, which had been losing £10 million a day due to the action, settled the dispute by offering a 17 per cent increase. Callaghan would later define this as 'the heaviest blow, which did much to determine the course of events in the winter of 1978' (Callaghan, 2006, p 534; Lopez, 2014, p 83).

As Roy Hattersley informed the House of Commons, this was not the first time the government's 5 per cent pay norm had been breached. Smaller companies had settled for higher amounts, supported by the Conservative Party, which saw the 5 per cent as an average (Hansard, 1978). Unlike its competitors, British Leyland or Chrysler, Ford was a highly profitable company, and thus 'there was no economic or moral reason why Ford workers should have been subject to the [5 per cent norm]' (Holmes, 1985, p 135). However, as Callaghan (2006, p 534) argued, Ford was a 'bellwether … watched by other unions and highlighted by the press. Where Ford would go, the others would follow, and such a flagrant breach of the guidelines could not be ignored'.

Here, Ford's size and the prominence of the dispute, particularly in the national media, meant that it became a focal point or test of the incomes policy. Such considerations (along with political ones) led the opposition party to table a motion granting powers to the government to impose sanctions on the company (Butler and Kavanagh, 1980, p 120). Although the government narrowly won this vote, governmental inability or unwillingness to impose sanctions on the company 'open[ed] the floodgates' (Lopez, 2014, p 63). The settlement at Ford encouraged other workers to take industrial action, and the lack of sanctions imposed on Ford offered little incentive for companies to adhere to the 5 per cent cap.

> Oil and petrol-tank drivers threatened to strike over a 25% pay claim but settled for 20% …. lorry drivers struck [and] … settled for a 21% pay rise. The 5% pay policy was dead even before public sector workers struck on 22 January in favour of a £60.00 per week minimum wage. (Taylor, 2001, pp 122–3)

'The Winter of Discontent' was used to refer to a period of industrial unrest between December 1978 and February 1979. It denoted strikes in a wide variety of industries, such as hospital workers, gravediggers, oil tank drivers and refuse collectors. In total, almost 5.4 million days were lost to industrial action in January–February 1979 (Office for National Statistics, 2023).

As Lopez (2014, p 9) notes, 'images of rubbish piled in Leicester Square, striking gravediggers, and picketed hospitals eventually became the trenchant symbols that would embody the chaos of a decade'. Changes in the relationship between the state and vested interests, forged in the post-war consensus, were identified earlier in the decade, but became synonymous with 'overzealous' trade unions (Aldcroft and Oliver, 2000). King (1975) highlights notions of 'overload', whereby governments were increasingly seen as expendable, and the public 'increasingly bloody-minded', unsympathetic to what they saw as an inability of the government to deliver its promises. Such themes were echoed elsewhere and in an international context (for a discussion of such points, see Birch, 1984), but most scholars agreed with Samuel Brittan's analysis (1975, pp 131–2) that they represented 'particularly acute problems' in the UK. Brittan further notes an opinion poll commissioned for BBC *Panorama* in September 1974, which 'showed that 32 per cent of respondents thought that there was "a serious threat" to British democracy, and a further 33 per cent thought there was "some threat"'.

Framing

Seaton (1982, p 272) argues that 'union bashing is one of the conventions of the British media'. As such, paradoxical perceptions of trade unions developed during the late 1970s/early 1980s, whereby they were viewed as forming the 'extremist' elements of the Labour Party, while simultaneously being 'regularly attacked for their conservatism'. She points to one opinion poll in 1978 in which '82 per cent of all adults believed that the unions had too much power' and, in the same poll, '78 per cent also thought that unions were essential to protect the interests of workers'. This poll, by no means in isolation (see earlier, and Kirkland, 2017), was furthermore remarkable as it was set against historic levels of trade union membership/density.

Such notions were also noted prior to the industrial action of 1978–79. In 1978, one Labour MP, Giles Radice (1978, p 1), argued that

> Few institutions – with the possible exception of Parliament – are more constantly criticised than British trade unions. They are said to be the cause of strikes and the main reason for inflation. They are accused of being largely responsible for our poor economic performance. They are even alleged to be a threat to liberty and Parliamentary democracy.

The *Times* of 14 September 1977 came to the conclusion that 'the unions are the biggest national problem'.

These notions are supported by Derek Jameson, former editor of the *Daily Express*, who is quoted by Thomas (2007, p 271) as saying: 'we pulled every dirty trick in the book; we made it look like it was general, universal and eternal when it was in reality scattered, here and there, and no great problem'.

While there is much debate about its ability to influence public opinion, the reach of the media is undisputable. So prominent was the media at this time that William Rodgers (1984, p 178), who served as Transport Minister in the Callaghan government, would later note that the 'reporting of the [road haulier] strike by newspapers, television and to an extent radio was dramatic and had more impact on opinion than the public's own direct experience of the strike'.

Trade unions and industrial relations, like other aspects of news, are often simplified within media narratives. They are typically homogenised, as are the reasons for taking industrial action. Strikes and industrial action, too, are homogenised and such actions are presented as focusing solely on wages, despite government statistics 'used by television and industrial correspondents for other purposes … [which] reveal that between one quarter and one third of industrial disputes are about matters other than money' (Glasgow University Media Group, 1976, pp 20–21). Such themes encouraged and replicated perceptions of vested interests, though these were by no means new in the mid/late 1970s; a decade before the Winter of Discontent, Einzig (1969, p 37) had highlighted the prevailing narrative of 'the enemy within – the trade union's greed and short-sighted selfishness, which had been the main cause of Britain's decline'.

Such concerns, however, overlooked the more nuanced understandings held by the public. Analysis of Gallup opinion polls suggests that the public, many of whom would also be members of trade unions, did not share the same concerns about union power. They did not see the unions as opposed to their own interests, or holding the country for ransom as later narratives would posit, but were supportive of the notion of a Social Contract in 1974 and sympathetic towards union aims. Even in 1979, when the public overwhelmingly viewed the trade unions as 'too powerful', this did not equate to overall negative perceptions; at no point during the decade did more respondents to polling suggest that trade unions were a 'bad thing' rather than a 'good thing' – though an equal number of respondents held each view in January 1979 (Kirkland, 2017, pp 78–9).

Given these differences, it was important for those opposed to the trade unions to link their causes in some way – by homogenising their actions and in doing so increase the threat level posed by the industrial action. Doing so ignored the sectoral differences but could be used to present the trade unions as too powerful and a challenge to democracy, akin to the government in 1926 arguing that the TUC was plotting a revolution (see Chapter 6).

Such homogenisation allowed the media and those unsympathetic to the strike to focus on a single entity. There was no distinction between the different unions undertaking different actions at different times, but rather the creation of a singular 'enemy'. Such reductionist understandings are significant and enabled newspapers to present the dispute as a battle, routinely drawing upon notions of the Second World War. The *Daily Mail* depicted the strike at Ford as

'ALL-OUT WAR ON JIM'S 5%' (Lopez, 2014, p 80). Having run the headline 'Britain under Siege' on 8 January, from 19 January the *Mail* incorporated the tagline 'Britain under Siege' to its reporting of events (Greig and Porter, 1979).

The notion of homogenising the union movement was important. Unlike the General Strike of 1926, the events of 1978–79 arose organically; they were not coordinated or conducted by a single group. In 1926, the TUC orchestrated the General Strike in support of the miners; there was no similar rallying cry driving support for actions in 1979. The goals of the actions – for example, levels of wage claims – differed between industries.

The media's reporting was also contradictory, again to maximise the notion of disruption. Two articles, both in the *Daily Mail*, emphasise this point. The first, entitled 'The Union's Hospital Will Not Be Hit', centred upon the decision to continue working at Manor-House Hospital during the municipal worker's strike (*The Daily Mail*, 1979a). The criticism levied here was that this particular hospital was protected from industrial action as it predominantly treated union members. The second article, published just five days later, had the headline 'Sick Old Man Left in the Snow' and criticised the trade unions this time for not attending a retired miner and husband of a former nurse (*The Daily Mail*, 1979b).

Such narratives were not confined to the popular press but were also used within the Conservative opposition. As Saunders (2012, pp 25–6) notes, the 1979 Conservative manifesto was 'remarkably light on policy'. Rather, Thatcherism in the 1970s can be seen as descriptive rather than prescriptive – a narrative that cleared the way for policy responses, rather than a policy programme in its own right. As such, it was directed not just against the Labour Party but against rival analyses within her own party, which favoured conciliation of the unions, constitutional reform and/or the active pursuit of coalition.

Nuances were lost as newspapers used the language of war. Headlines and sub-headings such as 'Battle of Britain 79', 'Britain under siege', 'It's guerilla warfare' and 'No mercy until further notice' appeared in the press. Elsewhere, the printed press sensationalised stories: despite reassurances from Liverpool's Chief Medical Officer, who 'insisted there was no short-term threat to public health but ... if the strike dispute continued for months then burials might have to take place at sea', the headlines of the *Times* and the *Telegraph* were 'bodies may be buried at sea' and the *Daily Mail*'s was 'with bodies piling up in the cities' mortuaries some may have to be buried at sea' (Thomas, 2007; Kirkland, 2017, p 76).

The media's presentation of events was very much set within this framework. Although it has been criticised as 'simplistic', this does not mean that they were unimportant. As Hay notes, the narratives surrounding the Winter of Discontent were important in establishing the framework for Thatcher's election victory. Hay (1996, p 255, original emphasis) argues: 'It must be emphasised that state projects must respond to this narrative *construction of crisis*, and not necessarily to the conditions of contradiction and failure that in fact underlie it.'

The iconic 'Crisis? What Crisis?' headline, plastered on the front page of the *Sun* newspaper on 11 January, was attributed as a quote to James Callaghan and used to suggest that the government was out of touch with events. However, as the article later noted, Callaghan never uttered these words, indeed, the phrase had been used three days earlier in the *Daily Mail* (Thomas, 2007, p 269).

Outside of the reporting, the *Sun* newspaper used other means at its disposal to foster anti-union feelings:

> On four days: 15 Monday, 20 Saturday, 23 Tuesday and 24 Wednesday, January, the developments were so bad that the newspaper had to temporarily move the 'page three girl' to page five. This was done simply to maximise the impact of the strike upon the newspaper['s] readers. On the first two occasions, she was returned the next day, and in the Saturday edition, the newspaper still found space on page three to advertise 'Paradise on the Isle of Wight', a Ladbroke Holiday brochure. (Kirkland, 2017, p 77)

Key events were highlighted and presented as being typical of trade unions. Callaghan (2006, p 534), talking about events at a London hospital, noted that 'unreasonable behaviour' was 'resorted to by only small groups of public sector workers ... but although they were not typical, such examples when highlighted by press and television brought the good name of trade unionism in dispute'.

The relationship between the 'Labour Party and capitalist press had often been tense' (Sheperd, 2013, p 109). Throughout the crisis the media was able to blame the unions for causing the strikes while presenting the Labour government as looking weak. The *Daily Mail* referred to Callaghan as an 'ostrich Prime Minister' who had his head buried in the sand, who was off having a 'junket in the tropics' (he was attending a finance meeting in Guadeloupe) rather than dealing with the crisis at home (Kirkland, 2017, p 74).

Changes in newspaper readership and partisanship were also important. In 1969, when the *Sun* was sold to Rupert Mudoch, it had a readership of 1 million and supported the Labour Party. By 1973, the paper boasted a readership of 3 million, and it overtook the *Daily Mail* as the most read paper in 1978. The transition from Labour to Conservative affiliation, however, did not occur immediately; the newspaper backed the miners over Heath, and in 1975 it ran a 'Meet the Unions' series. The shift started in 1976, when it began to attack the left of the Labour Party and Callaghan's economic record over the IMF crisis. It did not, though, overtly support the Conservatives until the Ilford North by-election in 1978, pronouncing that 'it is Margaret Thatcher, not Jim Callaghan, who speaks for Britain today' (Sheperd, 2013, pp 111–12).

Crisis resolution

Immediate resolution to individual instances of industrial action occurred at a local level. As mentioned earlier, the Ford workers settled in December 1979 and other industries quickly did the same, albeit with settlements exceeding the 5 per cent pay norms. The notion of crisis, however, had extended beyond individual industries to become a national crisis. In the House of Commons, opposition parties supported a vote of no confidence in the government, which it lost on 28 March 1979, leading to an election in May. The crisis led to the fall of the Callaghan government, the second time an elected government had lost due to the actions of the trade unions in just over five years. Taylor (1982, p 191) highlights the prevailing narrative:

> Less than five years after the fall of Heath, the credibility of a Labour government was shattered at the hands of organized labour when unions smashed through a Labour government's flimsy 5 per cent pay guidelines in the 'winter of discontent' with widespread disruption of the community. The Labour Party could no longer boast of its special relationship with the unions, which ensured harmony and goodwill.

Such arguments fed into wider narratives of British decline – drawing upon the earlier works of King (1975) and Brittan (1975). The trade unions 'soon became the scapegoats for Britain's poor economic performance ... the press and media writers led the campaign against them' (Aldcroft and Oliver, 2000, p 88). Such narratives were simplified, overlooking the heterogeneity within the union movement or the complex nature of trade union power. Taylor (1982, p 191) goes on to note that for the most part, the unions and the TUC itself 'remain weak, fragmented bodies, vulnerable to the ups and downs of the labour market in an economy faced by almost constant crisis'.

These narratives and ideas link to the notions of revolution and overthrow of the state expressed in Chapter 6 on the General Strike of 1926. Here, the media utilised the same language as it did in wartime, heightening the situation and creating an enemy that had to be defeated at all costs.

Despite such nuances, the narrative of overzealous or overly powerful unions came to dominate British politics. In its 1997 manifesto, the Conservative Party (1997 [2001]) referred to 'A country once brought to its knees by over-mighty trade unions', while Tony Blair (1997), as part of the New Labour rebranding, penned an article in the *Times* entitled 'We won't look back to the 1970s', which promised not to reverse the industrial relations legislation of the 1980s.

Hay (quoted by Black and Pemberton, 2009, p 561) elaborates on his assertion that the 'Winter of Discontent' is best viewed as constructed. In doing so he argues that

> Policymakers respond not to crises themselves, but to their construction. This is not to trivialise the extent of the real crisis that existed, so much as to show how it came to be responded to in the manner in which it did. But it is to argue that we misunderstood the nature of the crisis at the time and, to some extent, we continue to do so today.

Here Hay acknowledges that the nuances – some of which have been highlighted earlier – were overlooked in the simplification of the construction of the discourse. However, once this discourse becomes dominant, it, rather than the crisis per se, shapes policy discussion. Much of the reporting, as discussed earlier, homogenised events in diverse locations. Many individuals had little or no first-hand experience of the effects of the Winter of Discontent. Rather, a national media presence offered such understandings – through the lens of journalists and editors – and in doing so, homogenised processes of industrial relations.

The term 'Winter of Discontent' was only used retrospectively, its coinage stemming from a newspaper editorial on election day, 3 May 1979, written by the editor of the *Sun* newspaper, Larry Lamb, to denote the optimism associated with the new Conservative government and encourage readers to vote for Thatcher (Martin, 2009, p 64; Lopez, 2014, p 21). Although the period Lamb identifies lasted only a few months, its effect upon the British political imagination has spanned decades. Hay (1996, pp 253–4) argues that:

> If there is indeed such a thing as a collective British political imagination, then it is surely to be found in the mythology which surrounds the 'Winter of Discontent'. Moreover, if this collective imagination resides anywhere, then it surely lingers in the enduring popular resonances and connotations of a new political lexicon spawned in the winter of 1978–9. This discursive regime enlists characters as diverse as Richard III, 'Sunny Jim' Callaghan and St Francis of Assisi in the recounting of the tale; of how the country was 'held to ransom'; of how 'the dead were left unburied' and of how the 'bins were left unemptied' during a 'winter of discontent' in which 'Britain was under siege' from 'militant trade unionists' and their 'communist leaders' while the Prime Minister disdainfully 'abandoned the sinking ship', jetted to Guadeloupe, 'sunned himself' and complacently returned to pronounce 'crisis, what crisis?'

As new ideas emerge, so too must old ideas be reconsidered or declared irrelevant. The myths of over-powerful trade unions, willing and able to exercise excessive power, challenged key tenets of the post-war consensus, and in particular the tripartite relationship. Although the precise end date of the consensus is contested, it is clear that by the mid-1980s a new neoliberal economic paradigm was emerging. Thatcher (1993, p 167) famously rejected notions of consensus, arguing that consensus amounted to 'the process of abandoning all beliefs, principles, values and policies in search of something in which no one believes, but to which no one objects'. The new paradigm, introduced by Thatcher and accepted by the Labour Party in the 1990s, had three key tenets: 'markets should rule under the guidance of entrepreneurs, with minimal intervention from government; taxes and public spending, and in particular the redistributive effect of direct taxation, should be kept down; and trade unions should have as marginal a role as possible' (Crouch, 1997, p 352).

This change, from one consensus to another, has been described as a paradigm shift. In his work outlining paradigm shifts, Hall (1993) draws upon the example of Britain in the 1980s. The Winter of Discontent (or at least the collective imagination surrounding it) helped to facilitate such changes. The general election of 1979, instigated following a vote of no confidence in Prime Minister Jim Callaghan, enabled Thatcher to demonstrate the political coalition for an anti-union agenda. The Conservative victory – of 43 seats – offered her a workable majority (something that Wilson and Callaghan lacked in the 1970s) and enabled her to bring forward legislation aimed at weakening the powers of the trade unions (see Chapter 11).

Although Hall (1993, p 287) refrains from stating that the election of the Conservative government in 1979 was the crucial turning point – earlier (p 284) he identifies the election as a 'key component … [but] not the only component' – he notes that 'policy failures associated with the stretching of the Keynesian paradigm, culminating in the collapse of incomes policy during the winter of 1979, probably contributed more to the Conservative's electoral victory that May than did the positive appeal of monetarism'. In outlining the third-order change that occurred in the following decade, he notes:

> By the end of the 1970s, a decade of tortuous negotiations over incomes policies had rendered both the trade unions and neocorporatist arrangements increasingly unpopular. The government seemed impotent in the face of continuing economic problems and powerful unions. Monetarism offered a simple but appealing prescription for all of these dilemmas. Its advocates argued that the government could discipline the unions and eliminate inflation, the most serious economic problem of the 1970s, simply by adhering to a strict target for the rate of growth of the money supply. In the face of such a target, the unions would have to reduce their wage demands in order to avoid unemployment. In short, monetarism was presented as a doctrine that could restore the authority of the government as well as resolve Britain's economic problems. (Hall, 1993, pp 286–7)

Legacy

Thomas (2007, p 265) notes that the Winter of Discontent was used to present a 'right-wing memory of the 1970s constructed since 1979 … of a harder, nastier decade than most people thought at the time'. He earlier quotes a *Daily Mail* article some 25 years later, which summarises this understanding of the decade:

> rampant inflation, industrial chaos, economic disasters. … Economically, the UK was the sick man of Europe. As Germany and France prospered, inflation here was running at third world levels … Unemployment had breached the one million barrier for the first time since the 1940s … the all-powerful unions held sway … and families were under financial siege. (*Daily Mail*, 17 March 2004, quoted by Thomas, 2007, p 263)

Although much attention has rightly been placed on the effects of the crisis on the trade unions, the Labour Party and the relationship between the two, notions of the end of the post-war consensus also impacted upon the Conservative Party, for it too had been involved in its formation. Thatcher (1993, p 8) used the crisis to shift understandings not just in the minds of the public but also within her party. For Thatcher:

> The final illusion – that state intervention would promote social harmony and solidarity or, in Tory language 'one nation' – collapsed in the 'winter of discontent' when the dead went unburied, critically ill patients were turned away from hospitals by pickets, and the prevailing social mood was one of snarling envy and motiveless hostility.

Such understandings further shape understandings of post-crisis politics. The Conservative Party, and Thatcher in particular, would 'often refer to the failures of [the 1970s] in the hope of dramatizing their alleged successes after 1979' (Tiratsoo, 1998, p 163). In particular, the Thatcher government's defeat of the miners in 1984–85 has been used to demonstrate the changes within industrial relations and enabled the government to put in place more restrictive trade union legislation (see Chapter 11).

This links to wider notions of myth generation and the politics of remembering. When such narratives are used in contemporary society, for instance, they are not accompanied by forensic analysis of the events in question. Rather, once such myths or assumptions have become dominant, they are frequently used as the basis for all further consideration. This is not to say that revisionist understandings cannot displace such ideas, but rather that such a revision is difficult and timely (on this point, see the discussion in Black and Pemberton, 2009). Certainly in the short term, (some) agents can shape, or even manufacture, crises to suit their own goals; for example, Thatcher (1995, p 414) herself noted that without the Winter of Discontent 'it would have been far more difficult to achieve' industrial relations reform in the 1980s.

The crisis of 1978–79 is often used as a barometer for other instances of strike action and has subsequently also been exploited politically by the Conservative Party to highlight, and attack, the close links between the Labour Party and the trade unions (Hay, 1999b, pp 38–9; Lopez, 2014). The crisis also prompted widespread debate within the Labour Party and the relationship between the party and the unions 'emerged as a central issue' in the 1992 leadership election (Howell, 1992/93, p 17).

Such discourses still dominate British politics. Following an increase in industrial disputes and days lost due to industrial action in the early 2020s, commentators drew parallels with the industrial relations of the 1970s, using the narratives and imagery highlighted earlier. The Conservative Party, and in particular Boris Johnson, promoted such comparisons when promising not to 'roll over and surrender' to the unions, while others in his party presented the unions as threatening '"a summer of discontent" that would "take Britain back to the seventies"' (Bale, 2023, p 253). Such links were frequently used within the media; these were not confined to the right-wing press (what

Bale identifies as 'the [Conservative] Party in the media') but their usage demonstrates how entrenched the language used to describe the 'myths' of the 1970s has become (Elliott, 2022; Massey, 2022; The FT, 2022; Warner, 2022).

Conclusion

The Winter of Discontent demonstrates the subjective element of crisis. Much of the public lacked direct experience of the key events but, through the narratives of industrial action in the press, were presented with notions of over-powerful trade unions holding the country to ransom. Such narratives, embedded through the use of wartime terminology, placed 'Britain under siege' and argued that traditional economic and democratic structures were at risk throughout the crisis. Such notions recall the presentation of the 1926 General Strike as a revolution (see Chapter 6) and heighten the salience afforded to events.

Linked to this, the trade unions, through being blamed, were excluded from debates. They were not able to present their ideas in the same way as newspaper journalists and politicians did. Nuances were lost through the homogenisation of industrial action. The unions could not contribute technical or specialist knowledge as the bankers or financiers did in the 1970s, and were thus unable to contribute to narratives of the crisis or to the new emerging paradigm.

The legacy of the crisis is also important and recast through the definition of the Winter of Discontent. Such terminology was not used during the strikes, but rather to symbolise the optimism that a new government, led by Margaret Thatcher, offered the country. In doing so, the events of the winter became synonymised with wider structural problems of the decade, such as Heath's 'who governs' election of February 1974. Again, these narratives presented the idea of trade unions as anti-democratic and set the path for the anti-union legislation of the 1980s.

Further reading

For an account of the framing of the debates see Colin Hay's (1996) 'Narrating Crisis: The Discursive Construction of the "Winter of Discontent"' and James Thomas's (2007) '"Bound by History": The Winter of Discontent in British Politics 1979–2004'. Both explore the constructed elements of the Winter of Discontent.

On the legacy of the crisis see Maria Lopez's (2014) *The Winter of Discontent: Myth, Memory, and History*. Lopez demonstrates how narratives of the Winter of Discontent underpin much of contemporary narratives surrounding industrial relations.

Peter Hall's (1993) 'Policy Paradigms, Social Learning, and the State: The Case of Economic Policymaking in Britain' discusses how paradigms shift and are replaced. Hall argues that following the events of the 1970s Thatcher was able to introduce a new economic paradigm to Britain.

For a wider understanding of the economics of Thatcherism see Andrew Gamble's (1988) *The Free Economy and the Strong State* or the edited collection of works *The Legacy of Thatcherism: Assessing and Exploring Thatcherite Social and Economic Policies* by Stephen Farrall and Colin Hay (2015).

Contemporary accounts of the crisis can be found in Prime Minister James Callaghan's *Time and Chance* (2006) and the leader of the opposition Margaret Thatcher's (1995) *The Path to Power*. For a unionist perspective see Jack Jones's (1986) *Union Man*.

11

The Miners' Strike, 1984–85

Overview

This chapter explores the Miners' Strike of 1984–85. In 1984, in a dispute over the reorganisation of the coal mining industry, miners walked out in a year-long dispute over jobs. The crisis demonstrated tensions between the mining union and the government, but also within the mining union itself, where tensions centred upon the lack of a national ballot for strike action. Support for the strike was less forthcoming in Nottinghamshire and the Midlands, where many coal mines remained open but were subject to picketing and intimidation.

The government presented the strike as anti-democratic and militant, drawing upon the memories of the 1970s. The strike was framed using wartime language, and clashes between police and miners were blamed upon the strikers. This led to notable incidents and disputes over the police tactics used during the strike.

Defeat for the miners cemented many of the narratives employed in the 1970s and enabled Thatcher to expedite policies of 'rolling back the state'. It also led to the decline of the industry; the workforce declined by 90 per cent in the decade from 1985, while the number of collieries fell from 170 to just 8 by 2005.

Introduction

The Conservatives fought the 1979 general election campaign on the basis of Labour's inability to govern the economy and the rising number of days lost due to industrial action. Hugo Young (1990, p 130) quotes the incoming Prime Minister Margaret Thatcher as saying, 'Never forget how near this nation came to government by picket. Never forget how workers had to beg for the right to work'. Although its broader economic policies may not have been fully developed in 1979, the new government was acutely aware of the need to prepare for the prospect of more strikes. Its understandings reflected the narrative that the previous Conservative government, under Edward Heath, had been brought down by the National Union of Mineworkers (NUM). In opposition, Thatcher had established her position, even prior to the Winter of Discontent, that 'one day we would have to face another miners strike' (Thatcher, 1993, p 340).

Thatcher was not content to fight the miners in the same manner that Heath had attempted. She acknowledged that the miners had won that battle, though importantly saw this as receding from the public imagination following the Winter of Discontent and images of 'militant' trade unions. Discussions in opposition focused on the tactics used in industrial action, and Thatcher (1995, pp 437–8) promised to 'make secondary picketing unlawful and to review trade union immunities'. The Conservative Party's 1979 election manifesto expanded this point, arguing that the government was also willing to 'make any further changes that are necessary so that a citizen's right to work and go about his or her lawful business free from intimidation or obstruction is guaranteed' (The Conservative Party, 1979).

In 1977, the Conservative Party introduced the Stepping Stones programme. Developed by Keith Joseph, 'the key ideologist of early Thatcherism', this offered the Conservatives a 'framework within which to understand and publicise the nature and scale of the problems facing Britain'. It was 'intended to provide the intellectual basis of a major campaign to educate the British public about the parlous state of the British economy, and the extent to which this could be directly attributed to the Labour Party, socialism and trade unionism' (Taylor, 2001, p 109; Dorey, 2014, p 98). Thatcher (1995, p 421) argued that 'without it the rest of our programme for national recovery would be blocked'.

The programme argued that monetarism alone was insufficient and required 'a political strategy … to challenge collectivism' (Taylor, 2001, p 109), though this programme had been halted by October 1978, and Thatcher (1995, p 422) later admitted that had Labour Prime Minister Jim Callaghan called an early election the Conservative manifesto would not have included any 'significant measures on union reform'. In the last few months of 1978, key figures in the party either accepted the provisions of Stepping Stones or diluted their opposition to campaigning on such issues. For example, Jim Prior, then Conservative employment spokesperson, accepted the use of public funding to cover the costs of secret pre-strike ballots. In early January, Thatcher (1995, pp 424–5) advanced the key principles of the policy, arguing that 'The unions have [had] tremendous power over the years … this is what the debate has got to be about – how unions use their power'.

In addition to the Stepping Stones, the Ridley Report was formulated in 1977 by the Economic Reconstruction Group think tank. This was a 'blueprint for an ideologically inspired Tory attack on the trade unions' (Rawsthorne, 2018, p 157; see also Saville, 1985). This plan, written following the end of the Heath government, recommended building stockpiles of coal at power stations and sourcing ways of ensuring that coal continued to be transported, utilising non-unionised lorry drivers. It also proposed cutting public finances available to those on strike to increase the costs to the unions and those on strike. Thatcher was acutely aware of the problems faced by the Heath government and keen to reduce the leverage the miners had over other areas of the economy. From 1981, the government began 'steadily and unprovocatively' to build up stockpiles of coal 'which would allow the country to endure a coal strike' (Thatcher, 1993, p 341).

The Report 'described the mines as the "most likely" area for conflict between a future Conservative government and the unions, and it anticipated some tactics – the circumvention of rail transport by road hauliers or the deployment of a more centralised police force – that were used in 1984' (Viven, 2019, p 125). Hain and McCrindle (1984) argue that the government's preparations for the strike demonstrate:

> all the hallmarks of a carefully-planned strategy … Anti-union laws; restrictions on picketing; the extension and centralisation of police powers; new social security regulations to ensure that families of people on strike cannot survive on state benefits; the use of US style management tactics … Followed by the deliberatively provocative appointment of MacGregor;[1] the creation by government policy of regional unemployment; the deliberate shift in energy policy toward nuclear power, the curbing of local authorities' ability to protect their communities from the worst effects of redundancy and the collapse of heavy industry; the use of the media to discredit and abuse the leadership of any union likely to mount serious resistance.

Conservative criticisms, however, were not simply confined to the industrial relations of the 1970s but represented 'a critique of the entire post-war political economy of Britain'. Fundamental to this system were 'the trade unions and collective regulation of industrial relations'. Such an understanding 'viewed and identified Keynesian demand management, the goal of full employment, the mixed economy, powerful trade unions and a rigid labour market as the central problems of the British economy' (Howell, 2005, p 135). The proposed solution is exemplified by what Gamble (1988) terms the 'free economy and strong state'.

Claims that the government was actively seeking confrontation are countered by Viven (2019, pp 121–3), who argues that much of the initial literature was written from positions favourable to the miners, which oversimplifies the narratives that the Conservatives or Thatcher wanted to 'take on' or 'fight' the miners. Viven acknowledges that his focus is narrow, centred only on the position of the government, but cites the 'Authority of Government' group, which met between 1975 and 1977, as offering a more pessimistic understanding of industrial relations. Led by Lord Carrington, who would later be Thatcher's first Foreign Secretary, the group offered a negative understanding of the government's ability to defeat the miners. Carrington (quoted by Viven, 2019, p 125) argued, 'There might be advantages in saying in our report that the Government cannot win a Miners' Strike, but it can make sure everyone else

[1] Ian MacGregor was appointed Head of the National Coal Board in March 1983, following a role reorganising British Steel, cutting employment by over half, reducing employment by approximately 95,000 jobs from an initial workforce of 166,000 over the period 1980–83 (Phillips, 2014, p 125).

suffers from it ... if you could not win, then you should not try'. Viven's analysis offers similarities with the notions of preparedness in the nine months prior to the General Strike of 1926 (see Chapter 6):

> Ministers and officials anticipated and, to some extent, prepared for a strike from an early stage. However, this does not mean that they had clearly worked-out plans for achieving their victory over the NUM in 1984/5. The very fact that a potential strike was discussed so much reflected uncertainty about what would, and should, happen. There were multiple plans, some of which, such as the quixotic suggestion that enthusiasts who ran narrow-gauge railways might be recruited to drive coal trains, bore little relation to what the government ultimately did. (Viven, 2019, p 122)

However, when faced with the prospect of a strike in February 1981, the government backed down and increased investment in the coal industry. Arthur Scargill (quoted by Adeney and Lloyd, 1986, p 2), who did not become president of the NUM until the following year, claimed, 'the government sidestepped the issue because they realised they could not win'.

It also outlines the distinction that Viven (2019, p 124) highlights between the rhetoric of Thatcher and the actions of her government. The landslide victory in the 1983 election offered Thatcher more confidence and allowed 'a greater emphasis on action rather than reflection'. Yet neither Scargill's nor Viven's comments should be taken as a reflection on the government's desires to defeat the miners or instigate widespread union reform, both of which remained. Rather, it can be explained by a pragmatic understanding of politics: conflict and defeat in 1981 would have led to Thatcher facing the same problems that Heath experienced after 1972.

The 'climb down' led to three important changes within government. First, Nigel Lawson replaced David Howell as Energy Secretary and stockpiles of coal were 'rapidly and deliberately' built up. Second, and in sharp contrast to her predecessor, Heath, Thatcher committed the government to continuing the policy – there would be no U-turns as there were after Heath 'lost' to the miners in 1972. The final change in the government approach was the restoration of 'management's right to manage' (Adeney and Lloyd, 1986, p 3).

At the same time, widespread changes were taking place within the mining industry. 'Between May 1979 and March 1984 thirty-six collieries closed, a reduction of 24 per cent, while the number employed in the industry fell by 23 per cent' (Howell, 2012, p 150).

The 1980s were not the first time coal mines were declared uneconomic or asked to close. Between 1957 and 1975 the number of collieries fell from 822 to 241, and the number of miners fell from 704,000 to 245,000 (Turner, 1985, p 167). Much of this was done with the support of the NUM. While many of these mines closed due to exhaustion, the right-wing leadership of the NUM still accepted the plans of different governments to deindustrialise. Outside the industry, full employment meant other jobs and opportunities existed; the union remined loyal to the Labour Party and believed that the party saw a future in the industry, as demonstrated in the 1974 'Plan for Coal'.

The 1980s differed, however. The leadership of the NUM had shifted with the election of Scargill as president in December 1981, unemployment in 1984 peaked at 11 per cent and the Thatcher government, as demonstrated by the Ridley Plan, was intent on 'taking on' rather than working with the NUM (Turner, 1985, p 172; Office for National Statistics, 2019).

The catalyst for the strike, however, proved to be the 1983 election. Thatcher again replaced her Energy Secretary, opting for Peter Walker, having promoted Lawson to Chancellor of the Exchequer. Thatcher informed Walker that 'sometime during the course of the next parliament the miners' leader, Arthur Scargill, would mount a challenge to the Government' (Young, 1990, p 366).

The coal industry became managed from within the centre of the British government. Ian MacGregor's appointment as chairman of the National Coal Board on 1 September 1983 prompted the formation of a 'miscellaneous Cabinet committee … to monitor the coal industry. This was transformed to the Cabinet Ministerial Group on Coal (CMGC) on 14 March 1984, chaired by the Prime Minister and attended by ministers responsible for each of the key departments of state' (Beynon and Hudson, 2021, p 108).

Ahead of the strike, the government was keen to downplay arguments that a 'hit list' of pit closures had been drawn up, and disputed the figures claimed by the NUM and Scargill. Although Scargill's figures (of 75 pit closures, with the loss of 64,000 men) were broadly correct, publicly the government suggested 'a much smaller programme of shrinkage, possibly extending only to twenty pits was being contemplated' (Phillips, 2014, p 117).

In 1983 Peter Walker, the Energy Secretary (Beynon and Hudson, 2021, p 108), had informed colleagues that 'Mr MacGregor had it in mind over the three years 1983/5 that a further 75 pits would be closed … There would be no closure-list but a pit-by-pit procedure. The manpower at the end of that time in the industry would be down to 138,000 from 202,000'. MacGregor, too, consistently claimed that 'Scargill was exaggerating the threat and misleading his members' (Beynon and Hudson, 2021, p 108). Thatcher (1993, p 343) later admitted that the government's 20,000 figure for job losses was only partial and that MacGregor informed her of plans to cut the workforce by 44,000 over two years and 64,000 over three years. Such planning was also being undertaken by Scargill, who argued that the disproportional nature of the first past the post electoral system left little room for Parliament to oppose a government which had received less than 50 per cent of the vote. Ahead of the 1983 election, Scargill told the NUM conference in Perth:

> I am not prepared to accept policies proposed by a government elected by a minority of the British electorate. I am not prepared to quietly accept the destruction of the coal industry, nor am I willing to see our social services utterly decimated … This totally undemocratic government can now easily push through whatever laws it chooses. Faced with possible Parliamentary

> destruction of all that is good and compassionate in our society, extra-Parliamentary action will be the only course open to the working class and the Labour movement. (NUM, 1983)

Such rhetoric confirmed Thatcher's assertion that the NUM was part of the 'undemocratic left'. She regarded Scargill's rejection of the legitimacy of government as an attack not only 'against the government, but against anyone standing in the way of the Left, including fellow miners and their families, the police, the courts and the rule of Parliament itself' (Thatcher, 1993 pp 339–40). Thatcher argued that one 'myth' created in the 1970s was that the mining union should be treated as a 'special case' in British politics, unrestrained by economic reasoning (on the issue of a special case see Winchester, 1972). She contended that mining strikes were political, rather than economic, noting that 'from 1972 to 1985 the conventional wisdom was that Britain could only be governed with the consent of the trade unions. No government could really resist, still less defeat, a major strike; in particular a strike by the miners' union' (Thatcher, 1993, p 377).

Just as in 1974, the official strike action in 1984 was preceded by an overtime ban. Importantly, this action did not require a ballot; however, support for the ban was far from unanimous and there was 'evidence of disunity' (Howell, 2012, p 152). Issues of legitimacy and unity were to play an important role in subsequent events.

The trigger event for the strike was the announcement, without consultation, in March 1984 of the closure of the Cortonwood colliery in South Yorkshire, and the 'government's intention to close a further twenty pits', resulting in 20,000 redundancies. The decision to close Cortonwood with just five weeks' notice came as a shock to the workforce, as 'miners had been transferred from nearby Elsecar just weeks before, and £1 million had recently been invested in new machinery'. On 5 March, at a Yorkshire Area Council meeting of the NUM, it was argued that 'if Cortonwood pit was not safe from closure, neither were many others'. A week later, miners in Kent and Scotland – many of whom were already in local disputes – took part in a national stoppage. South Wales also came out, so by 12 March, 99 pits covering more than 96,000 workers 'had shut down production' (Sutcliffe-Braithwaite and Tomlinson, 2023, p 59).

The strike would become 'one of the most bitter and protracted industrial disputes in British history', lasting until the following March. Eighty per cent of 'Britain's miners downed tools and the majority would remain on strike for the next twelve months' (Bailey and Popple, 2011, pp 20–21).

The Miners' Strike in 1984 differed from those in the 1970s. 'The 1984 strike was, for the first time, a strike for jobs, whereas the strikes of the 1970s had been about wages. The impact of this was to push the communities, which had historically formed around the pit, into action' (Buckley, 2015, p 421). Goodman (1985, p 15) succinctly adds that 'the future of work was at the core of [the strike]. To remove a pit from a mining community is to snap the lifeline to a job'.

Controversially, Scargill drew the mandate for the strike from ballots undertaken in 1981. There was no national ballot called. In 1984, a divisive decision led to a situation whereby some collieries were working while others were on strike. This resulted in tensions between miners and communities in Yorkshire and Nottinghamshire in particular. Those on strike attempted to disrupt and effectively close operations and collieries that remained working. This led to legal challenges, and on 14 March 1984, the High Court granted an injunction to the National Coal Board which prevented Yorkshire miners from protesting outside their area. A day later, and two weeks after the announcement at Cortonwood, a miner, David Jones, 24, died at Ollerton in Nottinghamshire. Jones was killed during 'violent episodes when pickets tried to stop the pit from working'. This tragic incident also became the subject of legal challenges; two days after Jones's death, the National Coal Board (NCB) was given leave to bring action for contempt against the Yorkshire area of the NUM for defying the High Court ruling on secondary picketing. The incident set the tone for the difficulties within the strike, as the *Mirror*'s industrial editor noted: 'Within a few weeks, the strike had become deeply entangled with the law, the police, with picket line martyrdom and a continuing bitter tussle between strikers and working miners' (Goodman, 1985, p 77).

Framing

The Miners' Strike differed from other industrial disputes. From the outset, the media coverage was greater than any previous strike. Such coverage had a polarising effect, which at the time was likened to US coverage of the Vietnam War (Goodman, 1985, p 78). Just as in the case of the Winter of Discontent, media framing of the strike soon became synonymous with notions of war. Within the strike, events were 'conceptualised as battles', Orgreave being the most famous of these (see later). Military roles were ascribed to Scargill, who was labelled as a 'general' and 'dictator'. Although such language was used explicitly in the right-wing press such as the *Daily Mail*, the *Express* and the *Sun*, it extended to other papers too. Left-leaning papers, although 'less explicit in framing the strike as a war, avoiding the lexical item "war" in direct reference to the strike, … similarly maintained a war framing by invoking aspects of the frame, in both language and image, as well as through other pragmatic strategies' (Hart, 2017, p 13).

The decision not to call a national ballot fostered accusations of anti-democracy. Such narratives were not confined to those outside the NUM; for example, Ted McKay, the North Wales area secretary, used such arguments to criticise Scargill within the union and also in the press. Speaking to the local press (quoted by Gildart, 2009, p 142), he argued that 'I am concerned that people who don't believe in the ballot box can overturn the democratic decisions of those who do'.

Notions of the union, and Scargill in particular, being undemocratic were used to denounce the strike. The *Sun* planned on 15 May to publish its front page with 'a picture taken of Scargill at a rally in Mansfield with his arm outstretched in a pose reminiscent of Adolf Hitler. The picture was to be accompanied by the headline "Mine Fuhrer"'. This was only averted when the printers refused to print the image, leading to the paper being published without the picture or headline (Hart, 2017, pp 4–5).

Framing the dispute as a war, supported by the notion of Scargill as a dictator, was akin to the notions of revolution put forward in government publications in 1926 (see Chapter 6) or the media presentation of strikes during the Winter of Discontent (see Chapter 10). This linked to notions of democracy and was the basis for Thatcher's equivalency of the miners with the Argentine Junta in her much publicised 'enemy within' reference.

The media, just as it had during the 'Winter of Discontent' (see previous chapter), sensationalised the coverage of the strike. Philo (1995, pp 38–41) recalls the experiences of people on picket lines, both striking miners and police, who describe the strikes as largely good-natured and even boring. He later argues that 'it is something of an indictment of news journalism that after coverage virtually every day for a year such a large proportion of people had no idea what a typical picket line was like'.

Discourses of association with violence were commonplace and served to increase the tensions surrounding the strike. Philo (1995, p 38) further argues:

> Virtually all the people who were interviewed thought that most picketing shown on television news had been violent, but whether they believe that most picketing was really like this was another matter. The extent to which they believed in the television version of the world depended on several factors, particularly on whether they had access to alternative accounts. No one who had actually been to a picket line thought that picketing was mostly violent.

Despite such accounts, newspapers continued framing the strike using narratives of 'war'. In September 1984, the *Guardian* ran with the headline 'Men at the Front of Scargill's Total War'. Such themes were echoed in the *Star* and the *Express*, whose headlines were, respectively, 'Battle front pickets face 8,000 police' and 'Now it's murder ... this was not industrial action. This was not picketing. This was murder'. Such language denoting 'The "bloody", "bitter" pit "war"' was used regularly within the tabloid press (Wade, 1985, p 274).

The violence was presented as one-dimensional, stemming from the actions of the trade union and the union alone. The 1984–85 Miners' Strike was not the first time that the state or media had equated strikes or industrial action with violence. Such tactics were used in the 1970s to delegitimise the trade union movement as respectable corporatist partners within the post-war settlement and demonstrate their excessive powers. Violence was further linked to notions of the unions as being undemocratic and equated to notions of disorder – a further means of limiting public support for the trade unions (Kelliher, 2021, p 22).

In 1984–85, television viewers were 'bombarded with nightly pictures of picket line violence [making] it difficult not to conclude that it was the miners who were the aggressors, and that it was only intimidation which prevented a return to work' (Samuel, 1986, p 34). Speaking about the events at the infamous 'Battle of Orgreave', Clement (2015) notes: 'The media coverage of these events notoriously adjusted the audience view of events so it appeared as if the miners had charged the police – causing their civilised reaction to re-impose order – when in fact later enquiries proved the police culpability for the violence that day.'

The government, for its part, sought to minimise the potential risks and costs to the state by presenting itself as neutral within the strike. In her memoirs, Thatcher (1993, p 347) notes that:

> I repeatedly made it clear that prime responsibility for dealing with the strike lay with the managements of the NCB and those other nationalised industries involved – the CEGB, BSC, and British Rail. – They operated within financial and other constraints set by government and statute. But so much was at stake that no responsible government could take a 'hands-off' attitude: the dispute threatened the country's economic survival. Consequently, I tried to combine respect for the freedom of action with clear signals as to what would or would not be financially and politically acceptable.

Far from government claims of neutrality, Phillips (2014, p 118) highlights a discrete phase of the strike, 'May to October, [when] the striking miners were isolated from other groups of unionized workers and inhibited in their construction of broader social and political anti-government alliances'. Here a paradox emerges: the government was keen to isolate the miners to present the dispute as one contained with an industry – a position that was reinforced following the banning of secondary picketing in 1980 – yet saw and presented the eventual defeat of the miners as a government triumph over a wider 'militant, irresponsible, trade union movement' (Buckley, 2015, p 420). It was only by framing and encouraging others to frame the strike as a major national event, equating to wartime or crisis, that exceptional responses such as the coordination of a national policing exercise could be justified.

Thatcher's rhetoric and action undermined such arguments of neutrality. The government had close links with the breakaway Democratic Union of Mineworkers, both during the strike (even though the UDM was only officially formed in December 1985) and after (Daniels, 2019). This was in stark contrast to the government's approach to the NUM. Although refraining from the language of 'enemy within' in her conference speech in 1984, following the failed IRA bombing of her hotel in Brighton, Thatcher still praised those who were continuing to work during the dispute: 'The sheer bravery of those men and thousands like them who kept the mining industry alive is beyond praise. "Scabs" their former workmates call them. Scabs? They are lions!' (Thatcher, 1984 [2023]).

Although Thatcher's direct involvement in public was rare, other Cabinet ministers had greater public influence; the Home Secretary offered unlimited support for the police, while Norman Tebbit offered a link to other industrialists who 'got windy' and kept the management of British Steel 'away from the courts'. Yet, despite the government's claim that it was not deeply involved in the strike, it acted 'through the agency of others'. The government took care to stress 'that the NCB was in charge of negotiations, that the police were responsible for order, the courts for the law, public and private corporations for securing their own supplies of labour and materials'. Such narratives 'worked' (that is, became accepted), albeit with a few discrepancies – for example Thatcher's intervention in a 1984 pay offer to British Rail when she was 'concerned to ensure [the offer] did not make the miners' offer look bad' (Adeney and Lloyd, 1986, pp 202–3).

Outside of ministers, who are expected to receive intense press attention, key differences and inequalities existed between the interactions the NUM and the NCB had with the media: 'The National Union of Mineworkers had only one press officer, who was inaccessible because of the pressure of dealing with over one hundred journalists each day. This compared with the forty press officers employed by the National Coal Board' (Wade, 1985, p 280). This links to the arguments set out in Chapter 2 that key actors can have unequal powers to present and communicate their ideas during times of crisis.

Crisis resolution

The tactics used to police the strike became as contentious as the strike itself. Beynon and Hudson (2021, pp 97–8) describe how:

> During the strike, over 20,000 miners were arrested or hospitalised. Two were charged with murder. Over 200 miners served time in custody, including the President of the Kent miners, who spent two weeks in jail. A total of 995 miners were victimised and sacked. Two miners were killed on picket lines, two died on their way to the picket lines, and three teenage children died in Yorkshire foraging for coal. In the coalfield areas, convoys of police vans – 40 or 50 at a time with motorcycle outriders – became regular features of the roads and motorways. There was a powerful and deep sense of oppression: the unnerving upset of liberal sensibilities. Mining villages were cut off by the police.

According to Goodman (1985, pp 118–20), responses to previous strikes 'offered no real parallel. There had been nothing, hitherto, on the scale of the Miners' Strike'. Rather, there existed a 'virtual military command system', with police officers, 'specifically trained to contain civil disorder' being accommodated in army barracks in Yorkshire, Nottinghamshire and Derbyshire.

The experience of the strike differed from region to region and from pit to pit. Goodman (1985, pp 79–82) notes the experience of Markham Main colliery in Armthorpe in Doncaster. Initially, relations between miners and pit managers were good. The strike was 100 per cent adhered to. Pickets of six – in line with Trades Union Congress (TUC) guidance – were positioned by arrangement with management. In return, the local coal board 'made no attempts to incite men back to work'. However, such cordiality changed in July following the breakdown of national talks and 'a government decision to force the pace for a return to work'. A month later, strike-breakers from outside the area were transported to the colliery under armed police protection. In order to support their activities, the police moved the official pickets. Tensions escalated, police numbers escalated and, eventually, after five days of escalating tensions, the police, reinforced with 52 transit vans and in full riot gear, charged the miners.

Such instances were not unique. At another Doncaster colliery, Hatfield, the return of two miners to work at a pit that again had no history of trouble drew 400 police, again in riot gear. The police had been recruited nationally, from the Metropolitan Police, Manchester and Sussex (Goodman, 1985, p 86).

The conflict was a mobilisation of the 'state against the miners' (Beynon and Hudson, 2021, p 97). The traditional local approach to policing was subsumed by a centrally coordinated operation orchestrated from the National Reporting Centre in Scotland Yard. Oversight for policing was divided between local police authorities (comprised of local councillors and magistrates), the Home Secretary and chief constables (Thatcher, 1993, p 347). In total, 1.5 million police from 43 forces were deployed (Elliott, 2004, p 5).

Outside of the police tactics on picket lines, attempts were made to prevent striking workers from picketing certain locations, roadblocks established to prevent 'flying pickets' and police transportation used to facilitate the movement of workers in and out of places of employment.

Clashes occurred at high-profile sites, such as Orgreave, near Rotherham. Orgreave was symbolic – it was the first and only nationally coordinated picket, located at a coking plant. This led to a change in police tactics. The miners were directed into a field and blocked off. They were faced down by police in riot gear, and behind the police line were further police mounted on horses. One reporter from Radio Sheffield (quoted by Beynon and Hudson, 2021, p 118) recalls: 'Looking up and suddenly seeing two lots of horses sweeping in from the left and the right simultaneously on the pickets. It was like a scene of war, a battle. They swept; the police went forward. The miners obviously didn't realise what had hit them.'

Phillips (2014, pp 118–19) draws upon the work of Beynon, who notes that the strike exhibited three phases: 'initial division of the coalfields, between working areas and striking areas, followed by a "face off" between striking miners and the government and then the long "entrenchment", with divisions in communities in all coalfields as striking miners slowly returned to work'. Drawing upon the minutes of the CMGC, Phillips argues that the phases overlapped, and that through this group, 'Thatcher and her ministers were determined to defeat the NUM by covertly intervening in the strike in a number of ways'.

Plans were discussed that would have deepened the state's involvement in the strike. In July 1984 the government explored options to break other points of industrial unrest. Akin to the tactics used by the government in 1926 (see Chapter 6), the Thatcher administration 'examined the possibility of declaring a state of emergency to allow military personnel to move coal imports and other materials through the ports to break a short-lived but economically damaging strike by dock workers' (Phillips, 2014, p 117).

Throughout the strike, the police were used to ensure that those workers who wanted to, particularly in the coalfields of Nottinghamshire and other areas that had not undertaken strike action, could continue to work. The cutting of welfare payments to the families of those on strike, along with the promise of Christmas bonuses, meant that 'by December some 40,000 of the strikers had gone back to work, and by late February the National Coal Board was claiming that over half the NUM's membership were no longer on strike. Hardship had driven many men back' (Macbeath, 1985, p 197; also see Clement, 2015).

Speaking on *Panorama*, Thatcher (1993, p 351) remarked that the 'police are upholding the law. They are not upholding the government. This is not a dispute between miners and the Government. This is a dispute between miners and miners'. Ministers were keen to publicly insist 'that the dispute was between the NUM and the NCB. This was tenuous, given state ownership of the industry and the NCB's obligation to operate within the financial and policy framework established by the government, and the CMGC minutes clearly demonstrate that non-intervention was a fiction' (Phillips, 2014, pp 128–9).

By early 1985, it was clear that the government and country could survive the winter without rationing coal or undertaking power cuts as were necessary in 1973–74. The remaining miners returned to work after 51 weeks of being on strike, without any compensation and at a cost of approximately £9,000 per miner (Pelling, 1987, p 309).

Legacy

The defeat of the miners in 1984–85 had a much wider significance than the outcome of previous disputes. There were no government U-turns or elections (such as those of February 1974 or 1979) in which the government could be replaced and alternative ideas/policies offered; there was no means of challenging the political status quo. Thatcher (1993, p 377–8) saw victory in the strike as reinforcing her government's policies, noting that 'the strike certainly established the truth that the British coal industry could not remain immune to the economic forces which applied elsewhere'. It further established that 'Britain could not be made ungovernable by the Fascist Left ... [it] demonstrated just how mutually dependent the free economy and a free society really are'.

The reorganisation of the mining industry took a very different path from previous reorganisations. The 1980s were not the first decade to see large numbers of mines close and miners made redundant. However, unlike the 1960s, 'the redundancies of the 1980s were not accompanied by major state intervention aimed at attracting new industries. In fact, the funding made available was minimal' (Beynon and Hudson, 2021, p 162). The pace of change was drastic; between 1985 and 1995, 90 per cent of the workforce was lost from the mining industry. The number of collieries fell from 170 to just 8 by 2005 (Beatty, Fothergill, and Powell, 2007, p 1654). The mining industry was privatised in 1994 under John Major. Such was the lack of support for the industry, the House of Commons Employment Committee (quoted by Beynon and Hudson, 2021, p 161) argued that, in light of the 1992 colliery closures, 'there was insufficient thought given to or account taken of the major employment consequences to close the pits'.

The miners' (and larger trade union movement's) ability to instigate widespread political changes diminished with the defeat in 1985. The strike of 1984–85, importantly, also differed from 1926 (see Chapter 6) as the defeat of the miners was not coincidental, but rather formed 'the core of the government's strategy. It was planned years in advance' (Foster, 2004, p 40). The idea of preparing for a strike also became associated with Thatcher personally (Viven, 2019, p 122); though, as Viven notes, this overlooks other actors and simplifies the process of decision making. He argues that:

> [m]uch planning was secret. Some documents found their way into the archives even when their authors had written 'we dare not risk the enclosed note getting into the official machine', but one must assume that others were destroyed and that there were times, particularly in the period immediately preceding the strike, when a deliberate decision was taken not to record some discussions. (Viven, 2019, p 122)

Instigating a crisis within the mining industry and defeating the mining unions thus offered scope for the paradigm shift identified by Hall (1993). For Thatcher, the experience of this strike, along with the wider crisis of the 1970s (see Chapter 10), dismantled the Keynesian economic understanding of a mixed economy and state support for industry. Victory against the miners ensured that 'governments thereafter did not fear trade union resistance to their economic policies or have to risk their governing competence in confrontations over wage demands' (Thompson, 2014, p 63).

The opposition found in the miners and their supporters has subsequently been seen as embodying a wider opposition to Thatcher and Thatcherism, particularly from those sympathetic to the miners' cause. Partly, this is the legacy of the importance of the NUM historically, but it has been used elsewhere to reflect the decline in regional support for the Conservatives and even moves towards devolution and constitutional change granting greater powers for local communities (Wiliam and Collinson, 2024).

There were also legacies in terms of how disputes were policed. The Miners' Strike paved the way for a more 'hands-on' approach from the police, tactics which were replicated in the anti-poll tax demonstrations of 1990 and 1995 protests over the exportation of veal cattle (Briggs, 1998, p 211). Such tactics were 'new' and affected perceptions of the police. A National Recording Centre took responsibility for coordinating the police response to the strikes away from local forces, and tactics such as 'roadblocks, riot control tactics, police support units, their deployment of dogs and mounted police raised a great deal of opposition' (Briggs, 1998, p 92).

Controversies over the nature of the policing of the strike did not abate with the end of the strike. Since that time, there have been numerous campaigns to establish an inquiry into the conduct of the police during the strike. In 1991, this question was the subject of an early-day motion in the House of Commons, and it was subject to a parliamentary debate in 2022 (UK Parliament, 1991 [2024]; Hansard 2022). Other key events from the Thatcher period, such as the Hillsborough football disaster, have subsequently been opened to a public inquiry, but governments have refused to hold an inquiry into key events in the Miners' Strike, such as the Battle of Orgreave (BBC News, 2024).

Narratives of the strike, along with the 1979 Winter of Discontent, were subsequently used to advocate for more restrictive legislation. Thatcher passed legislation in 1988 protecting workers who refused to take part in industrial action and in 1990 to grant powers to employers to dismiss those who take part in unofficial action (Daniels, 2023). Post-Thatcher memories of the strike have been used to debate further restrictions; the Conservative Party especially '[stoked] public debates on the allegedly disruptive nature of strikes' to justify imposing more restrictive measures on union activity, especially strikes, such as the 2016 Trade Union Act (Gallas, 2018, pp 250–51).

Conclusion

The Miners' Strike demonstrates the subjective nature of crises in multiple ways. First, as Chapter 2 argues, the narratives surrounding crises are subjective. During the Miners' Strike, Thatcher and the government, protected by their positions, were able to argue that the state remained neutral during the strike. This further demonstrates the argument made in Chapter 2 that crises lead to an expansion of the state.

The second element of subjectivity relates to the ability to present your argument. Within crises, narratives are not subjected to scrutiny in the same manner as normal policy making. Crises demand faster action and allow for narratives to be more readily accepted. Through the government's effective links with the media (and the lack of resources available to the NUM), government narratives became dominant and accepted during the crisis – though these have been challenged subsequently. In addition to this, through blaming the trade unions – just as in the Winter of Discontent – union views could be marginalised or delegitimised from debates.

The crisis also demonstrates the links between narratives and outcomes, emphasising the importance of controlling such narratives. Framing the strike using war terminology narratives offered legitimacy for the use of force against those on strike. Just as in the case of 1926, the strikes became presented as akin to revolution, threatening the norms of democratic government. According to the government's narrative, this was the rationale and justification for the police becoming involved in the strike. Such tactics were in contrast to other strikes, including those within the Winter of Discontent (see Chapter 10), or the steel strike of 1980.

Further reading

For a good overview of the strike and the issues surrounding it see Martin Adeney's and John Lloyd's (1986) *The Miners' Strike 1984–85: Loss without Limit* or Huw Beynon and Ray Hudson's (2021) *The Shadow of the Mine: Coal and the End of Industrial Britain.*

Other publications have explored regional aspects of the strike, such as Ralph Samuel, Barbra Bloomfield, and Guy Boanas (1986), *The Enemy within Pit Villages and the Miners' Strike of 1984–5* or Jim Phillips's (2012) *Collieries, Communities and the Miners' Strike in Scotland 1984–85.* Such works emphasise the disaggregated nature of the strike, and emphasise how diverse groups contributed to it.

On the broader issue of trade unions in the 1980s and subsequent legislation, competing accounts can be found in Derek Aldcroft and Michael Oliver's (2000) *Trade Unions and the Economy: 1870–2000* and Chris Howell's (2005) *Trade Unions and the State: The Construction of Industrial Relations Institutions in Britain 1890–2000.*

The issue of the miners' strike is addressed in both Margaret Thatcher's (1995) *The Downing Street Years* and the biography of her written by *Guardian* journalist Hugo Young (1990) *One of Us.* For a critical account of the political response to the strike see Tony Benn's (1995) *The Benn Diaries 1940–90.*

The *Mirror*'s industrial correspondent Geofrey Goodman's (1985), *The Miners' Strike* offers a journalist's account of the strike, while there are numerous records of miners publishing or contributing to the publishing of such works. On this, see for instance Brian Elliott's (2004) *Yorkshire's Flying Pickets in the 1984–85 Miners' Strike: Based on the Diary of Silverwood Miner Bruce Wilson.* Or Jonathan Symcox's (2011) *The 1984/5 Miners' Strike in Nottinghamshire*, written by the grandson of John Lowe, chairman of Clipstone Colliery's strike committee.

12

The 7/7 London Bombings, 2005

Overview

This chapter explores the London Bombings of 2005. During the morning rush hour on 7 July, three bombs exploded on London's underground network ('the tube'). A fourth bomb was detonated on a bus about an hour later. These bombs claimed the lives of 56 individuals and led to a shutdown of London's transportation system.

Further attempted attacks two weeks later led to the largest ever UK manhunt and the death of an innocent Londoner. As fears of the unknown spread, media coverage focused on the resilience of London and praised the capital's ability to stand up to terrorists, linking 2005 with notions of the 'Blitz spirit'.

Two broad narratives emerged, the first of which emphasised the role of agency, arguing that the bombers were acting alone to undertake criminal activities, the second highlighting structural factors such as religion, integration or UK foreign policy. By focusing on different aspects, these two arguments served, respectively, to reinforce and shift paradigms. Narratives highlighted notions of resilience, tensions between quick answers and questions of national security. The outcome of this was that blame was deflected away from both government and security services, further preventing any knee-jerk reactions.

Introduction

On the morning of 7 July, four bombs were detonated in a coordinated attack on London's transportation system. Three bombs exploded on the London underground network ('the tube') with a fourth exploding on a bus in Tavistock Square shortly afterwards. The bombings represented the 'most costly single attack on London since the Second World War' (Kelsey, 2015, p 2). The three bombs on the underground network – the first on a Circle line train between Aldgate East and Liverpool Street, the second on a Piccadilly line train between King's Cross and Russell Square and the third on a train at Edgware Road station – exploded within a minute of each other. The fourth, on a bus near Tavistock Square, exploded almost an hour later (House of Commons, 2006; *The Independent*, 2015). The attacks claimed the lives of 56 individuals – including the four perpetrators – and injured a further 770, making it the deadliest attack since the 1988 Lockerbie bombing (Allen and Bryan, 2011, p 263; Hoskins, 2011, p 270).

There was no warning of the attack. Information relating to the attacks developed in a piecemeal fashion. Initial reports suggested that the incidents could be a result of a power surge, though the scale of events led to this being discounted. By 9:15 the Metropolitan Police feared 'up to nine underground stations had been hit', and there were no guarantees that further incidents would not occur. Nor could guarantees be offered that London was the only target; bomb scares were reported in cities including Birmingham, Brighton, Edinburgh, Manchester and Sheffield (Stern et al, 2014, pp 410–12).

The bombings came at a time when there was a widespread 'institutional belief that the threat of terrorism had subsided'. In May, the Joint Terrorism Analysis Centre had reduced the threat level from 'Severe General', meaning that an attack was a 'priority' and 'likely', to 'Substantial', meaning that an attack was 'only "likely"'. This decision was 'made on the basis of available evidence that there was "not a group with both the current intent and capability to attack the UK"' (Hewitt, 2008, pp 86–7).

The bombings were carried out by four men, three of whom were second-generation British citizens, born in West Yorkshire, while the fourth was born in Jamaica but moved to the UK as a baby. These profiles, along with others known to have committed or attempted to commit terrorist attacks, demonstrate that 'there is not a consistent profile to help identify who may be vulnerable to radicalisation' (House of Commons, 2006, p 31).

The fear of future attacks almost turned into reality when, two weeks later, on 21 July, five more would-be bombers set out to attack London's transport network. Of the five, one bomber failed to go through with the plan and dumped his bomb in a park in West London, three boarded underground trains, at Warren Street, Shepherds Bush, and Oval, while the fifth boarded a bus in Shoreditch, East London. None of the bombs detonated, and no one was injured. The four men disappeared 'and the UK's biggest ever man hunt [began]'. All five men were arrested within the next eight days (*The Guardian*, 2008).

A day later, with the capital on high alert, a further fatality occurred when an innocent Brazilian, Jean Charles de Menezes, was shot seven times at Stockwell station by police who had adopted a 'shoot-to-kill' policy. 'Initial witness reports [which] said that De Menezes was wearing a suspiciously large padded jacket on a hot day, had vaulted the ticket barriers, and kept running when asked to stop' were inaccurate; De Menzes had 'picked up a free paper and swiped his Oyster card' (Younge, 2015). Menezes was not a bomber, but an electrician on his way to fix a broken fire alarm.

Terror attacks – and others globally – represent what Kaldor (2013) identifies as 'new wars'. These are fought by both state and non-state actors and differ from old wars as they are fought in the name of identity rather than for geopolitical interests or ideology.

Such understandings were acknowledged by the government. Speaking in 2007, Labour's Home Secretary, John Reed (quoted by Hellmuth, 2016, p 139) said:

> In terms of intention, we are now facing a completely unconstrained enemy … spurred on by a perverse perception of morality to achieve an ever greater extent of civilian carnage … In our history … we have faced enemies before … But – compared to today – they were constrained by the second element of threat – capability … Nowadays, science has expanded capability out of all recognition … Along with unconstrained intent, today's world allows potential access to almost unlimited destructive capability.

Equally understood by the government was that the new wars, and in particular the tactics used by those engaged in such activities, differed substantially from previous threats to British security – principally 'the Troubles' in Northern Ireland (Hellmuth, 2016, p 138). Such distinctions help to distinguish the attacks in 2005 from other crises, such as both world wars or the prospect of civil war in Ireland following the Third Home Rule Bill (see Chapter 4), but also from the terrorist threat in Northern Ireland, for which most anti-terror legislation on the statute books prior to 2001 was designed.

Yet these were not the first attacks, but were linked to attacks in the US on 11 September 2001 (9/11), which claimed the lives of 67 Britons, and Madrid in 2004. Each of these events impacted the government response, though, as Thomas (2012, p 58) notes, it was only after 2004 that the 'government rethought the scale of its response', largely in response to the Madrid bombings, which demonstrated that 'Europe, and thus Britain, had no special immunity from the terrorism of the 9/11 variety' (Hewitt, 2008, p 98).

In response to these attacks, the government commenced its counter-terrorism (CONTEST) strategy, a five-year 'strategy designed to "reduce the risk from international terrorism so that our people can go about their business freely and with confidence"'. This strategy contained four principal areas: prevention, pursuit, protection and preparedness, with a recognition that a 'complete elimination of terrorism was impossible, rather policies of containment were adopted' (Hewitt, 2008, pp 98–9).

Such attacks demonstrated broader issues. They further showed how interconnected the political systems of Western states were in this conflict. They also supported Kaldor's arguments about the declining importance of state actors in these conflicts; the attacks on London were not the first involvement Britain had in what became labelled as 'the war on terror': 11 out of the 19 individuals involved in the 9/11 attacks were residing in the UK when the attacks were being planned (Hellmuth, 2016, p 139).

Following the 9/11 attacks, the government passed the Anti-Terrorism Crime and Security Act. These extended provisions contained in earlier acts and strengthened police powers to 'obtain disclosure of information and those relating to the identification of suspects; provision against inciting religious hatred' and extended controls over 'weapons of mass destruction'. However, the most controversial aspect was the power given to the Home Secretary to 'certify non-UK nationals who he believed to be a risk to national security and suspected of being international terrorists'. If individuals could not be returned to their home country due to risk of 'torture or ill-treatment', they could be detained. Such powers contradicted rulings of the European Court of Human Rights, meaning the UK had to enter derogations from certain aspects of the European Convention on Human Rights 1950 and the International Covenant on Civil and Political Rights 1996 (Shah, 2005, pp 403–4).

Framing

One of the key differences between this crisis and others in this book was the raw material, obtained from people's phones, which was incorporated into the coverage of events without being produced by journalists or filmmakers. Within six hours of the attacks, the BBC had 'receive[d] more than one thousand photographs and 20 videos from members of the public'. Such means of reporting is now not uncommon and is particularly evident in such disasters where news crews are not present at the event's origin; however, such incorporation of footage was 'virtually unheard of before 7/7' (Lorenzo-Dus and Bryan, 2011, p 25; also see Katz and Liebes, 2007).

This does not mean that journalists and editors could not act as gatekeepers despite the technological advancements in recording events (Reading, 2011). Narrative or framing of remembrance drew directly upon those who survived the attack, and in doing so the media encouraged such survivors to present narratives which 'emphasised their victimhood' (Brown, Allen, and Reavey, 2015, p 423). Here, newspapers used the images of those caught up in the attacks to present individuals as both victims of the attacks and victims of wider political tensions. Brown, Allen and Reavey (2015, pp 433–4) recall the story of John Tulloch, whose image was used, against his wishes, by the *Sun* newspaper in November 2005 in support of anti-terror legislation, and a subsequent article in the *Daily Mail* attacking Blair's policies and an independent inquiry into the bombings. The authors quote Tulloch's displeasure at the stories: 'I'm faced with Rupert Murdoch's mob and others, err, just using me, constructing me, reconstructing me, at the very same time I'm trying to reconstruct myself.'

Such reporting lacked an immediate response from experts (often understood as politicians) – the Mayor of London was in Singapore, having attended the ceremony awarding the Olympic Games to London the previous day, and the Prime Minister was in Gleneagles, hosting a G8 summit – and was limited to criticising terrorism. In many respects, newspapers, which were largely not seeking to fill space continually reporting events in 'real time', had the advantage of processing events prior to printing editions. This allowed much more sophisticated understandings of events to be discussed:

> Newspapers engaged collectively in connecting the bombings to historical episodes, the most prevalent of which – the 'blitz spirit' idea – was used as a shorthand to explain their contemporary reactions and resilience. Ideas of Britishness were also used to comment on the bombers. As offset against 'a virulent brand of Islam', these ideas helped newspapers to reflect on the motivation behind the incident. In short, the constructed context in which voiced condemnation and solidarity emerge in reporting is significant. (Matthews, 2016, p 187)

Official framing took two forms, with one narrative emphasising the role of agency and the other structures. The first promoted the events as criminal activity, reserving blame for the individuals who carried out the attacks (and others who assisted). In doing so, it promoted a 'business as usual' approach, arguing that incorporating large-scale changes into daily lives was akin to acknowledging victory for the terrorists. Such narratives emphasised the resilience of Londoners in particular. In the second narrative, structural issues, such as the 'war on terror' or policies of multiculturalism, were identified. Those advocating such narratives rejected the conclusions of returning to normal and advocated changes in policies, either stopping involvement in foreign conflicts or more restrictive policies on immigration and a reversal of the government's current multiculturalism approach.

Kelsey (2015, pp 66–71) undertakes a content analysis of 257 newspaper articles within 16 mainstream British newspapers between 8 July and 8 August, covering the period not just of the bombings but also of the failed attacks on 21 July and the shooting of Jean Charles de Menezes. In doing so, he points to declining importance placed upon notions of the Blitz or wartime spirit, as later articles were 'more likely to provide critical discourses that questioned the relevance, applicability or compatibility of Blitz spirit analogies in 2005. Critical articles were more common later in the sample and were less likely to occur immediately after the bombings'.

One key tension in the discourses associated with the far right and the political mainstream was the homogenisation of actors in the former's account. By suggesting that the attacks were the product of the Islamic religion, the far right argued that the Islamic faith was one of aggression that encouraged violence and destruction (Rehman, 2007, pp 833–4). Such understandings noted that threats to ordinary Britons remained large within society, hence the need for radical revisions to policies of multiculturalism, and so on. The importance of language is important, as Klausen (2009, p 404) notes:

> 'Jihad' has many meanings, ranging from improving oneself in the image of God to taking up armed struggle for Allah. 'Jihad' refers here to terrorism – violent acts or the threat of violence with a political purpose – in the name of Allah. The term 'jihadi' is used in place of the more common terms, 'Islamist' or 'Islamic', because it captures the movement's rejection of democracy and existing state institutions in

> favour of a political religious utopia. It is also the term that Al Qaeda and the terrorists inspired by Al Qaeda use to describe themselves.

Reassuring a public who were all too aware of what a future attack might mean, was juxtaposed against notions of continuing or 'business as normal'. The challenge for the government was to simultaneously demonstrate that lessons would be learnt, that those who lost their lives did not do so in vain, and that in the future police and security services would be able to prevent such an atrocity from occurring on British soil, while simultaneously demonstrating that there was no need for an overhaul of daily lives, that democratic politics would continue to shape British society and that there was no 'giving in' to terrorist demands.

Linked to the tone of initial reporting were the ideas or themes of 'business as usual' or 'resilience' – encouraged by the rhetoric of politicians. Such narratives were linked to an understanding of the Blitz. Indeed, the words 'anxiety' and 'fear' were more likely to occur in articles mentioning the Blitz than not.

> Even when the monolithic view of unfazed Londoners became more complex, with some consideration of other emotions, this would nearly always occur within the context of the Blitz mythology. When combining the number of references to 'anxiety' or 'fear', they are still less frequent than either 'defiance' or 'resilience' alone. (Kelsey, 2015, p 72)

Such narratives, highlighting the role of agency, are summarised by Durdoie (2007, p 429), who outlines the isolation of the individuals responsible for the atrocities; they did not consult with family and friends, meeting in the local gymnasium rather than a religious place of worship. While little comfort to the families of the victims, this resonates with ideas of blaming agency and responding to the threat through the mantra 'business as usual'.

> In the end, [the bombers] acted alone – in isolation – a form of private gesture against a world they appeared to feel little connection to, let alone ability to influence. … The real truth, then, about the London Bombings may be that they were largely pointless and meaningless. The bombers were fantasists – want-to-be terrorists – searching for an identity and a meaning to their lives. They hoped to find it in a global cause that was not their own, but that appeared to give expression to their nihilistic sense of grievance. Islam was their motif, not their motive.

Notions of resilience were used to support moderate policy responses – in contrast to the rhetoric of blame undertaken by the far right (Jones and Smith, 2006, p 1091).

The links between Islam and narratives relating to the bombings were seized upon by far-right political parties and groups such as the British National Party (BNP). Groups such as the BNP used the crisis to challenge mainstream multiculturalism, which 'argues that the crimes of the few extremists do not represent the Muslim mainstream' (Wood and Finlay, 2008, p 710). Wood and Finlay explore six articles written by BNP leaders and published on the party's website in the month after the bombings. The authors conclude that 'the BNP use[d] the London Bombings in order to work up versions of both Muslims and liberal multi-culturalism such that they both present a threat to white people and the nation' (Wood and Finlay, 2008, p 712).

Others, such as George Galloway, who was elected to Parliament after winning the seat of Bethnal Green and Bow in the 2005 general election, linked the 7/7 bombings and Blair's support for the US-led 'war on terror'. Such narratives were generated across the political spectrum, becoming 'mainstream', despite no mention of the Iraq War in the 'martyrdom video' released shortly after the attacks by one of the bombers, and suspected ringleader, Mohammad Sidique Khan (Durdoie, 2007, pp 427–8).

New Labour's foreign policy had been based on notions of the UK as a 'global player'; a leader within both the EU and the global community. Designed 'to counter public perceptions that Old Labour had been "weak" on defence, [narratives defending New Labour's foreign policy] sought to espouse the benefits of strong and decisive leadership, and to locate Britain's national interests in the pursuit of an active role in world affairs'. In doing so, Blair promoted a more humanitarian understanding of foreign policy, proclaiming an 'ethical dimension' to foreign policy (Kettell, 2013, p 267).

This was based upon ideas of liberal interventionism, set out in Blair's 1998 Chicago speech. Here, Blair argued that due to globalisation, economic changes in one geographical location have consequences around the world. Such interconnectedness leads to a reimagination of national interests and how these can be advanced when they are (or have the propensity to be) challenged by events in other countries/regions. Nation states, including Britain, now must work together – either through international organisations such as the United Nations or the North Atlantic Treaty Organization or ad hoc 'coalitions of the willing' – to advance their own interests (Plant, 2008).

Blair later came to incorporate the idea of universal human rights and a shared international morality into this philosophy. Here, the protection of such rights lies not just with the nation states but with the wider international community. If one nation state intentionally infringes human rights, or through neglect allows such rights to be infringed, the international community has an obligation to protect the human rights of those within the state. States have a duty not just to respect the rights of those in other states by forbearing from interference of their own with such rights, but they also have a positive duty to protect such rights when they are infringed by the government of the right holders (Plant, 2008, p 154).

Blair sought to frame his foreign policy as progressive and 'pose the available policy choices in terms of a false dichotomy between vigorous action or passivity'. In the spring of 2006, he argued that critics of New Labour's foreign policy adhered to 'a doctrine of benign inactivity' and saw US foreign policy since 9/

11 as a 'gross overreaction' before denouncing such positions as 'a posture of weakness', which 'Instead of challenging the extremism ... panders to it and therefore instead of choking it feeds its growth' (Kettell, 2013, p 273).

New Labour remained adamant that the attacks were not linked to its foreign policy – in particular, the ongoing war in Iraq. In doing so, the government's response marked a significant shift in its media framing of the war on terror. Involving an overt fusion of humanitarian and security themes, the amended discourse now sought to promote the virtues of strong leadership and interventionism via an increasingly elevated emphasis on the importance of values and ideas as key weapons in the fight against terrorism (Kettell, 2013, p 273).

In contrast, other narratives emphasised the role of agency in the attacks, which were carried out by four individuals. Such arguments posited that without these individuals – who had killed themselves in the process of carrying out the attacks – there was a limited chance of further attacks (due to the possibility of copycat or sympathetic replications the prospect of an attack could not be discounted completely). The question posed by this narrative was not about a particular religion but about how notions of religion were (mis)used to encourage such behaviours. Emphasis here was placed on finding such 'terrorist camps' – principally overseas – and eradicating the recruiting and training of such individuals. At the heart of these arguments were questions about a lack of integration. As Gordon Brown (quoted by Somerville, 2007, p 41) argued following the attacks, 'we asked anew whether we had done enough to encourage and support the integration of people of different ethnicities and faiths into our country and suddenly dry debates about citizenship and Britishness had both a meaning and urgency for our times and for our generation'.

Crisis resolution

Most of London's transportation network was shut down: the entire tube network and bus services in the central 'Zone 1'. Bus services restarted in the afternoon, as did most mainline services. The tube service resumed at 5 am the following day, allowing for enhanced checks overnight in depots (Stern et al, 2014, p 412).

The fact that most Londoners returned to work using the public transportation system the following day was widely commended as a display of resilience, of not playing into the terrorists' hands (Durdoie, 2007, p 430). Such discourses of resilience were linked to notions of presumed national identity (Bean, Keranen, and Durfy, 2011).

In other areas, the need to prevent knee-jerk reactions was clear. In any policy, there exists a need to balance issues of security and civil liberties. As English (2009) notes, heavy-handed responses risked further escalation of violence and eroding the middle ground, which in turn risked increasing the number of people sympathetic or willing to commit terrorist activity.

The government was acutely aware of these dangers and pursued policies of wider engagement to bolster policies of multiculturalism and combat far-right narratives. Prior to 7/7, the government 'lacked engagement with

Muslim communities over counterterrorism ... one immediate response [to the bombing] was a new commitment to consultation with Muslim communities that led to the "Preventing Extremism Together" working groups' (Thomas, 2012, p 59). Government ministers undertook listening exercises in 'towns and cities with large Muslim communities', involving over '100 Muslim community leaders in a shift from counter-intelligence to prevention' (Klausen, 2009, p 405).

Responses to other narratives of blame were also offered. The language of the far right was rejected by the 'Preventing Extremism Together' Working Groups (2005 [2007]), established in the autumn of 2005. These noted:

i. The atrocities of 7/7 were not committed by 'the Muslim community', but a group of individual criminals (ab)using Islam to justify terrorism. We must, therefore, avoid any language that implicates Islam and the Muslim community as a whole and holds them responsible for the atrocities.
ii. The phrase 'Islamic extremism' is offensive – there may be a very small fringe element who claim to follow Islam, but that does not make Islam as a whole, a religion followed by over a billion people, an extremist religion. The Government must provide a lead in decoupling Islam and Muslims from such pejorative phrases that implicate the whole religion/community.
iii. The language suggests that the terrorism we are facing today is 'a Muslim problem' – created by Muslims and to be resolved by Muslims. The WG is of the view that the problem is underlined by a multiple and complex set of causes that need to be more widely owned and addressed by society as a whole – with, of course, the Muslim community playing an important role.

A later national report in 2006, *Countering International Terrorism: The United Kingdom's Strategy* (Home Office, 2006), further emphasised this community approach. It praised the great contribution of the British Muslim community to British society and summarised its approach using four words: 'Prevent, Pursue, Protect and Prepare' (Klausen, 2009, p 406).

Alternative paradigms, stemming largely from far-right groups or conspiracy theories, failed to generate sufficient support to challenge mainstream political thinking. The decline of the BNP (see, for example, Goodwin, 2014; Startin, 2014) in part helps to explain how any substantive change or social learning has failed to materialise. The lack of a unified narrative or alternative hindered the prospect of a paradigm shift. Even those who argued for multiculturalism retreated, failing to produce a coherent strategy or narrative that could act as an alternative (Joppke, 2014).

Such arguments also suffer from failing to promote workable alternatives. In 2011, David Cameron denounced multiculturalism as an idea in a speech in Munich, arguing that it had 'encouraged different cultures to live separate lives, apart from each other and the mainstream' and advocating instead for a 'muscular liberalism'. The experience of policy, however, was more nuanced.

In certain areas, where multiculturalism was embedded, it was difficult to replace and rhetoric was not translated into policies (Tremblay, 2019, pp 152, 218). This fits with Hall's (1993) understanding of paradigm shifts – that blame in and of itself is insufficient to offer such a shift; rather, the new paradigm must both be able to explain the problems and offer a coherent challenge to existing policies.

The government's approach of blaming individuals also absolved it and others of blame. The government rejected links between its foreign policy and the terrorist attacks. By accepting no linkages between the actions of the West and terrorism, Blair presented terrorism as emanating from 'decades of alienation, victimhood and political oppression in the Arab and Muslim world', while the West was perceived as

> a passive, progressive and wholly benign entity; a victim of the irrationality and insecurities of the Islamic world … by ruling out foreign policy as a causal factor, this framing also served to preclude any critical analysis of the direction that it had taken under New Labour, and foreclosed any consideration of policy change. (Kettell, 2013, p 273)

However, the attacks saw a change in government rhetoric around the 'war on terror'. The post-7/7 discourse fused themes of humanitarianism and security, promoting 'virtues of strong leadership and interventionism via an increasingly elevated emphasis on the importance of values and ideas as key weapons in the fight against terrorism' (Kettell, 2013, p 273).

Nor did the government wish to pass blame onto security services. Although 7/7 led to questions relating to the UK's counterterrorism capabilities, the government 'rallied to the aid of MI5 and the police and deflected calls for the establishment of an independent public inquiry to investigate the bombings' (Hewitt, 2008, p 88).

As the Intelligence and Security Committee (2009, p 5) noted: 'It is important that the public know as much as possible, but we must also ensure that what we publish does not undermine the efforts of MI5, MI6 and GCHQ in the fight to counter the very real threat we all still face from terrorism.'

Tensions exist between the need for quick answers and complete accounts of events. Complex investigations take time. Yet politicians are vote maximisers and conscious of electoral cycles and public opinion, which encourage them to focus upon the short term. In addition to this, a lack of, or incomplete or contradictory evidence leads to speculation and conspiracy theories aimed at delegitimising or reducing public trust in government and official institutions (Bartlett and Miller, 2010). This situation was particularly relevant, as both the UK and US had recently faced charges that they had manipulated 'intelligence to fit policy, which may involve ignoring or downplaying intelligence which does not assist in the advancement of a preferred policy' over accounts of weapons of mass destruction in Iraq prior to invading in 2002–3 (Phythian, 2005, pp 362–3).

Such tensions are borne out in the preface to the 'official Account of the Bombings', printed in May 2006, which notes that its account is:

> not yet the full picture. Some material has been withheld to avoid prejudicing current or possible future prosecutions, the ongoing police investigation, to protect intelligence relationships, sources and techniques and to avoid providing information that could help future terrorists. The police investigation remains very much a live one, and further information may emerge. (House of Commons, 2006, p 1)

Speaking at the publication of the Intelligence and Security Committee's (2009) *Review of the Intelligence on the London Terrorist Attacks on 7 July 2005* Report in 2009, the chairman, Kim Howells (2009), offered two examples of why such reporting needed to be incomplete:

> We cannot publish the exact numbers of people that MI5 can keep under surveillance at any one time, as this would tell our enemies the extent of MI5's capability and they might be able to use this information to their advantage. Similarly, for example, we cannot publish the name of an individual if it could lead to one of MI5's sources being identified, as this might put lives in danger.

Terrorists, however, seek to instil fear to drive such changes, and here we need to be careful not to 'reorganize society around the presumption of similar events taking place. To do so would be to normalise extremes and thereby to marginalise what is normal. This would effectively "do the terrorists' job for them", by institutionalizing instability' (Durdoie, 2007, p 430).

However, dismissing any potential for changes or making normative claims or warning against such changes risked downplaying events, dismissing the notion of crisis and redefining events purely in terms of criminal activity. Such ideas are linked to the 'bad apples' argument, which exclusively blames agents (see Chapter 2). Operational lessons – such as the need for radio communication in the underground network – were also needed to reassure the public. Such themes were discussed at a local (devolved) level. In part this can be explained by the devolved nature of government, with counterterrorism being a national policy but aspects such as transport or policing falling under the remit of the Mayor of London. The report from the Greater London Assembly (2006), although accepting that 'such an attack could happen in any country, in any city, at any time', argued that:

> There is an overarching, fundamental lesson to be learnt from the response to the 7 July attacks, which underpins most of our findings and recommendations. The response on 7 July demonstrated that there is a lack of consideration of the individuals caught up in major or catastrophic incidents. Procedures tend to focus too much on incidents, rather than

on individuals, and on processes rather than people. Emergency plans tend to cater for the needs of the emergency and other responding services, rather than explicitly addressing the needs and priorities of the people involved.

We argue in this report that London's emergency plans should be re-cast from the point of view of people involved in a major or catastrophic incident, rather than focusing primarily on the point of view of each emergency service. A change of mindset is needed to bring about the necessary shift in focus, from incidents to individuals, and from processes to people.

Legacy

The government claimed that legislation brought in after the attacks, principally the 2006 Terrorism Act, which initially proposed extending the period for which the police could hold a suspect without charge from 14 days to 90 – though this was reduced to 28 during the passage of the legislation – and created a new offence 'encouragement of terrorism', did not represent a direct response to the London attacks in July 2005. While significant portions of the bill may have been prepared before the 7/7 attacks, consultations with security agencies after the bombings and the piecemeal assembly of the bill in the autumn of 2005 indicate a more direct response than the government claimed (Hewitt, 2008, pp 53–55; Hellmuth, 2016, p 155).

The nature of the drafting of the bill also differed from other pieces of legislation, as the government frequently met counterparts in the Conservative and Liberal Democrat parties. Although not on the same scale as the coalition governments forged during both world wars, this demonstrates a greater willingness to consult on matters of national security.

The attacks in July 2005 led to amendments to existing terrorist legislation rather than a wholesale rethink of the legislation. Writing at the end of the decade, Klausen (2009, p 404) defines the 2000 Terrorism Act as the 'primary anti-terrorism legislation'. However, procedurally, the attack prompted a greater awareness of the 'home-grown' threat, as demonstrated by the linkages between social policy and policing.

For critics of the government's approach, the crisis and wider 'war on terror' marked a change in British policing and perceptions of terrorism. It signified a shift which has resulted in certain Muslim communities being identified as 'new suspect communities', replacing the Irish population (Pantazis and Pemberton, 2009; Awan, Spiller, and Whiting, 2019, p 25).

However, such views are challenged by Greer (2010, pp 1172–5), who argues that such a shift has not occurred. Greer argues that the language used within the legislation is not 'expressly directed against Muslims or Islam' and that some of the legislation that forms the basis of Pantazis's and Pemberton's thesis originated prior to the 9/11 attacks in the US. Greer rejects the assertion that discourses or official labelling have created the linkages between Islam and such attacks. In doing so, he draws upon the words of one of the London bombers who made such assertions. He further notes that far from an official labelling, the language used has been challenged in various official capacities:

> It is not clear that even in its heyday, the term 'war on terror' unproblematically captured the approach the United Kingdom took to the al Qaeda-7/7-type terrorist threat. For example, there has been 'widespread opposition within MI5' to the 'war on terror' rhetoric for many years and, in 2009, the term was criticized by the then Foreign Secretary David Miliband. (Greer, 2010, p 1175)

In addition to the legislation, the aftermath of the bombings saw a reorganisation of the Home Office. This split the existing Home Office into two: a smaller Home Office would retain responsibility for police, immigration and border control. Emphasis 'would now be placed on security and counterterrorism' while tangential concerns such as prisons, criminal justice and constitutional affairs became the domain of the newly created Ministry of Justice (Hellmuth, 2016, p 158).

However, plans to reorganise in response to the terrorist threat were highlighted in Labour's 2005 election manifesto (written before the attacks took place). This acknowledged that closer working between security and law enforcement was needed; it promised, from 2006, to bring together 4,000 specialist staff to tackle terrorism, drugs and people trafficking, while greater powers were to be offered in the form of 'new control orders' and effective house arrest limiting the contacts of those suspected of plotting 'terrorist outages' (The Labour Party, 2005, pp 45, 53).

One area where the legacy of the crisis did represent a significant break with the past is through notions of remembrance. Prior to 2005, high-profile events, such as the Birmingham pub bombings of 1974 or the Manchester Bombing of 1996, were commemorated with plaques. However, in the wake of the 7/7 attacks, 52 stainless steel pillars – one for each victim – were erected in Hyde Park as an official memorial. The London Bombings then took on a significance akin to that of either world war. The 'terrorist attacks attained new hyperbolic significance. More than a loss of innocent life, they became attacks perpetrated by an apocalyptic enemy of civilisation. Terrorism became the new global threat against which national, and civilised, identities could be juxtaposed' (Heath-Kelly, 2015). However, as Heath-Kelly (2015) notes:

> there is no space for one victim of July 2005 in the official memorial landscape of London. The death of Jean Charles de Menezes at the hands of overzealous counterterrorism firearms officers (the Brazilian was shot seven times in the head at Stockwell tube station two weeks after 7/7) does not fit with the imagery of the good fight against terror. Good guys don't murder innocent Londoners.

This links to notions of the Blitz; London, in 1940 but also in 2005, was seen as an 'innocent victim' while leading politicians and newspapers emphasised the resilience of the capital and themes of business as usual. Though there was a significant difference from the Blitz; in 1940, this referred to the working classes, but in 2005 this idea was used 'to evoke the defiance of some of London's wealthiest workers' (Kelsey, 2015, pp 170–71).

The terrorist attacks, however, offer a different means of commemorating from earlier examples. Their memory has not yet been shaped by the revisionist accounts that subsequent generations offer to events (see, for instance, the differing accounts of the First World War in Chapter 5). In addition to this, the processes of remembrance and commemoration have been shaped by

> those who witnessed the events commemorated, or of their relatives who pass on the story, [which offer] a crucial element in shaping the commemorative object. With 7/7, there were numerous survivors of all four bombings who were able to offer accounts of their direct experiences, and there was a large number of photographic images, some taken at the scene by survivors using camera phones, others from broadcast media coverage. (Brown, Allen, and Reavey, 2015, p 429)

Other attacks have similarly been commemorated in this way. The Manchester Arena Bombing of 2017, in which 22 people lost their lives, led to the creation of a 'living memorial' garden, with 'personalised memory capsules, filled with memories and mementoes of them provided by loved ones' (Manchester City Council, 2024).

Conclusion

This chapter has highlighted the importance of narratives in affecting the outcomes of crises. By highlighting the agency of individuals involved in the crisis, the government was able to offer a paradigm-reinforcing narrative. Notions of resilience were praised, while discussions about structural issues were marginalised within policy making. A similar narrative was pursued in response to the banking crisis (see Chapter 13) – though influenced by those blamed – which again prioritised preventing certain agents from repeating their actions at the expense of structural changes.

It has also demonstrated the inequalities that can exist in narrative formation. The attacks occurred shortly after the Labour Party had won a 66-seat majority in the 2005 general election. Blair personally received a polling boost following the attacks (Ipsos MORI, 2005). This made it easier for the government to deflect opposition parties' narratives, such as the BNP's criticism of multiculturalism or critics of the government's foreign policy. The timing also made it harder for such groups to demonstrate an electoral coalition for their policies.

Further reading

For a detailed account of the bombings and the wider political issues see Steve Hewitt's (2008) *The British War on Terror.* Other useful sources include the relevant chapter in Dorle Hellmuth's (2016) *Counter Terrorism and the State: Western Responses to 9/11.* This situates the experiences of the UK alongside France, Germany and the US and in doing so offers a comparative understanding of the British government's approach to terrorism

Others have linked the war on terror to wider issues of foreign policy, for example Steve Kettell's (2011) *New Labour and the New World Order: Britain's Role in the War on Terrorism* and Raymond Plant's (2008) chapter 'Blair's Liberal Interventionism' in Matt Beech and Simon Lee's, *Ten Years of New Labour.*

Contemporary political accounts are somewhat harder to source. Given the nature of the attacks, emphasis is placed upon contemporary politicians, rather than protagonists, to offer accounts in memoirs. Tony Blair's (2010) *A Journey* only briefly touches on the events themselves (though it does explore the wider issue of terrorism in more depth) while Home Secretary Charles Clarke has not, yet, written an autobiography and the then Shadow Home Secretary Theresa May's autobiography focuses on her time in Downing Street. In lieu of such accounts, British Paralympian Martine Wright (2017), who was aboard the train at Aldgate, explores the event in her book *Unbroken.*

13

The Global Financial Crisis, 2007–8

Overview

This chapter explores the Global Financial Crisis (GFC) of 2007/8. As banking became more complicated, distinctions between retail and investment banking became less distinct. The collapse of the US subprime housing market demonstrated the vulnerability of linking these parts of the banking system. As interest rates increased, the number of people unable to repay mortgages also increased, leading to mortgage defaults. Such losses left banks increasingly reluctant to lend money to individuals and businesses and even other banks.

Initially those embroiled within the GFC looked to the state to recapitalise or, bail out, banks which could not receive funding needed for day-to-day activities. Such policies sought to encourage lending, reinflate the economy and promote growth. However, competing narratives emerged blaming such policies for the onset of a government spending crisis and promoted austerity economics.

Such understandings conflated cause and effect, ignored the fiscal shock generated by bailing out the banks and allowed the coalition government, elected in 2010, to pursue a programme of state retrenchment. Blame shifted from the banking sector – with a few individual exceptions – to focus on the recipients of government spending. In doing so, attention shifted away from issues such as banking regulation and systemic reform, entrenching the pre-crisis paradigm.

Introduction

The neoliberal reforms of the 1980s promoted a more liberal banking sector and one which was more heavily aligned to international markets and the US in particular. As early as 1981, the government sought to turn the mortgage markets into an 'engine of growth' (Oren and Blyth, 2019, p 611). The 'Big Bang' deregulation of 1986 further liberalised the banking sector, allowing UK banks to make riskier international investments and diluting the differences between savings and investment banks. This was the result of two pieces of legislation, the Financial Services Act and the Building Societies Act. Poser (1988, p 319) identified four components of this 'Big Bang':

- The abolition of fixed commission rates charged by members to their customers, and their replacement by negotiated rates.
- The elimination of the 'single capacity' system, which prevented Stock Exchange members from acting both as brokers – that is, agents – for customers and dealers – that is, principals – for their own accounts.
- The introduction of a new system for trading securities on the Stock Exchange.
- The lifting of restrictions on exchange membership, which enable major British and foreign financial institutions to become member firms of the London Stock Exchange.

The result of these policies was debt-fuelled economic growth, supported not just by the mortgage market but by expanding access to credit cards, bank loans and overdrafts, making consumer credit more readily accessible. Household debt grew by £768.37 billion, 783 per cent, between 1979 and 2008 (Sparkes and Wood, 2021, p 601).

Such increases left the economy inherently unbalanced. Credit became dominant, and access to credit was a key determinant of individuals' economic power; for example, the value of property failed to rise in line with earnings, meaning that some £800 billion had been spent 'stimulating house prices' (Ambrose, 2012, quoted by Kirkland 2015, p 519).

Further to this, such policies also led to changes in the way banks operated: faced with increased international competition and fewer opportunities for growth, banks pursued speculative investments and 'increased their leverage ratios as a means of protecting their margins'. Banks further pursued 'herding behaviour[s]', following the successes of rivals. They 'became evermore willing to ignore their own intuitive warning signs for fear of losing ground' to their competitors. Finally, banks adopted short-term views focusing on shareholder value and bonus culture, which placed greater emphasis on risk (Barber, 2021, pp 62–3; see also Peston and Knight, 2013, pp 16–17).

As shareholders, rather than customers, became prioritised, banks diversified their portfolios. Building societies adopted similar approaches, following processes of demutualisation, with banks such as Abbey National and Northern Rock as two of the largest undergoing such demutualisation. Distinctions between retail banking, which dealt primarily with members of the public through taking deposits and offering mortgage loans, and investment banking, which involved engaging with international markets, became increasingly opaque. One key implication of this was that depositors' money was increasingly used to fund investments in global markets.

Processes that became known as 'casino banking' moved quicker than regulatory frameworks. At the same time regulatory frameworks were becoming increasingly informal; in 1999 the US officially repealed the Glass–Steagall Act, which had required a separation of commercial and investment banks.

Under New Labour, the task of regulating such activities was split between the Treasury, the Bank of England (financial and monetary stability) and the Financial Services Authority (FSA), which addressed market confidence through compliance with regulation.

Important here were the links that emerged between investment and retail banking, with the former effectively subsidising the latter. Such dependency entailed that a problem in the investment side of banks would translate into the 'real economy' through a tightening of credit opportunities.

As banks grew in size, they created new ways of maximising their liquidity. One such way was through a process known as 'securitisation'. This essentially allows banks to transfer illiquid assets into liquid assets while simultaneously 'tapping new creditors, including pension funds, mutual funds and insurance companies, as well as foreign investors such as foreign central banks' (Shin, 2009a, p 310). Securitisation was traditionally seen as enabling the dispersion of credit risk away from large institutions (banks); however, following 2007/8, it was widely criticised for:

> multi-layered agency problems that took hold at every stage of the securitisation process, starting with the origination of the loan to the sale, warehousing and securitisation as well as the role of the credit rating agencies in the process. We could dub this less charitable view the hot potato hypothesis, which has figured frequently in speeches given by policy makers on the credit crisis. The motto would be that there is always a greater fool in the chain who will buy the bad loan. At the end of the chain, according to this view, is the hapless final investor who ends up holding the hot potato and suffers the eventual loss. (Shin, 2009a, p 312)

Although Shin warns against wholeheartedly accepting this 'hot potato' explanation, the narrative became popularised by policy makers and regulators. In doing so he notes that far from getting rid of the 'hot potato', banks positioned themselves last in the chain by issuing liabilities against such products.

The use of these new products saw a further layer of regulation that was provided by ratings agencies. They were responsible for determining the value of securitised bonds/investments. Such agencies were paid by the issuers of the bond, raising questions about their objectivity.

Underpinning these moves was a misbelief that risk both could and had been removed from the economic models used by financial institutions (Bell and Hindmoor, 2015, p 15). Linked to this was the implicit belief that regulators understood financial innovation and practices. Traders believed that 'governments would not let the system fail and would therefore move in to compensate them for any losses they made through excessive trading' (Crouch, 2011, p 101). Gamble (2009, p 1) notes that such confidence was not unique to Britain: across the Western hemisphere, 'everyone assumed each bubble could be managed and burst at the right time by appropriate action by the authorities'. The risks associated with such an approach were well-known to policy makers, but nonetheless encouraged as the only means of achieving non-inflationary growth (Oren and Blyth, 2019).

The subprime mortgage crisis in the US occurred when homeowners were unable to repay mortgages following increases in interest rates. As the number of defaults rose, so too did the number of foreclosures and the decline in house prices. This led to a tightening of liquidity; banks stopped lending to one another, demonstrating a lack of confidence in global markets. This had visible impacts on the UK banking sector. Northern Rock, which had little exposure to US subprime debt, nevertheless found itself unable to borrow money to 'roll over the short-term debt on which it relied' (Hay, 2011, p 15; Kirkland, 2022, p 77). It was the bank's exposure to borrowing that became problematic for Northern Rock, as 'only 23 percent of its liabilities were in the form of retail deposits. The rest of its funding came from a combination of short-term borrowing in the capital markets and securitized notes and other longer-term funding sources' (Shin, 2009b, p 102).

On 13 September 2007 the BBC reported that Northern Rock had sought financial support from the Bank of England, which offered assistance the following day. As news of this assistance spread, those who had deposits in Northern Rock, fearing for their savings (in 2007 the first £2,000 of deposits were fully insured and 90 per cent of amounts less than £35,000), rushed to withdraw their money, leading to Britain's first run on a bank in 150 years. Over the next few days, some £4.6 billion was withdrawn from Northern Rock (Public Accounts Committee, 2009, p 3; Shin, 2009b, pp 101–2).

Northern Rock was by no means the only bank to suffer as fears of contagion grew. If Northern Rock, the fifth largest mortgage lender in the UK, was vulnerable, then it was feared that other banks might be vulnerable too (Goldsmith-Pinkham and Yorulmazer, 2010). Bank lending soon dried up, posing problems not just for other financial institutions which, like Northern Rock, relied on short-term debt, but the real economy as businesses and individuals also struggled to borrow money on a short-term basis.

Problems in the banking sector further transcended into the wider economy. Banks adopted a much more stringent approach to borrowing and lending, which made it harder for individuals to obtain credit, fundamentally challenging an economic growth model that was reliant upon the continued availability and employment of such debt. This 'credit crunch', as it became known, led to tighter spending and lower consumption, unemployment increased, and the UK entered a recession in spring 2008, which would last for over a year.

To avert such problems and ensure that lending to the 'real' economy continued, the government injected money into the banking sector, through either guaranteeing loans or nationalisation. The Labour government initially sought to address the crisis by adopting a Keynesian approach to economic policy, although it was reluctant and keen to emphasise the limited time frame of investments, and noted it would abandon such measures should growth return to the economy (Hay, 2011, p 23; Kirkland, 2022, p 82). Alongside the bail-out of the banks, the government embarked on a process of 'quantitative easing', asking the Bank of England to purchase government debts, allowing greater government spending to boost the economy. In November 2009, £200 million of debts were purchased under the scheme. Such measures were used to 'increase the money supply and prevent the kind of deflationary slump that had followed the crash in 1929' (Gamble, 2010a, p 5).

Against Brown's views on the timing of cuts were those of the Treasury, which, just as in 1931 (see Chapter 7), advocated for quicker and deeper cuts to public spending. According to Gamble (2015, p 43), the Treasury 'quickly reverted to their standard approach to a fiscal crisis, arguing that there needed to be strong measures of retrenchment to maintain the UK's credibility with the markets, to allow the Government to continue to borrow at reasonable rates of interest'.

In 2009 the Treasury adopted policies of fiscal retrenchment. As the global crash generated a recession, tax receipts plummeted. In addition to this, the cost of bailing out the banks 'transformed the UK public finances. The clearest indicator of this change was the rise in the share of the public spending in GDP from 41 to 47 per cent' (Gamble, 2015, p 43). The government could respond by increasing taxation rates, reducing spending or increasing borrowing. Underpinning each option were predictions about the downturn: a short, sharp, 'V shaped' recession with a quick return to growth could justify increasing borrowing – which was Brown's preference. Brown argued that major cutbacks would inhibit a return to growth and that such policies should only come about after recovery was assured.

As large banks were nationalised, what was 'essentially [a] private – to the banking sector – crisis became a crisis of the state' or 'the nationalisation of the crisis' (Kirkland, 2017, pp 147–8; see also Blyth, 2013b). Attention mistakenly focused on the amount of money – some 35 per cent of GDP – used to support the banks. Such understanding confused cause and effect, as Blyth (2013b, pp 45–6) notes: 'to put it bluntly the state plugged a gap and stopped a financial collapse. It did not dig a fiscal ditch through profligate public spending'. Such measures were not unique to the UK; internationally, policies

> evolved from a brief flourishing of Keynesian thinking in 2008–2009 when [the Managing Director of the IMF] Strauss-Kahn called for a coordinated global fiscal stimulus amounting to 2 per cent of global GDP … [to] a shift towards prioritising restoring the public finances and addressing increased public debt though cuts in public expenditure and austerity policies. (Cliff, 2015, p 154)

In addition to this misdiagnosis, the crisis hit the ability of the state to finance programmes, due to lost taxation revenue caused by a lack of liquidity within the economy. Hay (2014, p 62) estimates that '70 per cent of the current account deficit in 2008–9 and 86 per cent in 2009–10 is attributable to lost taxation revenue alone'. The spending crisis was what Hay (2013, p 24) described as a 'second-order crisis' which stemmed from a lack of growth.

Framing

The economic crisis of 2007, also known as the GFC, has been said to have multiple causes. Four distinct arguments have been identified. The first views the crisis as an international crisis (French and Thrift, 2009), or at least one whose roots can be traced to the US (Duca, Muellbauer, and Murphy, 2010), and one which policy makers in Britain only had a little or indirect effect upon. The second view suggests that the crisis evolved from the accession of New Labour, and in particular Gordon Brown's time as Chancellor, and the promise of the 'ending of boom and bust' (Goodhart, 2008; Hodson and Mabbett, 2008; Kavanagh and Cowley, 2010, pp 19–23). The third and fourth arguments offer a slightly longer-term approach: the third views the GFC as stemming from Britain's withdrawal from the European Exchange Rate Mechanism (ERM) in September 1992 (Martin and Milas, 2013), while the fourth emphasises the shifts in the changes to financial markets and regulation that occurred in the 1980s (Kirkland, 2015). Though blame was not mutually exclusive, the Labour government blamed a combination of actors: the housing market in the US, the international financial system and the leadership of domestic banks.

Convergence on economic issues emerged following the 1980s. Terms such as a 'Thatcherite consensus' in the UK (see, for example, Coates, 2013 and Gudgin and Coutts, 2015) and ' Reaganomics' in an international sense symbolised such agreements. This point was made by Hay (2011, p 14), who argued that the crisis was just as much one of 'the Anglo-Liberal growth model as it is a specifically American crisis'. The transition of the UK's Labour Party to what Tony Blair and others termed New Labour further helped to cement the new paradigm that Hall (1993) identifies. Others, too, have noted the convergence between the two parties' economic policies under a Thatcherite consensus (Hay, 1999b; Heffernan, 2000), to the extent that Cameron, elected Conservative Party leader in 2005, was more comfortable positioning himself as the 'heir to Blair', rather than the heir of Thatcher or other Conservative Party leaders (Kerr, 2007, p 48; cf. Cliff and Tomlinson, 2007, who argue against the 'orthodoxy' that New Labour 'decisively renounced Keynesianism'). Brown adopted a scientific understanding of the economy and famously claimed to have 'ended boom and bust'. Such rhetoric left Labour 'unprepared to acknowledge that, after 15 uninterrupted years of economic growth, it might be sensible to have some margin of error in its plans for the possibility of an economic downturn' (Dolphin, 2011, p 3). Though this is not to say that prior to 2007 there were alternatives readily offered by politicians; light-touch regulation and prevailing spending plans were accepted across the political spectrum (Gamble, 2010a, p 7, 2010b, p 649). Such views were by no means confined to the UK; Gamble (2009, p 1) locates this confidence across the Western hemisphere – what Engelen and colleagues (2011) define as the 'great complacency' within financial markets and regulation.

A similar, confident theme was noted in the *Times*. On 21 August, the paper ran a story arguing that there was 'no historical reason why recent turmoil should spark a recession'. Here, Gerard Baker (2007) argued that although the scale of the 'US mortgage crisis' was unknown, intervention from the US Federal Bank (cutting interest rates) could prevent the crisis from affecting those 'whose only interaction with a financial institution is their monthly bank statement'.

Such confidence in the underlying model, and unwillingness to significantly alter the overarching framework, led to the policies of austerity, which came to dominate the decade after 2010 and defined the Conservative Party's response to the crisis. Although not the first political expression of the policies of austerity, it soon became 'constructed as a "common sense" response to the crisis' within political and media discourse (Basu, 2019, p 314; also see Berry, M. 2016). Though this not to say that the term was controversial. Others argued that defining the crisis as one of austerity was to misdiagnose: 'to see the British crisis ... as one of debt, is to mistake a symptom for the condition itself'. The distinction between different narratives is important, as the authors note, for if the crisis was 'conceived differently, as a *crisis of growth*, not a *crisis of debt*, then austerity and deficit reduction would be no solution at all' (Green, Hay, and Taylor-Gooby, 2015, p 3, original emphasis).

The initial crisis (or crises) within the banking system focused upon individuals. The decision to nationalise or bail out the banks led to enhanced scrutiny of the banks. In particular, it led to discussions about bankers' bonuses, which came to be termed 'bonuses for failure'. The *Telegraph* ran an article entitled 'Bonus Culture to Blame for Banking Crisis, say MPs' (*The Telegraph*, 2009), while the *Express* highlighted the 'controversial' £703,000 pension received by Fred Goodwin (*The Express*, 2009). This pension was set against the backdrop of Royal Bank of Scotland (RBS) making a record loss of £24 billion and being bailed out by the government. The focus on bonuses:

> presented the problems in [a] very individualistic manner; these payments were not so much the fault of regulators or the system of regulation, but those claiming the large bonuses. Pressure was placed on individuals to give up their bonuses, especially following the nationalisation of certain institutions, but calls for [legislation] to prevent such bonuses being offered were absent and when instigated at EU level ... challenged by the coalition government. (Kirkland, 2017, p 142)

Nor was Goodwin alone in such portrayals. Just as he became the face of the bonuses scandal, Bob Diamond, the Chief Executive of Barclays, became the face of another scandal – the LIBOR (London Interbank Offered Rate) scandal. Here, it was revealed that to conceal the financial position of Barclays, the bank had submitted false reports on the cost of borrowing (Monticini and Thornton, 2013). This made Barclays appear to be able to borrow money at cheaper rates, suggesting it was in a stronger financial position than it actually was. As Diamond later admitted, this was done to alleviate fears of Barclays also being nationalised (Kirkland, 2017, p 145).

Such understanding viewed the problems as stemming from agents, under the guise of 'bad apples'; the notion was that such actors were not representative of the sector as a whole. Partly, this was due to the simplistic understanding of events portrayed in the media and political rhetoric. Individuals were tangible – they could be seen in a manner which regulations could not, and they were also instantly recognisable. In contrast, debates and discussions surrounding regulatory frameworks were complicated – exemplified in the exchange between Mervyn King, the Governor of the Bank of England, and Conservative MP Michael Fallon in the Treasury Select Committee (2008, p Ev5) where Mr King was, twice, asked 'who was in charge?' in the crisis, before replying 'What do you mean by "in charge"? Would you like to define that?'

Partly, though, this individualisation was also due to the manner in which they behaved:

> If the former RBS boss (Goodwin) had wanted to make himself the epitome of bad boy bankers, the physical embodiment of the British end of the crisis, he could not have done a better job if he tried. His bizarre handling of the aftermath has involved the adoption of an anti-PR strategy in which he offers nothing in the way of explanation ... It has done nothing to aid understanding and has guaranteed that Goodwin be treated as the pantomime villain. (Martin, 2013, p ii)

Yet blame did not exclude such individuals from participating in debates about the wider regulatory framework. Their technocratic expertise was incorporated into discussions, which led to the prioritisation of both the prevailing pre-crisis economic orthodoxy and Conservative notions of austerity. As Mike Berry (2016, p 848) notes, the BBC's coverage of the crisis was dominated by 'City sources ... with the consequence that wide-ranging reforms to the sector were absent from debates'.

A similar pattern occurred in the printed media. Mullen (2021) explores the reporting of the GFC between 2008 and 2010, drawing upon articles in the *Guardian* (including the *Observer*) and the *Telegraph*. His analysis demonstrates that politicians formed the primary source of information for articles, followed by non-financial and financial corporations and the Bank of England. In contrast, those opposed to austerity or a retrenched state – the public sector, trade unions or anti-austerity activists – were marginalised, with these groups representing less than one tenth of all sources.

Basu (2019, p 318) argues that the narratives of austerity were not established until April 2009 – months after the origins of the crisis – and only after the banking bail-outs. Rather, as Basu notes, the pattern of shifting from a banking crisis to austerity was predictable and consistent with previous responses to economic crises that sought to maintain existing paradigms (see, for instance, Chapter 7). One contemporary was Naomi Klein (cited by Basu, 2019, p 318), who wrote in the *Guardian* in 2008:

> Nobody should believe the overblown claims that 'free market' ideology is now dead. During boom times, it is profitable to preach laissez-faire, because an absentee government allows speculative bubbles to inflate. When those bubbles burst, the ideology becomes a hindrance, and it goes dormant while government rides to the rescue. But rest assured: the ideology will come roaring back when the bailouts are done. The massive debt the public is accumulating to bail out the speculators will then become part of a global budget crisis that will be the rationalisation for deep cuts to social programmes and for a renewed push to privatise what is left of the public sector.

The dominance of the 'debt crisis' narrative was confirmed during the 2010 general election. Here both main parties, Labour and the Conservatives, promised to reduce spending and the national deficit through a combination of spending cuts and changes to taxation, albeit at different levels (Kavanagh and Cowley, 2010; Hay, 2013). The Labour Party (2010, p 0:4) promised in its manifesto to 'More than halve the fiscal deficit over the next four years [through] … cuts to lower priority programmes and fair tax rises'. The Conservative Party (2010, p 19) argued, 'Cutting the deficit is the most urgent task we need to undertake if we are to get the economy moving'.

The election results produced a hung parliament, with the Conservative Party holding the most seats. This led to the formation of a coalition government involving the Liberal Democrat and Conservative parties, which entrenched the idea of a debt crisis. The coalition agreement, which set the framework for the government, stated that 'The deficit reduction programme takes precedence over any of the other measures in this agreement, and the speed of implementation of any measures that have a cost to the public finances will depend on decisions to be made in the Comprehensive Spending Review' (The Coalition Government, 2010, p 35).

Such a shift, along with the formation of the coalition government between the Conservatives and Liberal Democrats, which was keen to blame the previous government for the economic difficulties faced, meant that the three largest parties in the UK – defined in terms of parliamentary seats – now accepted the narrative of a 'spending crisis'. This left little scope – outside of academia (for example, Hay, 2013) – for competing narratives and paradigm shifts to occur.

Understanding the crisis as a crisis of debt, and one that was particular to the UK, rested upon many prior assumptions, such as 'the relationships between debt and growth, debt and interest rates, or fiscal policy and growth' (Cliff, 2015, p 153). The GFC was therefore framed within the context of the existing paradigm, reducing the scope but also the necessity. Hall (1993) notes that one benefit of a new paradigm over the existing one is its ability to explain a crisis as a paradigm shift.

Upon coming into government, the coalition, led by David Cameron, planned an emergency budget to deal 'decisively with our country's record debts'. The budget set the ratio of spending cuts to tax increases at 4:1 – the same ratio as proposed by the Labour government in 1931 (Hansard, 2010).

The government presented notions of credibility as 'non-negotiable' and necessary, linking back to Thatcher's assertion that 'there is no alternative'. Although backdating much of the cuts, Chancellor Osborne embarked on an aggressive reduction in the size of the UK state. The newly created Office for Budget Responsibility (OBR) estimated that the plans would lead to government consumption falling to its lowest level of national income since 1948 (Cliff, 2015, p 168).

The importance placed upon the national debt, alongside the simple narratives peddled by politicians and the media, led to confusion between public and private debt. Such understandings appealed to the 'common sense'; readers understood, from their own lives, that debts needed to be repaid and if they weren't, bad things would happen. This helped to justify the government's actions. However, economically it overlooked significant differences between public (that is, government) and private (that is, individual and household) debt; most important, that a government has the ability to print money in order to satisfy its debts or to fund further spending commitments – this is essentially what the government asked the Bank of England to do in the process of quantitative easing. Governments, by virtue of their sovereignty, could further simply cancel the debt owed (though this, of course, would not be without future implications, such as inflationary pressures) in a way individuals cannot.

Linked to this, notions of debt – at least on an aggregate level – are not solely negative. Debts allow a range of functions to occur within modern economies, from day-to-day spending on credit cards to the purchase of houses through mortgages. Such nuances are lost in comparisons between public and private debt, which have at their core an assumption that all debt is equal. Yet at the same time as emphasising the need for Britain to pay down its debts, David Cameron rewrote his 2011 conference speech to remove references asking the public to pay off their own debts, for fears such moves would 'dampen consumer demand and worsen the recession' (Wintour, 2011).

The tension that existed was born partly from the subjective nature of macroeconomic policy. Much of the debate rested upon subjective questions, such as where the UK was in the economic cycle and what level of debt was 'acceptable'. Such subjectivity led to different institutions, such as the International Monetary Fund (IMF), the Organisation for Economic Co-operation and Development (OECD) and the UK government, using different methodologies for calculating metrics such as the output gap and potential growth rates (Cliff, 2015, pp 152–3). Underpinning this was a commitment to 'credibility', a term which 'is a social relationship as much as an economic relationship' (Hall, 2008, p 2).

Notwithstanding such problems, however, narratives conflating public and private debt became dominant. One article in the *Mail Online* had the headline 'It's even worse than we thought: cost of national debt to each family is a staggering £138,360' (Barrow, 2011). Other terms, too, were used erroneously: in 2013, Andrew Dilnot, head of the Office for National Statistics, rebuked David Cameron's claims that the government was 'paying down Britain's debt' and distinguished between public sector net debt and public sector net borrowing (*The Guardian*, 2013).

Just as they had been in 1931 (see Chapter 7), notions of debt were used to highlight 'excessive' government spending. Again, newspapers and media outlets appealed to the 'common sense' of readers and consumers to target those in receipt of government spending. Individuals were highlighted, and their family compositions were used as examples of Britain's 'something for nothing' culture.

By highlighting such themes, the media promoted the idea of austerity as 'common sense', helping to legitimise it within policy-making circles. This further heightened the urgency of deficit reduction (Berry, C, 2016; Basu, 2019). Where engagement with the public was afforded, this was limited. Basu (2019, p 315) highlights one BBC interactive feature entitled 'What Would You Cut?' which invited users to choose which government departments should have their budgets cut using a sliding scale. The only tax included was value-added tax (VAT) – widely accepted as the most regressive form of tax. In focusing on what to cut rather than the question of whether there should be any cuts in the first place, the feature 'closes down the space beyond the status quo' where alternative solutions might be explored.

Newspapers further sought to legitimate such arguments by asserting that those living off the state, on benefits, could live extravagant lives. It was reported that some people in receipt of benefits could be receiving large sums of money. Newspapers highlighted individuals and families who received benefits worth £23,000, £38,000 and even £60,000 per year, while talking about a 'benefits culture'. Such was the difference in the lives of those who received benefits, the *Sun* even asked if the welfare system had turned one man into a 'killer' (Kirkland, 2017, p 152).

Such narratives were not confined to the media. Politicians also presented those in receipt of state benefits as being lazy. George Osborne spoke about the need for fairness 'for the shift-worker, leaving home in the dark hours of the early morning, who looks up at the closed blinds of their next-door neighbour sleeping off a life on benefits', while Cameron argued that 'generations languish on the dole and dependency'. Politicians were keen to juxtapose such dependency against 'hard-working individuals', despite figures showing that 80 per cent of claimants spent 'at least three quarters of the past 4 years off unemployment benefit' (Mulheirn, 2013).

Crisis resolution

The Keynesianism introduced in the immediate aftermath of the crisis was limited, not just in terms of time (see Blyth, 2013b, p 54) but also Britain's privatised Keynesianism was modest in a comparative context; tax cuts rather than unemployment assistance was prioritised by the Labour government (Vis, van Kersbergen, and Hylands, 2011, p 348). Unemployment under New

Figure 13.1: British government deficit as a percentage of GDP

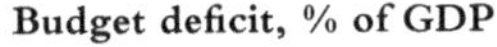

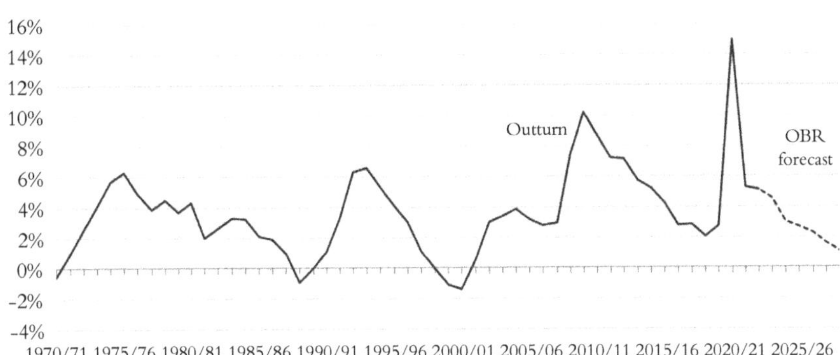

Source: House of Commons Library, 2024

Labour was seen as a secondary consideration to other policy measures. Unlike other Labour governments, New Labour's acceptance of the post-Thatcherite settlement emphasised macroeconomic indicators such as inflation and growth, which took precedence over unemployment. Clegg (2010, p 7) argues that the UK benefits system 'had become the least generous of all the most developed countries'. New Labour, and Gordon Brown in particular, were committed to notions of prudence, something that marked Brown out as a 'fiscally Conservative Chancellor' (Berry, C, 2016, p 71). Brown (2001, p 31) asserted that previous Labour governments were overburdened by spending commitments and that this required new 'economic approaches [that] have sought to learn from past errors'.

The problem, however, of linking the crisis to Britain's debts was that the UK government had run a budget deficit each year since 2001, and only on five occasions since 1970/71 had the government achieved a surplus (House of Commons Library, 2024). Here, Cameron's and the Conservatives' argument that they were paying down Britain's debts was misleading. Each year that Britain runs a deficit the overall debt levels increase; by reducing the deficit, the coalition government, and governments since (up to the COVID-19 pandemic) were slowing the rate at which British debts were growing, but they were still growing.

Craig Berry (2016, pp 69–71) notes that the coalition government and Conservative Chancellor George Osborne routinely missed deficit reduction targets, and such misses were largely responsible for the return to economic growth post-2013 (see Figure 13.1). Yet it did not follow that the narratives of austerity abated; the 2015 Conservative Party manifesto was more ambitious in its deficit reduction plans than the 2010 manifesto.

Austerity measures, then, failed to resolve the problem they were designed for. While the most severe austerity measures put in place under the coalition were backdated, subsequent Prime Ministers have promised to end (further) austerity. As Figure 13.1 demonstrates, the OBR estimates that Britain will continue to run a deficit in the short and medium term, meaning that any moves towards 'returning' to pre-crisis debt levels remain a long way off. As Blyth (2013b, p 229) notes, the application of the term 'austerity' during the crisis was less about fixing the economy and more about denying choices that existed within the crisis/economy as an economic ideology: 'Austerity doesn't work. Period.'

The existing neoliberal paradigm seemed unable to comprehend what had happened and even 'denied that such a crisis was possible in the first place' (Blyth, 2013b, p 54). Such lack of understanding, it could be argued, left fertile ground for a new paradigm to replace the existing one, one that could explain not only how the crisis occurred, but how it could be both resolved and prevented from occurring in the future. 'Although the events of 2007–08 were the kind of large systemic shocks ... many social scientists would expect to lead to a radical departure from the existing neoliberal paradigm to something new ... they did not' (Carstensen and Mattijs, 2017, p 431).

In practice, most changes were 'relatively superficial', with rhetoric failing 'to match reality'. Even the 'transformation' or 'shift' to austerity politics can be seen as reinforcing paradigms. Narratives of austerity offered an 'illusion of change in fiscal management [while] shielding from scrutiny the considerable effort by policymakers to actually prevent change in the way that the UK economy operate[d]' (Berry, C., 2016, p 2).

One important distinction between the narratives of crisis and links to paradigm shifts is that between agency and structure. By blaming agents, attention is confined to who occupies certain positions. Here, any changes focus on personnel rather than the structures within which they operate. Such focus leads to a more limited understanding of what changes need to be incorporated to alleviate the crisis and prevent future ones, which in turn offers greater support to the existing paradigm and reduces scope for new paradigms to emerge.

Through highlighting the actions of figures such as Fred Goodwin or Bob Diamond, it was argued that replacing bad agents would be sufficient to prevent a repeat of the problems. In some respects, it is easier to view agents, who are visible figures and thus can act as lightning rods for blame, than the rules or regulations that govern their actions, which are complex and difficult to understand or even see. The structural framework in which both Goodwin and Diamond (and the wider banking communities) operated was spared serious scrutiny, at least in the short term. This is especially true of the regulations governing the setting of the LIBOR rate; although Diamond and Barclays Bank received punishment for their roles in LIBOR rigging, such actions were confined to actors. That meant that:

> [r]ather than creating new and stronger legal frameworks governing market conduct, the Barclays settlements thus reproduce[d] the fiction of neutral market arbitration while recursively producing continued, post-scandal support for LIBOR amongst both financial-market participants and those charged with market oversight. (Ashton and Christophers, 2015, p 211)

Where structures were blamed, New Labour's response, through defining any interventionist measures as 'temporary', was to defend the existing paradigm. Brown, one of the key architects of New Labour, had little incentive to pursue a radical departure from the existing paradigm. Rather he, as other Labour Prime Ministers/Chancellors had done in times of crises, adopted a conservative rather than radical approach to an economic crisis. No new institutions were sought, but rather prosperity was to be achieved by securing the existing institutions (for example, banks were defended through bailouts as the cost of replacing them or letting them fail was deemed to be too great). Nor did there exist a desire to present the government as implementing something new; in the House of Commons, Brown sought accolades for saving the world, before swiftly correcting himself to state that the government had 'worked with other countries to save the world's banking system' (Kirkland, 2022, p 138).

Brown (2011, pp 23–4), after leaving office, claimed that his solutions/recommendations to overcoming the crisis were 'underpinned by my life-time commitment to fiscal responsibility, keeping deficits and debt as low as possible'. Such understandings support Baker's (2015, p 343) assertion that 'in the field of macroeconomic policy – both monetary and fiscal policy – many pre-crash beliefs remain prominent, there is little evidence of ideational sickness and inertia, and despite some policy experimentation, overarching policy frameworks and their rationales have not as yet been overhauled'.

Even under New Labour, powerful institutions such as the Treasury adopted positions which reduced the likelihood of a paradigm shift. Just as the Treasury's insistence on balanced budgets in the 1930s guided the initial response to the Great Slump, continued acceptance of the 'crowding out' theory – whereby government spending simply replaces more efficient private sector investment – which came to 'underpin government fiscal consolidation strategy … further [encouraged] the retreat from Keynesian approaches to managing the UK economy' (Cliff, 2015, p 169).

The retreat from the initial Keynesianism and lack of an overarching paradigm shift was further confirmed/secured following Labour's defeat in 2010. Upon defeat, the party largely accepted the narration of a 'spending crisis' and the parameters that this entailed. Ed Miliband, who became Labour leader after the party's defeat in the 2010 general election, 'failed to challenge the perception that the deficit crisis had been created by irresponsible public spending on the part of the previous Labour government' (Goes, 2016, p 178). Miliband even apologised for Labour's part in the banking crisis but ignored wider narratives of a spending crisis (Kirkland, 2022, p 153).

The redefinition of the GFC to one of spending and debt also reinforced the post-Thatcherite paradigm. Such framing and narration did not 'entail a change in economic paradigm'. Instead, it offered a

> simple diagnosis – deficit reduction and austerity – which is arguably quite in accordance with the liberal market disposition of recent British governments. The alternative crisis of growth discourse [represented] a

> far more challenging one. For it would entail rejection of the prevailing economic paradigm informing policy since at least the 1980s. More significantly still, it would almost certainly require a rejection of the old growth model and the search for a new one. (Green, Hay, and Taylor-Gooby, 2015, p 4)

Legacy

Conservative electoral success after 2010 ensured that narratives of a spending crisis and policies of austerity became the prevailing paradigm within British politics. Such understandings were confirmed in the 2015 general election, and while the 2017 and 2019 elections shifted attention to Brexit, the legacy of the crisis could be seen in the assertion by John McDonnell, Labour's Shadow Chancellor under Corbyn, that the 2017 and 2019 manifestos should be 'fully costed' (Sloman, 2024, p 26).

Austerity is not an even process. As highlighted in Chapter 7, government spending is naturally progressive, and any reductions are regressive, affecting the poorest areas. Fetzer (2019, p 3850) notes that areas with 'significant exposure to specific benefit cuts' saw a rise in support for the anti-EU party UK Independence Party (UKIP) after 2010. Fetzer argues that 'without austerity, Remain would likely have won the EU referendum'.

Other events have, however, overshadowed austerity and programmes of austerity. The COVID-19 pandemic (see next chapter)) led to an expansionist economic policy and greater emphasis upon Keynesian economic thought, promoting jobs and employment despite restrictions on the movement of people. Just as in 1914 the First World War displaced the Irish Home Rule Crisis, without the latter being resolved, so too have other events, including but not limited to Brexit and COVID-19, displaced arguments about austerity as the government undertook further quantitative easing measures and terminology such as 'key workers' challenged existing understandings of the economy.

As the next chapter demonstrates, such changes were temporary, and the 'end' of the COVID-19 crisis led to a new wave of austerity. Such a paradigm has now become a permanent feature of the British state, leaving it 'retrenched, reconfigured and broken' (Farnsworth, 2021). Important changes to people's lives have become normalised – for example, a reduced role of the state and local council provisions, especially reductions in work benefits, increases in privatisation (for example, Royal Mail) and the raising of the state pension age.

Conclusion

What was initially billed as a GFC has several parallels with other crises in this book. For example, the redefinition of the crisis links to the dichotomy between health and economic crises during COVID-19 (see Chapter 14). Initial understandings of the crisis were challenged and became accepted, as demonstrated through the 2010 general election.

Chapter 2 also argued that blame was not a precursor for exclusion from debates. During the GFC, individuals and institutions successfully argued that their expertise was crucial in understanding the crisis and finding solutions. Financial institutions, both commercial but also of the state, the Bank of England, the Treasury, and so on, were able to help generate narratives of the crisis and shape responses to it, as they were able to do following the Great Slump of 1931 (see Chapter 7). In doing so, these actors helped to minimise the blame placed upon structures and generate a paradigm-reinforcing narrative of the crisis.

The redefinition of the crisis led to austerity being presented as the solution. This was confirmed by the 2010 general election and the formation of the coalition government. Yet even by its own logic, austerity has not produced the solutions it was designed to do. That the crisis has abated, then, is due to other pressing concerns dominating the political agenda, such as COVID-19, which have subsequently challenged the logic of austerity (see Chapter 14).

Further reading

Howard Davies (2010), in his book *The Financial Crisis: Who Is Blame?*, Explores the reasons for the crisis by demonstrating the links between financial institutions and the everyday actions of citizens. Like Davies, Andrew Gamble, in his work *Spectre at the Feast* (2009), also traces the history of the crisis, situating this within other crises such as the 1931 Great Slump.

For an account of the economic and political consequences of the crisis, Craig Berry's (2016) *Austerity Politics and UK Economic Policy* maps out the impacts of the coalition government narrative of a debate crisis upon British economics. Others within the same *Building a Sustainable Political Economy* book series, published by Palgrave Macmillan, also explore elements of the UK economy post-crisis, including Jeremy Green, Colin Hay and Peter Taylor-Gooby's (2015) *The British Growth Crisis*, Scott Lavery's (2019) *British Capitalism after the Crisis* and Adam Barber's (2021) *UK Banks and the Lessons of the Great Financial Crisis*.

The role of the media in (re)framing the crisis as one of debt is explored by Paul 't Hart and Karen Tindall in their book *Framing the Global Economic Downturn: Crisis Rhetoric and the Politics of Recessions* (2009).

Key works from those involved, such as Gordon Brown's (2017) *My Life, Our Times* or Alistair Darling's (2011) *Back from the Brink*, demonstrate the difficulties in governing through the crisis. David Cameron's (2019) *For the Record* offers a contrasting account and spells out the arguments in favour of viewing the crisis as one of debt.

14

COVID-19

Overview

This chapter explores the effects of the COVID-19 pandemic since its discovery in late 2019. The virus, which emanated from China, spread to the UK in the first few months of 2020 and by July 2023 killed over 200,00 in the UK and led to the largest peacetime restrictions on freedom of movement the country had ever seen (BBC News, 2023a). Virtually all aspects of life were impacted as the population was encouraged to avoid all but essential travel. Millions were encouraged to work remotely (from home) and virtually all leisure activities were curtailed to avoid the spreading of the virus.

The imposition of lockdowns and changing rules in a fast-paced environment placed significant strain on the government to produce clear and effective messaging. Key themes of personal sacrifice for others more at risk of dying from the virus, for the NHS, and so on, were used to encourage people to adhere to rules that impinged upon their freedoms. At the height of the crisis, daily press conferences were held in Number 10 Downing Street to communicate the latest advice and any legal updates. Such briefings rested largely upon people having confidence in the expertise and legitimacy of scientists and politicians, something that was tested by a number of high-profile individuals flouting the guidance/rules.

As the economy shut down further, economic problems emerged as the UK entered into a recession three times worse than the crisis of 2007–8. Government support was offered to businesses, but narratives of the crisis pitted economic and health concerns against each another. The development of vaccinations reduced the risk to millions and allowed the opening of the economy in the latter half of 2022. Key institutions like the NHS were no longer at risk of being overrun by COVID admissions; however, the disease remains prevalent in society and has led to questions about how successful any 'resolution' has been.

Introduction

On 20 January 2020, Chinese Premier Xi Jinping acknowledged the existence of a deadly disease, a form of coronavirus. The virus, labelled 'COVID-19', spread rapidly across the globe, and over the next 12 months it was responsible for some 2.2 million deaths. COVID-19 also changed the daily lives of billions. Employment changed drastically for 3 billion adults while 'close to 1.6 billion young people had their education interrupted'. The scale of restrictions imposed by governments far exceeded what could be captured by economic indicators such as GDP (gross domestic product), unemployment or trade figures. The extent of the changes far exceeded anything previously experienced in most people's lives. The virus 'caused stress, depression, and mental anguish [on such a scale that] by the end of 2020, the largest part of scientific research on COVID-19 was dedicated to mental health' (Tooze, 2021, p 5).

The first reported case was confirmed in the UK on 29 January 2020 (Tooze, 2021, p 1), and 'the following day the threat level was raised from low to moderate' (Stanley, 2022, p 159). The scale of response was unlike any previous health or economic crisis faced by the UK. 'Never had economies such as the UK's been deliberately closed down to the extent that they were in the first half of 2020' (Davies et al, 2022, pp 1–2).

The extent of these restrictions generated tension between health and economic policies. Lockdowns, which had been employed in other countries to minimise human interaction and slow down the spread of the disease, impacted economic activity, particularly the hospitality and leisure industries, which were closed by such actions. Any financial measures introduced to support those affected would have to be paid for. After a decade of austerity, the Conservative government was ill-prepared to change track now. The narrative of COVID-19 quickly became 'health v the economy' (Stanley, 2022, p 159).

Unlike other crises explored in this book, blame, at least initially, was not widely assigned to specific agent(s). The problem was not that one individual or group of individuals had acted in a suboptimal or unruly manner, as they had been portrayed as doing in previous crises. Short of completely isolating from one another, the actions of individuals could not stop the spread of the disease – no action could be called off, as the discourses of the 1926 and 1984–85 strikes suggested; there were no deliberate actions, as in the case of the 7/7 bombings, that could have been prevented; and there were no political decisions which could simply be reversed, as in the case of both world wars or the Suez Crisis. Rather, the virus was transmitted irrespective of people's actions. It could not be legislated against; while legislation was enacted in an attempt to control the transmission of the virus, this was separate from making the virus illegal – for viruses exist in nature outside of human laws.

This is not to say that the issue of blame was uncontested. However, unlike other crises, debates focused not on the merits of the crisis, on who was right or wrong, but rather on questions about whether or not the virus (and, by extension, a crisis) existed at all. Again, this differs from previous crises – it is not a debate that can be summarised in phrases such as 'peers vs the people' or 'the enemy within', both of which accept the existence (if not legitimacy) of competing forces. Rather, those opposed to the government's policies aimed at overcoming, or managing, the virus tended to deny the existence of the virus in order to claim that other motives were driving national policies of lockdowns and vaccinations.

Such theories were largely propagated through unregulated social media, with different platforms offering an inconsistent approach to handling misinformation. Where they were presented on outlets capable of regulation by the UK regulator Ofcom, sanctions were imposed for 'disseminating content which "had the potential to cause significant harm to viewers"' (Allington et al, 2021, p 1764).

The existence of the crisis, like others discussed in this book, pitted the government against an external threat. Here, it became accepted that the government would have to increase its powers and exercise existing powers that were reserved for such occasions. In 2020, the government introduced the Coronavirus Act. This passed through both houses of Parliament in four sitting days. It saw a centralisation of power away from the legislature to the executive and contained three central provisions: 'To give further powers to the government to slow the spread of the virus, To reduce the resourcing and administrative burden on public bodies [and t]o limit the impact of potential staffing shortages on the delivery of public services' (Haddon et al, 2020).

COVID laws covered a wide range of activities impacting many aspects of daily life. The regulations covered restrictions on meetings (whether or not people were allowed to leave their homes, if so how many people could gather and where – for example, the 'rule of six' – what businesses were allowed to remain open and what restrictions, if any, were placed upon business operations), the wearing of face coverings (requiring people to wear face masks in public places, such as in shops or on public transport, with some exemptions on medical grounds), international travel restrictions and the need to test and, where appropriate, self-isolate (Barber, Brown, and Ferguson, 2022).

Governance was also centralised within the executive at the expense of the wider legislature. Importantly, here, unlike the emergencies of the First and Second World Wars, throughout the crisis the executive remained a single-party government and never formed a coalition. The first few months of the pandemic saw the emergence of 'Parallel governance structure(s)' as new committees were formed, comprising a few select ministers (though full membership was not disclosed) (Ward and Ward, 2023, pp 1180–81). Additionally, rather than receive parliamentary assent prior to legislation being implemented, the Act required the Secretary of State for Health and Social Care to report on the use of the powers every few months. In addition to this, the government used Statutory Instruments (SIs), which are long-standing conventions for delegated legislation within the UK political system. Between January 2020 and March 2022, the government laid 582 SIs relating to COVID-19. These accounted for 30 per cent of all SIs during this period (Hansard Society, 2022).

The spread of the virus in the UK appeared to be two weeks behind European countries such as Italy, where, by 25 February, 229 cases had been detected and 11 towns in Lombardy and Veneto had been put into lockdown. Yet, fearful of economic repercussions, the British Prime Minister had not comprehended the seriousness of the matter (Calvert and Arbuthnott, 2021, pp 137–42). That same evening, the Conservative Party hosted a 'black and white ball' fundraiser, where prizes included a tennis match with Prime Minister Boris Johnson, a day watching cricket with Chancellor Rishi Sunak and a lunch in a prison with the Justice Secretary Robert Buckland.

Privately, Johnson dismissed the importance of COVID. He labelled the pandemic as a 'scare story' and even suggested that the Chief Medical Officer, Chris Whitty, should 'inject him with the virus live on television to show how mild it was' (Bale, 2023, p 150). Throughout the pandemic, Johnson continued to be reluctant to impose restrictions. His adviser Dominic Cummings would later assert that Johnson regretted ordering the initial lockdown, and when faced with pressure to do the same later in 2020 claimed he would rather 'let the bodies pile high' (Sky News, 2021). Such attitudes are consistent with Johnson's libertarianism and 'anti-statism' (Tyler, 2021).

The sense of urgency was missing from the government. Later, on 25 February, the Health Secretary confirmed that, despite the data from Italy, 'The plan is still in the phase of "contain": we aim to contain the virus both abroad and here at home, and prevent it from becoming a pandemic, while of course ensuring that plans are in place should that happen' (Hansard, 2020b). The 'contain' phase lasted into March. At his press briefing in the second week of March, Johnson (2020) outlined that 'the best thing we can all do is wash our hands for 20 seconds with soap and water'.

Johnson missed five COBR[1] meetings in the first two months of the pandemic (Walker, 2020) – indeed, faced with the twin crises of floods and the pandemic, Johnson even went on holiday, something that Labour leader Jeremy Corbyn highlighted during Prime Minister's Questions (PMQs) when he noted:

> The Prime Minister was keen to pose for cameras when there was a crisis on during the election, but he often goes AWOL: he was late to respond to the London riots because he was on holiday; he was on a private island when the Iranian general was assassinated; and last week he had his head in the sand in a mansion in Kent. (Hansard, 2020a)

The UK's first national lockdown was only announced on 23 March, with legislation coming into effect on 26 March – two weeks after Italy's national lockdown and over a month after Europe's first regional lockdowns in Lombardy

1 COBR (commonly referred to as COBRA) is the Civil Contingencies Committee, which 'is convened to handle matters of national emergency or major disruption. Its purpose is to coordinate different departments and agencies in response to such emergencies' (Haddon, 2020).

and Vento (Sample, 2021). The delay in lockdowns enabled the virus to spread throughout the population. One estimate from Imperial College London and Oxford University estimated that the number of infections increased from 200,000 to 1.5 million in the nine days prior to the first lockdown (Calvert and Arbuthnott, 2021, p 9).

Although scientists argued that lockdowns were essential to stop the transmission of the virus, behavioural and political considerations impacted their timings. As the Deputy Chief Medical Officer, Jenny Harries (quoted by Finlayson, Jarvis, and Lister, 2023, p 339, authors' emphasis), warned in March 2020:

> Just because a lockdown is imposed doesn't mean that that is the right thing to do. Timing of an intervention is absolutely critical. *Put it in too early, you have a time period [where] people actually get non-compliant – they won't want to keep it going for a long time.*

Framing

Faced with these challenges, the government's unpreparedness and reluctance to act were well documented. That distinguishes this crisis from others in the book. It also challenges the assumptions spelled out in Chapter 2 that crises lead to a prioritisation of resources. Here, throughout the initial stages of the pandemic, the government was more reluctant than the public to impose measures such as lockdowns or restrictions on individuals' movements (Recchia, 2020).

Recommending 'banal' measures such as handwashing ensured that the crisis in its first period (from January to mid-March) was narrated in a 'low mimetic mode [which] cast the virus as an object of routine and mundane political management'. Johnson's instruction that the public should 'as far as possible, go about business as usual', presented the virus not as a critical incident or crisis but as one among a number of problems to be dealt with – a response that 'allowed the virus to spread unobstructed throughout the population' (Morgan, 2020, p 271). One estimate suggests that on 23 March alone there were 114,00 new cases, with a cumulative total of 527,00 since 16 February (Jit et al, 2020).

The crisis posed a new threat – something that the public had very little (if any) knowledge of. This lack of information, just as in the case of the First World War, increased the appetite and need for information (see Chapter 5). The government established daily press briefings to communicate key messages to the population. These briefings were used to update the public about changes in restrictions and the rate of infection among the general population (the 'R rate'). They were fronted by senior politicians (normally the Prime Minister or Health Secretary) and scientists.

The early press briefings (from 16 March to 16 May) were centred around four themes: the notion of 'unprecedented government activism', 'working to plan', 'national security, wartime unity and sacrifice' and following the 'scientific guidance' (Kettell and Kerr, 2021, p 11). The government was keen to portray new rules, laws and calls for action in a simple and easily digestible message – for example, the instruction 'stay home, protect the NHS, save lives' which was displayed visually as well as communicated orally at the press briefings.

Employment and work were the most affected areas of economic activity. Following the first lockdown in March 2020, there was a 'sudden popular realisation of whose work was essential to the everyday functioning of society'. New terms such as 'key workers' were used to denote such importance and encompassed not only those working in the NHS and risking their own lives to help others, but 'jobs usually considered "unskilled" such as delivery drivers, cleaners and supermarket workers' (Davies et al, 2022, p 77). The Office for National Statistics (2020) estimated that 10.6 million people, a third of the total workforce, 'were in key work occupations and industries'.

Alongside this shift in discourse, there was an outpouring of support for such workers. Newspapers rang out praises; the *Guardian* (2020) ran an editorial arguing that 'applause is not enough: cleaners, refuse collectors and food industry workers are playing a vital role in this crisis. They deserve better pay and conditions'. One opinion poll, reported in the *Daily Star*, noted that 60 per cent of the population took 'key workers [including nurses] for granted' prior to the pandemic and 45 per cent of respondents 'didn't give a second thought to the people collecting their weekly rubbish or delivering parcels'. The same report found that, as a result of COVID-19, three quarters of people 'now make a conscious effort to say thank you whenever they see someone providing a vital service' (Clemenson, 2020).

The most visible support for key workers was to be found in the Thursday night 'clap for carers'. Such an event began through an informal process, started when Annemarie Plas, who was inspired by similar rituals on the continent, posted details on social media which were picked up and shared by the celebrity Victoria Beckham and traditional media outlets. Claims were made that the clap 'united the nation', though it was increasingly seen as being political – with politicians too joining in. The weekly claps were called off by Plas towards the end of May as she felt it was becoming too politicised. Plas argued that more needed to be done on a formal level, such as increased funding for the NHS (Stanley, 2022, pp 163–4).

One study of the experiences of frontline workers, however, challenges some of the assumptions in the narratives of key workers as heroes. Such terms were often limited to those working in the NHS, ignoring other workers such as those who worked in supermarkets or in transportation. Labels such as 'heroes' were described as 'patronising', 'silly' and seen to detract from issues relating to funding (shortages) and their day-to-day work. While the sentiment of the Thursday evening clapping was appreciated, questions were asked about the sincerity of politicians instigating such measures (Kinsella et al, 2022, p 166).

As Kettell and Kerr (2021, p 11) note, throughout the virus there existed a tension between government ministers who wished to highlight the fact that they were simply 'following the science' and being guided by experts in the field, and simultaneously maximise the credit they received 'by hailing a range of "world-leading" activist measures'.

Although some communication to the general public was 'exemplary in its clarity', medical professionals complained about both the volume and content of communication, which undermined scientific understandings (Atkinson et al, 2020). Murphy (2020, p 47) argues that one policy in particular – that of decanting COVID-19 patients from hospitals into nursing homes without requiring testing, which continued until late April – demonstrated 'a distorted understanding – or perhaps, more accurately, interpretation – of COVID's pattern of behaviour'. Such policies, argues Murphy, were 'strong indicators that institutional priorities and anxieties were driving government and public health responses to COVID-19 rather than a grounded, evidence-based assessment of the risks and behaviour of the virus'. According to the Chair of the Health and Social Care Committee, Jeremy Hunt, 55 per cent of British deaths by May 2020 had occurred in nursing homes.

As the crisis progressed and lockdowns became extended, attention focused on the economic costs of COVID-19 regulations. Lockdowns placed huge economic constraints upon the country, whose economic model had been largely reliant upon the service sector, causing declining revenues across a wide range of sectors and the virtual collapse of the hospitality sector. Driven by falls in spending on 'restaurants, hotels, transport and recreation', the Office for National Statistics (2022b) estimated that GDP had shrunk by almost 20 per cent in the second quarter (April to June) of 2020.

To contextualise this, the fall in household spending over this period was the 'largest quarterly contraction on record', and the drop in GDP for the second quarter alone was almost three times the collective effect of the 2008–9 recession.

The distinction drawn between a health and an economic crisis painted a false dichotomy (see, for example, UCL, 2020; Escandon et al, 2021; Wenham, 2021; Fairclough, 2022). Proponents of such a distinction erroneously argued, either implicitly or explicitly, that health policy had no bearing on economic factors such as GDP. Such definitions did, though, have important implications for the framing of events. Just as in the case of the 2008 GFC, different distinctions and narratives sought to explain the crisis and offer responses for overcoming it. Following the events of 2008, the Conservatives' successful redefinition of events as a debt crisis emphasised notions of debt rather than growth (see Chapter 13). By presenting the two policy areas as distinct, it was argued that what was primarily a health crisis had become an economic crisis. It was therefore argued that an acceptable level of risk or health trade-offs must be accepted in order to alleviate the economic problems faced by business owners, particularly in the hospitality sector.

Such ideas were put forward by Chancellor Rishi Sunak (2020) in the autumn of 2020. Sunak declared in the Autumn Statement that there was now 'an economic emergency' and that COVID had created a situation that was 'clearly unsustainable over the medium term' (the UK was forecast to have borrowed 19 per cent of its GDP, £394 billion, in 2020 alone).

Similar concerns, this time at a microeconomic level, led Sunak to launch his 'Eat Out to Help Out' scheme in August 2020. Through this, the government subsidised the purchase of meals and soft drinks to eat in certain dining establishments on certain nights of the week to boost the hospitality industry. The cost of the scheme was £840 million (BBC News, 2023b).

Giving evidence to the COVID-19 inquiry, Patrick Vallance, the government's Chief Scientific Adviser, argued that the government's flagship 'Eat Out to Help Out' scheme in the summer of 2020 'completely reversed' previous government messages that mixing between households, particularly indoors, was high risk. Government scientists claimed they were omitted from the discussions surrounding the scheme and only learnt about it after it was announced by the government (BBC News, 2023b).

Another defining feature of the COVID crisis was the lack of adherence to the rules by senior government ministers. On Friday 27 March 2020, pictures emerged of Johnson's senior adviser, Dominic Cummings, dashing from Downing Street to attend to his wife, who had contracted the virus. In an apparent breach of the rules, which stated that if one family member had contracted COVID-19, the household was expected to isolate, Cummings returned to work and further 'skirted the rules again that evening by driving his family 264 miles up to Durham to stay on his parents' farm'. Cummings would later claim that this journey north was to allow for childcare for his four-year-old *should* he and his wife both become incapacitated (Calvert and Arbuthnott, 2021, p 234, emphasis added).

Although senior figures tried to excuse Cummings's behaviour (see for instance BBC News, 2020), the act of driving halfway across the country ran in stark contrast to the simple government message 'Stay Home. Protect the NHS. Save Lives', which dominated the early briefings. Less than a week earlier, Jenny Harries (England's Chief Medical Officer) had been asked for her advice to parents if they became ill. Dr Harries replied, 'If the individuals do not have access to care support, formal care support or access to family, they will be able to work through their local authority hubs' (*The Telegraph*, 2020).

Cummings was not alone; Health Secretary Matt Hancock resigned in June 2021 after pictures and video emerged of him having an extramarital affair and breaking social distancing guidance (BBC News, 2021b). Other politicians to breach the guidance included MP Margaret Ferrier, who lost the SNP whip after travelling between Glasgow and London while knowingly symptomatic with COVID, and Shaun Bailey (Conservative) who stepped down from two London Assembly roles over attending a party in breach of lockdown rules in December 2020 (Dimsdale, 2022).

Such scandals threatened to generate a legitimation crisis, whereby citizens withdraw legitimacy from the political-administrative system, which in turn could challenge wider political stability (Ibsen, 2019, p 801). Polling indicated that the vast majority of people watched or knew about the daily televised COVID briefings and the government's messages regarding the rules (Statista, 2021). The briefings presented the rules as 'simple message(s)' and, two days prior to Mr Cummings's trip, politicians argued that these were 'clear' (for example, Hansard, 2020c).

Cummings later admitted that the episode 'undermined public confidence' in the handling of COVID-19 (BBC News, 2021a). The breaking of the news story led to confidence in the national government's handling of the pandemic decreasing in England. Scotland and Wales – where health policy is a devolved matter – saw 'no similar decrease'. Indeed support for the devolved administrations was consistently higher than the national government throughout COVID (Bland, 2020; Macfarlane, 2024).

Crisis resolution

Crises require immediate action to achieve resolution. The government's initial slow response to COVID-19 was due to a downplaying of the importance of the crisis. However, after this initial phase, once the idea of lockdowns was taken seriously, the government rapidly increased spending on protective equipment and tools designed to overcome the virus (for example, 'test and trace' and vaccinations).

The government's main response to the crisis consisted of a lockdown to try and prevent the transmission of the virus. The first nationwide lockdown was announced on 23 March 2020, coming into force from the 26th. This was eased in June and replaced with a localised or tiered approach. A second English lockdown was announced on 31 October and commenced on 5 November for four weeks. Controversially, the government allowed mixing of three households over the Christmas period, over a five-day grace period, despite areas such as London being in the highest 'tier' of lockdown restrictions, before a third English lockdown came into force on 6 January 2021 (Institute for Government, 2021).

Although the exact impact of lockdowns is hard to gauge, the UK followed a pattern in which 'a succession of … lockdowns, curfews, closures, and circuit breakers were applied with initial but unsustained success' (Pawson, 2023, pp 140, 152). Lockdowns did, however, appear to save the NHS from being overburdened (or collapsing), acting as a mechanism to 'buy time' ahead of the development and roll-out of a vaccination programme. The first vaccination was given on 8 December 2020.

Government coordination relied upon an expansion of the state. In addition to the lockdown measures outlined earlier, the state expanded its estimates of the additional government spending as a result of COVID-19, ranging from £310 to £410 billion. Funding was used for the Jobs Retention Scheme or 'furlough scheme', which helped businesses cover the costs of employees' wages, business loans and guarantees. Funding was also used, more successfully, to help research and pay for vaccinations. Total spending as a proportion of the economy had 'grown to its highest sustained level since the 1970s' (Brien and Keep, 2022).

Such spending lacked the normal scrutiny and had varying degrees of success. The state funded, to the tune of £37 billion, a 'test and trace' scheme which sought to identify if individuals had been in close contact with someone who self-reported having COVID-19 to allow them to isolate and thus reduce the spread of the disease.

However, such an expansion was not without problems; in rapidly growing welfare payments, the government failed to exert robust checks on spending. Analysis conducted by Oxford University's Centre for Evidence-Based Medicine estimates that £1 in every £3 spent by the government on COVID contracts was lost due to fraud. The cost of 'twenty-eight contracts worth *£4.1 billion* went to firms with known political connections, while 51 worth *£4bn* went through a "*VIP lane*" for companies recommended by MPs and peers, a practice the High Court ruled was unlawful' (Johnson, 2024, original emphasis).

Such questions were also asked during the crisis. The Public Accounts Committee widely criticised the money spent on 'test and trace', concluding that 'there is still no clear evidence of NHST&T's overall effectiveness; and it's not clear whether its contribution to reducing infection levels – as opposed to the other measures introduced to tackle the pandemic – can justify its "unimaginable" costs' (Public Accounts Committee, 2021).

Some responses to crises actively seek to uphold the status quo – for example, the change in government in 1931 following the 'Great Slump' (see Chapter 7). The government's response to and subsequent framing of COVID-19 fits into the latter category. Jarvis (2022, pp 24–5) notes that underpinning the construction of the COVID narrative were 'a series of important, but distinct, claims about temporality'. Such claims prevented alternative discourses of COVID-19 from gaining traction and prevented widespread critique of the government's handling from emerging during the worst of the crisis. Yet they also enabled the government to control the narrative post-COVID, which in turn helped mitigate against a paradigm shift.

Prior to the pandemic, austerity was the key macroeconomic paradigm (on this issue see Stanley, 2022; Hastings, 2023). The pandemic led to a vast increase in government borrowing and debt, which dwarfed the quantitative easing programme introduced in the wake of the 2008 crisis, yet for the Conservative government this was still viewed within the prism of austerity and the need to 'balance the (nation's) books'. In his 2022 Autumn Statement, Jeremy Hunt (2022) argued that 'The furlough scheme, the vaccine roll-out, and the response of the NHS did our country proud – but they all have to be paid for'. However, just as Osborne had done a decade earlier (see Berry, C. 2016), the austerity was intended to be back-loaded. According to Hunt, debt would peak only in 2025–26 (importantly after the next general election), before falling later in the decade.

As yet, there has been little sign of wider adoption of some of the language used to define social relations during COVID-19. Faced with mounting industrial action in the summer of 2022 and beyond, the government and sympathetic media outlets have abandoned the terminology of key workers, favouring instead a return to the classifications based on education, such as 'low-skilled' workers. These policies deliberately prevent a paradigm shift and stop social learning from occurring.

Such pre-existing narratives were further reinforced by the language used to describe public sector workers' involvement in pay claims in 2023 and 2024. Language drew upon an understanding of industrial disputes in the 1970s and 1980s and largely overlooked the contribution that professions such as doctors, nurses, railway workers and teachers made during the pandemic (see, for example, Partington, 2023).

Nor did the pandemic generate any radical long-term shifts in public opinion. Sacrifices were framed as being made in the short term, allowing a return to normal. Even the Thursday night clapping, which saw the largest engagement, with almost seven in ten respondents to a YouGov poll conducted in May 2020 saying they had taken part, saw mixed public responses, with just under half (44 per cent) seeing the event as 'politicised', and just three quarters (73 per cent) believing that 'they and their neighbours were being sincere in their appreciation' (Manthorpe et al, 2021, p 1444). However, there was little appetite to continue the exercise; 63 per cent of respondents in the same poll agreed that the clapping should end, while half of respondents (50 per cent) saw the weekly event as less meaningful than it had been a few weeks before (YouGov, 2020).

Other economic crises, such as 1979, led to a new economic paradigm as they required a new means of conceptualising what went wrong. In the 1980s, monetarism, it was argued, could explain the economic problems Britain faced in a way that Keynesian economics was unable to do. In 2020–21, there was no similar need. The economic crisis this time was 'deliberate' (Stanley, 2022, p 165); it did not occur due to policy failures or unintended outcomes of existing policy – it was widely known and understood that by pursuing lockdowns and restricting people's movements, economic activity would decrease. Yet this was the trade-off that was accepted within the government. A recession was induced in order to preserve future, post-COVID, growth. As Stanley (2022, p 165) continues, 'productive economic activity was deliberately frozen with the hope of preserving it, so that it could be thawed and reanimated at a later date' when the health risks associated with the pandemic had been mitigated. Here, then, the economic problems were not a challenge to the existing growth model; they were not delegitimised in the same manner as previous paradigms and therefore were viewed as providing the best understanding of a successful economic model.

In other areas too, COVID has failed to generate widespread changes. Initial understandings of the government's approach to COVID-19 argued that a new Keynesian economic paradigm was emerging. The spending programmes associated with the furlough scheme and loan guarantees to businesses were understood as marking a rupture from the prevailing neoliberal paradigm. Such 'exceptional monetary policies' were compared to the stimulus packages agreed upon in the wake of the 2008 GFC (Davies and Gane, 2021, p 15).

Yet, just as the 2008 GFC failed to instigate a long-term paradigm shift, austerity policies returned as these facilitated a return to 'normal', neoliberal, policy making (see the previous chapter and Hay, 2013). Just as in the decade following the financial crisis, and in the case of the UK especially after 2010, questions of 'sustainability' and inflation offered a revisionist understanding of the stimulus package offered by the government. Such ideas rested upon an understanding of a 'COVID–Keynesianism' crisis and facilitated a return to fiscal conservatism, in particular through promoting understandings of prudence and calls for the Bank of England to address rising inflation (Wood, Ausserladscheider, and Sparkes, 2023, p 20).

In other ways, the COVID crisis holds parallels with the Irish Home Rule crisis. Although vaccinations have been able to provide some protection for the population, COVID-19 continues to be a health issue, and its wider implications are not yet settled. Indeed, it has become commonly accepted within political discourse that it would be almost impossible to return to a pre-COVID scenario whereby there were no illnesses or deaths attributed to COVID-19. Instead, other issues, such as the cost-of-living crisis or the war in Ukraine, have come to dominate the political discourse. Although neither are viewed in the UK to the same degree as the First World War, which is often credited with preventing civil war on the island of Ireland in 1914 (see Chapter 5), both have been able to shift media and political discourses away from COVID without first requiring an apparent 'resolution' to the crisis.

Setting a date as the 'end' of the crisis is arbitrary and not based on scientific evidence or modelling. Claims of the pandemic being 'over' are contested. The editorial of the *Lancet* in January 2023 was entitled 'The COVID-19 Pandemic in 2023: Far from Over' (*The Lancet*, 2023, p 79). Equally, COVID rates in other countries, especially those where access to vaccinations is lower, demonstrate that there exists the potential for a new strain of the virus to spread to countries such as the UK.

Legacy

Given the short time frame between the crisis losing salience and the writing of this book, unpacking COVID's legacy is full of uncertainties. How the crisis will come to be seen in the future will rely upon outcomes of policies that are still very much developing and revisionist accounts, as in the case of other crises, such as the First World War (see Chapter 5).

Although the crisis was unprecedented, much of the response was designed to maintain socio-economic relations. They promoted the existing capitalist structure rather than radically overhauling it; 'already powerful institutions were granted more power … already dominant firms were able to exploit their positions for higher profits' (Davies et al, 2022, p 4). Stanley (2022, p 158) further argues that although the crisis offered many opportunities, they were linked to the same questions about the state and nation, rather than representing a challenge to the relationship between the state and the market.

The previous section indicated that the pandemic largely failed to instigate a new paradigm shift. In this regard, words such as 'key workers' have been replaced to the extent that the last Conservative government sought to limit trade union powers in areas such as railways, through mandating 'minimum service' levels (Gov.UK, 2023).

The legacy of the crisis may also be dependent upon the new government elected in July 2024. Key elections following crises, such as 1945 after the end of the Second World War in Europe or the 2010 general election following the 2008 GFC, shift narratives and our understanding of both the crisis itself and its legacy.

However, unlike in other crises where elections have had a profound impact upon the crisis (for example, 1931 or 1979; see Chapters 7 and 10), the 2024 election came two years after the issue of COVID had dissipated from media and political salience. The term 'COVID' appeared just five times in Labour's 2024 general election manifesto: once in relation to waiting times, once to the broad COVID Inquiry established by the previous government, once to future pandemic planning and twice to negative notions of COVID contracts. One of these references pledged to appoint a 'fixed term COVID Corruption Commissioner' (The Labour Party, 2024, p 19).

Just as in the case of the London Bombings, some of the material needed to assess the crisis is highly specialist and requires forensic examination (see Chapter 12). Questions of what worked, to what extent policies worked and what did not are highly specialised. Obtaining a scientific or research-led understanding of the events of COVID-19 is time-consuming. An official inquiry was launched in October 2022 and, at the time of writing (autumn 2024), is currently still gathering evidence, with a further inquiry also taking place in Scotland (UK COVID-19 Inquiry, 2024). The publication of these reports may offer a further means for understanding the legacy of, or shifting discourses relating to, COVID-19, though doing so would require the creation of a coordinated political will to return to a crisis that has lost salience within the media and public.

Conclusion

As Chapter 2 demonstrated, crises lead to the prioritisation of a particular policy area. In the case of COVID-19, health policy was promised through slogans such as 'protect the NHS'. These policies came at the expense of economic policy; by introducing measures including lockdowns and restrictions on travel and leisure activities, the government knowingly restricted economic growth, causing a recession in order to achieve more salient priorities in health policy.

Linked to this was an expansion of the state. Despite initial reluctance from ministers and even the Prime Minister as the crisis unfolded, it became politically necessary to expand the role of the state. Although the country was not seen as being threatened in the crisis as it had been in both world wars, restrictions were brought in to ensure the safety of the population. In addition to this, the state, through funding programmes, was crucial to finding a solution (that is, vaccines) to the crisis.

Such expansion, however, was framed as temporary. Ministers, including the Prime Minister, expressed their regret at having to impose restrictions on individual freedoms. By defining policies as temporary, the government was able to prevent a paradigm shift, demonstrating links between crisis narratives and paradigm shifts (or lack of them) introduced in Chapter 2.

The temporary nature of such restrictions and the timings of their easing also highlight the subjectivity of crises. Just as in the case of the Irish Home Rule Bill in 1914, there was little to suggest that the threats posed by COVID had abated when restrictions were eased (indeed, after the first easing of restrictions, subsequent lockdowns were imposed). Yet from the vantage point of mid-2024, the crisis has slipped from public salience as other issues (such as the cost of living) have gained importance.

Further reading

Although the literature relating to COVID-19 is still in its infancy, the key scholarly account of COVID is Adam Tooze's (2021) *Shutdown: How Covid Shook the World's Economy*. A British perspective of the crisis is also offered in the final chapter of Liam Stanley's (2022) *Britain Alone*. Key articles exploring the language and discourse of COVID include Alan Finlayson et al. (2023), 'COVID-19 and "the Public": UK Government, Discourse and the British Political Tradition', and Steven Kettel and Peter Kerr's (2021) '"Guided by the Science": (De)politicising the UK Government's Response to the Coronavirus Crisis'.

Many of those involved in government during COVID are yet to publish memoirs, some due to remaining in government post-COVID (such as Sunak). Boris Johnson is an exception to this; however, his autobiography, *Unleashed* (2024) offers a highly politicised account of the crisis. Noted for the speed at which the book was written, critics have viewed the comments on COVID as blame avoidance and attempts to dismiss rule breaking in Number 10 as malicious leaks.

Johnson's account is challenged by Jonathan Calvert and George Arbuthnott (2021), investigatory journalists from the *Sunday Times*, in their book *Failures of State*. As the title suggests, this blames Johnson and his wider government for a number of errors in the handling of the crisis, from missing COBRA meetings to the easing of restrictions in the summer of 2020.

15

Conclusion

Introduction

The crises covered in this book transcend different policy areas, but crises are a frequent and key part of modern Britain. They are also entities that, at least in a comparative context, have been downplayed. While crises have been explored individually, there have been fewer attempts to amalgamate and learn from recent British crises. This is less so in the European Union, for example (Dinan, Nugent, and Paterson, 2017; Matthijs, 2020; Riddervold, Trondal, and Newsom, 2021).

Such trends, however, are not unique to Britain, and many of the crises explored here directly involved other nation states. Other countries have also experienced crises that Britain has been immune to, presenting wider narratives and discourses of crises. Since the 1970s, discourses surrounding the crisis of the politics of liberal democracy have been explored in various guises (for example, Habermas, 1998).

In a British context, this change is often assimilated with understandings or notions of decline, to the extent that Williams (2000, p 20) argues that 'the question of relative economic decline has dominated peacetime politics in Britain for much of the twentieth century'. Such decline is well observed and by the early 1990s had become 'the central fact about British politics for a century, a major preoccupation of its public intellectuals and intermittently but increasingly of its political leaders' (Gamble, 1993, p xiii; see also English and Kenny, 2001). Such decline, at least in economic terms, is relative rather than absolute – Britain remains one of the largest economies in the world – but its position has been superseded first by the US and more recently by China, Germany, India and Japan. Notions of decline have not been confined to the economic sphere but are also linked to Britain's role in the world – starting with the decline and loss of empire and, more recently, international retrenchment following the Brexit process. Partly, this is to confuse notions of sovereignty and self-sufficiency. As Gamble (1993, p 3) later identifies, Britain 'abandoned self-sufficiency and became dependent for its survival on the wider world economy' – such themes were a key part of early classical economist thinkers like Adam Smith or David Ricardo.

Tomlinson (2009, p 228) argues that such an understanding of 'declinism' ignores wider changes. He contends that the term has become overused to the extent that advocates, over some 130 years, have argued that:

> Every industry or even company's failure to match performance in another country has been commonly treated not as part of the rough and tumble life of global capitalism, or even as the result of contingent error and miscalculation, but rather as a symptom of profound economic, but also political, social and cultural malaise.

A more nuanced account of what has gone wrong, incorporating some of the themes Tomlinson identifies, is required. In part, this can be achieved by offering an empirical examination of key events, such as crises.

Notions of declinism and crisis overlap. This is particularly true where blame has been appropriated. An example is the narratives of the 'British Disease' that emerged in the 1960s and 1970s and sought to blame the trade unions for a lack of productivity growth to match inflation (such themes are linked to the Winter of Discontent – see Chapter 10). Gamble (1993, p xv) suggests that understandings of declinism were made 'plausible' by a series of crises.

Others have sought to contextualise a series of events or crises through broader notions of change. Davis (2024, pp 6–7) argues that modernisation theorists reject the negative associations of crisis or declinism, but instead point to cyclical disruption and renewal. Although the term 'crisis' is used in such understandings, it 'ignores the progress that has taken place over the *longue duree*'.

This does not mean that crises are not worth exploring. Those entrapped within crises seek short-term solutions and prioritise a range of competing issues accordingly, rather than seek a 'big history' approach (Davis, 2024, p 7). For example, when faced with immediate security issues, such as in times of war, we would expect questions of climate change to be deprioritised. Crises are inherently short-term events that threaten/impose large-scale disruption to contemporary politics. Defining a set of events as a crisis generates an expectation that solutions will be sought and found and that the current situation will be only temporary. In contrast, longer-term trends can only be seen, viewed and analysed after the events – and when anomalies are removed. This may not be reflective of people's own experiences – for example, Davis draws upon increasing global life expectancy between 1900 and 2022. This reflects broader measures such as vaccination roll-outs, public health campaigns and scientific discovery. However, such improvements are not evenly spread, and certain aspects of them will not be felt by every single person or group of persons. Such nuances matter, especially in democracies where governments are elected based upon the day-to-day, often short-termist, concerns of voters. Governments, which periodically have to face electorates, may have little incentive for long-term planning but are frequently punished for short-term problems or crises.

Reducing history to long-term trends further denies agency, which, as Chapter 2 demonstrated, is important in crises. Longer-term trends, such as neoliberalism or globalisation, are often presented as inevitable, something that individuals must adapt or succumb to and hold little power to stop. Crises challenge this assertion in several ways; first, those involved in crises may have the power to generate and shift narratives – crises, by their definition, denote a failure, and new narratives to explain this are required (see Chapter 2). Second, crises can emphasise the role of agents in casting blame. For example, the terrorist attacks of 7/7 emphasised the role of the bombers – those who defied the law to detonate explosive devices on London's transportation network (see Chapter 12), equally the Global Financial Crisis (GFC) and subsequent debt narratives emphasised the role that senior bankers and welfare recipients played in the crisis (see Chapter 13).

The language of declinism is distinct from that of crises. Tracing the history of declinism back to the nineteenth century, scholars such as Gamble (1993) and English and Kenny (1999) present it as a historical, rather than political phenomenon – though this is not to say there are not political ramifications of such language. Declinism can therefore been seen as more gradual, more deterministic, with less (or limited) agency for contemporary politicians or actors; Britain has limited ability to stop or prevent other countries from growing their economies at a faster rate (and indeed has benefited from such growth – through the ability to purchase cheap manufactured goods from countries such as China and India).

There also exists a tendency to overstate the notion of decline – to assume a degree of homogeneity (for a critique of such understandings, see English and Kenny, 1999, p 261). Discourses of declinism are also politically motivated; they can bring together coalitions of like-minded individuals in an attempt to change the status quo. Ralston (2022, pp 668–9) notes that narratives of declinism in parliamentary discourse in the post-Second World War period did not match economic indicators. In particular, Ralston identifies a relative lack of a declinist narrative from the 1950s to the 1970s, 'when Britain's decline vis-à-vis other major powers was most steep'.

Crises, by contrast, are viewed as contemporary events (certainly until they are 'resolved'). As Chapter 1 establishes, they are predicated on the assumption that alternatives exist and could be implemented and that any decisions about how to respond require such trade-offs. Here, then, crises offer an alternative understanding to gradual declinism. Crises are key turning points, or 'moments of decisive intervention' (Hay, 1999a, p 317) that at least offer the potential for radical new action (for example, actions that could halt or reverse any decline).

As Hall (1993) argues, crises can generate new means of understanding or conceptualising the world around us. They can generate different policies with different objectives. The incorporation of such new paradigms is not simply about reversing existing trends – though alleviation from the crisis may be a significant factor in any shift – but about better understanding policy and ensuring the crisis is not repeated.

Another key difference between exploring crises and notions of declinism is the formers' ability to instigate change. Although crises are seen as inherently suboptimal (see Chapter 2), they are also seen as temporary events. They do not offer permanence in the same way narratives of declinism do. The saying 'in every crisis there is opportunity' is testimony to this. By their very nature, crises encourage and compel changes to the status quo in a manner that declinism does not. As Hall (1993) identifies, when a paradigm is challenged, the primary task of any replacing paradigm is to explain what has gone wrong before offering solutions.

As this book demonstrates, crises do not exist in isolation; they challenge existing understandings and can promote new ideas. Though this, of course, does not mean that new policies are infallible – the resolution to one crisis may lead to future crises. For example, incorporating the Irish Parliamentary Party into the coalition forged by the Liberals in 1910 to secure the passage first of the budget and then of what became the 1911 Parliament Act gave prominence to the question of Irish Home Rule, which itself became a crisis for the British state.

Hall (1993, p 277) notes that the best indicator of any policy at time-1 is the previous policy (at time-0). Crises can and do frequently disrupt such policies. Crises can lead to significant paradigm shifts that alter policies in certain areas, along with expectations of policy tools. Hall (1993, p 284) draws upon the example of the 1980s, where monetarism replaced Keynesianism and, in doing so, offered a new understanding of 'how the economy itself worked'. For example, advocates of monetarism disagreed that the state could reduce unemployment, in the long term, and argued that unemployment had a 'natural rate' determined by labour market conditions rather than by macroeconomic policies.

Crises are not the only means by which significant change occurs. Richards (2023) highlights ten turning points in his exploration of Britain since the end of the Second World War. Some of these (Suez, the 2008 GFC and COVID-19) overlap with the crises highlighted in this book. Others are related to them; for example, the election results of 1945 and 1979 can be seen as immediate products of the Second World War and the Winter of Discontent, respectively. Other turning points, such as the 1967 Abortion Act, cannot be defined as a crisis in the same manner, but rather would link to Hall's (1993) understanding of 'normal policy making'.

It is clear that an understanding of crises as an abstract concept helps to illuminate contemporary British politics. In this regard, this book takes as its starting point the need to answer the questions 'what did happen?' and 'why did it happen?' rather than focus on 'what should have happened?'; though, of course, crises are not inseparable from such normative questions. The reference points obtained by answering this question offer expectations, which, when unmet, can lead to a crisis (or multiple crises) being declared.

As Chapter 2 highlights, crises are reactionary events – they respond to events that have taken place. This means that some form of barometer must be identified to measure expectations (derived from understandings of how politics *should* operate) and set the current outcomes/scenario against these. As each chapter demonstrates, notions of blame are offered to denote who or what is responsible for such deviations (for example, the House of Lords in the Constitutional Crisis of 1909–10, see Chapter 3, or the trade unions in the case of the General Strike, Winter of Discontent or Miner's Strike, see Chapters 6, 10 and 11 respectively).

The purpose of this book is to demonstrate how crises occur, how they are framed, how blame is assigned, and how crises can be resolved. The 12 crises described also highlight the inequalities within crises. As Chapter 2 noted, this book is not designed to be a definitive account of every crisis in modern British politics. The choices of which crises to include are inevitably subjective, though this should not detract from the comparisons that can be made between these and other crises. Numerous other crises could also be explored if limitations of time and space did not apply.

Unpacking the concept and pathology of crisis in an empirical framework, this book makes seven observations, each of which will be discussed in turn:

- Crises are inherently unequal – they can generate their own inequalities but also draw upon existing inequalities.
- Crises, although suboptimal events, are subjective – they can be (re)defined by individuals/governments and created for political purposes.
- Crises are non-deterministic events – the parameters of policy can and do change within a crisis – for example, leaving the gold standard in 1931. This links to Hall's (1993) notion of social learning.
- Controlling (the media) narrative is important – for example, the 1926 General Strike and the 1956 Suez Crisis.
- The role of the state expands during times of crisis.
- Blamed groups are often, but not always, excluded from crises – for example, the House of Lords in 1910, the Ulster Volunteer Force in 1914, bankers in 2008.
- The 'resolution' to a crisis is subjective and again can be exploited for political purposes.

Although explored in terms of the crises outlined in the previous 12 chapters, these points also extend to other crises, which have not been explored in this book. As the term 'crisis' becomes increasingly used by the media and politicians to discuss contemporary events, a holistic understanding of the term will enable us to accurately dissect narratives and events.

Crises are unequal

The examples offered in this book further demonstrate inequalities within crises, especially over notions of blame and framing. Crises are inherently unequal events that can magnify existing inequalities. The ability of key groups to control the political agenda (for example, governments in both world wars through censorship and regulation, and reliance on pro-government sources such as the BBC, as well as creating the *British Gazette* during the General Strike of 1926) helped frame events in a particular manner and strengthened public support.

Inequalities may also exist for those caught up in the crisis. High-profile figures who are seen to be closer to the events, even if they did not directly generate problems themselves, can receive greater attention (for example, Anthony Eden during the Suez Crisis, having previously been Foreign Secretary, or Gordon Brown during the GFC, having previously been Chancellor of the Exchequer). Such individuals were blamed for more than their incumbency of powerful positions, but also the roles they played in determining policy prior to the crisis. In contrast, senior Conservatives were not blamed for the onset of COVID-19 despite the party being in government and thus in charge of health policy for the previous ten years, as it was accepted that the crisis emanated from an external source.

Inequalities also exist in terms of blame. In some crises explored in this book, blame has been levied at structures, homogenising those within certain groups (for example, trade unions). This offers greater propensity for paradigm shifts, such as that which occurred following the Winter of Discontent, than if individuals were blamed, as in the case of the 7/7 terrorist attacks. Here, the government was keen to downplay far-right narratives that sought to homogenise followers of the Islamic faith and instead emphasise the agency of the perpetrators. Such narratives allowed the government to promote the existing status quo and argue that making radical changes would play into the hands of terrorists.

Crises are subjective

The case studies explored here demonstrate that crises can be manufactured or utilised to promote particular agendas. Controlling narratives, especially those contained within the media, is important in this regard. Chapter 13 demonstrated that the change in narrative following the 2010 general election helped to focus attention away from a global crisis to one of UK government spending and helped to usher in austerity politics. Other narratives of crisis have also been important – for example, the government's success in framing the 1926 General Strike as a revolutionary event, both on BBC radio but also in its own publications, linking this to the First World War and enabling the government to present itself as the guarantor of democracy (see Chapter 6).

Some crises are localised and may not be equally felt by the entire nation – for example, the Irish Home Rule Crisis or the London Bombings of 2005. Other localisation may occur at an industry level, such as the 1984–85 Miners' Strike, which failed to impact upon coal supplies as an earlier strike in 1974 had done and was therefore arguably more localised than other crises (for example, the Second World War or the 2008 GFC, which transcended different sectors of the economy).

Even when the term 'crisis' is appropriate, differing parties within the crisis may disagree on the terms of the crisis. The Irish Home Rule Crisis could be viewed as a crisis of the UK state but also of democracy and self-determination for the population of Ulster (see Chapter 4). Another example of different perspectives leading to competing narratives within a single crisis is the distinction between a health and an economic crisis within the language and discourses surrounding COVID-19 (see Chapter 14).

Crises as non-deterministic events

As stated in Chapter 2, crises rest upon notions of choice(s). Crises are not simply limitations or deterministic events. By declaring or suggesting that a crisis has occurred and blaming others (either agents or structures), it is implied that alternative options could have been pursued. Key junctures in crises demonstrate this; for example, the calling of strike actions (as in the case of the General Strike or the Miners' Strike, see Chapters 6 and 11), declarations of war (see Chapters 5 and 8) or the actions of terrorists (see Chapter 12). In other crises, the choices involved may be less obvious or longer term, for example, COVID-19, which is largely understood to relate to the consumption of particular animals, or the Great Slump of 1931, which was linked to economic choices in the 1920s (see Chapters 14 and 7, respectively). Choices are not confined to aggregate or formal politics but transcend into our everyday lives; crises can also offer choices for our own involvement – for example, COVID led to individuals thinking about their interactions with others who might or might not be infected and the need to take appropriate precautions, such as vaccinations or meeting in well-ventilated areas. This is not to make judgements about the appropriateness or justification of such actions. It may be felt that avoiding any crisis (be it a national or individual/ personal one) is unrealistic, but avoiding any specific crisis certainly is.

Within crises, too, options exist which lead to policy choices. Perceived wisdom or particular narratives and assertions can, and do, change during crises. As Hall (1993) notes, crises happen because existing paradigms fail to explain what is occurring, thus requiring a new paradigm to emerge. Crises also challenge and change the constraints faced by policy makers; for example, the Labour government's belief that it could not leave the gold standard in 1931, a decision that was immediately taken following the formation of the national government (see Chapter 7).

Controlling narratives is important

Once a crisis is declared – and it is accepted that a crisis is occurring – then the key question is 'what kind of a crisis is it?' As Chapter 2 demonstrated, being able to define the terms and parameters of a crisis shapes what solutions can be offered and can gain public acceptance. The transition in 2010 from a financial or banking crisis to a debt crisis shifted the emphasis from regulation of a particular sector to austerity politics and a retrenchment of the state.

Narratives are shaped and disseminated through the media. Newspapers, radio and television, and more recently the internet and social media, are the mediums by which the majority of the population are able to keep abreast of events (in the absence of first-hand experience). Being able to shape such reporting is crucial in shaping the narratives of events. This is exemplified through the decision by both the government and the Trades Union Congress (TUC) in 1926 to create their own newspapers following the print workers' strike which prevented the printing of most national newspapers (see Chapter 6).

Narratives also set the tone for crisis resolution. By generating narratives, parameters of the crisis can be established; often, this is done through labelling or defining the crisis. For example, competing narratives following the economic crisis of 2007–8, of a GFC and a debt or spending crisis, offered two different approaches to resolving the crisis (see Chapter 13).

The role of the state

The state is a key actor in all crises. When caught up in a crisis, as in other emergencies, the population turns to the state (Stanley, 2022, p 160). The vast powers of the state, which exceed those of individuals and organisations (including governments), make it key to liberation efforts. These powers are often overt – for example, the state and the monopoly of the legitimate use of force during both world wars (see Chapters 5 and 8). Other powers held by the state – for example, the ability to (legally) print money – shaped responses to the GFC of 2008 and the financial response to the COVID-19 crisis (see Chapters 13 and 14).

The expansion of the state becomes necessary during times of crisis. In the initial responses to both the First World War and COVID-19, governments were opposed to extending the powers of the state vis-à-vis the pre-crisis period. Yet both Asquith's emphasis on 'business as usual' and Johnson's desire to achieve 'herd immunity' were overturned as the crisis deepened. Even where the crisis has been used to try and diminish the role of the state – for example, austerity following the 2007–8 GFC – this only came about after a large expansion of the state (through the bailing out of commercial banks) and even here, on its own terms, its success has been questioned, with national debt rising between 2010 and 2014/15 (Berry, C., 2016, p 74).

In each of these examples, the state was able to act as an independent player, removed from the crisis. In doing so, it was the saviour rather than orchestrator of events, for example, by utilising its financial power in terms of bank bailouts or reinflationary measures such as the 'Eat Out to Help Out' scheme. Preserving the idea of state independence was also important to the government in the 1984–85 Miners' Strike – with Margaret Thatcher being keen to present the state as separate from the crisis but able and willing to uphold (some would say abuse) the rule of law through engaging with the police service. By framing the state as neutral, the government attempted to legitimise its policy decisions.

The state and its institutions are far from immune from crises, though (on this point, see Richards, Smith, and Hay, 2014). An example was seen during the Irish Home Rule Crisis (see Chapter 4). As the state became the subject of crisis, its powers to effectively 'resolve' the crisis diminished. A civil war would mean that the state, normally the resolver of the crisis, was indeed fighting for its own political survival, akin to both world wars.

Government narratives also purported such threats during the 1926 General Strike, defining the strike action as 'revolution' in a bid to galvanise ordinary citizens into taking action (see Chapter 6). Such narratives, expressed through the government's own media, emphasised the threats to the state that were posed by the crisis.

The redefinition of the 2008 GFC as one of public debt following the election of the Conservative-led coalition government in 2010 offered an alternative conceptualisation of the state. Here, the (welfare) state, it was argued, was complicit in the crisis. Although blame was reserved for the New Labour governments of Blair and Brown, this narrative is distinct from others studied in this book. Through this discourse, the government was able to promote a neoliberal policy agenda and, through pursuing ideological policies of austerity, reduce the scope of the state in certain areas (for example, welfarism).

Blame can lead to exclusion

Blame is not objective, it is not applied after exploring issues and evidence scientifically. Blame does not wait for counter-proposals to be put forward exonerating certain groups or reasonable debate to take place. Blamed groups are often excluded from presenting their version of events – for example, trade unionists in 1979 in the Winter of Discontent or those committing acts of terrorism in 2005 (see Chapters 10 and 12 respectively). Crises are emergencies that require immediate actions; deliberation can often be suspended in such times, and checks are only applied after legislation is passed (see also Chapter 14 on COVID-19 for a further example of this).

Narratives of blame were shaped by the ownership of the media in 1926. In the absence of normal media circulation, the government was able to present the TUC as waging a revolution on the streets of Britain through both its own publication, the *British Gazette*, and the BBC, without engaging with counter-narratives (see Chapter 6). The rise of propaganda during the First World War is further evidence of this (see Chapter 5). Propaganda was used to depict and publicise atrocities committed by opposing forces, strengthening the resolve of ordinary Britons and members of the armed forces to deliver 'justice'.

However, blame only leads to exclusion if others are sufficiently placed to generate a new narrative or policy paradigm. As the 2008 GFC demonstrated, even during the first few years (prior to the 2010 general election), key institutions remained responsible for guiding the UK economy. Certain agents may have been excluded but key institutions such as the Treasury or Bank of England retained and even enhanced their powers due to the specialist knowledge and technical understandings that they were perceived to hold.

Resolutions are subjective

Not all crises are 'resolved'. Some, such as wars or strikes, have definite endings, dates that can be memorised and used to form a historical chronology (see

Chapters 5, 6, 8, 10 and 11). Others are less precise or easy to assign dates to – for example, COVID-19, which, although it has receded from national discussions and salience, continues to impact individuals, either through new infections or legacies of 'long COVID'. In addition to defining what constitutes a crisis, or when crises occur, defining when a crisis ends can also be heavily politicised. For example, politicians may seek to claim credit for 'resolving' a crisis or redefining the parameters of the crisis.

Crises and policies aimed at alleviating crises can also interact with one another. The Irish Home Rule Crisis that left Ireland on the verge of civil war in 1914 was tempered by the First World War and an understanding of a 'common enemy' in Germany. COVID-19 led to the reversal of a decade of austerity policies aimed at alleviating the GFC of 2008. However, here, the solution (or part of it) to one crisis may come at the expense of other crises. As Bailey (2024, p 135) notes, the quantitative easing programme pursued by the Bank of England during the COVID crisis shored up 'the ecologically unsustainable economic status quo at a potentially pivotal moment of critical juncture'.

Linked to this, the effects of some crises are not immediately felt. Some policies aimed at overcoming crises may be temporary– for example, the restrictions put in place during the world wars; others have longer effects, such as Thatcher's anti-union legislation following the Miners' Strike of 1984–85. Resolutions to one crisis may, in turn, lead to other crises; one resolution to the Suez Crisis was to push Britain towards the Eurobond market, which itself became the subject of a crisis over 60 years later. This is not to decry policy choices in the 1950s but to demonstrate that the resolutions to crises may have long-lasting implications.

Multiple crises may also exist simultaneously. These may be localised (in terms of policy or geographic area) or occur at a national or international level. Within this juncture, political actors must determine which resources are afforded to each crisis. While in the case of the Irish Home Rule Crisis, protagonists decided to defuse the situation in favour of a more pressing issue, in other cases, resources have been diverted from one crisis to another – for example from tackling climate change in the name of austerity (Feld and Fetzer, 2024).

Responses to one crisis may also affect others. For example, the terms of the peace treaty with Germany in 1919 fostered a series of events that have been blamed for the onset of the Second World War in 1939 (see Chapter 5 and Keynes, 1920).

Conclusion

As the frequency of crisis narratives has increased, understanding the pathologies and inequalities of crises is important not just in a historical sense but for contemporary understandings of British politics. As the previous chapters highlight, not all crises follow the same pathology, nor are all narratives of events accepted as constituting a crisis. Yet narratives of crises are powerful tools, which can enable groups to divert resources, alter existing policies or exclude certain groups from policy making.

By using 12 case studies from modern British history, this book has sought to develop and deepen existing understandings of crises. In doing so, its contribution is not just to British political history but to the existing literature on crises, exemplified in the seven criteria outlined earlier.

References

Adams, R.J.Q. (1986) The May Coalition and the Coming of Conscription, 1915–1916. *Journal of British Studies*, 25(3), 243–63.

Addison, P. (1977) *The Road to 1945: British Politics and the Second World War.* Quartet Books.

Adeney, M., and Lloyd, J. (1986) *The Miners Strike 1984–85: Loss without Limit.* Routledge & Kegan Paul.

Aldcroft, D.H., and Oliver, M.J. (2000) *Trade Unions and the Economy: 1870–2000.* Ashgate.

Allen, M.J., and Bryan, A. (2011) Remembering the 2005 London Bombings: Media Memory, Commemoration. *Memory Studies*, 4(3), 263–8.

Allington, D., Duffy, B., Wessely, S., Dhavan, N., and Rubin, J. (2021) Health-Protective Behaviour, Social Media Usage and Conspiracy Belief during the COVID-19 Public Health Emergency. *Psychological Medicine*, 51, 1763–9

Allison, G.T. (1969) Conceptual Models and the Cuban Missile Crisis. *American Political Science Review*, LXIII(3), 689–718.

Anderson, J., and O'Dowd, L. (2007) Imperialism and Nationalism: The Home Rule Struggle and Border Creation in Ireland, 1885–1925. *Political Geography*, 26(8), 934–50.

Andrews, M. (2019) Commemorating the First World War in Britain: A Cultural Legacy of Media Remembrance. *Journal of War and Culture Studies*, 12(3), 295–313.

Ashton, N.J. (2002) *Kennedy, Macmillan and the Cold War.* Palgrave Macmillan.

Ashton, P., and Christophers, B. (2015) On Arbitration, Arbitrage and Arbitrariness in Financial Markets and Their Governance: Unpacking LIBOR and the LIBOR Scandal. *Economy and Society*, 44(2), 188–217.

Asquith, M. (2014) *Margot Asquith's Great War Diary 1914–1916.* Oxford University Press.

Aster, S. (1976) *Anthony Eden.* Weidenfeld & Nicolson.

Aster, S. (1989) 'Guilty Men': The Case of Neville Chamberlain. In R. Boyce and E.M. Robertson, *Paths to War: New Essays on the Origins of the Second World War.* Macmillan, pp 233–68.

Atkinson, P., Gobat, N., Lant, S., Mableson, H., Pilbeam, C., Solomon, T., Tonkin-Crine, S., and Sheard, S. (2020) Understanding the Policy Dynamics of COIVD-19 in the UK: Early Findings from Interview with Policy Maker and Health Care Professionals. *Social Science and Medicine*, 266, doi:10.1016/j.socscimed.2020.113423.

Attlee, C. ([1954] 2019) *As It Happened*. Sharpe Books.

Awan, I., Spiller, K., and Whiting, A. (2019) *Terrorism in the Classroom: Security Surveillance and Public Duty to Act*. Palgrave Macmillan.

Bailey, D. (2024) 'Building Back Better' or Sustaining the Unsustainable? The Climate Impacts of Bank of England QE in the Covid-19 Pandemic. *British Politics*, 19, 134–53.

Bailey, M., and Popple, S. (2011) The 1984/85 Miner's Strike: Reclaiming Cultural Heritage. In L. Smith, P.A. Shackel, and G. Campbell (eds), *Heritage, Labour and the Working Classes*. Routledge, pp 19–33.

Baker, A. (2015) Varieties of Economic Crisis, Varities of Ideational Change: How and Why Financial Regulation and Macroeconomic Policy Differ. *New Political Economy*, 20(3), 342–66.

Baker, G. (2007, 21 Aug) No Historical Reason Why Recent Turmoil Should Spark a Recession; the Credit Crunch. *The Times*, p. 38.

Bale, T. (2012) *The Conservatives since 1945: The Drivers of Party Change*. Oxford University Press.

Bale, T. (2023) *The Conservative Party after Brexit: Turmoil and Transformation*. Polity.

Ball, S. (1988) *Baldwin and the Conservative Party: The Crisis of 1929–1931*. Yale University Press.

Ball, S. (2020, 7 May) *Two Days in the Commons Chamber That Took Churchill to No 10: The Norway Debate of May 1940* [online]. Available from Hansard Society: www.hansardsociety.org.uk/blog/two-days-in-the-commons-chamber-that-took-churchill-to-no-10-the-norway [Accessed 26 January 2024].

Ballinger, C. (2011) Hedgeing and Ditching: The Parliament Act 1911. *Parliamentary History*, 30(1), 19–32.

Ballinger (2012) *The House of Lords 1911–2011: A Century of Non-Reform*. Hart Publishing.

Barber, A. (2021) *UK Banks and the Lessons of the Great Financial Crisis*. Palgrave Macmillan.

Barber, S., Brown, J., and Ferguson, D. (2022) Coronavirus: Lockdown Laws. House of Commons Library Research Briefing Paper No 8875 [online]. Available from Parliament UK: https://researchbriefings.files.parliament.uk/documents/CBP-8875/CBP-8875.pdf [Accessed 12 September 2024].

Barnes, D., and Reid, E. (1982) *Governments and Trade Unions: The British Experience 1964–79*. Heinemann Educational Books.

Barrow, B. (2011) It's Even Worse Than We Feared: Cost of National Debt to Each Family Is a Staggering £138,360. Daily Mail Online [online]. Available from: www.dailymail.co.uk/news/article-1374668/UK-debt-crisis-Cost-family-staggering-138–360.html [Accessed 22 June 2023].

Bartlett, J., and Miller, C. (2010) *The Power of Unreason: Conspiracy Theories, Extremism and Counter-Terrorism*. Demos.

Bartlett, T. (2014) When Histories Collide: The Third Home Rule Bill for Ireland. In G. Doherty (ed), *The Home Rule Crisis 1912–14*. Mercier Press, pp 412–42.

Barron, H. (2010) *The 1926 Miners' Lockout: Meanings of Community in the Durham Coalfields*. Oxford University Press.

Basu, L. (2019) Living within Our Means: The UK News Construction of Austerity Frame over Time. *Journalism*, 20(2), 313–30.

BBC (2023) *The General Strike – 1926*. BBC [online]. Available from: www.bbc.co.uk/historyofthebbc/research/editorial-independence/general-strike [Accessed 27 March 2024].

BBC News (2020, 26 May) Dominic Cummings: 'He Didn't Break the Guidelines' Says Gove. BBC News [online]. Available from: www.bbc.co.uk/news/av/uk-52804626 [Accessed 30 January 2023].

BBC News (2021a, 27 June) Matt Hancock Quits as Health Secretary after Breaking Social Distance Guidance. BBC News [online]. Available from: www.bbc.co.uk/news/uk-57625508 [Accessed 25 January 2023].

BBC News (2021b, 26 May) Covid: I Left London during Lockdown Due to Security Threat – Cummings. BBC News [online]. Available from: www.bbc.co.uk/news/uk-politics-57257784 [Accessed 25 January 2023].

BBC News (2023a, 5 July) Covid Inquiry: The UK Pandemic in Numbers. BBC News [online]. Available from: www.bbc.co.uk/news/uk-51768274 [Accessed 3 June 2024].

BBC News (2023b, 11 December) Eat Out to Help Out: What Was the Impact of the Scheme? BBC News [online]. Available from: www.bbc.co.uk/news/uk-67658106#:~:text=The%20scheme%20may%20have%20contributed,scientific%20adviser%2C%20told%20the%20inquiry [Accessed 3 June 2024].

BBC News (2024) South Yorkshire Police Accused of Cover-Up over Miners Strike Files. BBC News [online]. Available from: www.bbc.co.uk/news/uk-england-south-yorkshire-68436258 [Accessed 9 September 2024].

Bean, H., Keranen, L., and Durfy, M. (2011) 'This Is London': Cosmopolitain Nationalism and the Discourse of Resilience in the Case of the 7/7 Terrorist Attacks. *Rhetoric and Public Affairs*, 14(3), 427–64.

Beatty, C., Fothergill, S., and Powell, R. (2007) Twenty Years On: Has the Economy of the UK Coalfields Recovered? *Environment and Planning A*, 39(7), 1654–75.

Beech, M., and Hickson, K. (2007) *Labour's Thinkers: The Intellectual Roots of Labour from Tawney to Gordon Brown*. Tauris Academic Studies.

Bell, S., and Hindmoor, A. (2015) Masters of the Universe but Slaves of the Market: Bankers and the Great Financial Meltdown. *British Journal of Politics and International Relations*, 17(1), 1–22.

Benn, T. (1995) *The Benn Diaries 1940–90*. Arrow Books.

Bennett, R., and Kottasz, R. (2012) Public Attitudes towards the UK Banking Industry following the Global Financial Crisis. *International Journal of Bank Marketing*, 30(2), 128–47.

Bentley, M. (2001) *Lord Salisbury's World: Conservative Environments in Late-Victorian England.* Cambridge University Press.

Berkowitz, D. A. (1997) *Social Meanings of News.* Sage.

Berry, C. (2016) *Austerity Politics and UK Economic Policy.* Palgrave Macmillan.

Berry, M. (2016) No Alternative to Austerity: How BBC Broadcast News Reported the Deficit Debate. *Media, Culture and Society*, 38(6), 844–63.

Bevan, A. (2008) *In Place of Fear.* Aneurin Bevan Society.

Beveridge, W. (1942) *Social Insurance and Allied Services* [The Beveridge Report] His Majesty's Stationery Office

Bevin, E. (1946) Trade Disputes and Trade Unions Bill HC Debate Wednesday 13 February 1946. Hansard [online]. Available from: https://hansard.parliament.uk/Commons/1946-02-13/debates/6c4000b1-636e-42a1-b1a8-f2ca34f983d2/TradeDisputesAndTradeUnionsBill [Accessed 6 December 2024].

Bew, P. (1998) *Ideology and the Irish Question: Ulster Unionism and Irish Nationalism 1912–1916.* Oxford University Press.

Beynon, H., and Hudson, R. (2021) *The Shadow of the Mine: Coal and the End of Industrial Britain.* Verso.

Biagini, E. (2014) The Third Home Rule Bill in British History. In G. Doherty (ed), *The Irish Home Rule Crisis 1912–1914.* Mercia Press. pp 412–42.

Bingham, A., and Conboy, M. (2009) The Daily Mirror and the Creation of a Commercial Popular Language: A People's War, A People's Paper? *Journalism Studies*, 10(5), 639–54.

Birch, A.H. (1984) Overload, Ungovernability and Delegitimation: The Theories and the British Case. *British Journal of Political Science*, 14(2), 135–60.

Black, L., and Pemberton, H. (2009) The Winter of Discontent in British Politics. *The Political Quarterly*, 80(4), 553–61.

Blagden, D. (2021) Roleplay, Realpolitik and 'Great Powerness' the Logical Distinction between Survival and Social Performance in Grand Strategy. *European Journal of International Relations*, 27(4), 1162–92.

Blair, T. (1997, 31 March) We Won't Look Back to the 1970s. *The Times*, p 20.

Blair, T. (2010) *A Journey.* Arrow

Bland, A. (2020) The Cummings Effect: Study Finds Public Faith was Lost After Aide's Trip. Thre Guardian [online] Available from: https://www.theguardian.com/politics/2020/aug/06/the-cummings-effect-study-finds-public-faith-was-lost-after-aides-trip [Accessed 15 July 2025].

Blaxill, L. (2013) Quantifying the Language of British Politics, 1880–1910. *Historical Research*, 86(232), 313–41.

Blewett, N. (1972) *Peers, the Parties, the People: General Election 1910.* Palgrave.

Blyth, M. (2013a) Policy Paradigms in Two Moments of Crisis. *Governance*, 26(2), 197–215.

Blyth, M. (2013b) *Austerity: The History of a Dangerous Idea.* Oxford Univeristy Press.

Bogdanor, V. (1997) *The Monarchy and the Constitution.* Oxford University Press.

Bogdanor, V. (2016) The IMF Crisis of 1976. Gresham College [online]. Available from: www.gresham.ac.uk/lectures-and-events/the-imf-crisis-1976 [Accessed 23 August 2021].

Booth, A. (1996) How Long Are Light Years in British Politics? The Labour Party's Economic Ideas in the 1930s. *Twentieth Century British History*, 7(1), 1–26.

Boughton, J.M. (2000) From Suez to Tequila: The IMF as Crisis Manager. *The Economic Journal*, 110(460), 273–91.

Boughton, J.M. (2001) Northwest of Suez: The 1956 Crisis and the IMF. *International Monetary Fund Staff Papers*, 48(3)

Bowman, T. (2007) *Carson's Army: The Ulster Volunteer Force 1910–22.* Manchester University Press.

Boyce, D.G. (1996) *The Irish Question and British Politics 1868–1986.* Macmillan.

Boyce, R. (1988) Creating the Myth of Consensus: Public Opinion and Britain's Return to the Gold Standard in 1925. In P.L. Cottrell and D.E. Moggridge (eds), *Money and Power: Essays in Honour of L.S. Pressnell.* Macmillan, pp 173–97.

Boyer, R. (2012) The Four Fallacies of Contemporary Austerity Policies: The Lost Keynesian Legacy. *Cambridge Journal of Economics*, 36(1), 283–312.

Boyle, P.G. (2001) Eisenhower, Eden and the Suez Crisis. In J. Hollowell (ed), *Twentieth Century Anglo-American Relations.* Basingstoke. pp 166–79.

Brien, P., and Keep, M. (2022, 29 March) Public Spending during the Covid-19 Pandemic. House of Commons Library [online]. Available from: https://researchbriefings.files.parliament.uk/documents/CBP-9309/CBP-9309.pdf [Accessed 24 January 2023].

Briggs, J.E. (1998) *Strikes in Politicisation.* Routledge.

Brittan, S. (1977) The Economic Contradictions of Democracy. *British Journal of Political Science*, 5(2), 129–59.

Broadberry, S.N. (1986) *The British Economy between the Wars.* Basil Blackwell.

Broadberry, S., and Howlett, P. (2009) The United Kingdom during World War I: Business as Usual? In S. Broadberry and M. Harrison (eds), *The Economics of World War I.* Cambridge University Press, pp 206–34.

Bromley, M. (1999) Was It the Mirror Wot Won It? The Development of the Tabloid Press during the Second World War. In N. Hayes and J. Hill (eds), *'Millions Like Us?' British Culture in the Second World War.* Liverpool University Press, pp 93–124.

Brooke, S. (1992) *Labour's War: The Labour Party and the Second World War.* Oxford University Press.

Brookes, R. (1985) The Little Man and the Slump: Sidney Strube's Cartoons and the Politics of Unemployment 1929–31. *Oxford Art Journal*, 8(1), 49–61.

Brown, G. (2001) The Conditions for High and Stable Growth and Employment. *The Economic Journal*, 111(471), 30–44.

Brown, G. (2011) *Beyond the Crash: Overcoming the First Crisis of Globalization.* Simon & Schuster.

Brown, G. (2017) *My Life, Our Times.* Vintage

Brown, S.D., Allen, M., and Reavey, P. (2015) Remembering 7/7: The Collective Shaping of Survivors' Personal Memories of the 2005 London Bombing. In: A.L. Tota and T. Hagen (eds), *Routledge International Handbook of Memory Studies*. Routledge, pp 428–44.

Buckley, S.B. (2015) The State, the Police and the Judiciary in the Miners' Strike: Observations and Discussions, Thirty Years On. *Capital and Class*, 39(3), 419–34.

Buitenhuis, P. (1987) *The Great War of Words: British, American and Canadian Propaganda and Fiction, 1914–1933*. University of British Columbia Press.

Buitenhuis, P. (2000) J.B. Priestley: The BBC's Star Propagandist in World War II. *English Studies in Canada*, 26(4), 445–72.

Bullock, A. (1960) *The Life and Times of Ernest Bevin Volume I: Trade Union Leader 1881–1940*. Heinemann.

Burk, K. (1982) *War and the State: The Transformation of British Government 1914–1919*. George Allen & Unwin.

Burn, G. (1999) The State, the City and the Euromarkets. *Review of International Political Economy*, 6(2), 225–61.

Burns, C., and Tobin, P. (2016) The Impact of the Economic Crisis on European Environmental Policy. *Journal of Common Market Studies*, 54(6), 1485–94.

Burton, A. (1995) Projecting the New Jerusalem: The Workers Film Association, 1938–1946. In P. Kirkhan and D. Thomas (eds), *War Culture: Social Change and Changing Experience in World War Two*. Lawrence & Wishart, pp 73–84.

Burton, J. (2019) The 1918 Election and Its Relevance to Modern Irish Politics. *Studies: An Irish Quarterly Review*, 108(429), 93–103.

Butler, D., and Kavanagh, D. (1980) *The British General Election of 1979*. Palgrave.

Callaghan, J. (1976, October) Leader's Speech Blackpool, 1976. British Political Speeches [online]. Available from: www.britishpoliticalspeech.org/speech-archive.htm?speech=174 [Accessed 24 July 2020].

Callaghan, J. (2006) *Time and Chance*. Politico's Publishing.

Calvert, J., and Arbuthnott, G. (2021) *Failures of State: The Inside Story of Britain's Battle with Coronavirus*. Harper Collins.

Cameron, D. (2019) *For the Record*, William Collins

Campbell, F. (2005) *Land and Revolution: Nationalist Politics in the West of Ireland 1891-1921*. Oxford University Press.

Campbell, S. (2017) 'We Are the People': Protestant Identity and Collective Action in Northern Ireland, 1968–1985 In L. Bosi and G. De Fazio (eds), *The Troubles in Northern Ireland and Theories of Social Movements*. Amsterdam University Press, pp 91–110.

Cannan, E. (1932) The Demand for Labour. *The Economic Journal*, 42(167), 357–70.

Caporaso, J. (2018) Europe's Triple Crisis and the Uneven Role of Institutions: The Euro, Refugees and Brexit. *Journal of Common Market Studies*, 56(6), 1345–61.

Carstensen, M.B., and Mattijs, M. (2017) Of Paradigms and Power: British Economic Policy Making since Thatcher. *Governance*, 31(3), 431–47.

Castle, B. (1993) *Fighting All the Way*. Macmillan.
CATO (1940) *Guilty Men*. Victor Gollancz.
Caulfield, M. (1995) *The Easter Rebellion: The Outstanding Narrative History of the 1916 Rising in Ireland*. Gill & Macmillan
Chamberlain, A. (1936) *Politics from the Inside*. Cassell
Chase, E.P. (1929) House of Lords Reform since 1911. *Political Science Quarterly*, 44(4), 569–90.
Church, R., and Outram, Q. (1998) *Strikes and Solidarity: Coalfield Conflict in Britain 1889–1966*. Cambridge University Press.
Clark, L. (1996) 'Civilians Entrenched': The British Home Front and Attitudes to the First World War 1914–18. In I. Stewart and S.L. Carruthers (eds), *War, Culture and the Media*. Flicks Books, pp 38–53.
Clegg, D. (2010) Labour Market Policy in the Crisis: The UK in Comparative Perspective. *Journal of Poverty and Social Justice*, 18(1), 5–17.
Clegg, H.A. (1985) *A History of British Trade Unions since 1889 Volume II: 1911–1933*. Clarendon Press.
Clemenson, M. (2020, 18 November) Six in Ten Brits Admit They Took Key Workers for Granted before Coronavirus Pandemic. *Daily Star* [online]. Available from: www.dailystar.co.uk/news/latest-news/six-10-brits-admit-took-23029038 [Accessed 4 July 2022].
Clement, M. (2015) Thatcher's Civilising Offensive: The Ridley Plan to Decivilise the Working Class. *Civilising Offensives*, 4(1), 1–10.
Cliff, B. (2015) The UK Macroeconomic Policy Debate and the British Growth Crisis. In J. Green, C. Hay, and P. Taylor-Gooby (eds), *The British Growth Crisis*. Palgrave Macmillan, pp 151–73.
Cliff, B., and Tomlinson, J. (2007) Credible Keynesianism? New Labour Macroeconomic Policy and the Political Economy of Coarse Turning. *British Journal of Political Science*, 37(1), 47–69.
Clynes, J.R. (1937) *Memoirs*. Hutchinson & Co.
Coates, D. (2013) Labour after New Labour: Escaping the Debt. *British Journal of Politics and International Relations*, 15, 38–52.
Cockett, R. (1991) The Observer and the Suez Crisis. *Contemporary Record*, 5(1), 9–31.
Cohen, S., and Young, J. (1973) *The Manufacture of News: Social Problems, Deviance and the Mass Media*. Constable.
Cole, G. (1948) *A History of the Labour Party from 1914*. Routledge.
Cook, A.J. (1926) *The Nine Days*. Warwick Digital Collection [online]. Available from: https://cdm21047.contentdm.oclc.org/digital/collection/strike/id/1901 [Accessed 27 March 2024].
Cook, C. (1976) *A Short History of the Liberal Party 1900–1976*. Macmillan.
Cooley, T.F., and Ohanian, L.E. (1997) Postwar British Economic Growth and the Legacy of Keynes *Journal of Political Economy*, 105(3), 439–72.
Cross, C. (1963) *The Liberals in Power 1905–14*. Barrie and Rockliff with Pall Mall Press.

Crouch, C. (1997) The Terms of the Neo-Liberal Consensus. *The Political Quarterly*, 68(4), 352–60.

Crouch, C. (2011) *The Strange Non-Death of Neoliberalsim.* Polity

Crowson, N. (1997) *Facing Fascism: The Conservative Party and the European Dictators, 1935–1940.* Routledge

Cull, N.J. (1995) *Selling War: The British Propaganda Campaign against American 'Neutrality' in World War II.* Oxford University Press.

Daniels, S. (2019) The Thatcher and Major Governments and the Union of Democratic Mineworkers, c. 1985–1992. *Historical Studies in Industrial Relations*, 40, 153–85.

Daniels, S. (2023) How Consecutive Conservative Governments Destroyed Union Rights – A Timeline of the UK's Anti-Strike Laws since the 1970s. The Conversation [online]. Available from: https://theconversation.com/how-consecutive-conservative-governments-destroyed-union-rights-a-timeline-of-the-uks-anti-strike-laws-since-the-1970s-198178 [Accessed 9 September 2024].

Darling, A. (2011) *Back From the Brink.* Atlantic Books

Daunton, M. (2007) *Trusting Leviathan: The Politics of Taxation in Britain, 1799–1914.* Cambridge University Press.

David, E. (1970) The Liberal Party Divided 1916–1918. *The Historical Journal*, XIII(3), 509–33.

Davies, H. (2010) *The Financial Crisis: Who Is to Blame.* Polity.

Davies, W., and Gane, N. (2021) Post-Neoliberalism? An Introduction. *Theory, Culture and Society*, 38(6), 3–28.

Davies, W., Dutta, S.J., Taylor, N., and Tazzioli, M. (2022) *Unprecedented? How Covid-19 Revealed the Politics of Our Economy.* Goldsmiths Press.

Davis, A. (2024) *Political Communication: An Introduction for Crisis Times.* Polity.

Deacon, A. (1976) *In Search of the Scrounger: Occasional Papers on Social Administration 60.* G. Bell and Sons.

Dearing, J.W., and Rodger, E.M. (1996) *Agenda Setting.* Sage.

Dennis, P. (2021) *Decision by Default: Peacetime Conscription and British Defence 1919–39.* Routledge.

Dietl, R. (2008) Suez 1956: A European Intervention? *Journal of Contemporary History*, 43(2), 259–78.

Dimsdale, C. (2022, 12 January) Who Had to Resign for Breaking Covid Rules? The MPs and Government Advisors Who Quit over the Restrictions. *The I* [online]. Available from: https://inews.co.uk/news/covid-rules-resign-who-mps-government-advisers-quit-restrictions-1396505 [Accessed 25 January 2023].

Dimsdale, N.H. (1981) British Monetary Policy and the Exchange Rate 1920–1938. *Oxford Economic Papers*, 33 (Supp), 306–49.

Dimsdale, N., and Horsewood, N. (2014) *British Financial Crises since 1825.* Oxford University Press.

Dinan, D., Nugent, N., and Paterson, W.E. (2017) *The European Union in Crisis.* Palgrave Macmillan.

Doherty, G. (2014a) *The Home Rule Crisis 1912–14.* Mercier Press.

Doherty, G. (2014b) Liberal Public Discourse and the Third Home Rule Bill. In G. Doherty (ed), *The Home Rule Crisis 1912–14*. Mercier Press, pp 81–101.

Doherty, J. (2019) *Irish Liberty, British Democracy: the third Irish Home Rule crisis, 1909-14*. Cork University Press

Dolphin, T. (2011) *Debts and Deficit: How Much Is Labour to Blame?* Institute for Public Policy Research.

Dorey, P. (2014) The Stepping Stones Programme: The Conservative Party's Struggle to Develop a Trade-Union Policy, 1975–79. *Historical Studies in Industrial Relations*, 35, 89–116.

Dorey, P. (2016) 'Should I Stay or Should I Go?' James Callaghan's Decision Not to Call an Autumn 1978 General Election. *British Politics*, 11(1), 95–118.

Dorey, P., and Kelso, A. (2011) *House of Lords Reform since 1911: Must the Lords Go?* Palgrave Macmillan

Duca, J.V., Muellbauer, J., and Murphy, A. (2010) Housing Markets and the Financial Crisis of 2007–2009: Lessons for the Future. *Journal of Financial Stability*, 6(4), 203–17.

Durbin, E. (1985) *New Jerusalems: Labour Party and the Economics of Democratic Socialism*. Routledge.

Durdoie, B. (2007) Fear and Terror in a Post-Political Age. *Government and Opposition*, 42(3), 427–50.

Dutton, D. (2004) *A History of the Liberal Party*. Palgrave.

Dutton, J.E. (1986) The Processing of Crisis and Non-Crisis Strategic Issues. *Journal of Management Studies*, 23(5), 501–17.

Eada, C. (1943) *The End of the Beginning: War Speeches by the Right Hon. Winston S. Churchill C.H., M.P.* Cassell.

Earley, J.S., and Lacy, W.S.B. (1942) British Wartime Control of Prices. *Law and Contemporary Problems*, 9(1), 160–72.

Eatwell, R. (1971) Munich, Public Opinion and Popular Front. *Journal of Contemporary History*, 6(4), 122–39.

Eatwell, R., and Wright, A. (1978) Labour and the Lessons of 1931. *History*, 63(207), 38–53.

Einzig, P. (1969) *Decline and Fall? Britain's Crisis in the Sixties*. Macmillan.

Elliott, B. (2004) *Yorkshire's Flying Pickets in the 1984–85 Miners Strike: Based on the Diary of Silverwood Miners Bruce* Wilson. Wharncliffe Books.

Elliott, L. (2022, 11 December) Sunak and Hunt Face a Return of the 70s' Winter of Discontent. It Didn't End Well Then. *The Guardian* [online]. Available from: www.theguardian.com/business/2022/dec/18/rishi-sunak-and-jeremy-hunt-face-a-rerun-of-the-70s-winter-of-discontent#:~:text=Britain%20is%20facing%20its%202022,wage%20deals%20risk%20entrenching%20inflation [Accessed 6 June 2023].

Ellison, M., Sargent, T.J., and Scott, A. (2019) Funding the Great War and the Beginning of the End for British Hegemony. In T. Sargent, G. Hall, M. Ellison, A. Scott, H. James, E. Dabla-Norris, M. DeBroeck, N. End, M. Marinkov, and V. Gasper (eds), *Debt Entanglements between the Wars*. International Monetary Fund, pp 59–79.

Engelen, E., Ertuk, I., Froud, J., Johal, S., Moran, M., Nilddon, A., and Williams, K. (2011) *After the Great Complacence: Financial Crisis and the Politics of Reform.* Oxford University Press.

English, R. (2009) *Terrorism and How to Respond.* Oxford University Press.

English, R., and Kenny, M. (1999) British Decline or the Politics of Declinism? *British Journal of Politics and International Relations*, 1(2), 252–66.

English, R., and Kenny, M. (2001) Public Intellectuals and the Question of British Decline. *British Journal of Politics and International Relations*, 3(3), 259–83.

Escandon, K, Rasmussen, A.L., Bogoch, I., Murray, E.J., Escandon, K., Popescu, S. V., and Kindrachuk, J. (2021) COVID-19: False Dichotomies and a Comprehensive Review of the Evidence Regarding Public Health, COVID-19 Symptomatology, SARS-CoV-2 Transmission, Mask Wearing and Reinfection. *BMC Infectious Diseases*, 21(1), 710.

Fairclough, I. (2022) The UK Government's 'Balancing Act' in the Pandemic: Rational Decision-Making from an Argumentative Perspective In S. Oswald, M. Lewinski, S. Greco, and S. Villata (eds), *The Pandemic of Argumentation.* Springer, pp 225–46.

Fanning, R. (1985) Anglo-Irish Relations: Partition and the British Dimension in Historical Perspective. *Irish Studies in International Affairs*, 2(1), 1–20.

Fanning, R. (2013) *Fatal Path: British Government and Irish Revolution 1910–1922.* Faber & Faber.

Farnsworth, K. (2021) Retrenched, Reconfigured and Broken: The British Welfare State after a Decade of Austerity. *Social Policy and Society*, 20(1), 77–96.

Farrall, S. and Hay, C. (2015) (eds.) *The Legacy of Thatcherism: Assessing and Exploring Thatcherite Social and Economic Policies.* Oxford University Press.

Feld, I., and Fetzer, T. (2024) Performative State Capacity and Climate (In)Action. *CESifo Working Paper No. 10990.* SSRN [online], Available from: https://ssrn.com/abstract=4756072 [Accessed 11 September 2024].

Ferrall, C. (2015) *Writing the 1926 General Strike: Literature, Culture, Politics.* University of Wellington.

Fetzer, T. (2019) Did Austerity Cause Brexit? *American Economic Review*, 109(11), 3849–86.

Finlayson, A., Jarvis, L., and Lister, M. (2023) COVID-19 and 'the Public': UK Government, Discourse and the British Political Tradition. *Contemporary Politics*, 29(3), 339–56.

Finn, M. (2010) Local Heros: War News and the Construction of 'Community' in Britain, 1914–18. *Historical Research*, 83(221), 520–38.

Fletcher, M.E. (1958) The Suez Canal and World Shipping, 1869–1914. *Journal of Economic History*, 18(4), 556–73.

Foote, G. (1997) *The Labour Party's Political Thought.* Macmillan.

Foster, J. (2004) Prologue: What Kind of Crisis? What Kind of Ruling Class? In J. McIlroy, A. Campbell, and K. Gildart (eds), *Industrial Politics and the 1926 Mining Lockout.* University of Wales Press, pp 15–43.

French, S.L., and Thrift, N. (2009) A Very Geographical Crisis: The Making and Breaking of the 2007–2008 Financial Crisis. *Cambridge Journal of Regions, Economy and Society*, 2(2), 287–302.

Fuller, E.W., and Whitten, R.C. (2017) Keynes and the First World War. *Libertarian Papers*, 9(1), 1–37.

Gallas, A. (2018) The Politics of Striking: On the Shifting Dynamics of Workers' Struggles. In J. Nowak, M. Dutta, and P. Birke (eds), *Workers' Movements and Strikes in the Twenty-First Century*. Rowman & Littlefield, pp 237–54.

Gamble, A. (1988) *The Free Economy and the Strong State: The Politics of Thatcherism*. Macmillan.

Gamble, A. (1993) *Britain in Decline: Economic Policy, Political Strategy and the British State*. Macmillan.

Gamble, A. (2009) *The Spectre at the Feast: Capital Crisis and the Politics of Recession*. Palgrave Macmillan.

Gamble, A. (2010a) The Political Consequences of the Crash. *Political Studies Review*, 8(1), 3–14.

Gamble, A. (2010b) New Labour and Political Change. *Parliamentary Affairs*, 63(4), 639–52.

Gamble, A. (2012) Inside New Labour. *British Journal of Politics and International Relations*, 14(3), 492–502.

Gamble, A. (2015) Austerity as Statecraft. *Parliamentary Affairs*, 68(1), 42–57.

Garside, W.R. (1990) *British Unemployment 1919–1939*. Cambridge University Press.

Gilbert, C. (2002) From One Crisis to the Other: The Shift of Research Interests in France. *Journal of Contingencies and Crisis Management*, 10(4), 192–202.

Gilbert, M. (1970) *The Roots of Appeasement*. Plume

Gildart, K. (2009) Mining Memories: Reading Coalfield Autobiographies. *Labor History*, 50(2), 139–61.

Glasgow University Media Group (1976) *Bad News*. Routledge & Kegan Paul.

Glynn, S., and Booth, A. (2020) *Modern Britain: An Economic and Social History*. Routledge.

Goes, E. (2016) *The Labour Party under Ed Miliband: Trying but Failing to Renew Social Democracy.* Manchester University Press. Political Studies Association [online]. Available from: www.psa.ac.uk/sites/default/files/conference/papers/2016/PSA2016EGoes.pdf [Accessed 19 July 2021].

Goldsmith-Pinkham, P., and Yorulmazer, T. (2010) Liquidity, Bank Runs, and Bailouts: Spillover Effects during the Northern Rock Episode. *Journal of Financial Services Research*, 37, 83–98.

Goodhart, C. (2008) The Background to the 2007 Financial Crisis. *International Economics and Economic Policy*, 4(4), 331–46.

Goodman, G. (1985) *The Miners' Strike*. Pluto Press.

Goodman, G. (2003) *From Bevan to Blair: Fifty Years Reporting from the Political Front Line*. Pluto Press.

Goodwin, M.J. (2014) Forever a False Dawn? Explaining the Electoral Collapse of the British National Party (BNP). *Parliamentary Affairs*, 67(4), 887–906.

Gorst, A., and Johnman, L. (1997) *The Suez Crisis.* Routledge.

Gorst, A., and Kelly, S. (2000) *Whitehall and the Suez Crisis.* Routledge

Gov.UK (2023) Minimum Service Levels: Issuing Work Notices, a Guide for Employers, Trade Unions and Workers. gov.uk [online]. Available from: www.gov.uk/government/publications/minimum-service-levels-msl-issuing-work-notices/minimum-service-levels-issuing-work-notices-a-guide-for-employers-trade-unions-and-workers#:~:text=1.-,Introduction,rely%20on%2C%20during%20strike%20action [Accessed 8 August 2024].

Greater London Assembly (2006, June) *Report of the 7 July Review Committee.* London Assembly [online]. Available from: www.london.gov.uk/sites/default/files/gla_migrate_files_destination/archives/assembly-reports-7july-report.pdf [Accessed 12 December 2023].

Green, J. (2020) *The Political Economy of the Special Relationship: Anglo-American Development from the Gold Standard to the Financial Crisis.* Princeton University Press.

Green, J., Hay, C., and Taylor-Gooby, P. (2015) *The British Growth Crisis: The Search for a New Model.* Palgrave Macmillan.

Greer, S. (2010) Anti-Terrorist Laws and the United Kingdom's 'Suspect Muslim Community': A Reply to Pantazis and Pemberton. *British Journal of Criminology*, 50(6), 1171–90.

Gregory, A. (2008) *The Last Great War: British Society and the First World War.* Cambridge University Press.

Greig, G., and Porter, R. (1979, 8 January) Britain under Siege. *Daily Mail*, p 1.

Grieve, D. (2018) Dominic Grieve QC MP: A Backbencher's View of Brexit. The Constitution Society [online]. Available from: https://consoc.org.uk/publications/dominic-grieve-backbenchers-view-brexit/ [Accessed 17 November 2023].

Grube, D. C. (2022) Why Governments Get It Wrong: And How They Can Get It Right. Pan Books.

Gudgin, G., and Coutts, K. (2015) Should the UK Continue to Follow Liberal Economic Policies? In J. Green, C. Hay, and P. Taylor-Goby (eds), *The British Growth Crisis: The Search for a New Model.* Palgrave Macmillan, pp 17–42.

H.D.H. (1919) The Reports of the Coal Industry Commission. *The Economic Journal*, 29(115), 265–79.

Habermas, J. (1998) *Legitimation Crisis.* Polity.

Haddon, C. (2020) CORB (COBRA). Institute for Government [online]. Available from: www.instituteforgovernment.org.uk/explainer/cobr-cobra [Accessed 4 August 2024].

Haddon, C., Hogarth, R., Marshall, J., Nice, A., and Ghazi, T. (2020) Coronavirus Act 2020. Institute for Government [online]. Available from: www.instituteforgovernment.org.uk/article/explainer/coronavirus-act-2020 [Accessed 25 June 2025].

Hain, P.L. (1991) *The United States, Great Britain and Egypt, 1945–1956.* University of North Carolina Press.

Hain, P., and McCrindle, J. (1984) One and All: Labour's Response to the Miners. *New Socialist*, 20, 44–6.

Halifax, S. (2010) 'Over by Christmas': British Popular Opinion and the Short War in 1914. *First World War Studies*, 1(2), 103–21.

Hall, P. (1993) Policy Paradigms, Social Learning, and the State: The Case of Economic Policymaking in Britain. *Comparative Politics*, 25(3), 275–96.

Hall, R. (2008) *Central Banking as Global Governance.* Oxford University Press.

Hanna, E. (2009) *Great War on the Small Screen: Representing the First World War in Contemporary Britain.* Edinburgh University Press.

Hansard (1907, 10 May) Old Age Pension Bill HC Deb 10 May 1907. Hansard [online]. Available from: https://api.parliament.uk/historic-hansard/commons/1907/may/10/old-age-pensions-bill [Accessed 10 November 2022].

Hansard (1911) Parliament Bill HC Debate 24 July 1911 vol 28 cc1467–84. Parliament.uk [online]. Available from: https://api.parliament.uk/historic-hansard/commons/1911/jul/24/parliament-bill [Accessed 5 September 2022].

Hansard (1926, 5 May) British Gazette. Hansard House of Commons Debate 05 May 1926 Vol 195 [online]. Available from: https://api.parliament.uk/historic-hansard/commons/1926/may/05/british-gazette [Accessed 24 March 2024].

Hansard (1927, 23 June) Trade Disputes and Trade Unions Bill. House of Commons Debate Vol 207 [online]. Available from: https://hansard.parliament.uk/commons/1927-06-23/debates/2d1cfcb5-894e-40e4-8c80-6cbe225e9a29/TradeDisputesAndTradeUnionsBill [Accessed 26 March 2024].

Hansard (1938, 5 October) Policy of His Majesty's Government. Hansard [online]: Available from: https://api.parliament.uk/historic-hansard/commons/1938/oct/05/policy-of-his-majestys-government [Accessed 19 March 2024].

Hansard (1940, May 7) Conduct of the War Volume 360. Hansard [online]. Available from: https://hansard.parliament.uk/Commons/1940-05-07/debates/ee7fb681-43ae-4a17-a06f-cdf0a62e1ce2/ConductOfTheWar?highlight=amery#contribution-cbd93cdd-d08c-41cf-a39e-f8fd4721db13 [Accessed 26 January 2024].

Hansard (1956, 30 July) Suez Canal. Hansard Vol 557 [online]. Available from: https://hansard.parliament.uk/Commons/1956-07-30/debates/7ae2d024-d773-4d84-8e75-dfb2a7d56bf3/SuezCanal [Accessed 16 May 2023].

Hansard (1978, 13 December) Counter-Inflation Policy Volume 960. Hansard [online]. Available from: https://hansard.parliament.uk/Commons/1978-12-13/debates/8245b10c-ffa9-4856-aeb1-cbaed91a3d5d/Counter-InflationPolicy [Accessed 7 June 2023].

Hansard (2010, 22 June) Financial Statement. UK Parliament [online]. Available from: https://hansard.parliament.uk/Commons/2010-06-22/debates/10062245000001/FinancialStatement [Accessed 10 October 2024].

Hansard (2020a, 26 February) Oral Answers to Questions: Prime Minister. Hansard [online]. Available from: https://hansard.parliament.uk/commons/2020-02-26/debates/6A733918-AC43-4143-A629-0BA4AF5A932B/Engagements [Accessed 24 January 2023].

Hansard (2020b, 26 February) Coronavirus Volume 672. Hansard [online]. Available from: https://hansard.parliament.uk/commons/2020-02-26/debates/B0FE8C31-77D5-40AA-97AF-BBA8FB620A95/Coronavirus [Accessed 24 January 2023].

Hansard (2020c, 25 March) Engagements: Volume 674. Hansard [online]. Available from: https://hansard.parliament.uk/Commons/2020-03-25/debates/E02BF9C1-538F-49C0-B79D-3CC56E2B6309/Engagements [Accessed 1 September 2023.

Hansard (2022, 29 June) Miners Strike 1984–85: UK Wide Inquiry. Hansard [online]. Available from: https://hansard.parliament.uk/commons/2022-06-29/debates/232B075F-FAC9-4C77-A310-8E601A0A9731/MinersStrike1984-85UK-WideInquiry [Accessed 10 September 2024].

Hansard Society (2022, 17 June) Coronavirus Statutory Instruments Dashboard, 2020–2022. Hansard Society [online]. Available from: www.hansardsociety.org.uk/publications/data/coronavirus-statutory-instruments-dashboard [Accessed 20 June 2022].

Harkness, D. (1996) *Ireland in the Twentieth Century*. Red Globe Press.

Harmon, M.D. (2019) A War of Words: The British Gazette and British Worker during the 1926 General Strike. *Labor History*, 60(3), 193–202.

Harris, J. (1994) Beveridge's Social and Political Thought. In J. Hills, J. Ditch, and H. Glennerster (eds), *Beveridge and Social Security.* Oxford University Press, pp 23–36.

Hart, C. (2017) Metaphor and Intertextuality in Media Framings of the (1984–1985) British Miners' Strike: A Multimodal Analysis. *Discourse and Communication*, 11(1), 3–30.

Hart, P. (2002) Definition: Defining the Irish Revolution. In J. Auguestein (ed), *The Irish Revolution, 1913–1923*. Palgrave Macmillan, pp 17–33.

Hart, P. 't. Tindall, K. (2009) *Framing the Global Economic Downturn: Crisis Rhetoric and the Politics of Recessions.* ANU Press

Hartman, P. (1976) Industrial Relations in the News Media. *Industrial Relations Journal*, 6(4), 4–18.

Harvardi, J. (2014) *Projecting Britain at War: The National Character in British World War II Films.* McFarland & Company

Hastings, A. (2023) Are We 'All In This Together'? Reflecting on the Continuities between Austerity and the COVID-19 Crisis. In M. Steer, M. Davoudi, M. Shucksmith, and L. Todd (eds), *Hope under Neoliberal Austerity: Responses from Civil Society and Civic Universities.* Cambridge University Press, pp 137–43.

Hay, C. (1995) Rethinking Crisis: Narratives of the New Right and the Construction of Crisis. *Rethinking Marxism*, 8(2), 60–76.

Hay, C. (1996) Narrating Crisis: The Discursive Construction of the 'Winter of Discontent'. *Sociology*, 30(2), 253–77.

Hay, C. (1999a) Crisis and the Structural Transformation of the State: Interrogating the Process of Change. *British Journal of Political and International Relations*, 1(3), 317–44.

Hay, C. (1999b) *The Political Economy of New Labour: Labouring under False Pretences?* Manchester University Press.

Hay, C. (2001) The 'Crisis' of Keynsianism and the Rise of Neoliberalism in Britain: An Ideationalist Approach. In J.L. Campbell and O.K. Pederson (eds), *The Rise of Neoliberalism and Institutional Analysis*. Princeton University Press, pp 193–218.

Hay, C. (2010) Chronicles of a Death Foretold: The Winter of Discontent and Construction of the Crisis of British Keynesianism. *Parliamentary Affairs*, 63(3), 446–70.

Hay, C. (2011) Pathology without Crisis? The Strange Demise of the Anglo-Americn Growth Model. *Government and Opposition*, 46(1), 1–31.

Hay, C. (2013) Treating the Symptom Not the Condition: Crisis Definition, Deficit Reduction and the Search for a New British Growth Model. *British Journal of Politics and International Relations*, 15(1), 23–37.

Hay, C. (2014) A Crisis of Politics in the Politics of Crisis. In D. Richards, M. Smith, and C. Hay (eds), *Institutional Crisis in 21st Century Britain*. Palgrave Macmillan, pp 60–78.

Heath, E. (1998) *The Course of my Life: The Autobiography of Edward Heath*, Hodder & Stoughton.

Heath-Kelly, C. (2015, 7July) How 7/7 Changed the Way Britain Mourns Victims of Terrorism. The Conversation [online]. Available from: https://theconversation.com/how-7-7-changed-the-way-britain-mourns-victims-of-terrorism-43975 [Accessed 21 May 2023].

Heffernan, R. (2000) *New Labour and Thatcherism: Political Change in Britain*. Palgrave Macmillan.

Hellmuth, D. (2016) *Counter Terrorism and the State: Western Responses to 9/11*. University of Pennsylvania Press.

Hewitt, S. (2008) *The British War on Terror*. Continuum Publishing.

Hickson, K. (2004) The Postwar Consensus Revisited. *The Political Quarterly*, 75(2), 142–54.

Hickson, K. (2020) *Britain's Conservative Right since 1945: Traditional Toryism in a Cold Climate*. Palgrave Macmillan.

Hindmoor, A. (2019) *12 Days That Made Modern Britain*. Oxford University Press.

Hobsbawm, E. (1994) *Age of Extremes: The Short Twentieth Century: 1914–1991*. Michael Joseph.

Hobson, B. (2013) Foundation and Growth of the Irish Volunteers, 1913–14. In F.X. Martin (ed), *The Irish Volunteers 1913–1915: Recollections and Documents*. Merrion, pp 19–55.

Hodson, D., and Mabbett, D. (2008) UK Economic Policy and the Global Financial Crisis: Paradigm Lost? *Journal of Common Market Studies*, 47(5), 1041–61.

Holmes, M. (1985) *The Labour Government 1974–79: Political Aims and Economic Reality*. Palgrave Macmillan.

Home Office (2006|) Countering International Terrorism: The United Kingdom's Strategy Gov.uk [Online] Available From: https://www.gov.uk/government/publications/countering-international-terrorism-the-united-kingdoms-strategy [Accessed 12 September 2025]

Horgan, J.J. (1911) *Home Rule: A Critical Consideration.* Maunsel & Co.

Horne, A. (1989) *Harold Macmillan: 1894–1956: Volume 1: The Making of a Prime Minister.* Macmillan.

Horne, J., and Kramer, A. (1994) German 'Atrocities' and Franco-German Opinion, 1914: The Evidence of German Soldiers' Diaries. *Journal of Modern History*, 66(1), 1–33.

Hoskins, A. (2011) 7/7 and Connective Memory: Interactional Trajectories of Remembering in Post-Scarcity Culture. *Memory Studies*, 4(3), 269–80.

House of Commons (2006, 11 May) *Report of the Official Account of the Bombings in London on 7th July 2005.* The Stationery Office.

House of Commons Library (2024) The Budget Deficit: A Short Guide. House of Commons Library [online]. Available from: https://commonslibrary.parliament.uk/research-briefings/sn06167/#:~:text=Since%201970%2F71%2C%20the%20government,as%20the%20chart%20below%20shows [Accessed 20 March 2024].

Howell, C. (1992/93) Family or Just Good Friends? The Changing Labour Party–Trade Union Relationship in Britain since 1979. *International Journal of Political Economy*, 22(4), 17–35.

Howell, C. (2005) *Trade Unions and the State: The Construction of Industrial Relations Institutions in Britain 1890–2000.* Princeton University Press

Howell, D. (2012) Defiant Dominoes: Working Miners and the 1984–5 Strike. In B. Jackson and R. Saunders (eds), *Making Thatcher's Britain.* Cambridge University Press, pp 148–64.

Howells, K. (2009, 19 May) Could 7/7 Have Been Prevented? Intelligence and Security Committee [online]. Available from: https://isc.independent.gov.uk/wp-content/uploads/2021/01/20090519ISCPressRelease-7-7Review.pdf [Accessed 25 June 2025].

Hunt, J. (2022, 17 November) The Autumn Statement 2022 Speech. Gov.uk [online]. Available from: www.gov.uk/government/speeches/the-autumn-statement-2022-speech [Accessed 25 January 2023].

Ibsen, M.F. (2019) The Populist Conjuncture: Legitimation Crisis in the Age of Global Capitalism. *Political Studies*, 67(3), 795–811.

Innes, J. (2003) Legislating for Three Kingdoms: How the Westminster Parliament Legislated for England, Scotland and Ireland, 1707–1830. In J. Hoppit (ed), *Parliaments, Nations and Identities in Britain and Ireland, 1660–1850.* Manchester University Press, pp 15–47.

Institute for Government (2021) Timeline of UK Coronavirus Lockdowns, March 2020 to March 2021. Available from: www.instituteforgovernment.org.uk/sites/default/files/timeline-lockdown-web.pdf [Accessed 12 September 2024].

Intelligence and Security Committee (2009) *Could 7/7 Have Been Prevented?: Review of the Intelligence on the London Terrorist Attacks on 7 July 2005*. London.

Ipsos MORI (2005) MORI Political Monitoring July 2005. Ipsos [online]. Available from: www.ipsos.com/en-uk/mori-political-monitor-july-2005 [Accessed 25 June 2025].

Jackson, A. (1992) Unionist Myths 1912–1985. *Past and Present*, 136(1), 164–85.

Jackson, A. (2004) *Home Rule: An Irish History 1800–2000*. Phoenix.

Jalland, P. (1980) *The Liberals and Ireland: The Ulster Question in British Politics to 1914*. Harvester Press.

James, R.R. (1969) *Memoirs of a Conservative: J.C.C. Davidson's Memoirs and Papers 1910–37*. Weidenfeld & Nicolson.

Jarvis, L. (2022) Constructing the Coronavirus Crisis: Narratives of Time in British Political Discourse on Covid-19. *British Politics*, 17(1), 24–43.

Jeffreys, K. (1991) May 1940: The Downfall of Neville Chamberlain. *Parliamentary History*, 10(2), 363–78.

Jenkins, R. (1954) *Mr Balfour's Poodle*. William Heinemann.

Jessop, B. (2017) The Organic Crisis of the British State: Putting Brexit in Its Place. *Globalizations*, 14(1), 133–41.

Jessop, B. (2018) Valid Construals and/or Correct Readings? On the Symptomatology of Crises. In B. Jessop and K. Kino (eds), *The Pedagogy of Economic, Political and Social Crises*. Routledge, pp 49–72.

Jit, M., Jombart, T., Nightingale, E.S., Endo, A., and Abbott, S. (2020, May) Estimating the Number of Cases and Spread of Coronavirus Disease (COVID-19) Using Critical Care Admissions, United Kingdom, February to March 2020. *Eurosurveillance*, 25(18). Eurosurveillance [online]. Available from: www.eurosurveillance.org/content/10.2807/1560-7917.ES.2020.25.18.2000632#html_fulltext [Accessed 25 June 2025].

Johnson, B. (2020, 9 March) *Prime Minister Statement on Coronavirus (Covid-19): 9 March 2020*. UK Government [online]. Available from: www.gov.uk/government/speeches/pm-statement-on-coronavirus-9-march-2020 [Accessed 24 January 2023].

Johnson, B. (2024) *Unleashed*. William Collins

Johnson, L. (2024) Covid Fraud Cost Each Adult £1,000. Collateral Global [online]. Available from: https://collateralglobal.org/article/covid-fraud-cost-each-adult-1000/ [Accessed 20 September 2024].

Johnson, M. (2008) The Liberal War Committee and the Liberal Advocacy of Conscription in Britain, 1914–1916. *The Historical Journal*, 51(2), 399–420.

Jones, D.M., and Smith, M.L.R. (2006) The Commentariat and Discourse Failure: Language and Atrocity in Cool Britainnia. *International Affairs*, 82(6), 1077–1100.

Jones, J. (1986) *Union Man*. Harper Collins

Jones, J.H. (1926) The Report of the Coal Commission. *The Economic Journal*, 36(142), 282–97.

Joppke, C. (2014) The Retreat Is Real – but What Is the Alternative? Multiculturalism, Muscular Liberalism, and Islam. *Constellations*, 21(2), 286–95.

Kaldor, M. (2013) In Defence of New Wars. *Stability*, 2(1), 1–16.

Katz, E., and Liebes, T. (2007) 'No More Peace!' How Disaster, Terror and War Have Upstaged Media Events. *Intenational Journal of Communication*, 1, 157–66.

Kavanagh, D., and Cowley, P. (2010) *The British General Election of 2010*. Palgrave.

Kelliher, D. (2021) Class Struggle and the Spatial Politics of Violence: The Picket Line in 1970s Britain. *Transactions of the Institute of British Geographers*, 46(1), 15–28

Kelly, M. (2013) Home Rule and Its Enemies. In A. Jackson (ed), *The Oxford Handbook of Modern Irish History*. Oxford University Press, pp 582–602.

Kelsey, D. (2015) *Introduction: The Politics of Remembering and the Myth of the Blitz*. Palgrave Macmillan.

Kerr, P. (2007) Cameron Chameleon and the Current State of Britain's 'Consensus'. *Parliamentary Affairs*, 60(1), 46–65.

Kersaudy, F. (1990) *Norway 1940*. St Martins Press.

Kettell, S. (2011) *New Labour and the New World Order: Britain's Role in the War on Terrorism*. Manchester University Press

Kettell, S. (2013) Dilemas of Discourse: Legitimising Britain's War on Terror. *British Journal of Politics and International Relations*, 15, 263–79.

Kettell, S., and Kerr, P. (2021) 'Guided by the Science': (De)politicising the UK Government's Response to the Coronavirus Crisis. *British Journal of Politics and International Relations*, 24(1), 11–30.

Keynes, J.M. (1920) *The Economic Consequences of the Peace*. Harcourt, Brace & Howe.

Keynes, J.M. (1936) *General Theory of Employment, Interest and Money* Macmillan and Co.

Keynes, J.M. (1978) The Economic Consequences of Mr Churchill. In E. Johnson, and D. Moggridge (eds), *The Collective Writings of John Maynard Keynes Volume 9: Essays in Persuasion*. Royal Economic Society, pp 207–30.

Kindleberger, C.P., and Aliber, R.Z. (2005) *Manias, Panics and Crashes: A History of Financial Crises*. Wiley.

King, A. (1975) Overload: Problems of Governing in the 1970s. *Political* Studies, 23(2–3), 284–96.

Kinsella, E.L., Hughes, S., Lemon, S., Stonebridge, N., and Sumner, R.C. (2022) 'We Shouldn't Waste a Good Crisis': The Lived Experience of Working on the Frontline through the First Surge (and beyond) of COVID-19 in the UK and Ireland. *Psychology and Health*, 37(2), 151–77.

Kirkland, C. (2015) Thatcherism and the Origins of the 2007 Crisis. *British Politics*, 10(4), 514–35.

Kirkland, C. (2017) *The Political Economy of Britain in Crisis: The Trade Unions and the Banking Sector*. Palgrave Macmillan.

Kirkland, C. (2022) *Labour's Economic Ideology since 1900: Developed through Crises*. Bristol University Press.

Kirkland, C., and Deva, S. (2023) Weakness, Not Crisis: Brexit and the UK Constitution. *British Politics*, 18(4), 603–22.

Kitson, M. (2013) End of an Epoch: Britain's Withdrawal from the Gold Standard. In R. Parker and R. Whaples (eds), *Routledge Handbook of Major Events in Economic History*. Routledge, pp 127–37.

Klausen, J. (2009) British Counter-Terrorism after 7/7: Adapting Community Policing to the Fight against Domestic Terrorism. *Journal of Ethnic and Migration Studies*, 35(3), 403–20.

Klein, L.R. (1966) *The Keynesian Revolution*. Macmillan.

Korte, B. (2001) The Grandfathers' War: Re-imagining World War One in British Novels and Films of the 1990s. In D. Cartmell, I.Q. Hunter, and I. Whelham (eds), *Retrovisions: Reinventing the Past in Film and Fiction*. Pluto Press, pp 120–31.

Koss, S. (1976) *Asquith*. Allen Lane.

Kunz, D.B. (1991) *The Economic Diplomacy of the Suez Crisis*. University of North Carolina Press.

Kunz, D. (2003) The Importance of Having Money: The Economic Diplomacy of the Suez Crisis. In W.R. Louis and R. Owen (eds), *Suez 1956: The Crisis and Its Consequences*. Oxford University Press, pp 215–32.

Kyle, K. (1991) *Suez*. Weidenfeld & Nicolson.

Kyle, K. (2011) *Suez: Britain's End of Empire in the Middle East*. I.B. Tauris.

Kynaston, D. (2008) *Austerity Britain, 1945–1951*. Bloomsbury.

Laffan, M. (1989) Weimar and Versailles: German Foreign Policy, 1919–33. In M. Laffan (ed), *The Burden of German History 1919–45: Essays for the Goethe Institute*. Methuen, pp 81–102.

Lavery, S. (2019) *British Capitalism after the Crisis*. Palgrave Macmillan

Laybourn, K. (1990) *Britain on the Breadline: A Social and Political History of Britain between the Wars*. Alan Sutton.

Laybourn, K. (1993) *The General Strike of 1926*. Manchester University Press.

Laybourn, K. (1996) *The General Strike: Day by Day*. Sutton Publishing.

Laybourn, K. (2002) *Fifty Key Figures in Twentieth Century British Politics*. Routledge.

LBC/IRN (1978) PM Speaks to TUC Conference LBC/IRN London Broadcasting Company [online] Available from: https://learningonscreen.ac.uk/lbc/search/index.php/segment/0010500466003 [Accessed 14 July 2025]

Le May, G.H. (1979) *The Victorian Constitution*. Duckworth.

Levy, J.P. (2006) *Appeasement and Rearmament: Britain 1936–1939*. Rowman & Littlefield.

Lloyd, S. (1980) *Suez 1956*. Hodder and Stoughton.

Lloyd George, D. (1909, 30 July) Limehouse Speech. Parliament UK [online]. Available from: www.parliament.uk/about/living-heritage/evolutionofparliament/houseoflords/parliamentacts/collections/limehouse/ [Accessed 5 October 2022].

Lloyd Geroge, D. (1938) *War Memoirs of David Lloyd George: Volume I*. Odhams Press.

London Evening Standard (1910, 28 November) The Lords and the People, p 13.

Lopez, T.M. (2014) *The Winter of Discontent: Myth, Memory, and History*. Liverpool University Press.

Lorenzo-Dus, N., and Bryan, A. (2011) Recontextualizing Participaatory Journalists' Mobile Media in British Television News: A Case Study of the Live Coverage and Commemorations of the 2005 London Bombings. *Discourse and Communication*, 5(1), 23–40.

Loughlin, J. (1995) *Ulster Unionism and British National Identity since 1885*. Pinter.

Louis, W.R. (2003) The Tragedy of the Anglo-Egyptian Settlement of 1945. In W.R. Louis and R. Owen (eds), *Suez 1956: The Crisis and Its Consequences*. Oxford University Press, pp 43–72.

Lovell, J., and Roberts, B.C. (1968) *Short History of the Trades Union Congress*. Palgrave Macmillan.

Low, A., and Lapping, B. (1987) Did Suez Hasten the End of Empire? *Contemporary Record*, 1(2), 31–3.

Lowe, R. (1990) The Second World War, Consensus and the Welfare State. *Twentieth Century British History*, 1(2), 152–82.

Macbeath, I. (1985) The 1984–5 Coal Dispute: Newspapers. In A. Hetherington (ed), *News, Newspapers and Television*. Palgrave Macmillan, pp 197–225.

Macfarlane, E. (2024) The Impact of the Coronavirus Pandemic on Support for the SNP and Scottish Independence *Journal of Elections, Public Opinion and Parties* 1–22. https://doi.org/10.1080/17457289.2024.2395354

Mackay, R. (2003) *Half the Battle: Civilian Morale in Britain during the Second World War*. Manchester University Press.

Macmillan, H.P. (1931) *Report of the Committee on Finance and Industry*. HM Stationery Office.

Macmillan, H. (1966) *Winds of Change, 1914–1939*. Macmillan.

Macmillan, H. (2003) *The Macmillan Diaries: The Cabinet Years 1950–1957*. Macmillan.

Manchester City Council (2024) The Glade of Light Memorial. Manchester City Council [online]. Available from: www.manchester.gov.uk/info/500369/glade_of_light_memorial/8206/the_glade_of_light_memorial#:~:text=People%20and%20communities%20The%20Glade%20Of%20Light%20Memorial andtext=It%20honours%20the%2022%20people,space%20for%20remembrance%20and%20reflection [Accessed 25 June 2025].

Mansergy, N. (1965) *The Irish Question, 1840–1921*. Allen & Unwin.

Mansergy, N. (1991) *The Unresolved Question. The Anglo-Irish Settlement and Its Undoing 1912–72*. Yale University Press.

Manthorpe, J., Iliffe, S., Gillen, P., Moriarry, J., Mallett, J., Scroder, H., Currie, D., Ravalier, J., and McFadden, P. (2021) Clapping for Carers in the Covid-19 Crisis: Carer's Reflections in a UK Survey. *Health and Social Care in the Community*, 30(4), 1442–9.

Marr, A. (2007) *History of Modern Britain* [TV Series] BBC Production

Marriott, J. (1931) The Crown and the Crisis. *Fortnightly Review*, 130, 579–89.

Martill, B. (2017, 17 January) Britain Has Lost a Role and Failed to Find an Empire. UCL European Institute [online]. Available from: www.ucl.ac.uk/european-institute/news/2017/jan/britain-has-lost-role-and-failed-find-empire#:~:text=Dean%20Acheson%20famously%20remarked%20in,failed%20to%20find%20a%20role%22 [Accessed 28 September 2023].

Martin, C., and Milas, C. (2013) Financial Crises and Monetary Policy: Evidence from the UK. *Journal of Financial Stability*, 9(4), 654–61.

Martin, F.X. (1963) *The Irish Volunteers 1913–1915: Recollections and Documents*. James Duffy & Co.

Martin, I. (2013) *Making It Happen: Fred Goodwin, RBS and the Men Who Blew Up the British Economy*. Simon & Schuster.

Martin, T. (2009) The Beginning of Labor's End? Britain's 'Winter of Discontent' and Working-Class Women's Activism. *International Labor and Working-Class History*, 75(Spring), 49–67.

Marwick, A. (1982) Print, Pictures, and Sound: The Second World War and the British Experience. *Daedalus*, 111(4), 135–55.

Mason, A. (1969) The Government and the General Strike of 1926. *International Review of Social History*, 14(1), 1–21.

Massey, C. (2022, 2 December) *Winter of Discontent: How Similar Is Today's Situation?* The Conversation [online]. Available from: https://theconversation.com/winter-of-discontent-how-similar-is-todays-situation-195838 [Accessed 6 June 2023].

Matthews, J. (2016) Media Performance in the Aftermath of Terror: Reporting Templates, Political Ritual and the UK Press Coverage of the London Bombings, 2005. *Journalism*, 17(2), 173–89.

Matthijs, M. (2020) Lessons and Learnings from a Decade of EU Crises. *Journal of European Public Policy*, 27 (8), 1127–1136.

McConnel, J. (2013) *The Irish Parliamentary Party and the Third Home Rule Crisis*. Four Courts Press.

McCourt, D. (2014) *Britain and World Power since 1945: Constructing a Nation's Role in International Politics*. University of Michigan Press.

McDonald, G. (1975) The Defeat of the General Strike In G. Peele and C. Cook (eds), *The Politics of Reappraisal, 1918–1939*. St Martin's Press, pp 64–87.

McDonnell, D., and Valbruzzi, M. (2014) Defining and Classifying Technocratic-led and Technocratic Governments. *European Journal of Political Research*, 53(4), 654–71.

McIlroy, J., and Campbell, A. (1999) The High Tide of Trade Unionism: Mapping Industrial Politics, 1964–79. In J. McIlroy, N. Fishman, and A. Campbell (eds), *British Trade Unions and Industrial Politics: The High Tide of Trade Unionism, 1964–79*. Ashgate, pp 93–132.

McKibbin, R. (1975) The Economic Policy of the Second Labour Government 1929–1931. *Past and Present*, 68(1), 95–123.

McLaine, I. (1979) *Ministry of Morale*. George Allen & Unwin.

McLean, I. (2001) *Rational Choice and British Politics: An Analysis of Rhetoric and Manipulation from Peel to Blair*. Oxford University Press.

McLean, I., Spirling, A., and Russell, M. (2003) None of the Above: The UK House of Commons Votes on Reforming the House of Lords. *The Political Quarterly*, 74(3), 263–413.

Messinger, G.S. (1992) *British Propaganda and the State in the First World War.* Manchester University Press.

Miliband, R. (2009) *Parliamentary Socialism.* Merlin Press.

Miller, F.M. (1976) The Unemployment Policy of the National Government, 1931–1936. *The Historical Journal*, 19(2), 453–76.

Millis, H.A. (1928) The British Trade Disputes and Trade Unions Act, 1927. *Journal of Political Economy*, 36(3), 305–29.

Minkin, L. (1974) The British Labour Party and the Trade Unions: Crisis and Compact. *Industrial and Labor Relations Review*, 28(1), 7–37.

Minkin, L. (1991) *The Contentious Alliance: Trade Unions and the Labour Party.* Edinburgh University Press.

Mitchell, A. (1995) *Election '45: Reflections on the Revolution in Britain.* Bellew Publishing.

Mitchell, B.R., and Deane, P. (1971) *Abstract of British Historical Statistics* Cambridge University Press.

Moggridge, D. (1969) *The Return to Gold, 1925: The Norman Conquest of $4.86.* Cambridge University Press.

Monticini, A., and Thornton, D.L. (2013) The Effect of Underreporting on LIBOR Rates. *Journal of Macroeconomics*, 37(C), 345–8.

Morgan, E.V. (1952) *Studies in British Financial Policy, 1914–25.* Macmillan.

Morgan, K.O. (1971) *The Age of Lloyd George.* George Allen & Unwin.

Morgan, K.O. (1990) *The people's Peace: British History 1945–1989.* Oxford University Press.

Morgan, K.O. (2001) *Britain since 1945: The People's Peace.* Oxford University Press.

Morgan, K.O. (2009) 'Rare and Refreshing Fruit': Lloyd George's People's Budget. *Public Policy Research*, 16(1), 28–33.

Morgan, M. (2020) Why Meaning-Making Matters: The Case of the UK Government's COVID-19 Response. *American Journal of Cultural Sociology*, 8(3), 270–323.

Morris, A.J. (2015) *Reporting the First World War: Charles Repington, The Times and the Great War.* Cambridge University Press.

Morrison, H. (1960) *Herbert Morrison: An Autobiography by Lord Morrison of Lambeth.* Odhams Press

Morsy, L.A. (1993) The Role of the United States in the Anglo-Egyptian Agreement of 1954. *Middle Eastern Studies*, 29(3), 526–58.

Mulder, N. (2020, 26 March) The Coronavirus War Economy Will Change the World. Foreign Policy [online]. Available from: https://foreignpolicy.com/2020/03/26/the-coronavirus-war-economy-will-change-the-world/ [Accessed 9 January 2023].

Mulheirn, I (2013) The Myth of the 'Welfare Scrounger'. *The New Statesman* [online]. Available from: www.newstatesman.com/business/economics/2013/03/myth-welfare-scrounger [Accessed 4 March 2024].

Mullen, A. (2021) Media Performance in the 'Age of Austerity': British Newspaper Coverage of the 2008 Financial Crisis and Its Aftermath, 2008–2010. *Journalism*, 22(4), 993–1011.

Murphy, P. (2011) Britain as a Global Power in the Twentieth Century. In A. Thompson (ed), *Britain's Experience of Empire in the Twentieth Century*. Oxford University Press, pp 33–75.

Murphy, P. (2020) *COVID-19*. Palgrave Macmillan.

Murphy, R. (1986) Faction in the Conservative Party and the Home Rule Crisis 1912–14. *History*, 71(232), 222–34.

Murphy, R. (2001) *British Cinema and the Second World War*. Continuum.

Murray, B.K. (1973) The Politics of the 'People's Budget'. *The Historical Journal*, XVI(3), 555–70.

Murray, B.K. (1980) *The People's Budget 1909/10: Lloyd George and Liberal Politics*. Clarendon Press.

Nicholas, S. (1999) The People's Radio: The BBC and Its Audience, 1939–1945. In N. Hayes and J. Hill (eds), *'Millions Like Us?' British Culture in the Second World War*. Liverpool University Press, pp 62–92.

Nicolson, H. (1953) *King George V: His Life and Reign*. Constable.

Northedge, F.S. (1970) Britain as a Second-Rank Power. *International Affairs*, 46(1), 37–47.

Norton, P. (2012) Resisting the Inevitable? The Parliament Act of 1911. *Parliamentary History*, 31(3), 444–59.

NUM (1983) Presidential Address from National Union of Mineworkers. NUM [online]. Available from: https://num.org.uk/wp-content/uploads/2015/11/1993-Presidents-Address-28-06-1993-Arthur-Scargill.pdf [Accessed 11 September 2024].

O'Connor, E. (2016) British Labour, Belfast and Home Rule 1900–14. In L. Marley (ed), *The British Labour Party and Twentieth Century Ireland: The Cause of Ireland, the Cause of Labour*. Manchester University Press, pp 55–68.

O'Connor, J. (1987) *The Meaning of Crisis: A Theoretical Introduction*. Basil Blackwell.

O'Day, A. (1998) *Irish Home Rule 1867–1921*. Manchester University Press.

O'Domhnaill, R. (2004) Curragh Munity in Historical and Legal Perspective. *RUSI Journal*, 149(1), 80–84.

Office for National Statistics (1996, 8 January) *Labour Market Trends, January 1996*. The National Archives [online]. Available from: https://webarchive.nationalarchives.gov.uk/ukgwa/20160108025430/http://www.ons.gov.uk/ons/rel/lms/labour-market-trends--discontinued-/january-1996/index.html [Accessed 8 August 2022].

Office for National Statistics (2019, 2 September) Changes in the Economy since the 1970s. Office for National Statistics [online]. Available from: www.ons.gov.uk/economy/economicoutputandproductivity/output/articles/changesintheeconomysincethe1970s/2019-09-02 [Accessed 15 August 2022].

Office for National Statistics (2020, 15 May) Coronavirus and Key Workers in the UK. Office for National Statistics [online]. Available from: www.ons.gov.uk/employmentandlabourmarket/peopleinwork/earningsandworkinghours/articles/coronavirusandkeyworkersintheuk/2020-05-15 [Accessed 29 November 2022].

Office for National Statistics (2022a, 20 July) Retail Prices Index: Long Run Series: Annual Percentage Change. Office for National Statistics [online]. Available from: www.ons.gov.uk/economy/inflationandpriceindices/timeseries/cdsi/mm23 [Accessed 08 August 2022].

Office for National Statistics (2022b) GDP and Events in History: How the COVID-19 Pandemic Shocked the UK Economy. Office for National Statistics [online]. Available from: www.ons.gov.uk/economy/grossdomesticproductgdp/articles/gdpandeventsinhistoryhowthecovid19pandemicshockedtheukeconomy/2022-05-24#:~:text=The%20nationwide%20lockdown%20undertaken%20to,between%20April%20and%20June%202020 [Accessed 9 August 2022].

Office for National Statistics (2023) *Labour Disputes; Total Working Days Lost Due to Strike Action*. Office for National Statistics [online]. Available from: www.ons.gov.uk/employmentandlabourmarket/peopleinwork/employmentandemployeetypes/timeseries/bbfw/lms [Accessed 9 June 2023].

O'Hagan, L. (2020) 'Home Rule Is Rome Rule': Exploring Anti-Home Rule Postcards in Edwardian Ireland. *Visual Studies*, 35(4), 330–46.

Oliver, M.J., and Pemberton, H. (2004) Learning and Change in 20th-Century British Economic Policy. *Governance*, 17(3), 415–41.

Olusoga, D. (2019) *The World's War*. Head of Zeus.

Oren, T., and Blyth, M. (2019) From Big Bang to Big Crash: The Early Origins of the UK's Finance-Led Growth Model and the Persistence of Bad Policy Ideas. *New Political Economy*, 24(5), 605–22.

Owen, J. (1957) The Polls and Newspaper Appraisal of the Suez Crisis. *Public Opinion Quarterly*, 21(3), 350–54.

Packer, I. (2006) *Liberal Government and Politics 1905–15*. Palgrave Macmillan.

Pantazis, C., and Pemberton, S. (2009) From the 'Old' to the 'New' Suspect Community: Examining the Impacts of Recent UK Counter-Terrorist Legislation. *British Journal of Criminology*, 49(5), 646–66.

Parmentier, G. (1980) The British Press in the Suez Crisis. *The Historical Journal*, 23(2), 435–48.

Partington, R. (2023) Is the UK Really Facing a Second Winter of Discontent? The Guardian [online]. Available from: www.theguardian.com/uk-news/2022/dec/08/is-the-uk-really-facing-a-second-winter-of-discontent [Accessed 2 September 2024].

Pawson, R. (2023) Do Lockdowns Work? Evidence from the UK? In P. Eliadis, I.R. Naidoo, and R.C. Rist (eds), *Policy Evaluation in the Era-of Covid-19*. Routledge, pp 140–59.

Peace, D. (2004) *GB84*. Faber.

Pearson, J. (2002) *Sir Anthony Eden and the Suez Crisis: Reluctant Gamble*. Palgrave Macmillan.

Peden, G.C. (2012) Suez and Britain's Decline as a World Power. *The Historical Journal*, 55(4), 1073–96.

Pelling, H. (1960) *Modern Britain 1885–1955*. Thomas Nelson and Sons.

Pelling, H. (1980) The 1945 General Election Reconsidered. *The Historical Journal*, 23(2), 399–414.

Pelling, H. (1987) *A History of British Trade Unionism*. Macmillan.

Perkins, A. (2006) *A Very British Strike*. Macmillan.

Peston, R., and Knight, L. (2013) *How Do We Fix This Mess? The Economic Price of Having It All, and the Route to Lasting Prosperity*. Hodder.

Phillips, G.A. (1976) *The General Strike*. Weidenfeld & Nicolson.

Phillips, J. (2012) *Collieries, Communities and the Miners' Strike in Scotland 1984–85*. Manchester University Press

Phillips, J. (2014) Containing, Isolating, and Defeating the Miners: The UK Cabinet Ministerial Group on Coal and the Three Phases of the 1984–85 Strike. *Historical Studies in Industrial Relations*, 35, 117–41.

Philo, G. (1995) Audience Beliefs and the 1984/5 Miners' Strike. In G. Philo, *Glasgow Media Group Reader, Volume 2: Industry, Economy, War and Politics*. Routledge, pp 37–44.

Phythian, M. (2005) Intelligence, Policy-Making and the 7 July 2005 London Bombings. *Crime, Law and Social Change*, 44(4–5), 361–85.

Pigou, A.C. (1918) A Special Levy to Discharge War Debt. *The Economic Journal*, 28(110), 135–56.

Pigou, A.C. (1933) *The Theory of Unemployment*. Macmillan.

Pimlott, B. (1977) *Labour and the Left in the 1930s*. Cambridge University Press.

Pimlott, B. (1988) The Myth of Consensus: Echoes of Greatness. In L.M. Smith (ed), *The Making of Britain: Britain in Decline*. Macmillan, pp 129–41.

Pimlott, B. and Cook, C. (1982) *Trade Unions in Britsih Politics*. Longman.

Pimlott, B., Kavanagh, D., and Morris, P. (1989) Is the 'Postwar Consensus' a Myth? *Contemporary British History*, 2(6), 12–15.

Pirie, I. (2012) Representations of Economic Crisis in Contemporary Britain. *British Politics*, 7(4), 341–64.

Plant, R. (2008) Blair's Liberal Interventionism. In M. Beech and S. Lee (eds), *Ten Years of New Labour*. Palgrave Macmillan, pp 151–69.

Porritt, E. (1910) The British Labour Party in 1910. *Political Science Quarterly*, 25(2), 297–316.

Poser, N.S. (1988) Big Bang and the Financial Securities Act through an American's Eyes. *Brooklyn Journal of International Law*, 14(3), 317–38.

Powell, D. (1996) *The Edwardian Crisis: Britain 1901–1914*. Macmillan.

Preventing Extremism Together Working Groups (2005 [2007], October) 'Preventing Extremism Together Working Groups' August–October 2005. The National Archives [online]. Available from: https://webarchive.nationalarchives.gov.uk/ukgwa/20070506224440/http://www.communities.gov.uk/pub/16/PreventingExtremismTogetherworkinggroupreportAugOct2005_id1502016.pdf [Accessed 14 June 2024].

Public Accounts Committee (2009) The Nationalisation of Northern Rock. Parliament.uk [online]. Available from: https://publications.parliament.uk/pa/cm200809/cmselect/cmpubacc/394/394.pdf [Accessed 24 March 2024].

Public Accounts Committee (2021) 'Unimaginable' Cost of Test and Trace Failed to Deliver Central Promise of Averting Another Lockdown. Parliament.uk [online]. Available from: https://committees.parliament.uk/committee/127/public-accounts-committee/news/150988/unimaginable-cost-of-test-trace-failed-to-deliver-central-promise-of-averting-another-lockdown/ [Accessed 8 June 2023].

Pugh, M. (1974) Asquith, Bonar Law and the First Coalition. *The Historical Journal*, XVII(4), 813–36.

Pugh, M. (2012) Lloyd George's Coalition Proposal of 1910 and Pre-War Liberalism. *Journal of Liberal History*, 77, 18–23.

Radice, G. (1978) *The Industrial Democrats: Trade Unions in an Uncertain World*. George Allen & Unwin.

Ralston, R. (2022) Make Us Great Again: The Causes of Declinism in Major Powers. *Security Studies*, 31(4), 667–702.

Rapport, L. (1962) The State of Crisis: Some Theoeretical Considerations. *Social Science Review*, 36(2), 211–17.

Rawsthorne, P (2018) Implementing the Ridley Report: The Role of Thatcher's Policy Unit during the Miners' Strike of 1984–1985 *International Labor and Working-Class History*, 94 (Fall) 156-201

Reading, A. (2011) The London Bombings: Mobile Witnessing, Mortal Bodies and Globital Time. *Memory Studies*, 4(3), 298–311.

Recchia, G. (2020) Coronavirus: New Study Suggests UK Public Supports a Long Lockdown. The Conversation [online]. Available from: https://theconversation.com/coronavirus-new-survey-suggests-uk-public-supports-a-long-lockdown-136767 [Accessed 17 June 2024].

Rees, G. (1970) *The Great Slump*. Harper and Row.

Rehman, J. (2007) Islam, 'War on Terror' and the Future of Muslim Minorities in the United Kingdom: Dilemmas of Multiculturalism in the Aftermath of the London Bombings. *Human Rights Quarterly*, 29(4), 831–78.

Renshaw, P. (1975) *The General Strike*. Methuen.

Renshaw, P. (1982) The Depression Years 1918–1931. In B. Pimlott and C. Cook (eds), *Trade Unions in British Politics*. Longman, pp 98–119.

Richards, D., Smith, M., and Hay, C. (2014) *Institutional Crisis in 21st Century Britain*. Palgrave Macmillan.

Richards, S. (2023) *Turning Points: Crisis and Change in Modern Britain from 1945 to Truss*. Macmillan.

Richardson, H.W. (1967) *Economic Recovery in Britain 1929–32.* Weidenfield & Nicolson.

Riddervold, M., Trondal, J., and Newsom, A. (2021) *The Palgrave Handbook of EU Crises.* Palgrave Macmillan.

Ridley, J. (1992) The Unionist Opposition and the House of Lords, 1906–1910. *Parliamentary History*, 11(2), 235–53.

Riley, C. (2021) Why History Should Always Be Rewritten. In S. Lipscomb and H. Carr (eds), *What Is History Now?* Weidenfeld & Nicolson, pp 280–95.

Rodgers, W. (1984) Government under Stress: Britain's Winter of Discontent 1979. *Political Quarterly*, 55(2), 171–79.

Rogers, C. (2009) From Social Contract to 'Social Contrick': The Depoliticisation of Economic Policy-Making under Harold Wilson, 1974–75. *British Journal of Politics and International Relations*, 11(4), 634–51.

Russell, M., and Sciara, M. (2007) Why Does the Government Get Defeated in the House of Lords? The Lords, the Party System and British Politics. *British Politics*, 2(3), 299–322.

Saltzman, R. (2018) *Lark for the Sake of the Country: The 1926 General Strike Volunteers in Folklore and Memory.* Manchester University Press.

Sample, I. (2021) Covid Timeline: The Weeks Leading Up to First UK Lockdown. The Guardian [online]. Available from: www.theguardian.com/world/2021/oct/12/covid-timeline-the-weeks-leading-up-to-first-uk-lockdown [Accessed 12 September 2024].

Samuel, R. (1986) Introduction. In R. Samuel, B. Bloomfield, and G. Boanas (eds), *The Enemy Within: Pit Villages and the Miners Strike of 1984–5.* Routledge & Kegan Paul, pp 1–39.

Samuel, R, Bloomfield, B. and Boanas, G. (eds), *The Enemy Within: Pit Villages and the Miners Strike of 1984–5.* Routledge & Kegan Paul.

Sanders, D. (1990) *Losing an Empire, Finding a Role: British Foreign Policy since 1945.* Palgrave Macmillan.

Saunders, R. (2012) 'Crisis? What Crisis?' Thatcherism and the Seventies. In B. Jackson and R. Saunders (eds), *Making Thatcher's Britain.* Cambridge University Press, pp 25–42.

Saunders, R. (2020) Brexit and Empire: 'Global Britain' and the Myth of Imperial Nostalgia. *Journal of Imperial and Commonwealth History*, 48(6), 1140–74.

Saville, J. (1985) An Open Conspiracy: Conservative Politics and the Miners Strike 1984–5. *Socialist Register*, 22, 295–329.

Sayle, B. (2021) 'Popular Constitutionalism' and the Unionist Party during the 1911 House of Lords Crisis. *Parliamentary History*, 40(3), 521–42.

Schwarz, B. (1985) Conservatism and 'Caesarism', 1903–22. In M. Langan and B. Schwarz (eds), *Crises in the British State, 1880–1930.* Hutchinson, pp 33–62.

Seaman, L.C. (1993) *Post-Victorian Britain 1902–1951.* Routledge.

Seaton, J. (1982) Trade Unions and the Media. In B. Pimlot and C. Cook (ed), *Trade Unions in British Politics.* Longman, pp 272–90.

Searle, G.R. (2004) *A New England: Peace and War 1886–1918.* Clarendon Press.

Shah, S. (2005) The UK's Anti-Terror Legislation and the House of Lords: The First Skirmish. *Human Rights Law Review*, 5(2), 403–21.

Shaw, T. (1995) Eden and the BBC during the 1956 Suez Crisis: A Myth Re-examined. *Twentieth Century British History*, 6(3), 320–43.

Shaw, T. (1996) *Eden, Suez and the Mass Media: Propaganda and Persuasion during the Suez Crisis*. I.B. Tauris.

Sheffield, G. (2002) *Forgotten Victory: The First World War – Myths and Realities*. Headline.

Sheperd, J. (2013) *Crisis? What Crisis? The Callaghan Government and the British 'Winter of Discontent'*. Manchester University Press.

Shin, H.S. (2009a) Securitisation and Financial Stability. *The Economic Journal*, 119(563), 309–32.

Shin, H.S. (2009b) Reflections on Northern Rock: The Bank Run That Heralded the Global Financial Crisis. *Journal of Economic Perspectives*, 23(1), 101–19.

Shinwell, E. (1973) *I've Lived Through It All*. Victor Gollancz.

Shoemaker, P.J. (1997) A New Gatekeeping Model. In D. Berkowitz (ed), *Social Meanings of News*. Sage, pp 57–62.

Shrivasta, P., Mitroff, I.I., Miller, D., and Miglani, A. (1988) Understanding Industrial Crises. *Journal of Management Studies*, 25(4), 285–303.

Sky News (2021, 26 May) Dominic Cummings Tells Committee He Heard PM Say 'Let the Bodies Pile High' after Ordering Second Lockdown. Sky News [online]. Available from: https://news.sky.com/story/dominic-cummings-says-he-heard-pm-say-let-the-bodies-pile-high-12317584 [Accessed 16 August 2023].

Sloman, P. (2024) Labour, More or Less? Policy Reasoning in a Fiscal Register. *British Journal of Politics and International Relations*, 26(1), 22–38.

Smart, N. (1998) Four Days in May: The Norway Debate and the Downfall of Neville Chamberlian. *Parliamentary History*, 17(2), 215–43.

Smith, J. (1993) Bluff, Bluster and Brinkmanship: Andrew Bonar Law and the Third Home Rule Bill. *The Historical Journal*, 36(1), 161–78.

Snowden, P. (1934) *An Autobiography*. Ivor Nicholson and Watson.

Somerville, W. (2007) *Immigration under New Labour*. Bristol University Press.

Sparkes, M., and Wood, J. (2021) The Political Economy of Household Debt and the Keynesian Policy Paradigm. *New Political Economy*, 26(4), 598–615.

Speller, I. (2003) A Splutter of Musketry? The British Military Response to the Anglo-Iranian Oil Dispute, 1951. *Contemporary British History*, 17(1), 39–66.

Stamp, J.C. (1931) The Report of the Macmillan Committee. *The Economic Journal*, 41(163), 424–35.

Stanley, L. (2014) 'We're Reaping What We Sowed': Everyday Crisis Narratives and Acquiescence to the Age of Austerity. *New Political Economy*, 19(6), 895–917.

Stanley, L. (2022) *Britain Alone: How a Decade of Conflict Remade the Nation*. Manchester University Press.

Startin, N. (2014) Constrasting Fortunes, Differing Futures? The Rise (and Fall) of the Front National and the British National Party. *Modern and Contemporary France*, 22(3), 277–99.

Statista (2021, May) Did You Watch the UK Government's Daily Coronavirus Briefing? Statista [online]. Available from: www.statista.com/statistics/1111869/government-coronavirus-briefing-audience-uk/ [Accessed 1 September 2023].

Steed, A. (1996) British Propaganda and the First World War. In S.L. Carruthers and I. Stewart (eds), *War Culture and the Media: Representations of the Military in 20th Century Britain*. Flicks Books, pp 22–37.

Stern, E.K., Deverell, E., Fors, F., and Newlove-Eriksson, L. (2014) Post Mortem Crisis Analysis: Dissecting the London Bombings of July 2005. *Journal of Organizational Effectiveness: People and Performance*, 1(4), 402–22.

Stevenson, J. (1988) The New Jerusalem. In L.M. Smith (ed), *The Making of Britain: Echoes of Greatness*. Macmillan, pp 53–70.

Stevenson, J., and Cook, C. (2010) *The Slump: Britain in the Great Depression*. Pearson Education.

Stewart, A. T. Q. (1981) *Edward Carson*. Gill and Macmillan.

Stewart, I. (1996) Presenting Arms: Portrayals of War and the Military in British Cinema. In I. Stewart and L. Carruthers (eds), *War, Culture and the Media: Representations of the Military in 20th Century Britain*. Flicks Books, 75–90.

Stirling, A., and Laybourn-Langton, L. (2017) Time for a New Paradigm? Past and Present Transitions in Economic Policy. *The Political Quarterly*, 88(4), 558–69.

Summerfield, P. (2010) Dunkirk and the Popular Memory of Britain at War, 1940–58. *Journal of Contemporary History*, 45(4), 788–811.

Sunak, R. (2020) Spending Review Speech. Gov.uk [online]. Available from: www.gov.uk/government/speeches/spending-review-2020-speech [Accessed 11 September 2024].

Sutcliffe-Braithwaite, F., and Tomlinson, N. (2023) *Women and the Miners Strike, 1984–1985*. Oxford University Press.

Symcox, J. (2011) *The 1984/5 Miners' Strike in Nottinghamshire*. Wharncliffe Books

Symons, J. (1987) *The General Strike: A Historical Portrait*. The Cresset Press.

Taaffe, P. (2006) *1926 General Strike – Workers Taste Power*. Socialist Books. [online] Available From https://www.socialistparty.org.uk/articles/101424/08-09-2006/chapter-3-the-nine-months/

Tanner, D. (1990) *Political Change and the Labour Party*. Cambridge University Press.

Taylor, A. (2001) The Stepping Stones Programme: Conservative Party Thinking on Trade Unions. *Historical Studies in Industrial Relations*, 11(4), 109–33.

Taylor, A.J. (1965) *English History 1914–1945*. Clarendon Press.

Taylor, M. (2003) Colonial Representation at Westminster, c 1800–65. In J. Hoppit (ed), *Parliaments, Nations and Identities in Britain and Ireland, 1660–1850*. Manchester University Press, pp 206–20.

Taylor, P.M. (1999) *British Propaganda in the 20th Century: Selling Democracy* Edinburgh University Press.

Taylor. R. (1982) The Trade Union 'Problem' since 1960. In B. Pimlott and C. Cook (eds), *Trade Unions in British Politics*. Longman, pp 188–214.

Thatcher, M. (1984 [2023]) Speech to Conservative Party Conference. Margaret Thatcher Foundation [online]. Available from: www.margaretthatcher.org/document/105763 [Accessed 15 June 2023].

Thatcher, M. (1993) *The Downing Street Years*. Harper Collins.

Thatcher, M. (1995) *The Path to Power*. Harper Collins.

The British Gazette (1926a) The British Gazette No 5, 10 May 1926. Warwick Digital Collections [online]. Available from: https://wdc.contentdm.oclc.org/digital/collection/strike/id/515/ [Accessed 27 March 2024].

The British Gazette (1926b) The British Gazette No 4, 8 May 1926. Warwick Digital Collections [online]. Available from: https://wdc.contentdm.oclc.org/digital/collection/strike/id/439/rec/4 [Accessed 27 March 2024].

The British Gazette (1926c) The British Gazette No 8, 13 May 1926. Warwick Digital Collections [online]. Available from: https://cdm21047.contentdm.oclc.org/digital/collection/strike/id/520 [Accessed 27 March 2024].

The British Gazette (1926d) The British Gazette No 2, 6 May 1926. Warwick Digital Collections [online]. Available from: https://wdc.contentdm.oclc.org/digital/collection/strike/id/375/rec/11 [Accessed 27 March 2024].

The British Worker (1926, 5 May) The British Worker No 1. Warwick Digital Collections [online]. Available from: https://wdc.contentdm.oclc.org/digital/collection/strike/id/0/rec/3 [Accessed 27 March 2024].

The Coalition Government (2010) The Coalition: Our Programme for Government. HM Government [online]. Available from: https://assets.publishing.service.gov.uk/government/uploads/system/uploads/attachment_data/file/78977/coalition_programme_for_government.pdf [Accessed 23 June 2023].

The Conservative Party (1935) A Call to the Nation: the Joint Manifesto of the Leaders National Government (Stanley Baldwin, J. Ramsay MacDonald and Sir John Simon). Conservative Party Manifestos [online]. Available from: www.conservativemanifesto.com/1935/1935-conservative-manifesto.shtml [Accessed 23 August 2022].

The Conservative Party (1979) Conservative General Election Manifesto 1979. Margaret Thatcher Foundation [online]. Available from: www.margaretthatcher.org/document/110858 [Accessed 3 June 2023].

The Conservative Party (1997 [2001]) 1997 Conservative Party General Election Manifesto. PoliticalStuff.co.uk [online]. Available from: www.conservativemanifesto.com/1997/1997-conservative-manifesto.shtml [Accessed 6 June 2023].

The Conservative Party (2010) *Invitation to Join the Government of Britain*. Conservative Party.

The Daily Express (1926, 7 May) Premiers Message, p 1.

The Daily Mail (1926, 6 May) *The Daily Mail*. Warwick University Collection [online]. Available from: https://wdc.contentdm.oclc.org/digital/collection/strike/id/82/ [Accessed 27 Mach 2024].

The Daily Mail (1979a, 22 January) The Union's Hospitals Will Not Be Hit. *Daily Mail*, p 2.

The Daily Mail (1979b, 27 January) Sick Old Man Is Left in the Snow. *Daily Mail*, p 1.

The Earl of Ronaldshay (1928) *The Life of Lord Curzon: Volume III*. Ernest Benn Ltd.

The Express (2009, 15 May) Goodwin Pension: Minister Condemned. *The Express* [online]. Available from: www.express.co.uk/news/uk/101198/Goodwin-pension-Minister-condemned [Accessed 23 June 2023].

The FT (2022, 9 December) Britain's New Winter of Discontent. *The Financial Times* [online]. Available from: www.ft.com/content/a6c49ce9-4d3c-488e-9f62-8cdea4e7028f [Accessed 6 June 2023].

The Guardian (1931, 25 August) A National Government p 8

The Guardian (2008, 4 February) The July 21 Failed Bombings. *The Guardian* [online]. Available from: www.theguardian.com/uk/2008/feb/04/terrorism.world1 [Accessed 22 February 2024].

The Guardian (2013, 1 February) David Cameron Rebuked by Statistics Watchdog over Debt Claims. *The Guardian* [online]. Available from: www.theguardian.com/politics/2013/feb/01/david-cameron-rebuked-over-debt-claims [Accessed 22 June 2023].

The Guardian (2020, 30 March) Applause Is Not Enough. *The Guardian* [online]. Available from: www.theguardian.com/commentisfree/2020/mar/30/the-guardian-view-on-key-workers-applause-is-not-enough [Accessed 15 January 2023].

The Independent (2015, 7 July) 7/7 Bombings Timeline: How the Day Unfolded. *The Independent* [online]. Available from: www.independent.co.uk/news/uk/home-news/7–7-bombings-london-anniversary-live-timeline-how-the-day-unfolded-10369476.html[Accessed 15 December 2023].

The Labour Party (1929) Labour's Appeal to the Nation: 1929 Labour Party General Election Manifesto. Archive of Labour Party Manifestos [online]. Available from: www.labour-party.org.uk/manifestos/1929/1929-labour-manifesto.shtml [Accessed 28 August 2022].

The Labour Party (1935) 1935 Labour Party General Election Manifesto: The Labour Party's Call to Power. Labour Party Manifestos [online]. Available from: http://labour-party.org.uk/manifestos/1935/1935-labour-manifesto.shtml [Accessed 23 August 2022].

The Labour Party (2005) Britain Forward Not Back. Deryn [online]. Available from: https://manifesto.deryn.co.uk/labour-manifesto-2005-britain-forward-not-back/ [Accessed 22 February 2024].

The Labour Party (2010) *A Future Fair for All: The Labour Party Manifesto 2010*. Labour Party.

The Labour Party (2024) Change: Labour Party Manifesto. Labour Party [online]. Available from: https://labour.org.uk/wp-content/uploads/2024/06/Labour-Party-manifesto-2024.pdf [Accessed 22 August 2024].

The Lancet (2023) Editorial: The COVID-19 Pandemic in 2023: Far from Over. *The Lancet*, 401, 79.

The Liverpool Daily Post (1910, 13 Jan) Lordly Lawbreakers, p 7.

The Telegraph (1931, 25 August) The New National Government p 8

The Telegraph (2009, 15 May) Bonus Culture to Blame for Banking Crisis, Say MPs. *The Telegraph* [online]. Available from: www.telegraph.co.uk/finance/newsbysector/banksandfinance/5328193/Bonus-culture-to-blame-for-banking-crisis-say-MPs.html [Accessed 23 June 2023].

The Telegraph (2020, 29 May) Dominic Cummings: What We Know about His Drive to Durham and Coronavirus Lockdown. *The Telegraph* [online]. Available from: www.telegraph.co.uk/politics/2020/05/29/dominic-cummings-coronavirus-wife-castle-petition/ [Accessed 30 January 2023].

The Times (14 September 1977) It won't go away p 17

The University of Warwick (2023) General Strike Day 1: 4 May 1926. Warwick Digital Collections [online]. Available from: https://warwick.ac.uk/services/library/mrc/archives_online/digital/gs/timeline/day_1/ [Accessed 27 March 2024].

Theakston, K., and Gill, M. (2021) Theresa May Joint Worst Post-War Prime Minister, Say Historians and Politics Professors. Political Studies Association Blog [online]. Available from: www.psa.ac.uk/psa/news/theresa-may-joint-worst-post-war-prime-minister-say-historians-and-politics-professors [Accessed 10 July 2024].

Thomas, H. (1986) *The Suez Affair.* Weidenfeld & Nicolson.

Thomas, J. (2004) 'A Cloak of Apathy': Political Disengagement Popular Politics and the Daily Mirror 1940–1945. *Journalism Studies*, 5(4), 469–82.

Thomas, J. (2007) 'Bound by History': The Winter of Discontent in British Politics 1979–2004. *Media, Culture and Society*, 29(2), 263–83.

Thomas, P. (2012) *Responding to the Threat of Violent Extremism.* Bloomsbury Academic.

Thomas, S.E. (1931) *The MacMillan Report: A Short Summary of Its Main Points.* Waterlow and Sons.

Thompson, H. (2014) The Thatcherite Economic Legacy In S. Farrall and C. Hay (eds), *The Legacy of Thatcherism.* British Academy Scholarship, pp 33–68.

Thompson, M. (1948) *Official Biography of Lloyd George.* Hutchinson.

Thompson, P. (1992) *The Edwardians: The Remaking of British Society.* Routledge.

Thorpe, A. (1988) Arthur Henderson and the British Political Crisis of 1931. *The Historical Journal*, 31(1), 117–39.

Thorpe, A. (1991) *The British General Election of 1931.* Oxford University Press.

Thorpe, A. (2015) *A History of the British Labour Party.* Palgrave.

Tiratsoo, N. (1998) 'You've Never Had It So Bad?': Britain in the 1970s. In N. Tiratsoo (ed), *From Blitz to Blair: A New History of Britain since 1939.* Phoenix, pp 163–90.

Todman, D. (2013) *The Great War: Myth and Memory.* Bloomsbury Academic.

Tomlinson, J. (1990) *Public Policy and the Economy since 1900.* Clarendon Press.

Tomlinson, J. (1996) *Democratic Socialism and Economic Policy: The Attlee Years, 1945–1951*. Cambridge University Press.

Tomlinson, J. (1998) Why So Austere? The British Welfare State of the 1940s. *Journal of Social Policy*, 27(1), 63–77.

Tomlinson, J. (2009) Thrice Denied: 'Declinism' as a Recurrent Theme in British History in the Long Twentieth Century. *Twentieth Century British History*, 20(2), 227–51.

Tonge, J. (2005) *The New Northern Irish Politics?* Palgrave Macmillan.

Tooze, A. (2021) *Shutdown: How Covid Shook the World's Economy*. Penguin.

Toye, R. (2001) The Labour Party and the Economics of Rearmament, 1935–1939. *Twentieth Century British History*, 12(3), 303–26.

Toye, R. (2007) *Lloyd George and Churchill: Rivals for Greatness*. Macmillan.

Toye, R. (2023) *Age of Hope: Labour, 1945, and the Birth of Modern Britain*. Bloomsbury.

Treasury Select Committee (2008, 24 January) *House of Commons Treasury Committee: The Run on the Rock Volume II*. Parliament [online]. Available from: https://publications.parliament.uk/pa/cm200708/cmselect/cmtreasy/56/56ii.pdf [Accessed 23 June 2023].

Tremblay, A. (2019) *Diversity in Decline? The Rise of the Political Right and Fate of Multiculturalism*. Palgrave.

Turner, J. (1992) *British Politics and the Great War: Coalition and Conflict 1915–1918*. Yale University Press.

Turner, R.L. (1985) Post-War Pit Closures: The Politics of De-Industrialisation. *The Political Quarterly*, 56(2), 167–74.

Tyler, C. (2021) The UK and COVID-19. In J.N. Pieterse and H. Khondker (eds), *COVID-19 and Governance: Crisis Reveals*. Routledge, pp 125–38.

UCL (2020, 7 December) Choosing between the Economy and Covid-19 Is a False Dichotomy. UCL News [online]. Available from: www.ucl.ac.uk/news/headlines/2020/dec/choosing-between-economy-and-covid-19-false-dichotomy [Accessed 3 June 2024].

UK Covid-19 Inquiry (2024) Frequently Asked Questions. UK Covid-19 Inquiry [online]. Available from: https://covid19.public-inquiry.uk/frequently-asked-questions/ [Accessed 11 June 2024].

UK Parliament (2023) Erskine May: Basis of Modern Practice with Respect to Privilege. Parliament.uk [online]. Available from: https://erskinemay.parliament.uk/section/5852/basis-of-modern-practice-with-respect-to-privilege/ [Accessed 7 February 2023].

UK Parliament (2024) The Parliament Acts. Parliament.uk [online]. Available from: www.parliament.uk/about/how/laws/parliamentacts/ [Accessed 16 February 2024].

UK Parliament (1991 [2024) *Public Inquiry into Police Conduct during Miners Strike*. EDM 1016.

Vaisse, M. (1991) Post-Suez France. In R. Louis and R. Owen (eds), *Suez 1956: The Crisis and Its Consequences*. Oxford University Press, pp 335–40.

Vickers, R. (2008) Harold Wilson, the British Labour Party, and the War in Vietnam. *Journal of Cold War Studies*, 10(2), 41–70.

Virdee, S., and McGeever, B. (2018) Racism, Crisis, Brexit. *Ethnic and Racial Studies*, 41(10), 1802–19.

Vis, B., van Kersbergen, K., and Hylands, T. (2011) To What Extent Did the Financial Crisis Intensify the Pressure to Reform the Welfare State? *Social Policy and Administration*, 45(4), 338–53.

Viven, R. (2019) A War of Position? The Thatcher Government's Preparation for the 1984 Miners Strike. *English Historical Review*, 134(566), 121–50.

Wade, E. (1985) The Miners and the Media: Themes of Newspaper Reporting. *Journal of Law and Society*, 12(3), 273–84.

Walker, G. (2004) *A History of the Ulster Unionist Party: Protest, Pragmatism and Pessimism*. Manchester University Press.

Walker, P. (2020, 19 April) Boris Johnson Missed Five Coronavirus Cobra Meetings, Michael Gove Says. *The Guardian* [online]. Available from: www.theguardian.com/world/2020/apr/19/michael-gove-fails-to-deny-pm-missed-five-coronavirus-cobra-meetings [Accessed 24 January 2023].

Ward, J., and Ward, B. (2023) From Brexit to COVID-19: The Johnson Government, Executive Centralisation and Authoritarian Populism. *Political Studies*, 71(4), 1171–89.

Warner, J. (2022, 7 December) Winter of Discontent Spells Electoral Disaster for the Tories. *The Telegraph* [online]. Available from: www.telegraph.co.uk/business/2022/12/07/strikes-grim-result-failure-control-inflation/ [Accessed 6 June 2023].

Webb, S. (1932) What Happened in 1931: A Record. LSE Digital Library [online]. Available from: https://digital.library.lse.ac.uk/Documents/Detail/what-happened-in-1931-a-record-1932/99969 [Accessed 12 July 2021].

Wenham, C. (2021) What Went Wrong in the Global Governance of Covid-19? *BMJ*, 3, 372.

Wheatley, M. (2005) *Nationalism and the Irish Party: Provincial Ireland 1910–1916*. Oxford University Press.

White, D.M. (1997) The Gate Keeper. In D. Berkowitz (ed), *Social Meanings of News*. Sage, pp 63–71.

Wiliam, M., and Collinson, M. (2024) How the 1984 Miners' Strike Paved the Way for Devolution in Wales. The Conversation [online], Available from: https://theconversation.com/how-the-1984-miners-strike-paved-the-way-for-devolution-in-wales-221358 [Accessed 2 April 2024].

Williams, D. (1963) London and the 1931 Financial Crisis. *Economic History Review*, 15(3), 513–28.

Williams, M. (2000) *Crisis and Consensus in British Politics*. Macmillan.

Williams, P. (1983) *The Diary of Hugh Gaitskell 1945-1956* Jonathan Cape

Wilson, H. (1977) *A Prime Minister on Prime Ministers* Weidenfeld & Nicolson.

Wilson, R.J. (2015) Still Fighting in the Trenches: 'War Discourse' and the Memory of the First World War in Britain. *Memory Studies*, 8(4), 454–69.

Wilson, T. (1989) *Ulster: Conflict and Consent*. Basil Blackwell.

Winchester, D. (1972) The British Coal Miner Strike of 1972. *Monthly Labour Review*, 95(10), 30–36.

Wintour, P. (2011, 5 October) Cameron Rewrites Conference Speech to Remove Credit Card Pay-off Call. *The Guardian* [online]. Available from: www.theguardian.com/politics/2011/oct/05/cameron-speech-rewritten-credit-card-call [Accessed 26 June 2023].

Wollaeger, M. (2006) *Modernism, Media, and Propaganda: British Narrative From 1900 to 1945*. Princeton University Press.

Wood, C., and Finlay, W.M. (2008) British National Party Representations of Muslim in the Month after the London Bombings: Homogeneity, Threat, and the Conspiracy Tradition. *British Journal of Social Psychology*, 47, 707–26.

Wood, J.D., Ausserladscheider, V., and Sparkes, M. (2023) The Manufactured Crisis of COVID – Keynesianism in Britain, Germany and the USA. *Cambridge Journal of Regions Economy and Society*, 16, 19–29.

Wright, M. (2017) *Unbroken*. Simon & Schuster UK

Wrigley, C. (2012) Labour Dealing with Labour: Aspects of Economic Policy In J. Shepherd, J. Davis and C. Wrigley (eds), *Britain's Second Labour Government, 1929-31*. Manchester, pp 37–54

YouGov (2020) Survey Results. YouGov [online]. Available from: https://docs.cdn.yougov.com/cvz3k50tmj/Internal_ClapforCarers_200529.pdf [Accessed 25 June 2025].

Young, H. (1990) *One of Us*. Pan Books.

Younge, G. (2015) Shoot-to-Kill Won't Make Us Safe from Terror – Just Sorry. *The Guardian* [online]. Available from: www.theguardian.com/commentisfree/2015/nov/18/shoot-to-kill-terror-fear-prejudice-jean-charles-de-menezes [Accessed 10 September 2024].

Index

www.ingramcontent.com/pod-product-compliance
Lightning Source LLC
Chambersburg PA
CBHW081144020426
42333CB00021B/2660

* 9 7 8 1 5 2 9 2 3 2 0 0 4 *